ÉLIE BOUHÉREAU: THE COLLECTIONS AND COMMUNITIES OF
A HUGUENOT REFUGEE

Élie Bouhéreau

The collections and communities of a Huguenot refugee

Amy Boylan & Janée Allsman

EDITORS

FOUR COURTS PRESS

Typeset in 10.5 pt on 12.5 pt Ehrhardt by
Carrigboy Typesetting Services for
FOUR COURTS PRESS LTD
7 Malpas Street, Dublin 8, Ireland
www.fourcourtspress.ie
and in North America for
FOUR COURTS PRESS
c/o IPG, 814 N. Franklin St, Chicago, IL 60610

© The various contributors and Four Courts Press 2025

A catalogue record for this title is available from the British Library.

ISBN 978-1-80151-129-2

All rights reserved. No part of this publication may be reproduced, stored in or introduced into a retrieval system, or transmitted, in any form or by any means (electronic, mechanical, photocopying, recording, or otherwise), without the prior written permission of both the copyright owner and publisher of this book.

Printed in England
by CPI Antony Rowe, Chippenham, Wilts.

Contents

LIST OF ILLUSTRATIONS 7

ACKNOWLEDGMENTS 9

1 Introduction 11
  Amy Boylan and Janée Allsman

PART I: CONTEXT

2 Élie Bouhéreau (1643–1719): a biographical sketch 17
  Jean-Paul Pittion

3 'La Rochelle, notre commune patrie': the world of the Rochelais
  Huguenots before the Revocation of the Edict of Nantes 22
  Muriel Hoareau

PART II: COMMUNITY CREATIONS

4 John Locke and Élie Bouhéreau: an encounter 33
  Geoff Kemp

5 Abraham Tessereau's miscellany: Huguenot history-writing
  during the reign of Louis XIV 63
  David van der Linden

6 Psalms and sonnets in the correspondence between Élie Bouhéreau
  and Laurent Drelincourt 81
  Jane McKee

7 Religion and the singing of psalms: Huguenot worship music in
  eighteenth-century Dublin 98
  Eleanor Jones-McAuley

PART III: ECONOMICS AND DIPLOMACY OF EXILE

8 The envoy's wife: diplomatic sociability, family, and loss in the diary
  (1689–1719) of Élie Bouhéreau 116
  Amy Prendergast

Contents

9   Managing money in early modern Ireland: the financial accounting of Élie Bouhéreau, 1689–1717   132
Charles Ivar McGrath

10   Financial agent, secretary, protégé: Bouhéreau and the earl of Galway   149
Marie Léoutre

PART IV: LOSS, RETURN, AND RECONSTRUCTION

11   The lost notebooks of Élie Bouhéreau: reading, recording, and retrieving in the seventeenth century   161
Noreen Humble

12   The peregrinations of the archives of the Reformed Church of La Rochelle   177
Didier Poton

13   Stealing and selling Dr Bouhéreau's books in the long eighteenth century   190
Jason McElligott

LIST OF CONTRIBUTORS   210

INDEX   213

Illustrations

Plates appear between pages 128 and 129.

1 Map of La Rochelle in 1620, by Matthäus Merian, seventeenth century, 4 PL 194.
2 Isaac Baulot, *Mutus liber* (La Rochelle, 1677), title page.
3 The Reformed temple in Villeneuve, La Rochelle, built *c.*1630 and demolished on 1 March 1685 by royal decree.
4 List of books signed 'Bouhéreau, Docteur en Médecine, Rue des Augustins, A La Rochelle.' Bodleian Library, University of Oxford, 2025, MS Locke b.2., fo. 24.
5 Portrait of John Locke by John Greenhill, oil on canvas, 1672.
6 Moyse Charas, *Nouvelles expériences sur la vipere* (Paris, 1672), engraved title page.
7 Portrait of Laurent Drelincourt, artist unknown, oil on canvas, seventeenth century.
8 *Les Psaumes de David: retouchéz sur la version de Marot et de Béze* (Paris, 1701), title page.
9 *Les pseaumes de David mis en vers françois* (Dublin, 1731), frontispiece of King David playing the harp.
10 The Lady Chapel, St Patrick's Cathedral, Dublin.
11 Portrait of Henri de Massue, marquis de Ruvigny, earl of Galway (1648–1720).
12 Tanneguy Le Fèvre, *On the sublime* (Saumur, 1663), front pastedown and enleaf.
13 Confession of Faith of the Reformed Church of La Rochelle, 1571 (printed 1572).
14 Élie Bouhéreau's books in the old reading room of Marsh's Library, Dublin.
15 'List of missing books, 1828', Marsh's Library, MS ML 36, pp 86–7.
16 Élie Bouhéreau, *Traité d'Origéne contre Celse: ou défence de la religion chrétienne contre les accusations des païens* (Amsterdam, 1700), title page.

FIGURES

4.1 List of payments and 'Mr Bouhereau' on the last page of a notebook belonging to John Locke, compiled 1677–8. Bodleian Library, University of Oxford, 2025, MS Locke f. 15, p. 152. 53

5.1 Image from Abraham Tesserau's miscellany, 'Mémoires et pièces', vol. 1. Marsh's Library, MS Z2.2.9. 74–5

6.1 Letter from Laurent Drelincourt to Élie Bouhéreau, 6 August 1674. Marsh's Library, MS Z2.2.14 (13.2). 88–9

9.1 Élie Bouhéreau. The diary and accounts, Marsh's Library, Dublin, MS Z2.2.2. 'Accounts', fo. 1. 136

Acknowledgments

This book is the fruit of an international conference held 15–17 November 2019 at Marsh's Library in Dublin entitled 'Élie Bouhéreau & the World of the Huguenots'.

Mr Robert Yeoman in Canada and Dr Daniel Tierney of Bimeda Ltd generously covered the costs of the event, and Mr Mark Tierney of Crabtree Capital kindly sponsored an evening reception in St Patrick's Cathedral. All three are direct descendants of Élie Bouhéreau. The dean of St Patrick's Cathedral, Dr William Morton, very graciously granted permission for the reception to take place in the beautiful Lady Chapel, where Élie and his wife are buried. We wish to thank Mr Maurice Hennessey (a descendant of an Irish refugee who fled to France) for the excellent cognac used during the reception to toast Franco-Irish friendship.

We thank the Médiathèque Michel-Crépeau in La Rochelle and the Musée Rochelais d'Histoire Protestante for their assistance in verifying historical details and locating images for this volume, and Professor Derval Conroy for her expertise and support.

We acknowledge an award from University College Dublin College of Arts and Humanities towards the cost of translating two articles in this book from French into English, and we express our gratitude to Mr Rory Guinness and the trustees of the Lauchentilly Foundation for a grant towards the costs of publication.

We are grateful to the panel of international experts who conducted single-blind peer reviews of all the essays. Finally, we are very appreciative of the advice and encouragement of the Director of Marsh's Library, Dr Jason McElligott, the Deputy Director, Dr Sue Hemmens, and the Education & Outreach Officer, Ms Julie Burke.

Introduction

Élie Bouhéreau (1643–1719) had the misfortune to live in interesting times. In 1798, when she was ninety years old, his granddaughter, Jane Freboul, committed to paper the tale of her family's daring escape from France more than a century earlier. Her grandfather had been banished by King Louis XIV from his native city of La Rochelle to Poitiers for his Protestant faith. Soldiers had been quartered in the family home to pressure her grandmother Marguerite Massiot and her children to convert to Catholicism. We have few concrete details about the family's escape from France, apart from those in Jane's oft-repeated tale, as Bouhéreau's personal record of it has since been lost. We do know however, that it was just the beginning of a more than decade-long journey that would take him to England, the Swiss cantons, and across Europe before he and his family would find a new home in Dublin, Ireland. More specifically, they found their home at the nascent Marsh's Library, where the refugee Bouhéreau was appointed first keeper, a lifetime position that afforded his family income and lodgings on the premises and provided Ireland with its first public librarian.[1]

Bouhéreau and his family had suffered and lost a great deal as refugees. Bouhéreau did not, however, come to Dublin empty-handed. On the contrary, he somehow managed to smuggle his personal library of over 2,000 books and 1,250 letters, as well as the consistory records of the suppressed Reformed Church of La Rochelle out of France.[2] More remarkably still, most of these extraordinary book and manuscript collections survive, despite the dangers encountered by Bouhéreau, and subsequent threats to their existence over the centuries. This volume explores the worlds in which Bouhéreau lived, worked, worshipped, and was persecuted through an investigation of his remarkable collection of books and manuscripts.

Bouhéreau was born into a prominent family in the Reformed Church of La Rochelle, a stronghold of French Protestantism in south-west France. He was

---

1 Newport John Davis White, *Four good men: Luke Challoner, Jeremy Taylor, Narcissus Marsh, Elias Bouhéreau* (Dublin, 1927), pp 91–3. 2 The exact number of titles in Élie's original collection is uncertain; there are differing counts of the books he donated to Marsh's Library. In their analysis of the collection Benedict and Léchot provide a total of 2,022 titles based on Élie Bouhéreau's catalogue, but they do not include his manuscripts and periodicals. The 1707 act establishing Marsh's Library states a total number of 2,057. Jason McElligott suggests this includes sammelbands and so puts the total number closer to 2,300. See Jason McElligott's chapter in this volume and Philip Benedict and Pierre-Olivier Léchot, 'The library of Élie Bouhéreau: the intellectual universe of a Huguenot refugee and his family' in Muriel McCarthy and Ann Simmons (eds), *Marsh's Library – a mirror on the world: law, learning and*

shaped by the history, culture, and economics of this city, which a generation prior had been gutted by the infamous siege of 1628. Bouhéreau's family's affluence, largely derived from revenues from his mother Blandine Richard's salt fields on Ile de Ré, provided the means for him to live in Paris, travel abroad with his cousin, Élie Richard, fund his studies in theology and medicine, operate a large correspondence network, exchanging letters and packages with well over a hundred different people, and, of course, acquire many of the books that now reside at Marsh's Library. Some of the same skills, contacts, collections, and funds which enriched his youth ultimately also smoothed the path of exile for the adult Élie.

The son of a Reformed pastor, Bouhéreau initially prepared to follow his late father's example, studying theology at Saumur. While Bouhéreau ultimately chose medicine over the pastorate, his rigorous education and training at Saumur expanded his personal library and social networks.[3] He flourished there under the tutelage of classical scholar Tanneguy Le Fèvre (1615–72), who became a good friend – twenty-one of Le Fèvre's letters are addressed to Bouhéreau, and many of his tutor's books feature in Bouhéreau's library. Through Le Fèvre, Bouhéreau's intellectual circle widened, including Valentin Conrart (1603–75), a founding member of the *Académie française*, who encouraged him to produce a French translation of Origen's *Contra Celsum*.[4] Bouhéreau's surviving correspondence is brimming with references to books: receipts for books purchased; inquiries concerning books yet to be acquired; notes mailed alongside books sent, and reviews of books read, one even composed in sonnet form! As Jean-Paul Pittion and Ruth Whelan have shown, these letters illustrate the centrality of books to Bouhéreau's social universe and highlight his role in circulating these volumes among his friends and acquaintances, disseminating new knowledge from Saumur and Paris to his provincial contacts.[5]

libraries, 1650–1750 (Dublin, 2009), pp 169–75.   3 For more on Élie Bouhéreau's youth and studies, see Ruth Whelan, 'La correspondance d'Élie Bouhéreau (1643–1719): les années folâtres', *Littératures Classiques*, 71 (2010), 91–112; R. Whelan, 'Mère et fils: les lettres de Blandine Richard (1605?–1700) à Élie Bouhéreau (1643–1719)' in *Vérités de l'histoire et vérité du moi: hommage à Jean Garapon* (Paris, 2016); R. Whelan, 'Proposants et hommes de lettres en formation: la correspondance entre Paul Bauldry et Élie Bouhéreau (1662–1683)', *Bulletin de la Société d'Histoire du Protestantisme Français*, 159:1 (2013), 93–113; Jean-Paul Pittion, 'Intellectual life in the académie of Saumur (1633–1685): a study of the Bouhéreau collection, Dublin' (PhD, Trinity College Dublin, 1969). For the production, distribution and readership culture of his books: Benedict and Léchot, 'The library of Élie Bouhéreau', pp 169–75. For the erudite sociability expressed in his letters, see R. Whelan, 'Absent friends: the letters of Jacques Richier de Cerisy to Élie Bouhéreau' in *Le cabinet du curieux: culture, savoirs, religion de l'Antiquité à l'Ancien Régime* (Paris, 2013).   4 A defence of Christianity by Church father Origen against the pagan Celsus, who had argued that Christianity was irrational and corruptive. Élie Bouhéreau, *Traité d'Origéne contre Celse: ou défence de la religion chrétienne contre les accusations des païens* (Amsterdam, 1700).   5 Whelan, 'La correspondance d'Élie Bouhéreau'; Jean-Paul Pittion, 'Un médecin Protestant du dix-septième siècle et ses livres: anatomie de la collection Élie Bouhéreau à la bibliothèque Marsh De Dublin', *Irish Journal of French Studies*, 16:1 (2016), 35–58.

Bouhéreau's youth in La Rochelle, Saumur, Paris, and his youthful travels to Italy were largely free from religious persecution. Unfortunately, the parameters of the partial religious tolerance of the Edict of Nantes, which had provided Bouhéreau with enough space to cultivate his erudition, practise medicine, start a family, become a church elder, and widen his social world, painfully constricted his adult years. Creeping persecution changed the terms of peaceful co-existence for Huguenots like Bouhéreau again and again under Louis XIV. Marsh's collections retain copies of Bouhéreau's legal appeal, in conjunction with two of his cousins who were also Huguenot physicians, to restore their rights to continue to practise medicine without converting to Catholicism. Bouhéreau preserved the text of their appeal alongside that of its rejection. The loss of his profession was, unfortunately, not the worst ordeal for Bouhéreau. In 1683, Bouhéreau himself was expelled by royal decree from La Rochelle, and troops were stationed in his home during his forced absence, in the infamous *dragonnades*. The situation now untenable, Bouhéreau, his wife, mother, and all but two of their children managed their escape from La Rochelle. His youngest son Jean remained in La Rochelle but was rescued by Bouhéreau and brought to England two years later. His youngest daughter Madelon had previously been taken and placed in a convent to pressure the family to change religion. Bouhéreau was never able to arrange her release and, tragically, she died there in 1690 at the age of twelve, while the family was in exile.

Bouhéreau's many appreciative friends and acquaintances helped secure his livelihood in exile. He was encouraged to emigrate to the Netherlands, Germany or Switzerland, but initially chose England where he became the tutor to the duchess of Monmouth's children in 1686. From 1689 to 1692 he served as diplomatic secretary to Thomas Coxe, envoy extraordinaire to the Swiss cantons, and was subsequently secretary to Henri Massue de Ruvigny, later Lord Galway, who, as one of the lords justices to Ireland, ultimately helped him to secure his position as the first librarian of Marsh's Library in 1701.

While excellent scholarship has illuminated aspects of Bouhéreau's biography and collections,[6] he and his books and manuscripts remain seriously understudied. The recent publication of a critical edition of his surviving diary (1689–1719) and accounts (1704–17), held at Marsh's Library, by Marie Léoutre, Jane McKee, Jean-Paul Pittion and Amy Prendergast, and the ongoing digital transcription and forthcoming critical edition of his correspondence, however, are encouraging augurs that this improbable archive will be further explored in the future.

This volume establishes multiple entry points for future studies on the communities who composed and animated the Bouhéreau texts. Muriel Hoareau

6 On Bouhéreau's biography, see: Newport J.D. White, Léopold Delayant, 'Elias Bouhéreau of La Rochelle, first public librarian in Ireland', *Proceedings of the Royal Irish Academy*, 27C (1908), 126–58 and Muriel McCarthy, 'Élie Bouhéreau, first public librarian in Ireland', *Proceedings of the Huguenot Society of Great Britain and Ireland*, 27:4 (2001), 543–50.

examines the city of La Rochelle and the social, cultural and economic contexts that formed the young Bouhéreau. She describes the local particularities of the religious persecutions Bouhéreau and his coreligionists faced under Louis XIV. Jean Paul-Pittion provides us with a brief biography of Bouhéreau himself, helping us to apprehend the interplay between his life and his books and manuscripts.

The second part of the book, 'Community creations', contemplates what Bouhéreau's collections have yet to tell us about the scholarly, medical, and religious communities that he participated in before and after exile. Bouhéreau was at the centre of a network of family, college friends, pastors, authors and professionals, 'all seeking his help, his influence and his good word'.[7] Because of his networks, his reputation for erudition, and his embodiment of the cultural ideal of *honnêteté*, Bouhéreau contributed broadly, if often anonymously, to scholarly endeavours, and to the construction, revision, and conservation of Huguenot religious life and identity in France and the Refuge.[8] This section focuses particularly on what his collections reveal about these scholarly and religious practices of collaboration, community formation, historiography, and communal memory.

Geoff Kemp invites us into Élie Bouhéreau's meeting with the philosopher John Locke in La Rochelle in 1678, recounting that books the former commended to the latter, and the afterlife of their encounter. Kemp knits together the strands of the vast network of European physicians and intellectuals to which Locke and Bouhéreau belonged, uncovering their triangular relationship with the apothecary Moyse Charas (1619–98) as the latter innovated the use of cinchona bark, or quinine, as medical experts raced to refine their jealously guarded recipes for an antimalarial cure for kings and commoners alike. David van der Linden mines the two-volume miscellany of primary sources encompassing edicts, legal proofs, and eye-witness testimonies compiled by Bouhéreau's friend Abraham Tessereau to record the increasing persecution of Huguenots during the reign of Louis XIV. These groundbreaking unpublished accounts of the persecutions, willed to, and preserved by, Bouhéreau, have informed Huguenot historiography and collective memory for generations.

Two essays highlight the significance of psalm-singing for Huguenot communities, before and after the Revocation of the Edict of Nantes, underscoring their central role in worship and community identity. Jane McKee utilizes the correspondence of Élie Bouhéreau and Laurent Drelincourt to reveal the details of their uncredited role in co-editing Valentin Conrart's (1603–75) updated French translation of the ubiquitous 1562 Genevan psalter. Eleanor Jones-McAuley sounds the central role psalm-singing played in harmonizing the

7 Ruth Whelan, 'West coast connections: the correspondence network of Élie Bouhéreau of La Rochelle' in Vivienne Larminie (ed.), *Huguenot networks, 1560–1780: the interactions and impact of a Protestant minority in Europe* (New York, 2017), pp 155–71.   8 Whelan, *Les années folâtrées*.

Introduction

French and Irish identities of the Huguenot church in Dublin and shows how the very psalter that Bouhéreau contributed to was used by Dublin's Huguenot refugees and their descendants to worship and reconnect to their French roots.

In the third part, 'Economics and diplomacy of exile', three chapters mine Bouhéreau's diary and financial accounts for the forgotten political, cultural, and economic facets of the experience of exile. Each of these chapters makes use of the 2019 printed edition of the diary and financial accounts, hinting at its enormous untapped potential for the study of early modern economic, social, and diplomatic history.

Amy Prendergast casts light on the previously undervalued role that women played in diplomatic sociability. Through the experiences of Mary Coxe, wife of Thomas Coxe, recorded in Bouhéreau's diary, Prendergast explores the varied and diplomatically vital activities of embassy wives, which included accompanying their husbands at gatherings, playing hostess and entertainer, while also navigating the realities of pregnancy, childbirth and loss while on mission.

Two chapters use Bouhéreau's diary and financial accounts to investigate how his bookkeeping attests to the resilience of his pre-exile community connections, and the wider Huguenot community's ongoing care for its veterans, widows, orphans, and indigent in Dublin and the international Refuge. Ivar McGrath delves into the minutiae of Bouhéreau's accounting to reveal the consequence of quotidian transactions in the financial support network of the French Protestant community. Marie Léoutre focuses on Bouhéreau's role as the philanthropic arm of Henri de Massue de Ruvigny, earl of Galway, who served as lord justice of Ireland and was a leading figure of the Refuge. In addition to examining the details of Bouhéreau's charitable work on Galway's behalf, Léoutre brings to bear indices of the bond which developed between the two men despite their differences in social standing during the decades of their relationship.

While the Bouhéreau materials are exceptional for their contents and the relative completeness of the collection, particularly given the exigencies of exile, this volume also calls our attention to what has been lost, dispersed, or repatriated, in the fourth part, 'Loss, return, and reconstruction'. Noreen Humble pieces together the traces of Bouhéreau's lost notebooks through his meticulous notational system, partially preserved on the flyleaves of his books. Didier Poton's chapter recounts the remarkable odyssey of a large selection of the consistory records of the Reformed Church of La Rochelle to Marsh's Library, Dublin, and back again. Reviewing the inventory of the more than 372 documents, Poton relates their historical, political, and religious value, as well as what prompted Bouhéreau to risk carrying these precious papers with him into exile.

Jason McElligott tracks the theft of books from Bouhéreau's personal library at Marsh's Library. He examines which books were stolen, under what conditions, and when, to discover more about the practices of readership, management, and book theft at Marsh's Library in the eighteenth and nineteenth centuries.

By shedding light on the print and manuscript texts of Élie Bouhéreau this volume adds to our understanding of early modern practices of readership, worship, medicine, diplomacy, sociability, community construction and survival. That these collections of a provincial doctor contribute to such a wide range of fields emphasizes the value of studying those individuals whose impact remains lesser-known and often invisible due to the nature of collaborative work, or their marginal position in society. The diversity of Bouhéreau's collections and contributions point us not only backwards in time, but also forwards, as their untapped potential mirrors that of the erudite man who assembled and cared for them, their trajectories testifying to the often imperceptible ingenuity and resilience of communities experiencing persecution and exile.

Élie Bouhéreau (1643–1719): a biographical sketch

JEAN-PAUL PITTION

Élie Bouhéreau was a *réformé*, a member of the French seventeenth-century Reformed (Calvinist) churches, the *Églises Prétendues Réformées*, as they were officially termed. A physician from La Rochelle, he fled France at the Revocation of the Edict of Nantes and after years of roaming, found refuge in Ireland where he lived the rest of his life as the first librarian of Marsh's Library in Dublin.

He was born at 2 a.m. on 5 May 1643 in La Rochelle.[1] His father Élie senior was a pastor, just as his father had been before him. The son probably received his first education from a tutor, like many sons of the professional elite of the time.[2] He then was sent to acquire a classical education in a college of humanities from 1656 to 1662.[3] The *académie* of Saumur that he attended was one of four Protestant institutions of higher learning sponsored by *Églises réformées*.[4] Known throughout reformed Europe for its liberal theological doctrine, the *académie* was also reputed for the scholarship of its professors and the high standard of the teaching it provided.[5]

Élie Bouhéreau graduated with the *maîtrise-ès-arts* in 1659. While initially a *proposant en théologie*, he did not complete the two-year course in theology that led to a doctorate, although two of his close college companions and long-term friends, Daniel Henri Delaizement and André Lortie, did,[6] and became ministers of local churches. Élie subsequently resided in Paris in 1664, then

---

[1] He was baptized on Sunday, 10 May 1643, by pastor Flanc in the temple of the Reformed Church of La Rochelle in Villeneuve. His godfather was pastor Philippe Vincent, and his godmother was Jehanne Pajot, wife of Jehan Richard. Archives départementales de la Charente-Maritime, registres pastoraux de La Rochelle, I. 171–3, p. 145. http://www.archinoe.net/v2/ark:/18812/6fbc08f7344181e2ebfb92219986e454, accessed on 12 July 2024.
[2] Mathieu-Jules Gaufres, 'L'enseignement protestant sous l'édit de Nantes', *Bulletin historique et littéraire (Société de l'Histoire du Protestantisme Français)*, 47 (1898), 230–42. [3] Ruth Whelan, 'La correspondance d'Élie Bouhéreau (1643–1719): les années folâtres', *Littératures classiques*, 71:1 (2010), 94. [4] For more on Protestant institutions of higher learning at the time, see: Daniel Bourchenin, *Étude sur les académies protestantes en France au XVIe et XVIIe siècle* (Paris, 1882). [5] Jean-Paul Pittion, 'Être collégien à Saumur sous l'édit de Nantes' in Yves Krumenacker and Boris Noguès (eds), *Protestantisme et éducation dans la France moderne* (Lyon, 2014), pp 95–107. https://doi.org/10.4000/books.larhra.3642, accessed 11 July 2024.
[6] For more on the status of a *proposant en théologie* at this time see: Thomas Guillemin and Julien Léonard, 'Une identité d'entre-deux. Les proposants sous le régime de l'édit de Nantes', *Revue d'histoire du protestantisme*, 7:1 (2022), 9–64. For more on what the correspondence communicates about Élie's decision to abandon the ministerial path, see: Whelan, 'La correspondance d'Élie Bouhéreau', 94 and 99–100, and Ruth Whelan and Roger Zuber, 'West coast connections: the correspondence network of Élie Bouhéreau of La

travelled for five months in 1667 in Italy with his maternal cousin and close friend, Élie Richard, with whom he went on to study medicine in the principality of Orange.[7]

His medical degree from Orange entitled him to practise medicine, not 'urbi et orbi' but as *médecin ordinaire* for a town council or as attached to a noble household.[8] Élie had inherited land, which provided him an income from rent, but he nevertheless joined the health service run by the municipality of La Rochelle and started a medical practice. Some of his prescriptions, together with those of some of his colleagues are among his papers in Marsh's Library. He was by standards of the period, a competent and modern physician, prescribing both Galenic and chemical compositions, as well as a prudent practitioner, drawing on the experience he acquired in Orange where most of the training of future physicians was done in a charitable hospital founded by the town council.[9]

Soon after returning to La Rochelle, Élie married Marguerite Massiot, his cousin, and daughter of the prominent Massiot merchant family.[10] The couple settled in rue des Augustins and had eight children. In appearance, until the 1680s, Élie's life was not very different from that of other provincial professionals of the day. In reality, his religion set him apart from most other members of the local professional elite. From his ancestors Élie had inherited a deep commitment to the Protestant church. He was a stalwart member of the Protestant community of La Rochelle. In 1674 Élie was elected to the consistory of the Reformed Church of La Rochelle, serving as its secretary, and through correspondence, he kept informed of the life of regional *réformé* communities and devoted time to supporting them, often acting on their behalf.

What singles out Bouhéreau as opposed to the other local *réformé* elites, however, was his passion for books as a collector and reader. Whenever he could, he bought copies of *nouveautés* from Paris and Saumur booksellers. By the 1680s his library contained over 2000 volumes – a sizable number for the library of a professional of the times. His literary activity made Bouhéreau the pivot to a small provincial *respublica literaria*. He was in contact with the first secretary of the *Académie française*, Valentin Conrart, and when in Paris, participated in the latter's salons. But contrary to Conrart's circle which was multi-confessional, Bouhéreau's small republic of letters was primarily Protestant. Significantly, he once turned down an offer to correspond with a certain Vieux-Fourneau, a *réformé* who had recently returned to the Catholic Church.[11]

Rochelle' in Vivienne Larminie (ed.), *Huguenot networks, 1560–1780* (New York, 2018), pp 155–6 and 159–61. 7 Whelan, 'La correspondance d'Élie Bouhéreau', 94. 8 For more on conditions of medical practice in early modern France, see: Laurence Brockliss and Colin Jones, *The medical world of early modern France* (Oxford, 1997). 9 For more on this, see: Jean-Paul Pittion, 'Medicine and religion in seventeenth-century France: La Rochelle, 1676–1683' in Sarah Alyn Stacey and Véronique Desnain (eds), *Culture and conflict in seventeenth-century France and Ireland* (Dublin, 2004), pp 52–71. 10 Marguerite and Élie were wed on 4 November 1668. Whelan and Zuber, 'West coast connections', pp 156 and 166. 11 For the correspondence between the two men, see: Marsh's Library, MSS Z2.2.16 (7), 1–5.

The religious and cultural universe of Élie Bouhéreau abruptly changed in the 1680s, when Louis XIV abolished the Edict of Nantes. The edict, promulgated nearly a century earlier in 1598 by Henri IV, granted a number of civil and religious liberties to the Protestant minority. Its revocation in 1685 concluded nearly two decades of Louis XIV's personal reign during which, under the guise of administrative reform, Protestant liberties were increasingly restricted and the provisions of the edict gradually eroded. In 1683, when municipal health services were reorganized into medical faculties, a new faculty of medicine was set up in La Rochelle. To join it, physicians were required to sign a declaration of catholicity. Bouhéreau and his La Rochelle Protestant physician colleagues refused to sign it and were excluded from practice.[12]

Bureaucratic reform is often an occasion to exclude anybody who poses a threat, real or imagined, to authority. Louis, *le Roi très chrétien*, was an autocrat and an imperialist, in the old sense of the term. Under one king, there could only be one Law and one Faith: 'Un roi, une loi, une foi'. Many of the monarch's Protestant subjects harboured the illusion until the very day the Edict of Revocation was promulgated in 1685, that the monarch would not break the solemn promise made by his ancestor Henri IV. Bouhéreau must have realized early that this was an illusion. As secretary of the La Rochelle church, he had direct experience of the hardening attitudes of clergy and crown officials towards *réformés*. In 1683, anticipating what was to come and assigned to compulsory residency (*exilé*) in Poitou by a royal *lettre de cachet* after refusing to convert,[13] he had his books packed together with his own correspondence and the archives of the church of La Rochelle and had them dispatched to England.

Among Bouhéreau's papers now kept in Marsh's Library is a diary that he started after reaching England. The *Diary*, begins with the following terse statement: 'After the Revocation of the Edict of Nantes', 'at the end of 1685, and the various persecutions carried out against the Protestants in France, I gathered those of my family who I could and I travelled to England, in the month of January, 1686. It has since pleased the Lord to grant me the return of the remainder of my family, with the exception of the youngest of my daughters, who is still withheld from me, in a convent in La Rochelle, and for whose freedom I implore the Lord every single day.' In the margin, Bouhéreau later added 'She died there, the 8/18 May 1690' – the fate of many of these *nouveaux convertis* children taken away from their parents.[14]

In the first three years of an exile that was to last nearly three decades, Élie was tutor to the two surviving sons of the duchess of Monmouth. The duchess

---

12 For more on this, see: Jean-Paul Pittion, 'Un médecin Protestant du dix-septième siècle et ses livres: anatomie de la collection Élie Bouhéreau à la bibliothèque Marsh de Dublin', *Irish Journal of French Studies*, 16:1 (2016), 35–58.   13 Eugène Haag and Emile Haag, *La France Protestante*, 3 vols (Paris, 1873–82), ii, pp 420–1.   14 Marie Léoutre, Jane McKee, Jean-Paul Pittion and Amy Prendergast (eds), *The diary (1689–1719) and accounts (1704–1717) of Élie*

was the widow of the 'Protestant Duke', executed for rebellion in 1685. For a man of Bouhéreau's learning, tutoring two rowdy young aristocrats – the eldest of the two sons was aged nine – must have been a challenge. In 1688, the duchess remarried and changes in the household may have been one of the reasons why Bouhéreau left her service. He had, however, served in a Protestant household of committed supporters of William III. The connection helped: in 1689, Bouhéreau was offered the position of secretary to Thomas Coxe who was sent to the Swiss cantons as William III's envoy.

Coxe's embassy lasted three years. In the *Diary*, which starts when he joined Coxe in his journeys, Bouhéreau meticulously recorded day-by-day all that took place during the embassy. The parts that cover the journey are written in a fine, clear hand, evidence that the Marsh's copy is a good copy transcribed from daily notes on 'feuilles volantes', that is, loose sheets.

Coxe was tasked by William III to negotiate with the Swiss cantons, in the hope that the Swiss mercenaries in the service of Louis XIV might switch to the service of William III. All Coxe could achieve, and with some difficulty, were promises of neutrality. The cantons were not prepared to commit themselves any further. One of Bouhéreau's tasks was also to give passports to refugees who wanted to go to England and to recruit some to form Huguenot regiments to serve under Britain's flag. Some of these officers from Huguenot regiments of Foot and Horse are listed among those who fought during William III's Irish campaign.

Bouhéreau was already forty-three years of age when he returned with Coxe to London, where – to quote the *Diary* – 'God blessed me with finding my family in good health, after three years absence'.[15] The travels had been exhausting: Coxe's retinue had ridden and often walked for hours on end, sometimes on hardly passable mountain roads. They enjoyed some splendid official receptions, in particular in Zurich, but some of the inns where they stopped were little better than hovels.[15a]

Bouhéreau did not rest for long though. The war of the League of Augsburg that followed was now fought in Piedmont beginning in 1693 under the command of Henri de Massue de Ruvigny, a Protestant grandee and the former representative of the French Reformed Churches at court before the Revocation. Ruvigny had distinguished himself during Willam's Irish campaign, was appointed lieutenant-general in command of the British forces in Savoy, where Bouhéreau accompanied him in the same capacity as he had with Coxe.[16] Bouhéreau's *Diary* for this period is filled with narratives of sieges, of routine combats, of redoubts won and lost and of protracted negotiations. Following Catinat's victories, the duke of Savoy, Victor Amadeus, switched sides again, and

---

Bouhéreau: Marsh's Library Z2.2.2 (Dublin, 2019), p. 2.   **15** Ibid., 21 September / 1 October 1692, p. 179.   **15a** Ibid., 21/31 October 1689, p. 15.   **16** For more on Ruvigny, see: Marie Léoutre, *Serving France, Ireland and England: Ruvigny, earl of Galway, 1648–1720* (London,

to quote William Coxe 'began that system of art and dissimulation which was necessary to effect his perfect disentanglement'.[17] When in August 1696, France, Savoy, Spain and Austria signed the separate treatise of Vigevano, Bouhéreau followed Ruvigny back to Flanders and sailed back to London.[18]

The following year, Ruvigny, as Lord Galway, was appointed lord justice of Ireland. The Anglican archbishop of Dublin, Narcissus Marsh, was one of the other two appointed commissioners and with the support of Galway's patronage, Bouhéreau was offered the post of librarian of the 'Public Library' that the archbishop was founding in Dublin and which now bears his name. In 1703 Bouhéreau and his family moved to their permanent lodgings in the 'library of Saint Sepulchre', as it was then called.[19] The following year, his wife died aged 60. They had been married for thirty-six years. She was buried in the Lady Chapel, 'the French church of Saint Patrick'.[20]

Bouhéreau spent the last sixteen years of his life in Dublin. On Galway's behalf and separately from his librarian duties, in 1704 he was given the responsibility of managing the transfer and payment of their pensions to William III's Huguenot officers who had settled in Ireland. The *Diary* records a mix of personal and family events, such as the marriages of sons and daughters, the births and baptisms of grandsons, the hiring of 'valets', purchases of clothes, but succinctly and in a matter-of-fact way. It gives us no indication of how Bouhéreau felt as a refugee, particularly of his feelings at being exiled in a foreign land, one whose population was largely Catholic and where the Huguenots were very isolated compared to those in other lands of refuge.

Most of the last decades of his working life were spent classifying the books of Narcissus Marsh's newly founded library, and 'putting [them] in order in the Library, with the help of a Mr D'Agniel'.[21] To furnish it, in 1705 Marsh had acquired at auction the entire library of Bishop Edward Stillingfleet (1635–99). The task of sorting out and recording over 10,000 volumes must have been daunting.

Bouhéreau did not follow in his ancestors' footsteps and did not become a pastor of the Reformed Church. But he showed a similar commitment to the religious tradition he had inherited and true to his faith he chose exile rather than pro forma conversion. He worshipped with the small 'official' conforming Huguenot congregation at Saint Patrick's Cathedral until his death in 1719.[22]

2018). **17** William Coxe, *Private and original correspondence of Charles Talbot, duke of Shrewsbury, with King William, the leaders of the Whig party, and other distinguished statesmen; illustrated with narratives, historical and biographical* (London, 1821), p. 279. **18** Léoutre et al., *Diary and accounts*, p. 297. **19** Ibid., p. 375. **20** Ibid., p. 333. **21** Ibid., p. 353. **22** The terms of his employment at Marsh's Library stipulated that Bouhéreau serve as precentor in the cathedral; to this end, he obtained the grade of Doctor of theology from Trinity College in 1709, subsequently serving as precentor from 1709 to 1719. Ibid., pp 359–61.

'La Rochelle, notre commune patrie': the world of the Rochelais Huguenots before the Revocation of the Edict of Nantes

MURIEL HOAREAU

La Rochelle is not merely another provincial town in Huguenot history.[1] The name of the town evokes the resistance of Protestants against the Catholic royalty during a major event, the great siege of 1628.[2] Steeped in powerful symbolism, the Atlantic port is a veritable '*lieu de memoire*' (site of memory) for the native French Protestant diaspora. This chapter aims to recreate the context in which Élie Bouhéreau and the Protestants of La Rochelle found themselves before the 'great Refuge'. Many Huguenots that were exiled at the time of the Refuge were natives of La Rochelle. Among those remembered by history, one finds Paul Colomiès (1638–1692), Élie Bouhéreau's contemporary and librarian to the archbishop of Canterbury in Lambeth Palace, or in the following generation, Théophile Désaguliers (1683–1744), disciple of Isaac Newton, and later a custodian of the Royal Society and active member of the Masonic Grand Lodge of London.[3] Other descendants of Rochelais families forced into exile made a

Translated from the French by DCU Translation Services. 1 If the reader wishes to explore further some of the topics summarized in this article, they should consult the following valuable bibliographical references: Abraham Tessereau, *Histoire des Réformés de La Rochelle et du païs d'Aunis, depuis l'année 1660 jusqu'à l'année 1685, en laquelle l'Édit de Nantes a été révoqué* (Amsterdam, 1709); Louis Delmas, *L'Église réformée de La Rochelle, étude historique* (Toulouse, 1870); Philip Benedict, *The Huguenot population of France, 1600–1685: the demographic fate and customs of a religious minority* (Philadelphia, 1994); Kevin C. Robbins, *City on the ocean sea, La Rochelle, 1530–1650: urban society, religion, and politics on the French Atlantic frontier* (Leiden, 1997); Neil Kamil, *Fortress of the soul: violence, metaphysics, and material life in the Huguenots' New World, 1517–1571* (Baltimore, 2005); Mickaël Augeron, Didier Poton, Bertrand Van Ruymbeke, *Les Huguenots et l'Atlantique* (Paris, Presses de l'Université Paris-Sorbonne, 2009–12); Muriel Hoareau, Louis-Gilles Pairault, Didier Poton, *Huguenots d'Aunis et de Saintonge, XVIe–XVIIIe siècle* (Paris, 2017). 2 This historic event, which pitted France against England, intensified political issues such that it gained attention across all of contemporary Europe. The countless depictions and accounts that were created between 1627 and 1629 helped to drive, in France and in the Anglo-Saxon world, the lasting image of a rebellious Protestant city. See Christian Jouhaud, 'Imprimer l'événement: La Rochelle à Paris' in Roger Chartier (ed.), *Les usages de l'imprimé XVe–XIXe siècle* (Paris, 1987), pp 381–438. It should be noted that Marsh's Library preserves, in the Stillingfleet collection, a rich series of pamphlets devoted to the events in La Rochelle in the 1620s. 3 Paul Colomiès was the son of the doctor Jean Colomiès and grandson of Pastor Jérôme Colomiès, who was practising at the same time as Élie Bouhéreau's father. Théophile Désaguliers was the son of Jean Désaguliers, minister of Aytré, a town neighbouring La Rochelle. See R. Julian Roberts,

mark on the history of their places of refuge, such as the Godeffroys in Hamburg or the Faneuils in Boston.[4] Several thousand French Protestants coming from across the country also passed through the port at the time of the Refuge to leave France and travel to the Netherlands, Britain and North America. New Rochelle was founded in the latter in 1688 in reference to this place of origin.

Amid the hazards of exile, Élie Bouhéreau contributed to the memory of the Refuge, by preserving his personal library, but also his correspondence before 1685 and the archives of the Reformed Church of La Rochelle. This exceptional conservation effort, especially his willingness to transport these documents in their entirety, is proof of his strong attachment to his community and his native region.[5] The purpose of this chapter is not to write a biography of Marsh's Library's first librarian, but rather to study the environment in which he lived, up until his forced departure.[6] The local context shines a light on the particular trajectory of the Huguenots exiled from the province of Aunis, even as it elucidates the similarities of their experiences to those of Huguenots who left other regions in France.[7] Studying the environment specific to the Rochelais Protestants before the Revocation of the Edict of Nantes enables us to comprehend their material and immaterial culture, and to interrogate the influence their place of origin had on their individual and collective experience of exile.

'Colomiès, Paul (1638–1692), writer and librarian', https://www.oxforddnb.com/view/10.1093/ref:odnb/9780198614128.001.0001/odnb-9780198614128-e-5982, and Patricia Fara, 'Desaguliers, John Theophilus (1683–1744), natural philosopher and engineer', https://www.oxforddnb.com, *Oxford dictionary of national biography*, 2004, accessed 8 March 2024; Stephen W. Massil, 'Les bibliothécaires immigrés en Grande-Bretagne: Huguenots et quelques autres', *World Library and Information Congress: 69th IFLA General Conference and Council 1–9 August 2003*. Berlin, p. 21.   4 Jean Hiernard, Carl Alfred Godeffroy, Johann Diederich Hahn-Godeffroy, *Les Godeffroy, une famille au long cours: Orléans-La Rochelle-Hambourg (XVIe–XVIIIe siècle)* (Paris, 2018); Jonathan M. Beagle, 'Remembering Peter Faneuil: Yankees, Huguenots, and ethnicity in Boston, 1743–1900', *The New England Quarterly*, 75:3 (2002), 388–414.   5 Newport J.D. White, Léopold Delayant, 'Elias Bouhéreau of La Rochelle, first public librarian in Ireland', *Proceedings of the Royal Irish Academy*, 27C (1908), 126–58. This article states that the archives of the church of La Rochelle had been stored in a chest, together with Élie Bouhéreau's correspondence from before 1685, which demonstrates the will to preserve and transport this memory in its entirety. We have not identified, however, the source mentioned by White, stating that Élie Bouhéreau had expressed the wish that the documents relating to the church be returned to La Rochelle when the Protestant religion was once again tolerated in France.   6 Aside from the aforementioned reference, several studies have been dedicated to Élie Bouhéreau's years in France or the composition of his library before exile, in particular Ruth Whelan, 'La correspondance d'Élie Bouhéreau (1643–1719): les années folâtres', *Littératures classiques*, 71:1 (2010), 91–112, and Jean-Paul Pittion, 'Un médecin Protestant du dix-septième siècle et ses livres: anatomie de la collection Élie Bouhéreau à la bibliothèque Marsh de Dublin', *Irish Journal of French Studies*, 16:1 (2016), 35–58.   7 Recent work of historians highlights this comprehensive approach to the Refuge, in particular Owen Stanwood, *The global refuge: Huguenots in an age of empire* (New York, 2020). Numerous scientific research studies focus on the Huguenot culture, particularly Myriam Yardeni, *Le Refuge huguenot. Assimilation et culture* (Paris, 2002), and

THE MEMORY OF A PROTESTANT TOWN PROTECTIVE OF ITS INDEPENDENCE

To better understand the circumstances under which the Rochelais Huguenots lived in the second half of the seventeenth century, we must recall the origins of Protestantism in La Rochelle and place the Reformed community within the broader history that it safeguarded. Facing the sea, the town of La Rochelle is surrounded by marshy land that made accessing the town overland rather difficult for a long time. In the absence of a river leading inland, the port is above all connected to the nearby islands of the pertuis Breton inlet – Île de Ré and Île d'Oléron – and to other ports in the Atlantic. This location on the 'Atlantic frontier' and on strategic trade routes placed the city at the centre of geopolitical issues that pitted France against England throughout the Middle Ages and the Renaissance.[8] It is in this context that the port city progressively developed its own political culture throughout the fifteenth and sixteenth centuries, based on numerous privileges. This autonomy vis-à-vis the Kingdom of France could be seen in the administrative organization of the *corps de ville* (municipal government), which was based on the oligarchic power of a small number of powerful bourgeoisie families. It was also reflected in the economic power of the town and reached its peak with the development of Protestantism. From 1539, the Rochelais were won over by the ideas of the Reformation, which were gradually spreading. After the first Reformed Church was founded in 1557, the Rochelais population converted en masse to the Protestant religion under the reign of Henry II. Calvinism, which was adopted by the elite, rapidly became the majority religion but not without conflict with the Catholic population. During the French Wars of Religion, La Rochelle, a Protestant surety town since the peace treaty of Saint-Germain of 1570, served as a capital of the (Protestant) cause for a number of years. It harboured several leaders of the Huguenot party, including from its highest ranks, Jeanne d'Albret and her son, the future Henry IV. Besieged for several months in 1572–3 after the Saint Bartholomew's Day massacres, the city served, through the different civil wars which led to the Edict of Nantes in 1598, as a place of refuge for Protestants threatened in other French regions.

Although the Protestant city prospered under the reign of Henry IV, under the regency of Marie de Médicis, its power was less and less tolerated. After an initial embargo, which weakened it in 1621–2, La Rochelle was besieged by Cardinal Richelieu in 1628. At the end of a conflict that lasted more than a year,

---

Philip Benedict et al., *L'identité huguenote: faire mémoire et écrire l'histoire, XVIe–XXIe siècle* (Droz, 2014). More specific research was conducted on Protestants originating in the west of France and the La Rochelle region, in particular: Denise Bélanger, Jean Combes, Francine Ducluzeau, *Histoire des protestants charentais: Aunis, Saintonge, Angoumois* (Paris, 2001).
8 The term 'Atlantic frontier' is taken from Kevin C. Robbins, who elaborates on the analysis of the economic and geographic context of La Rochelle at the time of the Reformation in his

in which the English naval forces led by the duke of Buckingham confronted Richelieu's French army, La Rochelle surrendered, thousands of inhabitants having lost their lives before it ended in November 1628. The town lost all its privileges. It was still suffering the traumatic consequences of this great siege, which completely changed its demographics, when Élie Bouhéreau was born in 1643. In 1610, the flourishing Huguenot city had 22,000–23,000 inhabitants, around 80% of whom were Protestant. During the triumphal arrival of Richelieu at the end of 1628, only 5,400 inhabitants were on the census. It was not until around 1680 that the population recovered to the same level it had been at the start of the century, but from then on 80% of the inhabitants were Catholics.[9]

THE PROTESTANT MINORITY AFTER THE SIEGE AND BEFORE THE REVOCATION

The Protestant population became a minority, mainly due to the royal decision that stipulated that 'No person professing to be of the so-called Reformed Religion, and to be of any other than the Roman, Catholic & Apostolic Religion [...], will be welcome to take up new residence in the aforementioned town, unless they have already resided there previously, and were previously there before the arrival of the English'.[10] Like the Bouhéreaus, as well as the aforementioned Colomiès and Désaguliers families, the Protestant families living in the city in the second half of the seventeenth century had therefore been established there for several generations.[11] This situation probably increased the ties in a community that was already organized around a strong propensity to endogamy. The new generations of Protestants, however, lived in an urban area that was undergoing dramatic reconfiguration. With the exception of the towers that protected the entry to the port, all of the ramparts were demolished. All Protestant places of worship had been taken over by Catholics as part of an active counter-reformation policy. In 1648, La Rochelle became the seat of the Archbishop's palace: the Protestant Great Temple, which had been consecrated in 1603, was transformed into a Catholic cathedral. The only place of worship

publication *City on the ocean sea*. 9 This demographic data is taken from the following articles: Louis Pérouas, 'Sur la démographie rochelaise', *Annales. Économies, sociétés, civilisations*, 16:6 (1961), 1131–40, and Philip Benedict, 'La population réformée française de 1600 à 1685', *Annales. Économies, sociétés, civilisations*, 42:6 (1987), 1433–65. Kevin C. Robbins also demonstrates that urban density in La Rochelle was exceptionally high during the first decade of the seventeenth century compared to in Liverpool in the nineteenth century: the former had 500 people per hectare compared to 230 people per hectare in the latter. *City on the ocean sea*, p. 49. 10 *Déclaration du Roy sur la réduction de la ville de La Rochelle en son obéissance: contenant l'ordre & police que sa majesté veut y estre establie. Vérifié en Parlement le 15. janvier mil six cens vingt-neuf* (Paris, 1628), p. 28. 11 The pastoral registers record the baptism of a certain Pierre Bouhéreau in 1559. See Louis Delmas, *L'Église réformée de La Rochelle: étude historique* (Toulouse, 1870).

still permitted was a new, more modest temple, built in 1630 in the neighbourhood of Villeneuve, and which would be demolished in March 1685.[12]

The measures carried out against the representatives of the *Religion Prétendue Réformée* (R.P.R.), the 'So-called Reformed Religion', were increasingly coercive. From the Edict of Nîmes in 1629 at the beginning of the reign of Louis XIV, the royal determination was to maintain peace: the provisions of the Edict of Nantes were reaffirmed in 1643 and 1652. Catholic preachers roamed the town trying to convert individuals. Tensions between Catholics and Protestants primarily gave rise to local harassment and provocation.

From the beginning of the personal reign of Louis XIV, however, the Edict was applied strictly: the state's will for religious unification of the kingdom led to increasing oppression of the Protestant population. In contrast to other localities in the province, Protestantism was permitted for a long time in La Rochelle. But from 1679, pastors were expelled, forcing them into exile – André Lortie fled to England in 1682, Jean Désaguliers, pastor of the neighbouring commune of Aytré had to move to Guernsey in 1683. Restrictions also extended into everyday life via the violent *dragonnades*, which billeted soldiers in homes to pressure Huguenots to convert. Young Protestant girls were also taken from their parents and put into Catholic convents to be converted by force.[13]

The oppression was becoming more and more pernicious, including banning *réformés* from practicing certain professions. Corporations required a certificate of Catholicism and it became difficult, if not impossible, to practice liberal professions such as those of apothecary, midwife or doctor. In 1683, Catholic doctors, including Nicolas Venette, successfully excluded their Protestant counterparts, Élie Bouhéreau, Élie Richard and Jean Seignette from the medical profession.[14]

Facing increasing threats, which ended in the Revocation of the Edict of Nantes via the Edict of Fontainebleau in October 1685, the Rochelais Protestants were confronted with a Cornelian dilemma: convert to Catholicism, or go into exile in spite of the ban on leaving the kingdom for members of the R.P.R., and the confiscation of their assets if they were to contravene it. Some, for example Élie Richard, Élie Bouhéreau's close cousin, chose a third option which was to stay and practice their religion in private or in secret, while publicly adopting

---

12 It was in the area of this temple, near the Maubec gate, that Élie Bouhéreau's mother, Blandine Richard lived in the 1660s.   13 A daughter of Élie Bouhéreau was taken from her family in this way and died in a convent. The details of this practice appear in the documents from a case that had some repercussions at the beginning of the eighteenth century. It related to the daughter of Jean Ribaut and Françoise Lévesque, who was forced into a convent by Intendant Bégon in 1692. See: 'Puissance de l'amour maternel. Françoise Levesque, l'intendant Bégon, le marquis de La Galissonnière et Anne Ribaut', *Recueil de la commission des arts et monuments historiques de la Charente-Inférieure et société d'archéologie de Saintes*, 4th series (1893–14), ii, pp 60–70.   14 Jean-Paul Pittion, 'Medicine and religion in seventeenth-century France: La Rochelle, 1676–1683' in Sarah Alyn Stacey and Véronique Desnain (eds), *Culture and conflict in seventeenth-century France and Ireland* (Dublin, 2004), pp 52–71.

Catholicism as a façade.[15] Between 1681 and 1685, close to 3,000 Rochelais Protestants, almost two-thirds of the congregation, had thus left their native town, primarily going to England and the Netherlands (two destinations that accounted for 85% of all departures), but also to Switzerland, North America or Hamburg.[16]

The religious practices of the Rochelais Protestants hardly changed from the end of the sixteenth century to the time of the Great Refuge. Being Calvinist, the Aunis churches were organized according to the *Discipline des églises Réformées de France* (The discipline of the Reformed Churches of France). They were organized around several ministers and a consistory made up of approximately twenty deacons and elders who exerted significant control over the traditions of the congregation. Ecclesiastical discipline followed the precepts of the Confession of Faith of 1571, known as the *Confession de La Rochelle*, in addition to the guidelines of different synods. Historians regularly question whether members of the congregation personally adhered to this discipline.[17] The Reformation spread rapidly in this coastal region, where the network of Catholic clergy was relatively weak. Forms of devotion varied in this coastal and maritime environment.[18] Adhering to Calvinism didn't stop the spread of certain popular beliefs or practices inherited from several centuries of Catholicism. For example, the faithful believers experienced great difficulty in complying with the austere dictates of the Ecclesiastical discipline in relation to funeral rituals. Although all ceremonies related to burial were prohibited, Joseph Guillaudeau mentions in his journal that there were 3,000 people present at the burial of Minister Jacques Merlin in 1620.[19]

As the consistory archives of the seventeenth century have not been preserved, it is difficult to calculate the discrepancy between the instructions of the Church and their application by the faithful. However, other sources show that pastors seem to have undertaken an initiative to improve the morality of the faithful believers after the great siege. As such, sermons published in the years 1630–40 promoted strict moral standards, interpreting the great siege as a

---

15 Kees Meerhoff, 'Eloge de M. Richard, docteur en médecine: zones d'ombre dans la vie d'un médecin protestant à La Rochelle (1645–1706)', *Revue d'histoire du protestantisme*, 3:2 (2018), 213–41.   16 Forty-three per cent of the Protestants of Aunis and Saintonge emigrated to the Netherlands, 42% went to the United Kingdom, 8.7% to Switzerland, 3.5% to North America and 1.7% to Hamburg, according to Didier Poton, *Les Protestants de La Rochelle* (La Crèche, 2018), p. 26.   17 From demographic and statistical analyses, Philip Benedict demonstrated that the behaviour of the Protestant communities was consistent with the moral dictates of their churches: low rates of illegitimate births or conception before marriage, compliance with the 1662 ban on celebrating marriages during Advent or Lent, etc. Philip Benedict, 'The Huguenot population of France, 1600–1685: the demographic fate and customs of a religious minority', *Transactions of the American Philosophical Society*, 81:5 (1991), 111.   18 Didier Poton, 'Dévotion et piété maritimes huguenotes au XVIIe siècle: seureté du navigage ou manuel de prières pour ceux qui vont sur la Mer (1665)', *Religion et navigation: De l'Antiquité à nos jours* [online]. (Rennes, 2016).   19 'Diaire de Joseph Guillaudeau, sieur de Beaupréau (1584–1643), publié par M. Louis Meschinet de Richemond', *Société des*

consequence of certain deviances within the community.[20]

THE CULTURE OF A POWERFUL MINORITY

Like elsewhere in Europe, the spiritual life of Rochelais Protestants was punctuated by individual or family readings of the sacred texts. Reading the Bible and the Book of Psalms in the vernacular language only served to nurture the Rochelais Protestants' culture of books and writing. Bibles and New Testaments were part of the family inheritance, some copies even served as a medium for recording births and other events that were important for personal memory. Although not the preserve of the Protestants, a tradition of personal writing spread among the bourgeoisie class of the seventeenth century: two of Élie Bouhéreau's grand-uncles, Pierre and Joseph Guillaudeau, recorded political or weather events in their journals, punctuated by family events such as births, marriages and deaths. Evidence suggests a higher level of illiteracy among Catholics than Protestants across all social classes but a local study is needed on the literacy of the Rochelais people of the seventeenth century based on their religious affiliation.[21] Reading was taught in the '*petites écoles*' (village schools of the *Ancien Régime*), but also via the catechism. The *collège* of La Rochelle, founded by Jeanne d'Albret in 1571, declined in the seventeenth century due to a lack of resources and suitable teachers. Children of the wealthiest Protestant families generally continued their studies at the *académie* of Saumur where they received a humanist education centred around classic languages, theology and philosophy.[22]

The generations preceding Élie Bouhéreau were able to briefly frequent one of the first public libraries in Europe, opened in 1606 in the Saint-Yon temple and suppressed by Richelieu in 1628.[23] During the same period, printers from the town spread a number of religious, theological and controversial publications across all of Europe. While no Protestant printer could move to and set up shop in La Rochelle after the great siege, seventeenth-century scholars and notables could nevertheless call upon the services of the local Protestant bookseller and editor Pierre Savouret. Private libraries were also supplied by purchases from

archives historiques de la Saintonge et de l'Aunis (1908), p. 172. **20** Didier Poton, 'Aux origines d'une controverse entre protestants et catholiques à La Rochelle: *Sermon contre les danses* de Philippe Vincent (1634)', *Albineana. Cahiers d'Aubigné* (Paris, 2021), 257–72. **21** Such research would make it possible in particular to study the literacy rate of women according to their religious affiliation. It is notable that in Élie Bouhéreau's close circle women read and wrote, as indicated by the letters written by his mother Blandine Richard and his wife Marguerite Massiot in the correspondence kept at Marsh's Library. **22** Jean-Paul Pittion, 'Intellectual life in the *académie* of Saumur (1633–1685): a study of the Bouhéreau collection' (PhD, TCD, 1969). Yves Krumenacker and Boris Noguès (eds), *Protestantisme et éducation dans la France moderne* (Lyon, 2014). **23** This temple, which became a church in the seventeenth century, was situated in rue des Augustins, close to Élie Bouhéreau's home.

the bookshops in Saumur, or those made by Parisian correspondents. Élie Bouhéreau's library is among the most extensive of these, but it is not an isolated case. His cousin, Élie Richard, for example, had a library containing about 1,000 volumes.[24]

The presence of these private collections in the city reflected a form of intellectual vivacity: the decades that precede the Revocation were marked by the presence of a very active erudite and scientific milieu. Élie Bouhéreau's correspondence seems to indicate a certain literary exuberance, with the doctor acting as intermediary between his correspondents and the bookseller and editor, Pierre Savouret.[25] Paul Colomiès' *Bibliothèque choisie* was published by the same merchant-bookseller in 1682, with a printer's mark that contains the slogan *Vita sine literis* [sic] *mors est* ('Life without letters is death').

Primarily educated in Saumur, several Protestant scholars formed a group that devoted itself to different fields of knowledge, both classical and modern. The most renowned symbol of this scientific effervescence is *Mutus liber*, the famous book on alchemy published by Pierre Savouret in 1677 (see plate 2). An anonymous publication attributed to Doctor Isaac Baulot, but which was probably the result of group research, the *Silent book* is part of a long tradition of alchemy in the region.[26] Evidence of innovative and modern practice of medicine, pharmacy and chemistry in the town can also be found: 'Rochelle salt', a tartar salt, was invented there around 1650 by Jean Seignette, an apothecary, and his sons Jean and Élie, who developed its medical uses at the end of the century.[27]

Although the Rochelais Protestants lost their political power throughout the seventeenth century and were confronted by numerous legal and social constraints, the community was nevertheless developed in terms of its economic, social and cultural capital.

Despite progressive oppression from the royal administration, great financial power was amassed by a small number of Protestant families. In 1682, forty-six of the fifty-six main shipowners were Protestants. Even after the Revocation, powerful Protestant traders who had not not emigrated maintained an economic power that protected them from Catholic repression: Jacques Rasteau, Jehan Seignette and Pierre-Gabriel Admyrauld presided over the chamber of commerce in the eighteenth century. These traders learned to adapt to the changing maritime trade in the Atlantic during the seventeenth century. Colonial trafficking was progressively developing alongside the European and regional

[24] According to Meerhoff, *Relation des voyages faits en France,* Élie I Richard's grandson, Louis Richard Des Herbiers, donated his library to the town of La Rochelle in 1750, recreating a public library in the town more than a century after the Protestant library was confiscated by Richelieu.   [25] The network of Protestant authors that formed around Pierre Savouret did not disappear with the Revocation. It went on to continue its activity in Amsterdam.   [26] Kamil, *Fortress of the soul*, pp 378–9.   [27] Olivier Caudron, 'Découverte scientifique et succès commercial sous l'Ancien Régime: le "sel de Seignette" ou "sel de La

trade in wine and salt which up to that point had guaranteed the fortunes of the traders and the bourgeoisie from La Rochelle and Île de Ré.[28] Just like the population, the port had to recover from the great siege. After 1643, the year in which Élie Bouhéreau was born, the tonnage made a spectacular recovery thanks to a sharp increase in trade with the West Indies. The volume of goods passing through the port tripled between 1664 and 1686; by wandering along the banks of the port, the young Doctor Bouhéreau could pass by the boats loaded by the *Compagnie du Nord*, the *Compagnie du Sénégal*, and the East and West Indian companies.[29]

This lively trade contributed to the economic activity of the town and enriched the few traders who risked investing there.[30] As in the previous century, this created a flow of men, products and ideas that enlivened the port, the streets and their inhabitants. Scientists could procure exotic objects, which adorned their cabinets of curiosities, while apothecaries could obtain products from far away for their remedies. La Rochelle was a bustling transit town where one could hear the Aunis patois and French, but also English, Spanish, Portuguese, Flemish and German.

Alongside this opening to the Atlantic world, Rochelais Protestants were in contact with Huguenots throughout France and Europe. Élie Bouhéreau's correspondence offers an insight into these international intellectual networks that were observable from the sixteenth century and which developed in the following century.[31] In line with the educational instructions of Philippe Duplessis-Mornay, learning foreign languages and knowledge of the traditions and customs of other European countries was a vital part of young Rochelais' education. Pastors like Jacques Merlin studied in Geneva and travelled to the Netherlands or Great Britain before being assigned a church. Just like Élie Richard and Élie Bouhéreau, numerous young students from good families did their 'Grand Tour' of Europe before going into a profession.[32]

How did Élie Bouhéreau and his family look back on their life in La Rochelle? What memories did they have of their birthplace? While wandering the banks of Dublin's river Liffey, did the wind, the noise of the seagulls, or the range of smells sometimes remind him of the French port? The sources that are available to trace the biography of the first librarian of Marsh's Library do not enable us

Rochelle'", *Revue de la Saintonge et de l'Aunis*, 38 (2012), 35–47.   28 The fortune of Blandine Richard – Élie Bouhéreau's mother – came mainly from salt exploitation in Île de Ré. Whelan, 'La correspondance d'Élie Bouhéreau', 94.   29 Marcel Delafosse, 'La Rochelle et les Iles au XVIIe siècle', *Revue d'histoire des colonies*, 36:127–8 (1949), 238–81.   30 Marcel Delafosse et al., *Le commerce Rochelais de la fin de XVème siècle à la fin du XVIIème* (Paris, 1952).   31 Mark Greengrass, 'Informal networks in sixteenth-century French Protestantism' in Raymond Mentzer and Andrew Spicer (eds), *Society and culture in the Huguenot world, 1559–1665* (Cambridge, 2001), pp 78–97. Vivienne Larminie (ed.), *Huguenot networks, 1560–1780: the interactions and impact of a Protestant minority in Europe* (New York, 2018).   32 Élie Richard, *Relation des voyages faits en France, en Flandre, en Hollande et en Allemagne, 1708* (Paris, 2017).

to make sweeping statements on the personal feelings and emotions of this mature man exposed to exile. On the one hand, Élie Bouhéreau's writing and personal archives, like other 'ego documents' produced by contemporaries, left little room for expressing his innermost thoughts, and these documents make very few references to La Rochelle. The town appears sporadically in the journal, when he records the death of loved ones with whom he spent his childhood and who stayed in Aunis: 'I received a letter from Amsterdam, from the 5th of June, new style [a reference to the use of the Gregorian Calendar], in which I have been informed that Mr. Élie Richard, medical doctor, my first cousin, and my dear friend had died in La Rochelle, our shared Homeland.'[33] As the correspondence after 1685 has not been preserved, it is impossible to trace the connections that he may have maintained with his few friends and family members in France; after the Revocation, the majority of Élie Bouhéreau's correspondents were in the Netherlands or elsewhere in Europe.[34] Among his personal accounts, however, are references to goods that were transported by boat between La Rochelle and Dublin: spirits and 'papers': does the import of these typical products of the Charente region reflect the enduring nature of certain habits?[35]

The immaterial culture transported by the Huguenots in exile includes religious and spiritual practices, know-how passed down through generations, but also everyday practices like language or food. This cultural baggage embodies a form of continuity in the throes of expatriation. Born into the unstable context of a town undergoing drastic reconfiguration after the siege of 1628, where Protestants became a minority, Élie Bouhéreau took an eventful journey through the Europe of the League of Augsburg. His provincial life in La Rochelle was enlivened by a friendly, literary and intellectual correspondence

---

[33] 'J'ay reçu une lettre d'Amsterdam, du 5e de juin, nouveau style, où l'on me mande que Mr Elie Richard, Docteur en médecine, mon Cousin germain, et mon très cher Amy, etoit mort à La Rochelle, notre commune Patrie' He continues: 'We were raised together, studied together in Saumur, travelled together to Italy, Paris and elsewhere, and we always had a very close relationship', 'Nous avions été élevez ensemble, avions étudié ensemble à Saumur, avions fait ensemble le voyage d'Italie, et d'autres à Paris, et ailleurs, et avions toujours eu, l'un avec l'autre, une étroite liaison', Marie Léoutre, Jane McKee, Jean-Paul Pittion and Amy Prendergast (eds), *The diary (1689–1719) and accounts (1704–1717) of Élie Bouhéreau: Marsh's Library Z2.2.2* (Dublin, 2019), pp 340, 384, 386. [34] Élie Bouhéreau got his news from La Rochelle through his relatives who were living in the Netherlands; for example on 17 June 1710: 'I found out, via a letter that Madame Du Beignon wrote me from Amsterdam, dated the 27th of May, new style, about the death of Mr. Louïs Massiot, my brother-in-law, who was in La Rochelle.' 'J'y ai appris, par une Lettre, que Madame Du Beignon m'a écrite d'Amsterdam, du 27e de May, nouveau Style, la mort de Mr. Louïs Massiot, mon Beau-Frère, qui étoit à La Rochelle.' Ibid., p. 364. [35] In 1714 and 1715, the accounts show several imports of 'spirits' (probably cognac) and 'liqueurs'. Élie Bouhéreau sent Irish cider in return for these goods, which suggests that regular trading took place with one or several Rochelais correspondents, especially as the duties paid for 'documentation' and 'some packages' were also mentioned. Léoutre et al., *Diary and accounts*, pp 516, 524, 530, 534, and 552.

network that he most likely maintained in Ireland. Raised in the polyglot and cosmopolitan environment of the Atlantic port and well-versed in travel from the 'Grand Tour' that he completed in his youth, he knew how to adapt to different situations in England, then in Ireland, and how to settle with his family there. In both Élie Bouhéreau's journal and his last will and testament, this family unit emerges as responsible for the transmission of knowledge and religion.[36] This succession of generations traced the impact of the Refuge over time, and transcended material and geographical concerns.

---

[36] We can read, for example, in the last will and testament, cited by Newport J.D. White, 'Elias Bouhéreau of La Rochelle, first public librarian in Ireland', pp 149 and 150: 'I leave to my eldest son's keeping such Papers as concern the affairs of the family: and I bestow upon my youngest all such things as have any relation to sciences, and learning [...]. I shall leave you riches enough, if I leave you such a Treasure, as the favour of God is.'

John Locke and Élie Bouhéreau: an encounter

GEOFF KEMP

INTRODUCTION

Exile takes many forms, as do the encounters that expatriation brings, some being more conspicuous than others, although any might yield insight into human experience and interaction, whether among notable or less noted figures. Between November 1675 and May 1679, one of the most notable, John Locke, future author of the *Essay concerning human understanding* (1689–90), *Two treatises of government* (1689–90) and *Letter concerning toleration* (1690), lived and travelled in France. By his own account, Locke left his homeland for reasons of respiratory health, though self-exile came at a moment of regime reaction against the oppositionist politics of his patron, the earl of Shaftesbury. On departing, he began a journal bequeathing a day-by-day record of his travels and impressions in France.[1] He travelled south to Montpellier, after a year returned to Paris, then set out again in July 1678 to shepherd a young English tourist, Caleb Banks, along the Loire Valley and onward. In early September they reached La Rochelle, where Locke noted details of a medicinal remedy to which he attached the names 'Mr Richard & Dr Bouhereau of Rochelle' – the physicians Élie Richard and his cousin Élie Bouhéreau.[2]

The journal bore the barest details of the encounter and the two Englishmen soon continued their journey, but Locke subsequently received a list of French authors and books, signed, 'Bouhéreau, Docteur en Médicine, Rue des Augustins, A La Rochelle' (see plate 4).[3] Evidently Bouhéreau had been asked about reading as well as remedies and sought to respond. The list survives among Locke's papers in the Bodleian Library, where another item confirms further contact beyond the encounter in La Rochelle: a notebook with a list of payments of mysterious purpose, above which is written 'Mr Bouhereau'.[4] The evidence is modest but intriguing, inviting exploration of the connection

---

[1] Locke's journal entries for this period are printed in John Lough (ed.), *Locke's travels in France, 1675–9* (Cambridge, 1953). Entries relating to medical matters appear more fully in Kenneth Dewhurst, *John Locke, physician and philosopher: a medical biography* (London, 1963), pp 62–151. I am grateful for support in completing the present research to Marsh's Library, including a Maddock research fellowship, and to the Faculty of Arts, University of Auckland. [2] Bodleian Library, Oxford, MS Locke f. 3. Locke's journal, 1678, p. 279; Dewhurst, *John Locke*, p. 139; cf. Lough, *Locke's travels*, p. 231, fn. 1. [3] Bodleian Library, Oxford, MS Locke b.2. Papers relating to Locke's books and library, 1675–1704, fo. 24. [4] Bodleian Library, Oxford, MS Locke f. 15. A pocket memorandum book, 1677/78, p. 152.

between two figures notable, to their varying degrees, in the world of books and the world of the Huguenots. Tracing Locke's path to Bouhéreau also finds connections through encounters with individuals who featured in the lives of both men, inviting essays from the main path to that of the Parisian apothecary Moyse Charas, and more briefly to Locke's friend and Bouhéreau's later employer Thomas Coxe. The encounters yield insight into the lives and networks of Locke and Bouhéreau against the backdrop of France in the decade before Revocation, before either man achieved substantial recognition.

Élie Bouhéreau's notability is in the ascendant given publication of his own diary and related attention, although his life before 1689, when he began his journal, remains patchily known, the absence of an earlier Bouhéreau diary making Locke's perspective a rare source of insight.[5] The Englishman's notability probably can ascend little further than it has, his tolerationist fame alone meaning that in accounts of the Huguenot experience the non-Huguenot Locke has tended to eclipse the Huguenot Bouhéreau. Recent research augments older accounts in tracing engagement with the Huguenot world that was intellectual, political, and practical for Locke.[6] Among French-speaking Protestants, his close associate Jean Le Clerc, a Genevan refugee in Amsterdam, was instrumental in announcing the *Essay* through the 1688 'Extrait' or *Abrégé* and compiled the *Eloge* to Locke's achievement after his death.[7] The French translation of Locke's *Second treatise* (1690) in 1691 was by the Huguenot minister David Mazel.[8] Another Huguenot, Pierre Coste, became Locke's resident aide and translated several of his works into French before the author's death: the *Essay* (1690/trans. 1700), *Some thoughts concerning education* (1693/1695), and the *The reasonableness of Christianity* (1695/1696).[9] Coste was also the

---

5 Marie Léoutre, Jane McKee, Jean-Paul Pittion and Amy Prendergast (eds), *The diary (1689–1719) and accounts (1704–1717) of Élie Bouhéreau: Marsh's Library Z2.2.2* (Dublin, 2019).   6 See the following, and further notes below: John Marshall, *John Locke, toleration and early Enlightenment culture* (Cambridge, 2006); Delphine Soulard, 'Anglo-French cultural transmission: the case of John Locke and the Huguenots', *Historical Research*, 85 (2012), 105–32; Petter Korkman, 'Locke's civil philosophy in the early eighteenth-century république: an important footnote' in Sami-Juhani Savonius-Wroth, Paul Schuurman and Jonathan Walmsley (eds), *The Continuum companion to Locke* (London, 2010), pp 302–13; Robin Gwynn, *Huguenot heritage* (London, 1985), pp 83–6; Gabriel Bonno, *Les relations intellectuelles de Locke avec la France* (Berkeley, 1955); E.S. de Beer, 'The Huguenots and the Enlightenment', *Proceedings of the Huguenot Society of London*, 21:3 (1968), 179–95; Ch. Bastide, 'Locke et les Huguenots', *Bulletin de la Société de l'Histoire du Protestantisme Français*, 62:1 (1913), 60–3.   7 John R. Milton, 'Locke's publications in the *Bibliothèque universelle et historique*', *British Journal for the History of Philosophy*, 19:3 (2011), 451–72; Mark Goldie, 'The early lives of John Locke' in James G. Buickerood (ed.), *Eighteenth-century thought*, vol. 3 (New York, 2007), pp 57–87. The *Eloge* was translated as *The life and character of Mr John Locke* (London, 1706).   8 S.J. Savonius, 'Locke in French: the *Du gouvernement civil* of 1691 and its readers', *Historical Journal*, 47:1 (2004), 47–79; Robin Gwynn, *The Huguenots in later Stuart Britain*, 3 vols (Brighton, 2015–20), i, pp 357–8.   9 Soulard, 'Anglo-French cultural transmission', 117–22, 126–31; J.J.V.M de Vet, 'Coste, Pierre (1668–1747)', *Oxford dictionary*

sixth Huguenot tutor employed by Locke's Somerset friends Edward and Mary Clarke in a series instigated in 1686 as part of the project of advice that became Locke's book on education.[10] Posthumous publication of Locke's works was undertaken by the Huguenot Pierre Des Maizeaux.[11] It has long been recognized that Huguenots of the Refuge were an important presence in Locke's networks and played a key role in disseminating his writings to the European Republic of Letters.

These events lay in the future, however, in the province of other accounts. In the year Locke left England for France, the MP Sir Thomas Meres, whose wife was from a Huguenot family, declared in parliament that the Edict of Nantes had been 'violated upon 100,000 Protestants'.[12] Nevertheless, by the time Locke returned in 1679 the English could still refer to their neighbour as a regime of 'Toleration after the French Fashion', Roger L'Estrange's label for Catholic and Reformed co-existence without nonconformity.[13] It was with a pre-Revocation eye that Locke viewed the country, his journal ranging over sights and encounters, books and philosophical thoughts, medical gleanings and nature notes, husbandry and horticulture, as much as the political and religious state of France and condition of the Huguenots. Locke and Bouhéreau came together as medical men of literary inclination more than out of Protestant solidarity, and beyond ending persecution of the Huguenots it is uncertain how far they would have seen eye to eye about toleration. Admittedly we know more about Locke's views, though at the end of his life Bouhéreau justified having conformed on reaching exile in England as a duty to submit 'in our native country, to be Members of such a Reformed Body, as the Church of England now is' and not to adhere to 'distinct and separate Assemblies' which 'our Churches did highly disapprove'.[14] Nonetheless, he was unlikely to have disagreed that 'Strangers should not be vexed nor oppressed', Locke's scriptural echo in his letter on

---

of national biography (*ODNB*). **10** S.J. Savonius, 'The role of Huguenot tutors in John Locke's programme of social reform' in Anne Dunan-Page (ed.), *The religious culture of the Huguenots, 1660–1750* (Aldershot, 2006), pp 137–62; Bridget Clarke, 'Huguenot tutors and the family of Edward and Mary Clarke of Chipley, 1687–1710', *Proceedings of the Huguenot Society*, 27 (2001), 501–42. Savonius names the six as, in chronological order: 'D'eully (or Duelly), Passebon, de Grassemare (or Grasemar), de la Roque (or de Laroque), Dubois and Coste.' **11** Philip Milton, 'Pierre Des Maizeaux, *A collection of several pieces of Mr. John Locke*, and the formation of the Locke canon' in Buickerood, *Eighteenth-century thought*, pp 255–91; Diane Watts, 'Pierre Des Maizeaux: a life in exile' in Jane McKee and Randolph Vigne (eds), *The Huguenots: France, exile and diaspora* (Eastbourne, 2013), pp 155–72. **12** B.D. Henning, *The House of Commons, 1660–1690*, 3 vols (London, 1983), i, p. 54. **13** Roger L'Estrange, *Toleration discuss'd; in two dialogues* (London, 1679), p. 37; Mark Goldie, 'Toleration and the Huguenots' in Goldie, *Contesting the English polity, 1660–1688* (Woodbridge, 2023), pp 157–75. **14** Bouhéreau's will was among losses when the Public Record Office of Ireland was bombed in 1922; extracts are printed as appendix B in Newport J.D. White, 'Elias Bouhéreau of La Rochelle, first public librarian in Ireland', *Proceedings of the Royal Irish Academy*, 27C (1909), pp 126–58, at 148–50. In the months after arriving in London, Bouhéreau became an elder of the conformist Savoy Church, Westminster: Gwynn,

tolerance, penned in the weeks between the Revocation and January 1686, the month Bouhéreau and his family left for England.[15] In an earlier manuscript critique of Edward Stillingfleet's attack on separation from the Established Church, Locke remarked sardonically that leaving the 'Hugonot Church' for the Church of England would count as sinful separation on Stillingfleet's logic.[16] In practice, Locke, Bouhéreau and Stillingfleet were agreed there was no sin in the special case of Huguenot nonconformity, though reflect differing positions on the broader issue of nonconformist separation, a spectrum of acceptance, disapproval and rejection.[17] In summer 1705, Bishop Stillingfleet's 10,000 books arrived in Dublin. They would be added to 2,000 of Bouhéreau's own books designated for Narcissus Marsh's planned public Library, including the copy of the *Essay* that fed Stillingfleet's attack on Locke as accomplice to anti-Trinitarian heresy in the 1690s, Locke wondering at this 'strange Copy' with words 'so often different, from those I read'.[18] In 1707, the library's statutory settlement was overseen by the *Essay*'s dedicatee, Thomas, earl of Pembroke, as lord lieutenant of Ireland.[19] Bouhéreau's own collection contained no work by either Locke or Stillingfleet and his views on their contests are typically inscrutable.

The question of religious conformity and toleration recurs in what follows but Locke and Bouhéreau's encounter can be seen within the broader context of cultural contact and informational exchange of its time. Their connection has had little attention in accounts of Bouhéreau or the vast literature on Locke, whose main biographers do not mention it.[20] Lough's edition of Locke's journals in France relegated the relevant entry to a partly-rendered footnote, while an accompanying article on 'everything which bears on his reading' omits the

Huguenots in later Stuart Britain, ii, p. 298.   **15** John Locke, *A letter concerning toleration* (London, 1690), p. 38; Mark Goldie, 'The life of John Locke' in *Continuum companion*, pp 1–36, at p. 21; Léoutre et al., *Diary and accounts*, p. 3.   **16** Lord King, *The life of John Locke*, 2 vols (London, 1830), ii, pp 202–3. The manuscript, generally known as the 'Critical notes on Stillingfleet', was compiled by Locke and James Tyrrell: see John Marshall, *John Locke: resistance, religion and responsibility* (Cambridge, 1994), pp 97–110.   **17** Bouhéreau paid contributions to the nonconforming French church of Lucy Lane, Dublin, in the last dozen years of his life, indexed at Léoutre et al., *Diary and accounts*, p. 586; see also Jean-Paul Pittion, 'The question of religious conformity and non-conformity in the Irish refuge' in C.E.J. Caldicott, H. Gough and J.-P. Pittion (eds), *The Huguenots and Ireland* (Dun Laoghaire, 1987), pp 285–96, at p. 286. The recorded contributions postdated the 1692 Irish statute (4 Wm & Mary c. 2) permitting 'Protestant Strangers' to worship by 'Rites Used in their own Countries': *Acts and statutes made in a parliament begun at Dublin, the fifth day of October, Anno Dom. 1692* (Dublin, 1713), p. 3.   **18** John Locke, *Mr Locke's reply to the Right Reverend the Lord Bishop Worcester's answer to his second letter* (London, 1699), p. 320; Léoutre et al., *Diary and accounts*, p. 409; W.N. Osborough, '6 Anne, chapter 19: "settling and preserving a publick library for ever"' in Muriel McCarthy and Ann Simmons (eds), *Marsh's Library – a mirror on the world: law, learning and libraries, 1650–1750* (Dublin, 2009), pp 39–61, at p. 46; Neil Fairlamb, 'Stillingfleet, Edward (1635–99)' in *Continuum companion*, pp 113–16.   **19** Osborough, '6 Anne', pp 39–40.   **20** The three full-length biographies merely note Locke passing through La Rochelle: Henry Richard Fox Bourne, *The life of John Locke*, 2 vols (London, 1876), i, p. 400; Maurice Cranston, *John Locke: a biography* (Oxford, 1957), p. 177;

literary list.[21] Dewhurst's 'medical biography' supplies the journal entry but not the aftermath; Bonno noted the literary list in passing.[22] More recently, Jean-Paul Pittion has referred briefly to the initial encounter and, resulting from the present research, the literary list has been noted in Noreen Humble's work on Bouhéreau and, as a 'letter', has been printed in a ninth volume of the *Correspondence of John Locke* (2023), edited by Mark Goldie.[23] The latter places Bouhéreau before new generations of Locke scholars while inviting elaboration and examination of the encounter at La Rochelle and the connections linking the two men, revealed by following Locke's steps as he proceeded through France. The perspective to this extent is that of Locke but as a journey viewed through the lens of linkages to Bouhéreau's world.

LOCKE AND COXE: IN MONTPELLIER AND BEYOND

Locke's French journey had been cultural before actual, and slow progress initially. As a young Oxford don in 1659 he hailed the 'genius' of Jean-Louis Guez de Balzac, an author later listed by Bouhéreau, though Locke knew him in English translation, as his library records show.[24] Locke's many notebook references to his reading do not cite any books in French prior to 1676, as John Milton has observed.[25] He had first ventured abroad in the winter of 1665–6 to Cleves, and in autumn 1672 made a short visit to France, joining a friend from his medical studies, Dr John Mapletoft, in Lady Northumberland's entourage, which also included his relation Margaret Blomer.[26] Easing his own chest condition was a motivation, Blomer writing with alarm that 'you soe plainely tell mee that tis france must give you life'.[27] In the event, Locke spent a fortnight in Paris before deciding against continuing south, referring obscurely to duties with Shaftesbury back in England.

Three years later, having recently gained his medical degree, and after further preparatory noises about his health, Locke departed London for France on 12

Roger Woolhouse, *Locke: a biography* (Cambridge, 2007), p. 145. 21 Lough, *Locke's travels*, p. 231, fn. 1; Lough, 'Locke's reading during his stay in France', *The library*, 5th series, 8 (1953), pp 229–58, at p. 229. 22 Dewhurst, *John Locke*, p. 139; Bonno, *Relations intellectuelles*, p. 68. Bonno mistakenly supposed the list was given to Locke in La Rochelle in 1678. 23 Jean-Paul Pittion, 'Medicine and religion in seventeenth-century France: La Rochelle, 1676–83' in Sarah Alyn Stacey and Véronique Desnain (eds), *Culture and conflict in seventeenth-century France and Ireland* (Dublin, 2004), pp 52–71, at pp 53–4; Noreen Humble, 'Élie Bouhéreau (1643–1719): a scholar at work in his libraries', *Lias*, 44:2 (2017), 143–98, at p. 147; John Locke, *The correspondence of John Locke*, ed. E.S. de Beer and Mark Goldie, 9 vols (Oxford, 1976–2023), ix, pp 65–7. 24 Locke, *Correspondence*, i, p. 95; John Harrison and Peter Laslett (eds), *The library of John Locke* (2nd ed., Oxford, 1971), p. 79. 25 J.R. Milton, 'Life and works' in Jessica Gordon-Roth and Shelley Weinberg (eds), *The Lockean mind* (Abingdon, 2022), pp 7–11, at p. 8. 26 Cranston, *John Locke*, pp 81–4, and 145–6; Woolhouse, *Locke*, pp 60 and 111. 27 Locke, *Correspondence*, i, p. 343.

November 1675.[28] An added impetus was parliament that week having burned the anonymous *A letter from a person of quality to his friend in the country* and launched a hunt for those behind the 'scandalous, and seditious book'. In the event, neither Shaftesbury or his suspected assistant 'Pen-Man', Locke's role, was punished.[29] If Locke left to escape the metaphorical heat at home, healthier climate and broader horizons chiefly kept him from returning early. On 4 January 1676 he reached Montpellier, where he engaged a tutor in French for himself and an accompanying college friend, George Walls.[30] The southern city remained Locke's base until early 1677, his journal record ranging across subjects including its famous medical faculty and local olive oil and wine production, as well as the area's large Huguenot minority. From the Protestant physician Charles Barbeyrac, uncle of the later Lockean writer Jean Barbeyrac, he took the information that in recent times there were 'at least 160 churches pulled down' though 'They & the papist laity live together friendly enough in these parts.'[31] Protestants were deprived 'every day of something, some priviledg or other', Locke continued, his example being the Reformed Church authorities losing power to examine witnesses on oath. Under a marginal heading of 'Toleration', he added, 'If any one hold tenets contrary to their articles of faith, the King punishes him, soe that you must be here either of the Romish or their church', instancing a local man who risked being 'burnt as a Heretick' for Arian beliefs but escaped prison.[32] Locke's concern for the Huguenots accompanied a realistic grasp that Reformed Church discipline, like that of the church in England, ran counter to his developing views on toleration and the Trinity, as John Marshall has argued.[33]

In his early weeks in Montpellier, Locke encountered a fellow medically trained Englishman sympathetic to nonconformity, a younger man of subsequent importance in Élie Bouhéreau's life. This was Thomas Coxe, who thirteen years later would take the Huguenot refugee as his secretary on his three-year mission as envoy to the Swiss cantons. Locke's journal entry of 14 February 1676 noted a remedy for 'the pox or ill curd claps' imparted by 'Mr. Cox', who had learned it in Italy.[34] By July, Coxe was back in England with his father, the prominent physician Dr Thomas Coxe, Mapletoft writing to Locke that 'Dr. Coxe laments your not coming with his Son, but owns his obligations to you for the kindness you did him whilst you were together.' The nature of the

---

28 Lough, *Locke's travels*, p. 1. 29 *Journal of the House of Lords: volume 13, 1675–1681* (London, 1767–1830), 8 November 1675, pp 13–14, British History Online; John Locke, '*An essay concerning toleration*': *and other writings on law and politics, 1667–1683*, ed. J.R. Milton and Philip Milton, pp 97–118; Geoff Kemp, 'Politics, law, and constructive authorship: John Freke and "The most infamous libel that ever was written"', *Huntington Library Quarterly*, 84:4 (2021), 745–81, at 754–9. 30 Lough, *Locke's travels*, pp 16–17. 31 Ibid., pp 27–8. 32 Ibid., pp 40–1. 33 Marshall, *John Locke, toleration*, p. 184. 34 Dewhurst, *John Locke*, p. 64 (14 Feb. 1676). Lough omitted the text of the entry as a 'medical note': *Locke's travels*,

kindness is unclear: Locke was the elder by about eight years but Coxe the more seasoned traveller, 'more at home then I', as Locke remarked.[35]

Both Thomas Coxes would have been known to Locke before the encounter in Montpellier. Coxe senior was in effect 'grandparent' to Locke the medical man, having inspired the career of Locke's friend and mentor Thomas Sydenham, the 'English Hippocrates', who recalled the debt as well as lauding Mapletoft and Locke for assistance in his *Observationes medicae* (1676). Locke, whose laudatory verse to Sydenham for his work on fevers also appeared in the volume, had copies sent to Montpellier, giving one to Barbeyrac.[36] Dr Coxe, like Locke a Somerset man, had been physician to Parliament's forces from the earliest clashes of the civil war, where his famous Royalist counterpart was Dr William Harvey, the death of whose brother at the end of 1643 saw his widowed sister-in-law soon remarried – to Dr Coxe.[37] Mary Coxe was first cousin to Charles I's antagonist John Hampden and shared the family's Presbyterian commitments: her funeral sermon in 1679 was delivered by Richard Baxter.[38] The couple's eldest son, Thomas, the later envoy and employer of Bouhéreau, was probably born in 1645.

The younger Thomas Coxe is something of a neglected prodigy, often confused with Coxe senior and in accounts of Bouhéreau only noticed from 1689.[39] He followed his father into membership of the Royal Society in late 1663, proposed by Robert Boyle, ahead of gaining a medical degree.[40] Between 1665 and 1667 he played an important role in the Royal Society's experimental programme of animal blood transfusions, initiated by Locke's friend and teacher Richard Lower, at a time when Locke's own work on the relationship between blood and respiration led him to consider animal vivisection.[41] In October 1667,

---

p. 42, fn. 1.   35 Locke, *Correspondence*, i, pp 451 (28 June, Old Style) and 576.   36 Thomas Sydenham, *Observationes medicae* (London, 1676), sigs. A3r–v, A6r, c3r–c4r; Locke, *Correspondence*, i, p. 492 and 515. Locke's poem had first appeared in the 1668 second edition of Sydenham's *Methodus curandi febres* (1666).   37 Edwyn Sandys, *The declaration of Col: Edwyn Sandys* (London, 1642), p. 8; The UK National Archives, Kew (TNA), PROB 11/191/9. Will of Mathew Harvey; PROB 11/379/284. Will of Griffith Hatley; *The visitation of London, Anno Domini 1633, 1634, and 1635*, 2 vols (London, 1880–3), i, p. 363; Conrad Russell, 'Hampden, John (1595–1643)', *ODNB*; Roger French, 'Harvey, William (1578–1657)', *ODNB*; John Symons, 'Coxe, Thomas (c.1615–1685)', *ODNB*.   38 Richard Baxter, *A true believer's choice and pleasure. Instanced in the exemplary life of Mrs Mary Coxe, the late wife of Doctor Thomas Coxe* (London, 1680).   39 Christopher Storrs notes that Coxe had been 'on some sort of Grand Tour', remarking that 'Details of Coxe's life are scarce': 'Thomas Coxe and the Lindau project' in Albert de Lange (ed.), *Dall'Europa alle Valli Valdesi: Atti del convegno Il Glorioso Rimpatrio, 1689–1989* (Torino, 1990), pp 199–214 at p. 200. The present author is engaged in research towards a fuller account of the Coxes.   40 Thomas Birch, *History of the Royal Society*, 4 vols (London, 1756–7), i, pp 239, 322 and 324; Joseph Foster (ed.), *Alumni Oxonienses, 1500–1714* (Oxford, 1891), p. 310.   41 Thomas Coxe, 'An account of another experiment of transfusion, viz. of bleeding a mangy into a sound dog', *Philosophical Transactions*, 25 (6 May 1667), 451–2; Birch, *History of the Royal Society*, ii, pp 50, 112, 115, 123, 125, 133, and 161–2; Jonathan Walmsley, 'John Locke on respiration', *Medical History*,

Coxe junior was named by the Society alongside Lower, Robert Hooke and Edmund King to attempt animal-to-human blood transfusion; but instead he turned to travel abroad.[42] The Society's secretary Henry Oldenburg supplied him with a list of inquiries to pursue in Germany and Hungary, and he wrote to Boyle from Rome, although he seems to have spent most time in France, his travels there attested in 1671 by the London-based doctor and religious controversialist Louis Du Moulin, of the notable Huguenot family.[43] Coxe's earlier acquaintance with France and heterodox religious sympathies are suggested by his having translated from French in 1669 one of Du Moulin's manuscript treatises urging toleration in England.[44] The tract has not been identified, though Du Moulin's much-repeated position was an Erastian insistence on civil power in religion and that 'all Church-power is Popery', the motto he wanted on his tomb. When Du Moulin the Independent was challenged in print by Baxter the Presbyterian, each claimed that Dr Coxe was of their view, but his son appears to have been closer to Du Moulin.[45]

To look ahead from the perspective of 1676, two years later Thomas Coxe married the Lincolnshire heiress Mary Peachell, mentioned in Bouhéreau's diary (as 'Marie Péchel') and the subject of another chapter in the present volume.[46] Her inheritance quickly became absorbed into debts incurred by Coxe and his father in property speculations, to which was added political pressure in the 'Tory reaction' of Charles II's final years. Dr Coxe lost the presidency of the Royal College of Physicians in 1683 reportedly 'because he was a whig and would heare treason and not discover it'.[47] In mid-1684, the Coxes senior and junior left England, Dr Coxe dying near Calais in 1685 while his son with his wife and two children entered a wandering exile in France and the Low Countries.[48] In late 1684 or early 1685, Locke in exile in Holland briefly deputed Thomas Coxe junior in Orléans to assist their mutual friend Nicolas Toinard in efforts to

---

51 (2007), 453–76, at p. 472. The distinction of 'Mr' and 'Dr' Thomas Coxe is clear once recognized, though the son's activity has become often ascribed to the father, including in the Royal Society's online records: https://catalogues.royalsociety.org/CalmView/Record.aspx?src =CalmView.Persons&id=NA5012, accessed 24 June 2024.   42 Birch, *History of the Royal Society*, ii, p. 202.   43 Alfred Rupert Hall and Marie Boas Hall (eds), *The correspondence of Henry Oldenburg*, vol. 6 (Wisconsin, 1969), pp 75–8; Louis Du Moulin, *Jugulum causae* (London, 1671), part 1, pp 104–5.   44 N.H. Keeble and Geoffrey F. Nuttall (eds), *Calendar of the correspondence of Richard Baxter*, vol. 2, *1660–1696* (Oxford, 1991), pp 77 and 80. 45 Ibid., p. 85; Du Moulin, *Jugulum causae*, part 1, p. 248; Richard Baxter, *The difference between the power of magistrates and church-pastors* (London, 1671), p. 14. On Du Moulin, see Goldie, 'Toleration and the Huguenots', 168–74; Douglas Nobbs, 'New light on Louis Du Moulin', *Proceedings of the Huguenot Society of London*, 15 (1937), 489–509.   46 City of Westminster Archives Centre, London, Parish records of St Paul, Covent Garden (11 July 1678); Léoutre et al., *Diary and accounts*, p. 6. See Amy Prendergast's chapter in this volume. 47 TNA, PROB 11/380/334. Will of Thomas Coxe senior; Folger Library, Washington, DC, L.c. 1559. Newdigate newsletters, 8 July 1684 (digital file); Andrew Clark (ed.), *Life and times of Anthony Wood*, vol. 3 (Oxford, 1894), p. 76.   48 'Coxe, Thomas, 1615–1685', *ODNB*; Historical Manuscripts Commission (HMC), *Report on the manuscripts of the marquess of*

translate Locke's 'New Method' of note-taking, eventually seen into print by Le Clerc in the *Bibliothèque universelle* in 1686.[49] Coxe and his family returned to England at the revolution in 1688–9, as did Locke and also John Hampden, grandson of the 'patriot', who after agitation among the Huguenots at the start of the 1680s, a leading role in the Rye House Plot of 1683 and trial for treason after the 1685 Monmouth Rebellion had his services to William of Orange recognized by an offer to be envoy to the Swiss cantons for the new regime. He declined and instead proposed his relation Thomas Coxe for the post.[50] Hampden's close friend Nicolas Fatio de Duillier, the Swiss mathematician, did the same for Bouhéreau when approached by Coxe to be secretary.[51] It is possible Bouhéreau and Coxe were already known to each other through this circle, if not from Coxe's earlier travels in France. Locke too was offered an envoyship in 1689, to the elector of Brandenburg, but declined on health grounds.[52]

MOYSE CHARAS AND 'CHINA-CHINA'

In February 1677 the next vista in Locke's French journey was opened by a letter from Thomas Coxe junior in England, conveying a request from the wealthy merchant Sir John Banks to take charge of Banks' son, destined for Paris. A follow-up letter from Sir John indicated he had consulted on the matter with his friends Shaftesbury, Dr Coxe and also Samuel Pepys, with whom Caleb had spent a few months 'to weane him from home'.[53] It would be an oddity of subsequent correspondence to Caleb and Locke that Pepys addressed the former as 'Dear son'.[54]

Locke set off for Paris from Montpellier on 25 March but reached Paris only in early June, having languished for a month in Bordeaux with self-diagnosed 'tertian ague'. The term, relevant in what follows, denoted intermittent fevers within a three-day cycle, differing from 'quotidian' and 'quartan', the various

Downshire, vol. 1, part 1 (London, 1924), p. 73.   **49** Locke, *Correspondence*, ii, p. 647 and pp 701–2; John Locke, *Literary and historical writings*, in J.R. Milton, B. Chua, G. Kemp, D. McInnis, J. Spurr and R. Yeo (eds), *Literary and historical writings* (Oxford, 2016), pp 35–46. **50** William Seward, *Anecdotes of some distinguished persons*, 4 vols (London, 1796), iv, pp 419–42, at pp 441–2; White Kennett, *A complete history of England*, 3 vols (London, 1706), iii, p. 546. On Hampden, see Richard L. Greaves, 'Hampden, John (1653–1696)', *ODNB*; Justin Champion, 'Pere Richard Simon and English Biblical criticism, 1680–1700' in James E. Force and David S. Katz (eds), *Everything connects: in conference with Richard H. Popkin* (Leiden, 1999), pp 39–61 at pp 53–8.   **51** Fatio's account appears in the form of a letter of 1732 printed in *Anecdotes of some distinguished persons*, iv, pp 419–42, at pp 441–2. The letter as printed refers to 'Dr Boutreqeau', noting that the salary of £200 a year 'exceeded wt ye King allowed' and that Coxe arranged for Fatio to receive 'a considerable sum at ye Exchequer' to complete preparations. These details accord with the record made by Bouhéreau, naming Fatio: Léoutre et al., *Diary and accounts*, pp 2–3.   **52** Locke, *Correspondence*, iii, pp 573–4. **53** Locke, *Correspondence*, i, pp 462–5.   **54** J.R. Tanner (ed.), *Further correspondence of Samuel Pepys, 1662–1679* (London, 1929), pp 318–24.

cycles resulting from varying malarial parasites.[55] Locke's longstanding interest in the subject is reflected in notebook entries on 'febris intermittens' from the early 1660s and his verses acclaiming Sydenham's *Methodus curandi febres* (1666). As Locke continued to Paris, Sydenham wrote expressing alarm at the bloodletting and purging he had prescribed for himself, and prescribed instead the fresh air and exercise he would gain from riding to Calais, and from Dover to London, that is, to come home.[56]

Locke instead reached Paris, finding Caleb Banks in the care of a 'Monsieur Roseman', possibly the later emigré minister and translator Jean-Baptiste de Rosemont of the *réformée* family at Charenton.[57] Locke conveyed a Huguenot connection of his own in a letter soon after arriving, asking Boyle for a letter of introduction to Paris virtuosi to be directed to him, 'Chez Monsieur Charas maistre apothecaire rue de Boucherie dans le Fauxbourg St. German à Paris'.[58] This was Locke's address in Paris over the next two years and for a good part of this time he lodged there with Moyse Charas, apothecary, author and correspondent of Bouhéreau, a Protestant though later convert to Catholicism. At one point Locke was asked by a friend to send a copy of 'the book which your Land-lord Monsieur Charas hath printed'. This was Charas' 1,000-page *Pharmacopée royale* (1676), present in Locke's library along with Charas' earlier book, *Nouvelles expériences sur la vipere* (1672), both also in Bouhéreau's library, the work on vipers a gift mentioned in one of Charas' letters (see plate 6). The book carries Louis XIV's printed endorsement noting that Charas was apothecary to his brother, Philippe, Duc d'Orléans; Charas was also demonstrator at the Jardin royal des plantes médicinales (Royal garden of medicinal plants).[59] Locke made notes from the *Pharmacopée* and from conversation, including the treatment after Charas' wife fell and cut her face, 'so that the flesh of her cheek fell down below her mouth'. Locke also witnessed a viper killing young pigeons in an experiment probably staged by Charas. In the month he arrived in Paris, Locke's journal indicated another shared concern, that of intermittent agues, noting that, 'Mr. Charas, as he told me, has cured several quartans', having rarely failed with a dose of two drams in powder or infusion in white wine.[60] Drams of what was

---

55 Lough, *Locke's travels*, pp 136 and 143. 56 British Library, London. Add. MS 32554, fo. 119v; Locke, *Correspondence*, i, pp 488–9. 57 Locke, *Correspondence*, i, p. 483; Eugène and Émile Haag, *La France Protestante*, 10 vols (Paris, 1846–59), vii, pp 529–30; Gwynn, *Huguenots in later Stuart Britain*, i, p. 394. 58 Locke, *Correspondence*, i, p. 485. 59 Locke, *Correspondence*, i, p. 550; Harrison and Laslett, *Library of John Locke*, p. 105 (LL 662, 663 and 664); *Pharmacopée royale Galénique et chymique* (Paris, 1676); *Nouvelles expériences sur la vipère* (1672). For recent accounts of Charas' life and career, see F.W. Felix, 'Moyse Charas, maître apothicaire et docteur en médecine (Uzès 1619–Paris 1698)', *Revue d'Histoire de la Pharmacie*, 333 (2002), 63–80; Bruno Bonnemain, 'Moyse Charas, un maître apothicaire et docteur en médecine emblématique de son époque (1619–1698)', *Revue d'Histoire de la Pharmacie*, 391 (2016), 405–18. 60 Dewhurst, *John Locke*, pp 83, 88 and 119.

not specified but is revealed once we turn to Charas' letters held at Marsh's Library.

The twelve letters from Charas to Bouhéreau written between October 1677 and August 1679 make no mention of Locke but the one-sided correspondence sheds light on all three men's medical interests at this time, as well as being an untapped source on a famous episode in medical history linking the English and French courts. The contents and import of the letters invite another detour in following Locke's path.[61]

The letters show the Frenchmen's shared acquaintance with leading *réformés* such as Jean Claude and Abraham Tessereau, although their connection was first through their professional roles, between the experienced Parisian apothecary and the recruit to provincial medical practice, twenty-two years his junior. Their acquaintance clearly preceded the first extant letter, dated 29 October 1677, in which Charas updated Bouhéreau on a plan to visit England, announcing that departure was imminent and Bouhéreau could contact him through Christian Harel, Charles II's Dutch-born 'professor of chemistry'. In February 1678, Charas sent a belated report of the visit, an animated account of being 'extraordinarily well received' by the king, the Royal Society of Physicians, and the Royal Society, his *Pharmacopée royale* now being translated into English.[62] He had been attended particularly by 'Monsieur Frazer le fils' and his father, identifiable as the court physicians Charles Fraizer and Sir Alexander Fraizer, brother and father of Locke's later friend Carey Mordaunt, from 1689 countess of Monmouth.[63] Charas reported that the king's favour extended to sounding him out about a place at the English court. Charas demurred on account of his existing royal post but admitted being left in a quandary, asking Bouhéreau to treat the matter as confidential.

Locke knew of Charas' departure before Bouhéreau, having penned a letter of recommendation Charas carried to Dr Coxe, who probably helped him gain admission to one or both London societies.[64] Locke also sent two books with the apothecary in response to a request from Shaftesbury for works the dauphin might have used to learn Latin, thereby providing training in Latin and French simultaneously for his bright young grandson, the later third earl of Shaftesbury.[65] The first of the books Locke decided suitable was *Méthode pour*

---

61 Marsh's Library, Dublin, MSS Z2.2.17 (7) 1–12. Letters from Moyse Charas to Élie Bouhéreau (1677–1679). I am grateful to library staff for copies. On Bouhéreau's correspondence (though without attention to Charas), see Ruth Whelan, 'West coast connections: the correspondence network of Élie Bouhéreau of La Rochelle' in Vivienne Larminie (ed.), *Huguenot networks, 1560–1780: the interactions and impact of a Protestant minority in Europe* (New York, 2018), pp 155–69, at p. 157.   62 Marsh's Library, MS Z2.2.17 (7.2), Moyse Charas to Élie Bouhéreau, 23 February 1678.   63 Helen M. Dingwall, 'Fraizer, Sir Alexander, first baronet (1607?–1681)', *ODNB*; S.M. Wynne, 'Mordaunt [*née* Fraizer], Carey, countess of Peterborough and Monmouth (*c.*1658–1709)', *ODNB*.   64 Locke, *Correspondence*, i, p. 572.   65 Locke, *Correspondence*, i, p. 512.

commencer les humanités Grecques et Latines (1672), the work of the Saumur classicist Tanneguy Le Fèvre, who had presented his ex-student Bouhéreau with the copy now at Marsh's.[66] Locke also knew before Bouhéreau of at least one among Charas' English achievements, Mapletoft writing from London on 22 November (Old Style) of the Frenchman's attendance at the Royal Society's meeting that afternoon. Before Charas left England, Locke arranged for him to be presented with 'a knife bought by my order', reflecting a bond of interest and respect.[67]

In July 1678, the next letter from Charas to Bouhéreau opened another medical topic, revealing Charas' role in a notable development into which he drew his younger colleague.[68] This was the popularization of treating fevers with what Charas referred to as 'China-China', the variously designated cinchona, 'Jesuit's Powder', 'Peruvian bark', *cortex Peruvianus*, 'kinkina', or 'quinquina'. In modern terms, this was the prehistory of tackling malaria with quinine, part of the story of medicine's turn towards remedial specifics and away from evacuation of morbid humours through purging and bloodletting. Use of the bark as febrifuge was not entirely new, known not least to its Andean producers as well as Catholic colonizers (hence 'Jesuit's powder'). Its use in London and Paris by the early 1660s was attested by Boyle and Christiaan Huygens respectively.[69] Sydenham was cautious about possible dangers in *Methodus curandi febres* but in *Observationes mmedicae* remarked that the only genuinely specific remedy so far was 'Cortex Peruvianus'.[70] Charas' cure for quartans, incompletely recorded by Locke, almost certainly involved cinchona. The treatment was not described in *Pharmacopée royale* but in 1692 Charas would claim to have used cinchona 'depuis plus de quinze ans' (for more than fifteen years) using a dosage of up to two drams.[71]

A major vogue in use of the bark was inspired by the success of the English apothecary, Robert Talbor, sent by Charles II to the afflicted French court to apply his secret remedial recipe for agues. Full details of Talbor's method were only revealed around the time of his death in late 1681, when the French king

---

66 Lough, *Locke's travels*, p. 181. Locke acquired another copy, shipped to England just after visiting La Rochelle in September 1678: ibid., p. 239. The other work sent with Charas was *Examen de la maniere d'enseigner le Latin aux enfans* (1668). Locke's library catalogue lists both works, respectively LL 1082b and LL 1114.   67 Locke, *Correspondence*, i, p. 524; Lough, *Locke's travels*, p. 187.   68 Marsh's Library, MS Z2.2.17 (7.3), Moyse Charas to Élie Bouhéreau, 26 July 1678.   69 Wouter Klein and Toine Peters, 'The hidden history of a famous drug: tracing the medical and public acculturation of peruvian bark in early modern western Europe (*c*.1650–1720)', *Journal of the History of Medicine and Allied Sciences*, 71:4 (2016), 400–21; Robert Boyle, *Some considerations touching the usefulnesse of experimental naturall philosophy* (London, 1663), p. 46.   70 Sydenham, *Observationes medicae*, sig. b6r.   71 Charas, 'Nouvelle préparation de quinquina & la manière de s'en servir pour la guérison des fièvres [31 May 1691]', *Mémoires de L'Académie Royale*, 10 (1730), 92–8, at p. 93. Charas' 'astonishing' silence on cinchona in *Pharmacopée royale* has been ascribed to slow progress in medical chemistry but trade secrets probably played a part, described below: Saul Jarcho,

ordered 'Publication of the English Remedy, as the French called the Peruvian Bark, which at a great Rate he Purchased from Talbor, an English Emperick' – Boyle's summary in the second volume of *Medicinal experiments*, a book Locke put to the press.[72] A substantial literature has grown up around this episode, often dating Talbor's overseas mission to 1679 or later because of evidence that Charles II in 1679 and the dauphin and dauphine in 1680 took his remedy, or supposing that the story of his being sent to attend Charles' niece, Marie-Louise d'Orléans, also niece to Louis XIV, refers to the period after she became queen of Spain.[73] The stepmother of 'la petite mademoiselle' indicated that Marie-Louise had been treated in 1678, however, and an English government source narrows the date of the king's despatch and Talbor's cure 'to the amazement of that Court' to the weeks before 13/23 July.[74]

Charas' letter to Bouhéreau of 26 July 1678 offers novel insight into Talbor's visit and its impact from the standpoint of a French rival to this 'nouvel Athlas' (new Atlas). Charas complained that the 'medecin ou Apot Anglois' (English doctor or Apoth[ecary]) sent by the English king to 'Mademoiselle' had made a lot of noise and money but, while successful, Charas knew from his English visit that the remedy 'n'est fondé que sur le China-China, qu'il fait desguiser' (is only based on cinchona, which it disguises). He had reason to feel aggrieved, given his own trials of cinchona and service to Marie-Louise's father, but Charas' immediate concern was obtaining 'China-China' of fair price and quality. He suspected that imports (through Spain and Portugal) were being bought up at La Rochelle before St Malo, his usual source. Demand and price rose at this time, given the fame of Talbor and his attempts to buy up supplies of the bark in both England and France, according to *Le remède anglois* (1682), the 'official' account.[75] The letters at Marsh's show Charas engaging Bouhéreau in a shared enterprise to acquire and transport medicinal raw materials, initially and particularly 'China-China' but also other substances, including opiates – Charas became a noted self-experimenter.[76] The letters discuss prices and prospects for

Quinine's predecessor (Baltimore, 1993), pp 69–70. 72 Robert Boyle, *Medicinal experiments ... The second volume* (London, 1693), sig. A3v; Nicolas de Blégny, *Le remède Anglois pour la guérison des fièvres* (Paris, 1682). This 'official' account was translated as *The English remedy: Or, Talbor's wonderful secret* (London, 1682). 73 Uncertainty over the date is prevalent, in otherwise informative accounts: examples include, M.J. Dobson, 'Tabor [Talbor, Talbot], Sir Robert (*bap.* 1642, *d.* 1681)', *ODNB*; Dewhurst, *John Locke*, p. 60; Jarcho, *Quinine's predecessor*, pp 64–5; Klein and Peters, 'Hidden history', p. 413; T.W. Keeble, 'A cure for the ague: the contribution of Robert Talbor (1642–81)', *Journal of the Royal Society of Medicine*, 90 (1997), 285–90, at p. 288; Harold J. Cook, 'Markets and cultures: medical specifics and the reconfiguration of the body in early modern Europe', *Transactions of the Royal Historical Society*, 6th series, 21 (2011), 123–45, at p. 134; Laurence Brockliss and Colin Jones, *The medical world of early modern France* (Oxford, 1997), pp 292 and 312. 74 M. Bouvet, 'Talbot, vulgarisateur du quinquina en France', *Bulletin des Sciences Pharmacologiques*, 41 (1934), 165–80, at p. 166; HMC, *Calendar of the manuscripts of the marquess of Ormonde*, new series, vol. 4 (London, 1906), pp 444 and 449. 75 De Blégny, *Remède anglois*, p. 24. 76 Emma C. Spary,

shipping these goods to La Rochelle and onward to Paris, with comments on the effects, by land and sea, of the state of the weather and the state of war with Spain and the Netherlands and, during 1678, potentially with England.

Thanks to these efforts, by January 1679 Charas could boast to Bouhéreau of Talbor-like success with his own febrifuge, which he said had Parisian doctors and apothecaries guessing the remedy used 'China-China' but unable to be sure. Two months earlier, the *Journal des Sçavans* reported that Charas had a remedy he was keeping secret, which confirmed how far Bouhéreau had been taken into Charas' confidence.[77] In May 1679, Charas informed Bouhéreau of another planned visit to England from early June, reported elsewhere as an invitation to treat the fever 'd'une personne de qualité'.[78] His last extant letter to Bouhéreau, written from London on 10 August 1679, shows Charas further emulating Talbor, having treated several persons of quality with success while lining up a position at court: Sir Alexander Fraizer had assured him his services were desired, despite delays. Charas was ready to leave for Paris, checking that Bouhéreau wanted him to pay London prices for medical works including Sydenham's *Observationes*. It appears he did, as most of the suggested titles are in Bouhéreau's collection.[79] Charas also hinted at being in England in the autumn, presumably once in post, adding that Bouhéreau was too much of a friend not to share news with him of such great personal consequence.

Two weeks later, King Charles fell ill, was diagnosed with tertian ague, and 'his fits were put off, like mine, by the Jesuit's powder', remarked the dowager Lady Sunderland, possibly Charas' patient.[80] Richard Lower was among the royal doctors present, by later report resistant on behalf of physicians for fear 'it would spoil their practise'.[81] When Charles suffered a relapse in May 1680, the

---

'Opium, experimentation, and alterity in France', *Historical Journal*, 65 (2022), 49–67. Spary does not note that opiates were, among other things, used in febrifuges, being recommended by De Blégny, for instance: *Remède Anglois*, p. 125.   77 Marsh's Library, MS Z2.2.17 (7.8), Moyse Charas to Élie Bouhéreau, 16 January 1679; *Le Journal des Sçavans*, 6:33 (21 Nov. 1678), 422–3.   78 Marsh's Library, MS Z2.2.17 (7.11), Moyse Charas to Élie Bouhéreau, 18 May 1679; Bouvet, 'Talbot', p. 180.   79 Marsh's Library, MS Z2.2.17 (7.12), Moyse Charas to Élie Bouhéreau, 10 August 1679; Sydenham, *Observationes medicae* (London, 1676); Walter Charleton, *Exercitationes physico-anatomicae, de oeconomia naturali* (2nd ed., Amsterdam, 1659); Walter Charleton, *Exercitationes de differentiis & nominibus animalium* (2nd ed., Oxford, 1677); Thomas Bartholin, *Historiarum anatomicarum & medicarum rariorum centuria V et VI* (Copenhagen, 1661); Friedrich Loss, *Observationum medicinalium libri quatuor* (London, 1672); William Cole, *De secretione animali cogitate* (Oxford, 1674). See also Jean-Paul Pitton, 'Medicine in print in the early modern period: medical books in Marsh's Library, Dublin' in Danielle Westerhof (ed.), *The alchemy of medicine and print* (Dublin, 2010), pp 57–74, at p. 62. Locke owned Sydenham's book (LL 2814) and Charleton's *Exercitationes … animalium* (LL 668), in the same editions, and other works by all the authors except Loss/Lossius.   80 R.W. Blencowe (ed.), *Diary of the times of Charles the Second*, vol. 1 (London, 1843), pp 161–2.   81 Entry for 29 November 1694, E.S. de Beer (ed.), *The diary of John Evelyn* (London, 1959), p. 989. A variant recollection of Lower's attitude is found in Rudolph E. Siegel and F.N.L. Poynter, 'Robert Talbor, Charles II, and cinchona: a contemporary document', *Medical*

physicians were less hesitant and Charas was on hand. The king was 'at night prescribed a preparation of the Jesuits powder (extracted by one Monsieur Charras, a French apothecary, which hath had great success on several other people)', wrote the Privy Council clerk.[82] Charas was paid £54 3s. 6d., while Lower and four other physicians each received twice that amount, but further reward followed when on 22 July 1680 Charas was formally appointed the king's 'apothecary and operator in chemistry'.[83] Denization followed, with his wife and six children, and in 1682 Charas was involved in a project to establish a Huguenot community in Kent, but within a year he and his family left for Holland.[84] In October 1684, when the Carolina colonial project associated with Shaftesbury and Locke was encouraging Huguenot settlers, 3,000 acres was offered to 'Mr Charasse being a pson well skilled in Druggs & divers other secrets of nature.' A claim that Locke himself made the offer is not supported by the record involved but it seems possible the two men's prior association played some part.[85] Charas decided against leaving Europe and subsequently accompanied the Dutch ambassador to Spain, where his practice and religion brought him before the inquisition. Returning to France a Catholic convert in 1691, the details of his febrifuge were finally divulged before the *Académie Royale des Sciences* in Paris the following year.[86] Charas' contact with Bouhéreau evidently ceased several years before, though perhaps Bouhéreau thought back to the friendship in 1695 when with Lord Galway's regiment in Italy, as he dosed his fever for ten days with 'mon Quinquina'.[87]

In late summer 1678, Locke like Bouhéreau heard complaints about Talbor, possibly from Charas but demonstrably in a letter from Sydenham. Referring Locke to a cinchona-based remedy in *Observationes medicae*, Sydenham complained that Talbor had been 'an apothecary in Cambridg, wher my booke of practise have much obteyned', yet 'I never gott 10l by it, he hath gott 5000' and was 'now knighted'. As with Locke's note on Charas, the letter prescribes '2 dramms' of a substance left unnamed, in this case because the paper was cut away, presumably by Locke, at each point Sydenham would have referred to

History, 6:1 (1962), 82–4.   82 HMC, *Calendar of the manuscripts of the marquess of Ormonde*, 6th series, vol. 5 (London, 1906), pp 317–18 (15 May 1680). Charas appears to have been in England for some time, having attended the Royal Society on 25 March: Birch, *History*, iv, p. 30.   83 William A. Shaw (ed.), *Calendar of Treasury Books (CTB)*, vol. 6, *1679–1680* (London, 1913), p. 558; *Database of Court Officers, 1660–1837*: https://courtofficers.ctsdh.luc.edu/CHAMBER4.list.pdf, accessed 20 Feb 2024.   84 Felix, 'Moyse Charas', p. 69; Robin Gwynn, 'Strains of worship: the Huguenots and nonconformity' in David J.B. Trim (ed.), *The Huguenots: history and memory in transnational context* (Leiden, 2011), pp 121–52, at pp 123–8.   85 TNA, CO 5/288; 25 Oct. 1684, fo. 20r, Alexander Samuel Salley (ed.), *Records in the British Public Record Office relating to South Carolina 1663–1684* (Atlanta, GA, 1928), p. 312; Bertrand van Ruymbeke, *From New Babylon to Eden: the Huguenots and their migration to colonial South Carolina* (Columbia, SC, 2006), p. 34.   86 Felix, 'Moyse Charas', pp 69–70; Charas, 'Nouvelle Preparation de Quinquina'.   87 Léoutre et al., *Diary and accounts*, p. 244. Noreen Humble's chapter in the present volume notes further instances of

Peruviani corticis, the term on the relevant page in *Observationes*.[88] Such was the secrecy surrounding the race to perfect a cinchona-based remedy in 1678. At other times, Locke would make free and frequent reference and indeed use: in August 1679 he would treat Caleb Banks in England with cinchona, and in the 1680s, having 'allways found good successe' with 'Cortex Peru', Locke began contributing to his friend Dr Charles Goodall's project to write a history of 'quinquina', helping devise a survey to send to other physicians.[89]

The subject was a medicinal specific but the significance for the development of Locke's thinking was arguably wider. In a journal entry on 22 July 1678, with Talbor's triumphs the talk of medical circles, Locke declared that 'All doctors up to the present century seem to me to have failed' because their 'hypotheses of humours' addressed external symptoms of bile and phlegm, rather than using insights into the variable humours of men to support specific remedies for specific diseases, now the priority: 'I have no doubt that to cure each type of disease either a fixed method or fixed remedies are needed.'[90] In 1681, in a much-discussed journal entry about types of knowledge, he would divide demonstrable knowledge like mathematics and, for Locke, moral law, from an understanding of politics and prudence, 'the well management of public or private affairs depending upon the various and unknown humours, interests, and capacities of men'. It was knowable that men had a duty to be just but giving this practical effect required more than a sense of how men's humours and interests inclined to the needs of justice in general terms: 'whether this course in public or private affairs will succeed well, whether rhubarb will purge or quinquina cure an ague, is only known by experience', yielding probability not demonstrative certainty.[91] Contesting interpretations take this passage to link or divide Locke's major works, likewise the connection of moral framework, humours/interests, and empirical testing. The aim here is not to propose the 'English Remedy' as the key to unlocking Locke's thought, any more than rhubarb would. However, it is to see his period in France as a formative experience even when the ramifications were not immediately and fully obvious, with linkages between experience and thought similarly to be traced in his thinking on religious persecution and toleration as well as in his wider political and philosophical outlook. It was no insignificant step when Locke, in the *Essay concerning human understanding*, revised Francis Bacon's summary list of world-altering human developments from printing, gunpowder and the nautical compass to form the new trinity of printing, the compass and the 'right Use of *Kin Kina*'.[92]

Bouhéreau's continuing interest in quinine. 88 Locke, *Correspondence*, i (3 Aug. 1678), p. 601; Sydenham, *Observationes medicae*, p. 99. Talbor was knighted at Whitehall on 27 July 1678. 89 Locke, *Correspondence*, ii, pp 80, 272 and 696; iii, pp 231–3. 90 Dewhurst, *John Locke*, p. 136. 91 John Locke, 'Second tract on government', ed. Mark Goldie, *Political essays* (Cambridge, 1997), pp 281–2. 92 John Locke, *An essay concerning human understanding*, ed. Peter H. Nidditch (Oxford, 1975), 4.XII:12, p. 647.

LOCKE AND BOUHÉREAU: AN ENCOUNTER IN LA ROCHELLE

By the time Charas penned his last letter to Bouhéreau, Locke had left Paris on the journey that would lead to La Rochelle, departing with Caleb Banks on 9 July 1678 after Dr Coxe communicated the agreement of Caleb's parents to their son taking 'that which they call the little Tour of France'. Locke replied that he had expected to return to England but would not risk blame for shortcomings on Caleb's part when they returned, a revealing assessment after their time together.[93]

An important experience for Locke in that year of exploration in and around the capital had been attendance at meetings of *virtuosi* at the house of Henri Justel, the Huguenot *secrétaire du roi* and later royal librarian in England. In June 1681, a few months before leaving, Justel would write to Locke that 'les protestans de france ne peuvent pas subsister long temps' (the Protestants of France cannot survive for long).[94] Justel's mainly Protestant circle included the Catholic Toinard, whose wide-ranging activities first featured in Locke's journal on 21 April 1678, though not his alleged role in the recent seizure of Richard Simon's *Histoire critique du Vieux Testament* after prefatory material was passed to Bishop Bossuet.[95] As Locke journeyed from Paris with Caleb, Toinard updated him on news from the capital, including Talbor's return, and identified local contacts and guidance on the best route to take, advice having also come from Dr Coxe, likely gleaned from his son, to avoid along the Loire, 'the multitude of young unexperienced youths of our own Nation and Germans, that flock thither'.[96]

The pair journeyed south to the Loire at Orléans, where Caleb's non-aguish fever brought delay in which Locke wrote the journal entry on medical advance described earlier. In mid-August they stayed a week at Saumur, where Locke's notes were of local fruit production and 'very good' white wine, with no evident contact with the Protestant academy, Bouhéreau's alma mater.[97] Reaching Angers, they then retraced their steps through Saumur before leaving the Loire for Chinon and Richelieu, then south-west through Niort, where a Protestant bookseller's wife told Locke of 1,200 troops having been quartered on the town, before the Englishmen reached La Rochelle the following day, Friday 2 September.[98]

---

93 Locke, *Correspondence*, i, p. 572.   94 Locke, *Correspondence*, ii: p. 416.   95 Lough, *Locke's travels*, p. 191; Champion, 'Pere Richard Simon', p. 46. Champion's essay makes a persuasive case that the 'J. H.' to whom a radicalizing English translation-adaptation of Simon's *Histoire* was dedicated in April 1683 was John Hampden junior: pp 54–8.   96 Locke, *Correspondence*, i, pp 572–3, 593, 597, 603 and 607. Toinard would later assist the travels in France of Locke's cousin Anna Grigg, their correspondence when she lodged with the widow of the Huguenot theologian Moyse Amyraut in 1680 being the subject of Ch. Bastide, 'Locke et les Huguenots', *Bulletin de la Société de l'Histoire du Protestantisme Français*, 62:1 (1913), 60–3.   97 Lough, *Locke's travels*, pp 220–1.   98 Lough, *Locke's travels*, pp 229–30.

They would stay a week in La Rochelle, Locke giving his address as that of Jean Raullé, a Protestant banker involved in shipping, while noting a recommendation of 'Dalton, Irlandoise, the best inne'.[99] He summarized the city as having streets 'the straitest & largest I have seen in any town in France', with 'many good houses' and overhanging arches giving shelter from sun and rain. Local sea salt production was another topic of great interest to him, and after a note about tides, Locke remarked, 'This is the first time I ever saw the Ocean.' He also noted the city's safe harbour, though with access still confined by Cardinal Richelieu's 'banke of stones' from the siege. Locke was conscious of the city's turbulent history, a copy of Pierre Mervault's *Journal* of the siege being among books he boxed up before leaving Paris, the same 1671 Rouen edition that Mervault gave to Bouhéreau. Locke noted another outcome of the siege, the Catholic cathedral that was 'formerly the Protestants temple, built by the English & coverd with lead' with 'noe pillar to susteine the roof' despite its size.[100] On present constraints, he wrote that 'Noe Protestants are sufferd to set up trades (c'est a dire estre metrisé [*maitrisé*]) in Rochell, nor noe Protestants to live there that were not borne in the town.'[101] The source of this information was not named but may have been the 'Mr. Beaulot' who Locke appears to have met earlier in Angers and from whom he took other information, including numerous remedies, one cited from Charas' work, and that the 'endemial disease' of the La Rochelle region was 'colica' leading to paralysis, blamed on inferior white wine.[102]

The disease was evidently *colica Pictonum* or colic of Poitou, subject of *Traité de la populaire colique bilieuse de Poitou*, published at La Rochelle in 1673 by the local apothecary Jacques Boucher Beauval, who gave Bouhéreau the copy now at Marsh's.[103] 'Beaulot' is identifiable as Isaac Baulot, another apothecary practising in a city and profession where Protestants could not be masters. Baulot, grandson of an apothecary and son of a surgeon, had been an apothecary for at least thirty years under Catholic masters and their widows. Two months before his encounter with Locke, a new statute of La Rochelle's master apothecaries had been royally confirmed, reasserting restrictions against Protestants. A year later, only three Protestant apothecaries remained – Baulot, Beauval and Jean Seignette – and in November 1679, proceedings were brought preventing Baulot practising, anticipating the process which in 1683 suppressed the city's three Protestant physicians – Bouhéreau, Richard, and the former apothecary Seignette. In 1680 or 1681 Baulot left France, his son remaining in La Rochelle.[104] Three centuries later Isaac Baulot gained notice when his authorship

99 Locke, *Correspondence*, i, p. 603; Lough, *Locke's travels*, p. 230 fn. 1. 100 Lough, *Locke's travels*, pp 230–2; Lough, 'Locke's reading', p. 246. The building was destroyed by fire and demolition in the following decade. 101 Lough, *Locke's travels*, p. 230. 102 Dewhurst, *John Locke*, pp 139–40. 103 The cause was adulterating wines for sweetness and preservation with additives containing lead: Josef Eisinger, 'Lead and wine: Eberhard Gockel and the *colica pictonum*', *Medical History*, 26 (1982), 279–302. 104 The suppression of the La Rochelle apothecaries is traced in Maurice Soenen, *La pharmacie à La Rochelle avant 1803* (La Rochelle,

of *Mutus liber*, a pictorial work of 'philosophia hermetica' published at La Rochelle in 1677, was confirmed by reference to the inscription in the copy he gave to Bouhéreau (see plate 2). Long renowned as a work of mystical alchemy, the wording of the book's licence indicates less mystical concerns about marketability and, as Pittion argues, it may have been 'above all a handbook of experimentation' to test claims about the transmutation of metals.[105] The sharing of intelligence among Baulot, Bouhéreau and Locke points to the period's porous interface of alchemy, chemistry, 'new science', and the business of books: Locke owned numerous works of 'alchemia', though not the *Mutus liber*.[106]

On Tuesday 6 September, Locke's journal registered his other encounter with the La Rochelle medical fraternity, that with Bouhéreau and Richard, with Caleb Banks also likely present. Charas had possibly suggested they make contact, though there is no firm evidence. The result was a rather underwhelming note of a medicinal recipe not unlike many others Locke noted during his time in France: 'Sal prunella & peper are a certaine cure for that wch we call the pallate downe. Mr Richard & Dr Bouhereau of Rochelle', with the marginal note, 'Pallat fallen'. To the entry he added, 'This Dr Richard is the author of the treatise at the end of Lortie in answer to Rohault.'[107] Locke's minimalist journal entry clearly does not do full justice to the encounter with Bouhéreau, given subsequent contact. The medicinal advice was essentially a form of salt and pepper mouthwash for a sore throat, the fallen palate a reference to inflamed swelling of the uvula at the back of the mouth.[108] Élie Richard's treatise was *Reflexions physique sur la transsubstantiation, & sur ce que Mr Rohault en a écrit dans ses Entretiens*, which was appended with separate pagination to the La Rochelle minister André Lortie's 1675 work *Defense du sermon de Monsieur Hespérien*.[109] Lortie referred to the supplement 'by one of my friends' in his *Traité de la Sainte Cène* in 1674, saying it would rebut Rohault's contention that Descartes' principles supported transubstantiation, meaning Richard's work was caught up in attempts at suppression of Lortie's *Defense* on publication in 1675.[110] Locke nonetheless acquired a copy of the *Defense*, noting some passages in November 1677 that reached partway through its 288 pages, this pagination being noted by Locke, which suggests his copy lacked Richard's *Reflexions*.[111]

1910), pp 30–1 and 69–74. See also Pittion, 'Medicine and religion', pp 58–9. **105** Ibid., p. 54; Jean Flouret, 'A propos de l'auteur du *Mutus Liber*', *Revue Française d'Histoire du Livre*, 11 (1976), 205–11. **106** Harrison and Laslett, *Library of John Locke*, p. 292. **107** Bodleian Library, MS Locke, f. 3, p. 279; Dewhurst, *John Locke*, p. 139. The entry is given only in part in Lough, *Locke's travels*, p. 231 fn. 1. **108** The recommendation of forms of salt and pepper for a swollen uvula was not itself new; for instance, John Hartman, *The practise of chymistry* (London, 1670), p. 55. **109** André Lortie, *Défense du sermon de Monsieur Hespérien* (Saumur, 1675). Pierre Hespérien was a correspondent of Bouhéreau, see Marsh's Library, MSS Z2.2.17 (14) 1–15. Letters from Pierre Hespérien to Élie Bouhéreau (1672–5). **110** André Lortie, *Traité de la Sainte Cène* (La Rochelle, 1674), preface (no sig.); E. and E. Haag, *La France Protestante*, vii, pp 134–5. **111** Bodleian Library, MS Locke, f. 2, pp 350–1; Lough,

Bouhéreau's copy is marked 'don de l'autheur' (gift from the author). Lortie left for England in 1682 with his family, including Bouhéreau's god-daughter Marieanne, born two weeks after Locke's visit.[112] Élie Richard, remaining in La Rochelle, in 1712 composed an epitaph for Baulot's son Isaac, recalling a learned man with a love of books inculcated by his father.[113]

LOCKE AND BOUHÉREAU: LITERARY LIST AND PAYMENTS LIST

On 8 September 1678, Locke and Caleb left La Rochelle and resumed their tour, passing through Rochefort to reach Bordeaux then Toulouse before arriving at Montpellier in mid-October. It was decided to press on into Italy but by the time approval arrived from Caleb's parents 'old father Winter' blocked the passes, as Locke reported to Mapletoft, advising that letters could now 'keepe their old road to Mr. Charas's'. Arriving at Lyon, Locke engaged the services of a young Swiss man, Sylvester Brownower, who would be his chief aide and amanuensis over the next two decades.[114] At the end of November, the small party arrived in Paris, where they stayed for another five months, leaving the French capital for England at the beginning of May 1679. Locke's journal became less regular in these final months, though it indicates a variety of pursuits and interests, often shared with Toinard, who gave him sheets of his *Evangeliorum harmonia*. On 26 January Locke noted a treatment for gout involving a hot cloth and herbs that 'Mr. Claude' said 'never failes him', apparently Jean Claude, and in another notebook he recorded eight shillings 'given at Charenton'.[115] Just before departing Paris he wrote, without noting a source, 'The Protestants within these 20 years have had above 300 churches demolishd, & within these 2 months 15 more condemned.'[116]

Among the most intriguing records of this time is the short list of payments which Locke added to the last page of a book of memoranda whose other entries end by July 1678, when he began a new notebook. Locke wrote 'Mr Bouhereau' then below listed single, varying amounts for the dates December 9, 19 and 24, then '79 Jan 1', then January 12 and 23, March 9, 17 and 29, and April 11 and 22 –

'Locke's reading', p. 242.   112 Gwynn, *Huguenots in later Stuart Britain*, i, p. 349; La Rochelle Protestant BMS register, vol. I 56, f. 14v, at https://www.archinoe.net/v2/ad17/visualiseur/registre.html?id=170023073, image 1041/1493, accessed 25 June 2024. Marieanne in 1699 married Lawrence Brodbelt, who by his 1726 will left to her and their family his plantation on the island of Nevis, including 'all and singular houses mills buildings negros slaves utensills chattells and appurtenances whatsoever': TNA, PROB 11/61/221. Will of Lawrence Brodbelt (1726).   113 Louis-Étienne Arcère, *Histoire de La Rochelle*, 2 vols (La Rochelle, 1756–7), ii, p. 422.   114 Lough, *Locke's travels*, pp 232, 238 and 242; Locke, *Correspondence*, i, pp 625 and 628.   115 Locke, *Correspondence*, i, p. 651; Dewhurst, *John Locke*, p. 149; Lough, *Locke's travels*, p. 256 fn. 2, 258 fn. 6.   116 Lough, *Locke's travels*, p. 271. Lough notes that the figures broadly agree with those given in Haag and Haag, *La France Protestante*, x, pp 378–80.

John Locke and Élie Bouhéreau: an encounter

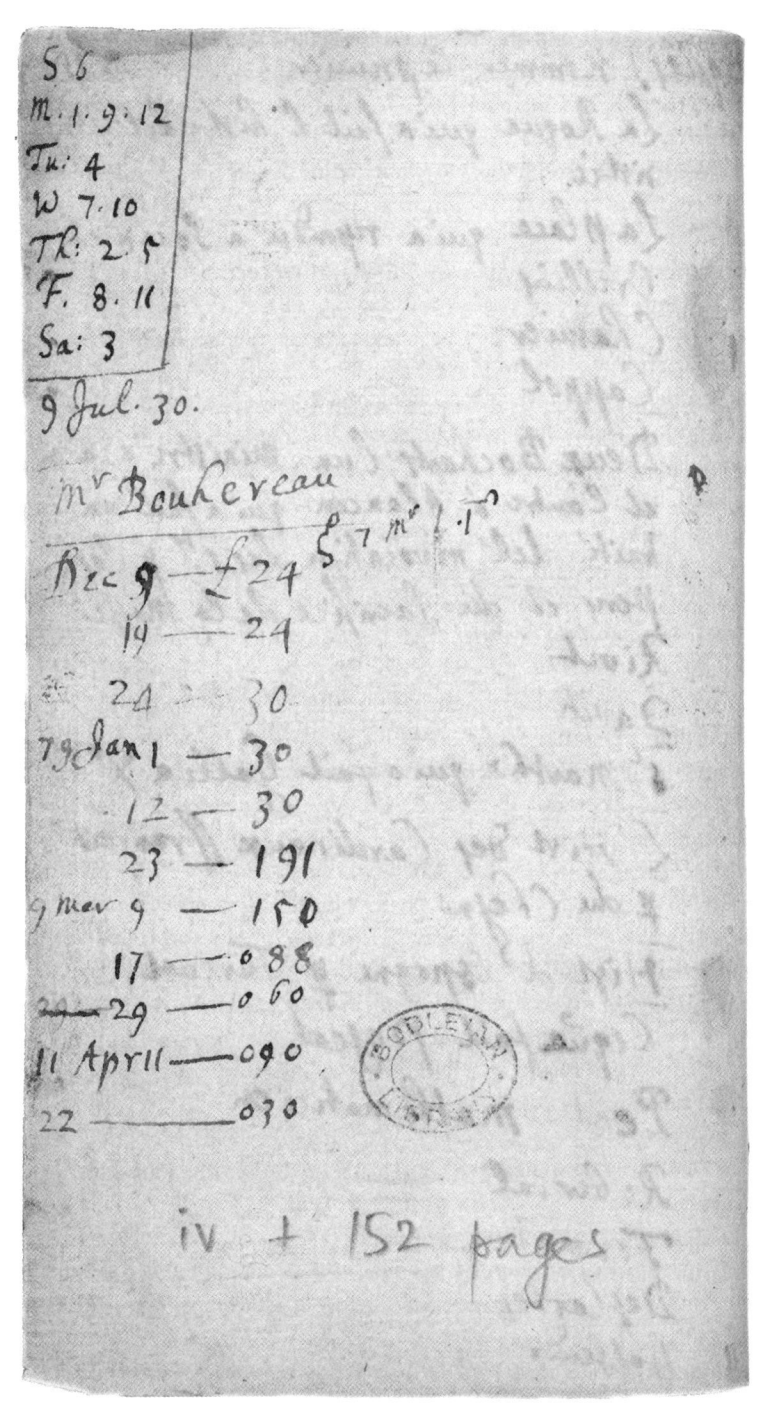

4.1 List of payments and 'Mr Bouhereau' on the last page of a notebook belonging to John Locke, compiled 1677–8 with this final page extending to 1679. Bodleian Library, University of Oxford, 2025, MS Locke f. 15, p. 152.

in other words, the period spent in Paris in 1678–9. The first payment has a '£' sign, which Locke used for livres in his French journals, and to its upper right is a rough note partly in shorthand, which could be read as 'rcd of Mr B Bnk'.[117] The nature of this continued connection with Bouhéreau is difficult to know for sure. It would seem there were payments from Caleb Banks to Bouhéreau via Locke, though the rogue 'B', the homonomy of 'Banks' and 'banks', and the general indeterminacy of the shorthand makes for multiple uncertainty. The varying amounts sum to 747 livres, which at the time was just over fifty-seven pounds sterling. Three of the eleven dates (23 January, 29 March, 11 April) coincide with journal entries by Locke noting the exchange rate, two concerning money forwarded from Sir John Banks for his son, though these and other sums listed in Sir John's accounts do not tally with Locke's list. The list's placement is itself puzzling, inserted at the end of a notebook otherwise completed months earlier. The immediately preceding pages contain book recommendations from Justel and a Mr 'Jaques', himself obscure, though earlier pages have some accounts with Caleb, including for books.[118] It seems unlikely Bouhéreau would have been dealing in books over several months, from December to April, and with a young man he had only recently and briefly encountered. It can at least be said that Bouhéreau's dealings with Locke extended beyond the remedy for sore throats.

The thought of Bouhéreau the book intermediary nonetheless leads to consideration of the other document confirming further connection with Locke after the encounter in La Rochelle. This was a single sheet signed by Bouhéreau, possibly an enclosure in a letter, now lost, in which he offered his own book recommendations. On the reverse, Locke wrote, 'Libri 79 Bouhéreau'.[119] We do not know more precisely when Locke received the list. Its date does not immediately align with the list of payments, which began in 1678, but it is possible the literary list found its way to Locke before he and Caleb left France. The general impression is of an informed answer to the question of which authors and books one should know to pass as conversant with stylish and influential writing in French, the suggestions ranging from modern *belles-lettres* to ancient authors in recent translation, travel literature and moral-theological essayists. The list reads as follows:

> Les Oeuvres de Balzac, de Sarrazin, et de Voiture. Les Entretiens de Voiture et de Costar. Toute la dispute de Costar et de Girac. Toutes les Traductions de Mr. d'Ablancourt; Son Minutius Felix, Son César, Son Tacite, Son Lucien, Son Thucydide, Son Marmol, &c. Le Quinte-Curce de Vaugelas. Les Ouvrages de Mr. de la Chambre, ou, du-moins, les

[117] Bodleian Library, MS Locke f. 15, p. 152. Locke's shift from 'Dr' to 'Mr' in his notes on Bouhéreau has no significance: he did the same in the earlier journal entry referring to Élie Richard.   [118] Bodleian Library, MS Locke, f. 15, pp 50–1 and 92–3.   [119] Bodleian Library, MS Locke b.2, fo. 24.

principaux; Sur-tout, les Caractéres des Passions: L'histoire de l'Académie Françoise, par Mr. Pellisson. La Vie de Socrate, par Mr. Charpentier; et tout ce qu'il a traduit de Xénophon. Quelques ouvrages de Mrs. de Port-Royal; comme les Lettres Provinciales, contre les Jésuites; Les Essays de Morale; &c. Quelques Relations choisies; comme celles que Mr. Thévenot a fait imprimer.
 Bouhéreau, Docteur en Médecine,
 Rue des Augustins. A La Rochelle
[Locke's endorsement:] <u>Libri 79</u> Bouhéreau

Locke as well as Bouhéreau would have been familiar with most of the suggested names, seven of whom were members of the *Académie française*, while a number of the titles named or implied are found in either or both of the two men's libraries.[120] These books are identified below, being those catalogued in the collection Bouhéreau left to Marsh's Library or listed in Harrison and Laslett's *Library of John Locke* (whose reference numbers are included).[121] Given the purpose of Bouhéreau's list and this exercise, only French-language editions are included, not the same authors in Latin or English translation, and details such as numbers of volumes are not generally indicated.

The Works of Jean-Louis Guez de Balzac, Jean-François Sarasin, Vincent Voiture.
BOUHÉREAU:
Balzac, *Les Oeuvres diverses du Sieur de Balzac* (Leiden, 1651)
Balzac, *Les Oeuvres de Mr. de Balzac* (Rouen, 1657)
Sarasin, *Les Oeuvres de Monsieur Sarasin* (Rouen/Paris, 1658)
Voiture, *Nouvelles oeuvres de Monsieur de Voiture* (Rouen/Paris, 1658)
LOCKE:
Balzac, *Oeuvres diverses. Augmentées en cette edition de plusieurs pieces nouvelles* (Amsterdam, 1664) LL 186d[122]

---

120 The Academy members were Balzac, Voiture, d'Ablancourt, Vaugelas, La Chambre, Pellisson, and Charpentier. I am grateful to Noreen Humble and Mark Goldie for help in analysing the list, though any mistakes remain my own.   121 Further details of any particular book or edition can be found in these catalogues. For accounts of Bouhéreau's collection, see Philip Benedict and Pierre-Olivier Léchot, 'The library of Élie Bouhéreau: the intellectual universe of a Huguenot refugee and his family' in M. McCarthy and A. Simmons (eds), *Marsh's Library: a mirror on the world. Law, learning and libraries, 1650–1750* (Dublin, 2003), pp 165–84; Pittion, 'Medicine in print'.   122 Locke's library lists featured another eight works by Balzac, including five volumes of letters, with four of the eight in English translation: LL 182–186d. All were published before 1665 except *Lettres choisies* (Amsterdam, 1678). He alluded in a note to owning a further Balzac title in translation, *The Roman* (London, 1652): Bodleian Library, Oxford, MS Locke, c. 1. Locke's ledger, 1671–1702, p. 434; Felix Waldmann, 'The library of John Locke: additions, corrigenda, and a conspectus of pressmarks', *Bodleian Library Record*, 26:1 (2013), 36–58, at p. 45.

Voiture, *Nouvelles oeuvres* (Paris, 1672) LL 3100
Voiture, *Les oeuvres* (Paris, 1672) LL 3102[123]

The conferences of Vincent Voiture and Pierre Costar
Not in Bouhéreau's or Locke's libraries.[124]

The dispute of Pierre Costar and Paul Thomas de Girac[125]
Not in Bouhéreau's or Locke's libraries.

The translations of Nicolas Perrot d'Ablancourt: his Minutius Felix, Caesar, Tacitus, Lucien, Thucydides, Marmol etc
BOUHÉREAU:
Les commentaires de Cesar (Paris, 1652)
Tacite de la traduction de N. Perrot Sieur D'Ablancourt (Paris, 1657)
L'histoire de Tacite, ou le suite des Annales (Paris, 1651)
La Germanie de Tacite (Paris, 1656)
Lucien de la traduction de N. Perrot Sr D'Ablancourt (Paris, 1655)
L'histoire de Thucydide, de la guerre du Peloponese; continuée par Xenophon (Paris, 1662)
Xenophon, *La Retraite des dix mille, ou l'expédition de Cyrus contre Artaxerxes* (Paris, 1658)
LOCKE:
Lucien de la traduction de N. Perrot Sr D'Ablancourt (Paris, 1678) LL 1822
Thucydides and Xenophon, *L'histoire de la guerre du Péloponnese* (Paris, 1678) LL 2986 (vols. 1 and 2) LL 3193 (vol. 3)[126]
Luis del Marmol Carvajal, *L'Afrique de Marmol de la traduction de N. Perrot, sieur d'Ablancourt* (Paris, 1667) LL 1912[127]

Quintus Curtius translated by Claude Favre de Vaugelas
BOUHÉREAU:
De la vie et des actions d'Alexander le Grand, Quintus Curtius de la traduction de Monsieur de Vaugelas (Paris, 1655)
LOCKE:
Not in Locke's library.

123 Locke also owned editions of Voiture's letters (LL 3099, 3102a) and poems (LL 3101) and a title not listed in Harrison and Laslett, *Library of John Locke*, this being *Conclusion de l'histoire d'Alcidalis et de Zelide* (Paris, 1668): Waldmann, 'Library', p. 46.   124 Marsh's Library has *Les entretiens de Monsieur de Voiture et de Monsieur Costar* (Paris, 1655) in Stillingfleet's collection. In 1704, Le Clerc wrote to Locke of having been outbid at auction for the *Entretiens*, which he also referred to as the '*Conferences de Voiture et de Costar*': Locke, *Correspondence*, viii, pp 210 and 323.   125 A series of exchanges after Paul Thomas de Girac published criticisms of Voiture's work in 1655, Costar defending his friend Voiture and being criticized in turn: Pierre Bayle, *Dictionary*, vol. 5 (2nd ed., London, 1738), pp 341–5. 126 The third volume carried the title, *L'histoire Grecque de Xenophon*, indicated in Locke's listing.   127 Marsh's Library has this edition in the Stillingfleet collection.

Works by Marin Cureau de la Chambre, at least the main ones; above all, *The Characters of the passions*
BOUHÉREAU:
Les Charactères des passions par le Sr. De la Chambre (Amsterdam, 1658)
LOCKE:
Not in Locke's library.

The history of the French Academy by Paul Pellisson.
BOUHÉREAU:
Pellisson, *Relation contenant l'histoire de l'Academie françoise* (Paris, 1653)
LOCKE:
Not in Locke's library.

The life of Socrates by François Charpentier and all he translated from Xenophon
BOUHÉREAU:
Les choses memorables da Socrate, ouvrage de Xenophon traduit de grec en françois. Avec la vie de Socrate (Paris, 1650)
LOCKE:
Les choses memorables da Socrate, ouvrage de Xenophon traduit de grec en françois. Par Mr Charpentier (Paris, 1657) LL 670
La vie de Socrate par Mr Charpentier, ouvrage de Xenophon traduict de grec en françois par Mr Charpentier (Paris, 1657) LL 671

Some works by the Port-Royal gentlemen, such as the *Provincial letters* **against the Jesuits, the** *Moral essays***, etc**
BOUHÉREAU:
Bouhéreau's library lacks Blaise Pascal's *Les Provinciales* and Pierre Nicole's *Essais de morale* but has works attributed to Port-Royal authors as follows. Bouhéreau and Locke also owned replies to Port-Royal works.
Antoine Arnauld, *Histoire et Concorde des quatres Evangelistes* (Paris, 1670)[128]
Arnauld, *Le Renversement de la Morale de Jesus-Christ par les erreurs des Calvinistes, touchant la justification* (Paris, 1672)
Arnauld, *La perpetuite de la foy de l'Église Catholique touchant l'Eucharistie, defendue contre le livre du Sieur Claude*, 3 vols (Paris, 1669–74)
Arnauld, *Nouveaux élémens de géométrie* (Paris, 1667)
Arnauld and Nicole, *La logique ou l'art de penser* (Paris, 1664)
Arnauld and Nicole, *Reponse generale au nouveau livre de M. Claude* (Paris, 1671).
Nicole, *L'art de parler: avec un discours dans lequel on donne une idée de l'art de persuader* (Paris, 1676)

---

[128] The copy in Bouhéreau's collection was given by Tessereau.

Claude Lancelot, *Abrégé de la nouvelle méthode presentée au Roy, pour apprendre facilement la langue latine* (Paris, 1679)
Lancelot, *Le jardin des racines Grecques* (Paris, 1682)
LOCKE:
Pascal, *Les Provinciales, ou les lettres écrites par Louis de Montalte à un provincial de ses amis, et aux RR. PP. Jésuites* (Cologne, 1669) LL 2030
Pascal, *Pensées* (Lyon, 1675) LL 2222a
Pascal, *Pensées* (Paris, 1678) LL 2222
Pascal, *Traité du triangle arithmétique* (Paris, 1665)
Nicole, *Essais de morale* (Paris, 1671) LL 2040a (Paris, 1673) LL 2040b (Paris, 1678–79) LL 2040
Nicole, *De l'éducation d'un prince* (Paris, 1670) LL 2085a
Arnauld and Nicole, *La logique ou l'art de penser* (Paris, 1674) LL 1803[129]
Arnauld, *Des vrayes et des fausses idées* (Cologne, 1683) LL 124
Lancelot, *Nouvelle méthode pour apprendre la langue Espagnole* (Paris, 1665) LL 1987
Lancelot, *Nouvelle méthode pour apprendre la langue Italienne* (Lyon, 1672) LL 1307

Some select travel relations, like those Mr Thévenot had printed
BOUHÉREAU:
Not in Bouhéreau's library.[130]
LOCKE:
Melchisédech Thévenot, *Relations de divers voyages curieux* (Paris, 1663) LL 2889
Melchisédech Thévenot, *Relations de divers voyages curieux* (Paris, 1672) LL 2889a
Melchisédech Thévenot, *Recueil de voyages* (Paris, 1681) LL 2890
Jean Thévenot, *Relation d'un voyage fait au Levant* (Rouen, 1665) LL 2888

Bouhéreau's list, as can be seen, indicated numerous works to be found in Locke's library, although the list was not particularly representative of either man's collection and differed in kind from the lists of recent publications which Locke received from associates such as Justel. Aside from the Port-Royal writers, the editions owned by Bouhéreau date mainly from the 1650s, probably works he came to know in late youth, whereas Locke's copies date from later, many from his time in France. They owned several titles in common, but none in the same editions.[131] Some of Locke's copies were acquired after 1678 but there seems no

129 Locke also owned the work in Latin (London, 1674), LL 1803a.   130 Several works by Melchisédech Thévenot and his nephew Jean Thévenot are in Marsh's Library but in the Stillingfleet and Marsh collections.   131 There is a copy of Charpentier's *La vie de Socrates* (Paris, 1657) among Bouhéreau's books in Marsh's Library, but it did not belong to him. It was previously in the library of Jean-Baptiste Colbert and was donated to Marsh's by the assistant librarian Robert Travers in the late nineteenth century, when it was added to

sign that the acquisition was inspired by Bouhéreau. Locke already owned many of the suggested books and more generally knew of the work of authors named, in the case of Melchisédech Thévenot probably knowing the author personally from Justel's circle.[132] Perhaps the most striking example of Bouhéreau telling Locke what he already knew was alluding to Pierre Nicole's *Essais*: Locke had lately undertaken an English translation of three of Nicole's essays to present to the countess of Shaftesbury.[133] A list of books he despatched to England before the 'little Tour of France' in 1678 included ten works suggested by Bouhéreau's missive.[134] Assuming the list arose from a request, Locke may have been checking his own grasp of the French literary landscape but it seems as likely the query was on behalf of his protégé Caleb Banks. Caleb more than Locke faced being quizzed on the matter on returning home and was of similar age to that at which Bouhéreau probably first met with many of the works. This surmise might also connect with the list of payments linking Bouhéreau and Banks, without solving the puzzle involved.

AFTER FRANCE

Locke's party arrived in London on 30 April 1679 (old style), the end of his journey and the encounter with Bouhéreau, although a possible re-encounter is considered later in this final section.[135] Locke's separation from Caleb Banks on reaching London was brief: he was called to the Banks family home in August to treat his erstwhile pupil for an ague, Locke prescribing 'kinkina' although with limited immediate effect, which Sydenham blamed on him also 'vomiting your patient'.[136] The patient recovered, though the sickly Caleb died in his thirties after a brief political career. His two years in France with Locke cost his father about £2,000.[137] Locke's contact with the Banks family faded as politics divided Shaftesbury and Sir John, and there is no extant correspondence with Locke after 1679. There are no further letters from the Coxes either, although there was further contact with Thomas junior, as we saw earlier and his envoyship provides the backdrop for the later moment of contact involving Locke and Bouhéreau.

Bouhéreau's diary provides the most sustained account of any period in Coxe's life, the two men's direct relationship concluding with the envoy's returning party going their separate ways in late July 1692, Coxe heading from

Bouhéreau's collection in the old reading room.   132 Thévenot added a passage to a letter from Toinard to Locke in 1680: Locke, *Correspondence*, ii, pp 229–30.   133 Jean S. Yolton (ed.), *John Locke as translator: three of the Essais of Pierre Nicole in English* (Oxford, 2000), p. 3. Yolton suggests a draft could have been complete by mid-1678.   134 Lough, 'Locke's reading', pp 244–8. The works were Nicole's *Essais*, Arnauld and Nicole's *L'Art de penser*, Pascal's *Lettres provinciales* and *pensées*, D'Ablancourt's Lucien and Thucydides/Xenophon, the 'Oeuvres de Voiture', Marmol's *Afrique*, and a volume of *Voyages* by each of the Thévenots. 135 Lough, *Locke's travels*, p. 275.   136 Locke, *Correspondence*, ii, p. 80.   137 D.C. Coleman, *Sir John Banks* (Oxford, 1963), p. 128.

the Hague to William III in Flanders with two Swiss aides and Bouhéreau soon travelling to London, where he was reunited with his family in late September (o.s.).[138] He was also soon reunited with Coxe's Swiss aides, who lodged with the Bouhéreau family in London, one for more than six months while seeking payment and royal favour he claimed had been promised by Coxe, without success.[139] The young Swiss, mentioned numerous times in Bouhéreau's diary, was Johann Jakob Heidegger, who turned instead to a career as an opera impresario and a long and famous association with George Frideric Handel.[140] Of the little previously known about his arrival in England, Heidegger's reported declaration that he 'came to England without a farthing' accords with Bouhéreau's record of loans to him.[141] Bouhéreau also loaned money to the other Swiss guest, 'de Muralt', apparently Béat-Louis de Muralt, who gained fame through his published letters about his experiences in England, the first dateable events aligning with Muralt taking a room with Bouhéreau.[142]

Coxe, meanwhile, was back in England by January 1693, claiming expenses of more than £3,000 and agreeing to join Sir Francis Wheler's expedition against French interests across the Atlantic but instead returning to Holland with his family in May.[143] His subsequent bid for the vacant post of envoy to Holland was rebuffed by Daniel Finch, earl of Nottingham, the Tory secretary of state, who claimed Coxe's earlier promise was a pretext to secure his Swiss expenses.[144] His diplomatic career over, Coxe remained in Holland or Flanders for some years, his wife being at the Hague in 1697 when Coxe arrived alone in Hamburg with unspecified 'goods' and a high fever from which he died two days later, on 22 June, the English resident Sir Paul Rycaut finding he had 'not above thirty shillings in mony'.[145]

---

138 Léoutre et al., *Diary and accounts*, pp 175 and 179.   139 Idem, pp 179 and 181; TNA, SP 44/100, fo. 391r.   140 Judith Milhous, 'Heidegger, Johann Jakob (1666–1749)', *ODNB*, which remarks that his early life is obscure and his date of arrival in London unknown. Bouhéreau met Heidegger's father, the theology professor Johann-Heinrich Heidegger, at Zurich in 1689 (Léoutre et al., *Diary and accounts*, p. 29), and in early 1690 met the son (p. 43), referred to on occasion in the *Diary and accounts* as 'young Mr Heidegger' (pp 75, 157 and 161) but otherwise simply as 'Mr Heidegger' or 'Heidegger'. Bouhéreau was friends with Heidegger senior, in 1689 receiving a copy of his *Consolatio Christiana martyryum* (Zurich, 1678), in 1690 his *De historia sacra*, 2 vols (Zurich, 1667–71), and in 1696 the newly published *Medulla theologiae Christianae* (Zurich, 1696) with a letter from Heidegger that remains within its pages. Heidegger also presented copies of his *Tumulus Tridentii Concilii*, 2nd ed., 2 vols (Zurich, 1690), and *Dissertationum selectarum ... Tomus III* (Zurich, 1690).   141 *The London Magazine*, vol. 48, October 1779, p. 453; Léoutre et al., *Diary and accounts*, pp 179–81. Unfortunately, a torn page in the manuscript diary obscures Bouhéreau's most extensive entry recording Heidegger's account with him: Marsh's Library, MS Z2.2.2, Diary, p. 57; Léoutre et al., *Diary and accounts*, pp 180–1.   142 Béat Louis de Muralt, *Lettres sur les Anglois et les François* (s.n., 1725), pp 130–2; Muralt, *Letters describing the character and customs of the English and French nations* (2nd ed., London, 1726), pp 67–8.   143 TNA, SP 44/98, p. 607; HMC, *Reports on the manuscripts of the late Allan George Finch*, vol. 5 (London, 2004), pp 46 and 61; TNA, SP 50/344, p. 50.   144 HMC *Finch*, 5: p. 74; TNA, SP 32/5 fo. 49r.   145 TNA, SP 82/19, fo. 77.

Ten days previously, 2/12 June 1697, Bouhéreau had begun his new life in Ireland, landing at Dublin with his family and his employer, Lord Galway.[146] His diary makes no mention of his former employer's demise; neither does it mention Locke, although it is possible there had been a further encounter between the two men five years earlier, just after Bouhéreau and Coxe parted at the Hague. Before leaving for England, Bouhéreau spent a fortnight in August 1692 in Amsterdam, 'where I have a large number of friends, especially from La Rochelle', one Dutch associate being 'Mr Guenelon, doctor of medicine, my friend'. Pieter Guenellon was also a friend of Locke's, who he probably met in Paris in 1678.[147] On 13 August 1692, the day before Bouhéreau's departure, Guenellon wrote in reply to questions Locke had sent on behalf of another friend – it was Dr Goodall's cinchona survey. Amsterdam physicians adjudged 'kina kina' 'un fort bon remede' if used prudently, wrote Guenellon. He then added that the letter would reach Locke by an intermediary, 'le bon Monsieur bouhereau de la Rochelle'.[148]

The letter was delivered, Locke noting on it that he sent an answer, though only in November (the letter is lost). He was in London when Bouhéreau arrived there on 21 September and for four weeks afterwards before retreating to the countryside until 18 November, when he returned to London for a week.[149] Possibly Locke and Bouhéreau met again but if so, neither saw reason to record the event, although neither man's journal was regular at this time – after arrival, Bouhéreau made no further entry until early November, when he noted receiving the final quarterly payment for his service with Coxe.[150] On 12 November, William Popple, translator of Locke's *Epistola de tolerantia* into the English *Letter*, reported to Locke that 'fourscore' ministers of the 'French Refugiez' in London were mounting a 'perfect Court of Inquisition': 'The cry is Socinianism', and 'My Lord G[alw]ay too is at the Head of the Party, and has complained to the King of the Growth of this Heresy'. Locke would remark that a French 'zeal for orthodoxy seems to be blazing more fiercely in our colder climate.' Among those accused of Socinian tendencies was André Lortie.[151] Bouhéreau's diary made no mention of the turmoil around him in London's Huguenot community, his infrequent entries preoccupied with his accounts with Heidegger and Muralt before, on 14 November 1693, recording that he had been appointed as secretary to accompany Lord Galway to Piedmont.[152]

---

146 Léoutre et al., *Diary and accounts*, p. 303.   147 Léoutre et al., *Diary and accounts*, p. 175; Locke, *Correspondence*, ii, p. 738 fn. 2.   148 Locke, *Correspondence*, iv, p. 493.   149 Léoutre et al., *Diary and accounts*, p. 179; 'Locke chronology', https://openpublishing.psu.edu/locke/chron/c1692.html, accessed 22 February 2024.   150 Léoutre et al., *Diary and accounts*, p. 179.   151 Locke, *Correspondence*, iv, pp 582 and 784; Robin Gwynn, 'Disorder and innovation: the reshaping of the French churches of London after the Glorious Revolution' in Ole Peter Grell, Jonathan I. Israel, and Nicolas Tyacke (eds), *From persecution to toleration: the Glorious Revolution and religion in England* (Oxford, 1991), pp 251–74, at pp 258–9.   152 Léoutre et al., *Diary and accounts*, p. 183.

Locke was by now a prolific published author, with nine works published in just four years and more soon to follow, although so far only the *Essay concerning human understanding* had named its author and made his reputation. As noted earlier, none of Locke's books was acquired by Bouhéreau, though few other publications in his collection date from after 1680 and fewer still in English – one exception is Locke's friend William Molyneux's *Case of Ireland* (1698) which Molyneux gifted to Bouhéreau as well as Locke.[153] The same was not true of Locke, who acquired Bouhéreau's translation of Origen from Greek, *Traité d'Origéne contre Celse* when finally published at Amsterdam in 1700, without making evident his views on the achievement.[154] Bouhéreau had been a passing presence in Locke's journey to notability, as had Locke in Bouhéreau's longer path to his own measure of recognition.[155]

---

153 William Molyneux, *The case of Ireland's being bound by acts of parliament in England, stated* (Dublin, 1698); Locke, *Correspondence*, vi, pp 376–7; Marsh's Library online catalogue www.marshlibrary.ie/catalogue; and see Benedict and Léchot, 'The library of Élie Bouhéreau', pp 169–71 and 179.   154 Harrison and Laslett, *Library of John Locke*, p. 199 (LL 2140).   155 As this volume went to press it was announced that Locke's journals have been digitised and are publicly available on the Digital Bodleian website at https:// digital.bodleian.ox.ac.uk.

Abraham Tessereau's miscellany: Huguenot history-writing during the reign of Louis XIV

DAVID VAN DER LINDEN

Stored in Marsh's Library since 1701 are two sprawling volumes filled with notes, manuscript copies, and printed publications that document the persecution of the Huguenots in France between 1656 and 1685. These papers were collected by Abraham Tessereau (1626–89), a Protestant lawyer from La Rochelle who served in the *parlement* of Paris (the kingdom's most important court of appeal), and who was a close friend of Élie Bouhéreau. The documents were to serve as the basis for a history Tessereau was preparing for publication, aptly titled 'Mémoires et pièces pour servir à l'histoire générale de la persécution faite en France contre ceux de la Religion Réformée' (Memoirs and documents to serve a general history of the persecutions in France against those of the Reformed religion).[1] Although the book never saw the light of day, Tessereau's two-volume miscellany is a valuable source of information for reconstructing how Protestant authors at the time of the Revocation began to write the history of the persecutions. The aim of this chapter, then, is not only to analyze Tessereau's narrative, but also to situate it within the larger world of Huguenot history-writing during the reign of Louis XIV.

As Philip Benedict has shown, the writing of Huguenot histories had seriously declined in the seventeenth century. The spectacular growth of the Reformed movement in the sixteenth century, followed by the Wars of Religion, had initially spurred a large number of Protestant authors to document the history of their community, in particular the persecutions they had suffered. These early works include the famous martyrology compiled by Jean Crespin, the *Livre des martyrs* (1554), as well as national histories of the troubles, such as the *Histoire ecclésiastique des Églises réformées de France* (1580) and Simon Goulart's *Mémoires de l'estat de France* (1576), which held the French monarchy responsible for the Saint Bartholomew's Day massacre. By the seventeenth

---

Research for this article was funded by the Dutch Research Council (NWO) under the VIDI grant 'Building peace: transitional justice in early modern France', as well as a Maddock research fellowship at Marsh's Library.   1 Marsh's Library, Dublin, MSS Z2.2.9 (vol. I) and Z2.2.10 (vol. II). Abraham Tessereau. Memoires et pieces pour servir a l'histoire generale de la persecution faitte en france contre ceux de la Religion reformee depuis l'année 1656 jusqu'a la revocation de l'édit de Nantes, faitte par celuy donné a Fontainebleau au moys d'octobre 1685.   2 Philip Benedict, 'Shaping the memory of the French Wars of Religion: the first centuries' in Erika Kuijpers, Judith Pollmann, Johannes Müller and Jasper van der Steen

century, however, such histories were hard to come by. The 1598 Edict of Nantes forbade both Catholics and Protestants to evoke the recent past, which was condemned to oblivion for fear of rekindling confessional tensions. In practice historians on both sides continued to write about the Wars of Religion, but Huguenot authors had to tread more carefully because it risked exposing their involvement in past wrongdoings, in particular the iconoclast revolts, massacres, and rebellions they had staged. Although in the privacy of their own studies Huguenot pastors and savants continued to compose histories, few of these were thus ever published for fear of undermining the position of the Protestant churches.[2] It is striking, for example, that between 1600 and 1750, virtually all local histories that discussed the religious wars were published by Catholic authors.[3]

This reluctance to evoke the past evaporated in the 1660s, when the Protestant churches came under increasing attack from Catholic clergy and the monarchy. Catholic clerics in particular dredged up the Wars of Religion to argue that the Huguenots were inherently seditious and had wrested their religious and civil liberties from the monarchy by force. The king, therefore, had a right – and some argued a divine duty – to curtail Huguenot freedoms and apply the Edict of Nantes in its strictest sense. It was in response to such partisan interpretations of the past that Huguenot authors again began publishing local and national histories.[4] The vast majority of these works were only published after 1685, however, and almost always from the safety of exile. The importance of Tessereau lies in the fact that he was one of the first refugee authors to compose a history of the persecutions. In fact, we can trace back Tessereau's activity as a historian to the early 1660s, when he began collecting documents that testified to the increasing pressure on the Huguenots while he also located evidence in the archives of the Protestant churches to help save them from closure by the Catholic authorities. Because Tessereau's history was never published, his miscellany has received little attention from modern historians.[5] This essay will argue, however, that Tessereau's archival approach and his contention that Catholics had knowingly plotted the downfall of French Protestantism – what I will call the 'Black Legend' of the Revocation – would have a profound impact on Huguenot historical consciousness as it developed in the Revocation era. As well-known refugee authors such as Élie Benoist and Pierre Jurieu gained access to Tessereau's miscellany, they exploited the documents he had gathered to

(eds), *Memory before modernity: practices of memory in early modern Europe* (Leiden, 2013), pp 111–25; Philip Benedict, 'La conviction plus forte que la critique: la Réforme et les guerres de religion vues par les historiens protestants à l'époque de la Révocation' in Philip Benedict, Hugues Daussy and Pierre-Olivier Léchot (eds), *L'Identité huguenote: faire mémoire et écrire l'histoire (XVIe–XXIe siècle)* (Geneva, 2014), pp 223–39, esp. 223–5. 3 Barbara B. Diefendorf, 'The scars of religious war in histories of French cities (1600–1750)', *French History*, 34:4 (2020), 453–74. 4 Benedict, 'La conviction'. 5 The only in-depth treatment is by Thomas Philip le Fanu, 'Mémoires inédits d'Abraham Tessereau', *Proceedings of the*

furnish their own histories, which in turn helped to cement his claim that the destruction of the Huguenot communities had been long in the making.

ABRAHAM TESSEREAU, LAWYER AND HISTORIAN

Most Huguenot historians writing in the Revocation era were refugee pastors, who had a direct interest in decrying the illegitimacy of the persecutions and lobbied to have Protestant worship in France re-established. The most prominent of these pastor-historians had taken refuge in the Dutch Republic, including Jean Claude, François Gaultier de Saint-Blancard, Pierre Jurieu, and Élie Benoist.[6] Abraham Tessereau cut a very different figure: he had been trained as a lawyer, not a theologian, and had subsequently pursued a career in court. But as we shall see, it was precisely Tessereau's legal training and his involvement in the campaign to save the Protestant churches that led him to take up his pen, writing a legal history of the persecutions that would have a remarkable impact on the refugee pastors who turned to Huguenot history-writing after the Revocation.

Little is known about Tessereau's early life. He was born in La Rochelle on 6 June 1626, the son of Françoise Franchard and Abraham Tessereau, and baptized a week later in the city's Protestant church of Saint-Yon. Tessereau's father was *pair de la commune*, a prominent city councillor, who took an active part in the defence of La Rochelle during the devastating siege of 1628.[7] Tessereau was thus born at a critical juncture in the city's history, and that of the French Reformed Churches more widely. In 1620 King Louis XIII had led his army across southern France to occupy the independent Protestant principality of Béarn, where he forcibly restored Catholic worship. Alarmed by this royal show of force, in December 1620 Protestant leaders headed by the Duke of Rohan met in La Rochelle, where they resolved to take up arms to defend the Reformed cause. Their uprising ended in spectacular defeat: between 1621 and 1629 royal armies besieged and occupied the rebellious Huguenot cities in southern France, including Montauban, Montpellier, and, most famously, La Rochelle.[8] The king forced the Rochelais to accept a humiliating treaty in November 1628, banishing the Protestant mayors and most prominent city councillors, including Tessereau's father, though they were allowed to return after six months.[9]

Huguenot Society of London, 15 (1937), 566–84.   **6** David van der Linden, *Experiencing exile: Huguenot refugees in the Dutch Republic, 1680–1700* (Farnham, 2015), pp 176–223.   **7** Léopold Gabriel Delayant, *Historiens de La Rochelle: études lues à la Société littéraire de La Rochelle de 1853 à 1860* (La Rochelle, 1863), p. 205.   **8** David Parker, *La Rochelle and the French monarchy: conflict and order in seventeenth-century France* (London, 1980); Kevin C. Robbins, *City on the ocean sea: La Rochelle, 1530–1650: urban society, religion, and politics on the French Atlantic frontier* (Leiden, 1997), pp 335–53. On the last war of religion, see Mack Holt, *The French Wars of Religion, 1562–1629* (Cambridge, 2005), pp 178–94.   **9** Delayant, *Historiens*

Tessereau must have left La Rochelle at some point to study law and obtain his degree, because on 7 June 1653 he became *secretaire et conseiller du roi* (secretary and councillor to the king) in the royal chancellery attached to the *parlement* of Paris. The chancellery was tasked with drafting, sealing, and expediting government acts, in particular decisions taken by the king and judgments issued by the *parlement*.[10] In his capacity as secretary Tessereau also turned to writing legal history: in 1676 he published the *Histoire chronologique de la grande chancellerie de France*, which meticulously recounted the origins of this royal institution as well as the duties and prerogatives of its functionaries. The preface offers a rare glimpse of Tessereau's historical method, since it noted that beginning in 1653, he had not only consulted previous works on the history of the chancellery, but had also gained access to its archives. This research resulted in a compendium of copied archival documents, including 'edicts, letters patent, declarations, *arrêts* (rulings), regulations, registers, and other pieces', which, Tessereau stressed, 'are proof of everything I have argued'.[11]

It was Tessereau's legal background and experience in archival research that would lay the groundwork for his later history of the persecutions, but equally important were his efforts to protect the Huguenot churches from closure. During the reign of Louis XIV, the toleration of France's Protestant minority came under serious pressure, as the king gradually stripped his Huguenot subjects of their religious, civic, and legal privileges as set out in the Edict of Nantes. Élisabeth Labrousse has aptly called this process a 'judicial Cold War': instead of outright persecution the monarchy relied on bans and harassment to persuade the Huguenots to abandon their faith.[12] A key episode in this campaign was the dispatch in 1661 of royal commissioners into all French provinces, known as the *commissaires de l'édit*. Composed of a Catholic and a Protestant magistrate, they were authorized to investigate local infractions of the Edict of Nantes and receive petitions from both confessions. Catholic clergy seized this opportunity to demand the closure of Huguenot churches, which, they argued, had been built in violation of royal edicts. Although the commissions were officially bipartisan, they often ended in a stalemate, because the commissioners sided with their own confessional community rather than find an equitable solution. These so-called *partages* were then referred to the king's council for arbitration, which generally ruled in favour of the Catholics.[13]

---

de La Rochelle, p. 205. See also Pierre Mervault, *Le journal des choses les plus memorables qui se sont passées au dernier siege de La Rochelle*, 2nd ed. (Rouen, 1671), p. 651.   10 Delayant, *Historiens de La Rochelle*, p. 205. On the chancellery and its secretaries, see Lucien Bély (ed.), *Dictionnaire de l'Ancien Régime* (Paris, 1996), pp 1144–5.   11 Abraham Tessereau, *Histoire chronologique de la grande chancelerie de France: contenant son origine, lestat de ses officiers, un recueil exact de leurs noms depuis le commencement de la monarchie jusqu'à present, leurs fonctions, privileges, prerogatives, droits & reglemens*, 2 vols (Paris, 1676), i, avertissement.   12 Élisabeth Labrousse, *Une foi, une loi, un roi?: essai sur la révocation de l'édit de Nantes* (Geneva, 1985), pp 119–24.   13 Ibid., pp 125–7; Patrick Cabanel, *Histoire des protestants en France*,

In 1661, however, the ultimate outcome of the commissions was still unknown, which meant the Protestant churches invested serious time and effort in fending off Catholic attacks. Huguenot consistories and provincial synods throughout France appointed trusted men with legal training, who were to gather and present the necessary documents to dispute Catholic allegations and convince the commissioners to uphold Protestant worship. When a commission arrived at La Rochelle in September 1663, the consistory thus relied on Tessereau's legal and archival expertise to save the church. Although at this point Tessereau mostly lived and worked in Paris, his family ties still bound him to the town where he had grown up: his mother lived in La Rochelle until her death in 1677, as did his brother Matthieu, and he remained an elder on the city's consistory. Tessereau's wife Louise Venaud, a Protestant noblewoman who owned large estates around Fontenay-le-Comte, also spent most of her time in La Rochelle, where the couple owned a townhouse. It was there that in October 1667 she gave birth to their son Abraham, who was baptized in La Rochelle's Protestant temple a few days later; sadly, the boy passed away in January 1671 at the tender age of three.[14]

Tessereau's main duty in 1663 involved the search for relevant documents. The Catholic commissioner, the intendant of the Aunis province Charles-Jean Colbert de Terron, a cousin of finance minister Jean-Baptiste Colbert, and his Protestant counterpart Isaac Isle, marquis de Loire, asked La Rochelle's Protestants to supply written evidence that their community had already worshipped in the years 1596–7, as stipulated by article nine of the Edict of Nantes. In response, Tessereau handed over extensive documentation drawn from the consistory archives of La Rochelle, in particular extracts from the baptism records covering the period 1559–95.[15] The church also submitted the acts of both national and provincial synods that had taken place in La Rochelle between 1581 and 1599, copies of marriage records from the years 1595–1600, and rulings by previous commissioners, who had granted the Protestants a cemetery and new place of worship following the siege of 1628. The overwhelming archival evidence succeeded in preserving Protestant worship at

---

XVIe–XXIe siècle (Paris, 2012), pp 547–50. The commissions were modelled on those appointed by Henry IV to implement the Edict of Nantes: Francis Garrisson, Essai sur les commissions d'application de l'édit de Nantes (Montpellier, 1964). 14 Delayant, Historiens de la Rochelle, p. 207; Bibliothèque du Protestantisme Français (hereafter BPF), Paris, MS 711, no. 41, Notarial procuration by Abraham Tessereau, Paris, 8 May 1682; Archives départementales de la Charente-Maritime (hereafter ADCM), La Rochelle, I 179, Baptism of Abraham Tessereau, 25 October 1667, fo. 47; ADCM, I 184, Burial of Abraham Tessereau, 16 January 1671, fo. 4v. I have not found evidence of other children. 15 Archives Nationales (hereafter AN), Paris, TT263B, fos. 1–7, Extracts of baptismal records, La Rochelle, 1559–1595. On Terron, see François Julien-Labruyère (ed.), Dictionnaire biographique des Charentais et de ceux qui ont illustré les Charentes (Paris, 2005), p. 336. On Isaac Isle, see Eugène and Émile Haag, La France protestante, ou vies des protestants français qui se sont fait un nom dans l'histoire, 10 vols (Paris, 1846–59), vi, pp 22–3.

La Rochelle: in December 1663 the commissioners agreed that the Huguenot church would not be demolished.[16]

The 1663 commission only marked the beginning of Tessereau's involvement in the legal campaign to safeguard the Protestant churches of his home region, the Aunis. Despite the small victory Tessereau had helped to score, La Rochelle's Huguenots faced a serious setback: intendant Colbert de Terron argued that their church should be marked as one of only two Protestant churches that the Edict of Nantes allowed in each *baillage* (bailiwick). This meant that in addition to La Rochelle's temple they could only retain one other church in the Aunis – Terron designated Marans as the second site of worship – and that the remaining eleven temples were forced to close. When the Protestant commissioner Isaac Isle objected to this decision, however, the commission resulted in a *partage* that was referred to the king's council.[17] As the fate of the Protestant churches hung in the balance, the synod of Aunis sent an envoy to Paris to lobby the royal council, but when after six months the king refused to take a decision, the synod instead appointed Tessereau as its official representative.[18] He would continue to serve as deputy throughout the 1660s and 1670s, often alongside delegates dispatched by other provincial synods, intervening with petitions and documents each time the Aunis churches came under threat. As the Aunis synod noted in 1675, Tessereau's task was 'to do what is necessary for the common good of the churches of this province and for the preservation of their right to worship; and also to present their complaints and to request redress for [Catholic] grievances which are made to them both as a community or as particular churches, in contravention of the Edict of Nantes'.[19] Tessereau's qualities did not go unnoticed by the other Huguenot churches, in particular the church of Paris located at Charenton, where he served as an elder on the consistory. In 1679, the provincial synod of Île de France nominated Tessereau as its deputy for church affairs at court, alongside Antoine de Massanes, who also served as secretary in the chancellery of the *parlement* of Paris.[20]

16 AN, TT 263B, fos. 24–31, Partage d'avis by Colbert de Terron and Isaac Isle, 20 December 1663.   17 AN, TT 263B, fos. 30–1, Partage d'avis by Colbert de Terron and Isaac Isle, 20 December 1663; Daniel Henri Delaizement, *Histoire des Reformés de La Rochelle, depuis l'année 1660 jusqu'à l'année 1685, en laquelle l'edit de Nantes a été revoqué* (Amsterdam, 1688), pp 18–25.   18 Delaizement, *Histoire des Reformés de La Rochelle*, pp 26–7.   19 ADCM, 300 J 235, Appointment of Abraham Tessereau as deputy for the Aunis churches, 4 December 1675. On the role of the deputies, see Solange Deyon, *Du loyalisme au refus: les Protestants français et leur député général entre la Fronde et la Révocation* (Villeneuve-d'Ascq, 1976), pp 75–84.   20 Orentin Douen, *La révocation de l'édit de Nantes à Paris, d'après des documents inédits*, 2 vols (Paris, 1894), i, p. 332; ii, pp 107–8, esp. fn. 2. Tessereau took over from Jacques Le Maçon, who had become too old to carry out his functions.

DOCUMENTING PERSECUTION

Tessereau's involvement in the defence of the Protestant churches meant that from the 1660s onwards he accumulated a large private archive, while in his capacity as secretary in the Paris chancellery he also had unprecedented access to the vast reservoir of state documents, in particular royal *arrêts* and decrees curtailing Protestant liberties. It is also noteworthy that in August 1674 he resigned his position as secretary and was honourably discharged, though not because of religious pressure: an edict issued by Louis XIV in February 1673 confirmed Protestants in their right to serve as royal secretaries. Only in January 1684 did the king revoke the privileges of Tessereau and the other Protestant secretaries in the Paris chancellery.[21] If anything, his resignation gave Tessereau more time to pursue his efforts to safeguard the Protestant churches, and in the process collect more documents.

In the early 1680s he thus became involved in protesting against the growing violence used by Catholic authorities. Between 1681 and 1685, the intendants of the Poitou, Aunis, Dauphiné, Béarn, and Languedoc successfully employed *dragonnades*, the quartering of Catholic soldiers on Protestant families to force them to convert.[22] Shocked by the first wave of violence and the mass abjurations that washed over the Poitou in 1681, Tessereau began collecting testimonies from affected Protestant communities in the region. The second volume of his miscellany contains over 200 depositions made by individual Huguenots before their local consistory, who recounted the violence they had suffered at the hands of Catholic soldiers. As Tessereau insisted in the preface to his 'Mémoires et pièces', these eyewitness accounts had been 'accurately and faithfully reported', showing readers 'unbelievable examples of cruelty and barbarity'.[23] Yet he soon reached the pessimistic conclusion that such evidence – either presented in writ to the king's council or printed to sway public opinion – made little difference. In a letter to his friend Élie Bouhéreau in La Rochelle, Tessereau wrote scathingly about those Protestants 'who believe to have a remedy for everything, when they say we must present petitions'. He reported that when Protestant deputies had protested against the Poitou *dragonnade* at court, the evidence they presented had simply been dismissed as *faits supposés* (alleged facts).[24]

21 Tessereau, *Histoire chronologique de la grande chancelerie*, p. 660. For the 1673 edict, see ibid., p. 614, article 12; the 1684 exclusion is referenced in Delayant, *Historiens de la Rochelle*, pp 207–8.   22 Labrousse, *Une foi, une loi, un roi?*, pp 173–7; Roy L. McCullough, *Coercion, conversion and counterinsurgency in Louis XIV's France* (Leiden, 2007), pp 125–79. 23 Marsh's Library, MS Z2.2.9, Avertissement, fo. 2. For an analysis of these depositions, see Caelinn Largey, 'Dragonnade in Poitou, 1681: a study of the Tessereau depositions in Marsh's Library, Dublin' (MA, Trinity College Dublin, 1981).   24 BPF, MS 713/2, Abraham Tessereau to Élie Bouhéreau, 8 September 1681. On Bouhéreau's correspondence network, see Jean Flouret, 'La correspondance du médecin rochelais Élie Bouhéreau (1643–1719)' in Pierre Albert (ed.), *Correspondre jadis et naguère* (Paris, 1995), pp 667–77; Ruth Whelan, 'West coast connections: the correspondence network of Élie Bouhéreau of La Rochelle' in Vivienne

The moment at which Tessereau decided to transform his vast collection of royal ordinances, consistory documents, petitions and personal testimonies into a full-fledged history of the persecutions remains difficult to pinpoint, but it seems likely that the idea only came to him once he had left France. Huguenot authors inside the kingdom had to be extremely cautious in writing about the persecutions, because a string of royal edicts forbade expressions of disrespect to the Catholic Church. For pastors in particular, publishing a condemnation of the persecutions could spell the end to their career, or even the closure of their church. This is not to say that Huguenot authors were uninterested in researching and writing the recent past; they simply had to be more cautious and often published their work abroad. In 1664, for example, the synod of Brittany elected pastor Philippe Le Noir from Blain to document the history of the Protestant churches in the province. Le Noir's goal was to prove the Huguenots' legal and historical right to worship in Brittany, just as Tessereau had collected documents for the Aunis churches. When the first *dragonnade* hit the Poitou, Le Noir began reworking his material into a four-part history of Brittany's churches, from their foundation in 1558 until his own time, but it was never published, because in 1685 he fled to the Dutch Republic and abandoned his manuscript.[25]

Huguenot pastors in Tessereau's home town of La Rochelle demonstrated similar caution. Prior to the Revocation, not a single author published a local history that discussed the Reformation, the Wars of Religion, or the recent persecutions under Louis XIV. Two pastors did compose a manuscript history of La Rochelle's Protestant community, but their works were only printed after the Revocation, by refugee publishers who had settled in the Dutch Republic. The first to undertake such a history was Philippe Vincent, who served as pastor at La Rochelle from 1626 until his death in 1651. He completed his *Recherches sur les commencemens et les premiers progrès de la Réformation en la ville de La Rochelle* in 1650, making extensive use of the consistory archives dating back to 1558 and the journal of an early convert to Calvinism, the baker Pierre Pacteau, who had chronicled events in the city until 1571. Vincent's manuscript was not published until 1693 though, by the Huguenot refugee bookseller Abraham Acher in Rotterdam.[26] The publication of Vincent's history was facilitated by another pastor, Daniel Henri Delaizement, who had served at La Rochelle until

---

Larminie (ed.), *Huguenot networks, 1560–1780: the interactions and impact of a Protestant minority in Europe* (London, 2017), pp 155–71.   25 Philip Benedict, 'The owl of Minerva at dusk: Philippe Le Noir de Crevain, a pastor-historian under Louis XIV' in Philip Benedict (ed.), *The faith and fortunes of France's Huguenots, 1600–85* (Aldershot, 2001), pp 248–76. 26 Philippe Vincent, *Recherches sur les commencemens et les premiers progrés de la Reformation en la ville de la Rochelle* (Rotterdam, 1693), Avertissement, and pp 1–4. Vincent's career is outlined in Delayant, *Historiens de La Rochelle*, pp 179–201. On Acher and refugee booksellers in the Dutch Republic, see Van der Linden, *Experiencing exile*, pp 51–62.

the Revocation had forced him into exile to the Dutch Republic, where he preached in Leiden's Walloon church. In 1688 Delaizement published a history of La Rochelle's Reformed community covering the period 1660–85. Aptly titled *Histoire des Reformés de La Rochelle*, it was sold under the guise of anonymity by the refugee bookseller Pierre Savouret in Amsterdam.[27] Scholars have often attributed this work to Abraham Tessereau, but a letter preserved in Geneva by the Rochelais merchant Jacques Barbaud clearly identifies Delaizement as the author.[28] The pastor also gifted a copy of his work to his friend Bouhéreau, who noted the pastor's name on the flyleaf.[29]

Like Delaizement, Tessereau only composed his history of the persecutions once he had reached the safety of exile. In November 1681 he obtained permission from Louis XIV to leave France and travel abroad for three years, ostensibly to visit foreign courts of law and write a comparative history of the European chancelleries, intended as a sequel to his acclaimed *Histoire chronologique de la grande chancellerie de France*. Yet in a letter sent to Bouhéreau upon arrival in London in May 1682, Tessereau admitted that the bleak religious outlook in France and his accumulating debts were the true reasons behind his sudden departure – he was unable to pay his wife's pension and claimed to be pursued by his creditors.[30] Once in exile, Tessereau did not immediately throw himself into the writing of Huguenot history. In July 1682 he announced to Bouhéreau that he was first hoping to finish another historical project. Prior to his departure he had borrowed from his friend a copy of the *Tables historiques* (1675), a universal history from Creation to the present day written by Jean Rou, a former Protestant *avocat* in the *parlement* of Paris. The work had been banned by Louis XIV for its supposed anti-Catholic slant, but Tessereau had a different axe to grind with the author: judging what Rou had written on ancient history to be 'of an appalling dryness', he had decided 'to augment it with several considerable commentaries', and to improve the sections on ecclesiastical history.[31]

Although it appears that Tessereau quickly abandoned both this project and his comparative European history of the chancelleries, the idea to instead write

---

27 Delaizement, *Histoire des Reformés*. On Delaizement's life, see the short notice in Julien-Labruyère (ed.), *Dictionnaire biographique des Charentais*, pp 769–70. See also Hans Bots, 'Liste des pasteurs et proposants réfugiés dans les Provinces-Unies' in Jens Häseler and Antony McKenna (eds), *La vie intellectuelle aux Refuges protestants* (Paris, 1999), p. 46 (fn. 234). **28** Bibliothèque de Genève, Geneva, MS Court 48, fos. 11–13, Jacques Barbaud to Élie Benoist, Kampen, March 1696. **29** Copy kept at Marsh's Library (second edition, 1689). Bouhéreau's note reads: 'Don de l'Auteur, Mr. Delaizamen.' **30** BPF, MS 713/2, Abraham Tessereau to Élie Bouhéreau, Paris, 11 May 1682, with a copy of the royal procuration allowing Tessereau to leave France, 3 November 1681; Abraham Tessereau to Élie Bouhéreau, London, 25 May 1682. His dire financial situation is also evident from BPF, MS 711, no. 41, Notarial procuration by Abraham Tessereau, Paris, 8 May 1682. **31** BPF, MS 713/2, Abraham Tessereau to Élie Bouhéreau, London, 5 July 1682. On Rou's *Tables*, see Michaël Green, *The Huguenot Jean Rou (1638–1711): scholar, educator, civil servant* (Paris, 2015),

a history of the persecutions occurred to him probably after the Revocation. He would also complete this work in the Dutch Republic rather than in England. Indeed, his correspondence reveals that Tessereau never fully adjusted to his new life in London. He was particularly worried by the increasingly hostile attitude of the English monarchy towards the Huguenot refugees, who predominantly worshipped at the non-conforming French stranger churches that followed the Reformed liturgy rather than conformed to the Church of England. Upon his arrival, Tessereau had also become a member of the non-conforming French church at Threadneedle Street.[32] Yet not all refugees followed his cue. Due to a lack of pulpits, many refugee pastors accepted reordination in the Church of England and ministered in the growing number of conforming French-speaking churches that sprung up in the capital. Among them was André Lortie, another refugee pastor from La Rochelle, who after his reordination began preaching at the conforming church of the Savoy.[33] Like many orthodox Calvinists from France, Tessereau viewed the Anglican Church as a halfway house to Catholicism, but his efforts to persuade Lortie to abandon his 'new episcopal ordination' proved fruitless. He was confirmed in his aversion of conformity by his friend and pastor Jean Claude from Paris, who in a letter to Tessereau admitted to be deeply shocked by the reordinations: 'The Episcopalians will forgive me if I say that they have done irreparable harm to the Reformation and consequently to themselves, but for our pastors it is a cowardice and a breach of trust for which posterity will blame them.' Claude singled out Lortie as the 'author and promotor of this shame', begging God to forgive the pastor.[34]

By the summer of 1686, Tessereau announced to Claude – who at the Revocation had been expelled from France and settled in The Hague – that he was planning to move to the Dutch Republic.[35] The exact date of his arrival is unknown, but by the winter of 1688 he had taken up residence in The Hague at the *Maréchal de Turenne*, a well-known inn at the centre of town.[36] A series of letters preserved with Tessereau's miscellany reveals that by December 1688 he had finished his history, and was now soliciting the editorial advice of two refugee pastors in the Dutch Republic: Daniel Henri Delaizement, who had baptized his son Abraham back in La Rochelle but now preached in Leiden, and Pierre Du Bosc from Caen, who ministered in the Walloon church of Rotterdam.[37] They

pp 75–81 and 185–95.   32 Le Fanu, 'Mémoires inédits d'Abraham Tessereau', 568; William and Susan Minet (eds), *Livre des tesmoignages de l'eglise de Threadneedle Street, 1669–1789* (London, 1909), p. 251.   33 Robin Gwynn, *The Huguenots in later Stuart Britain*, 3 vols (Brighton, 2015–20), i, pp 163–202, and 349–50 for Lortie's career in London.   34 BPF, MS 713/2, Abraham Tessereau to Élie Bouhéreau, London, 25 May and 24 September 1682; University Library, Leiden (hereafter UBL), BPL, MS 292/3, Jean Claude to Tessereau, Paris, 2 February 1684.   35 UBL, BPL, MS 292/3, Jean Claude to Abraham Tessereau, The Hague, 12 June 1686.   36 As is evident from a letter sent to Tessereau in December 1688. The address panel reads: 'A Monsieur Tessereau, à l'enseigne du marechal de Turenne dans la ruë qui va du fluwel bourgwal au Plain, à La Haye.' Marsh's Library, MS Z2.2.10, Daniel

both approved of Tessereau's manuscript. 'I have read it with a singular pleasure', Du Bosc wrote in June 1689. 'It is a complete history of the persecutions of our poor Churches, who will be eternally obliged to you for the care you took to collect documents of the horrible violence they have been subjected to.'[38] Yet despite this ringing endorsement the book was never published: when Bouhéreau finally visited his friend in October 1689, he noted in his diary that Tessereau had fallen 'dangerously ill' – he passed away before the year was up.[39]

THE BLACK LEGEND OF THE REVOCATION

Going through Tessereau's two volumes that served as the basis for his unpublished history, it is easy to see why Delaizement and Du Bosc heaped praise on the work: the 'Mémoires et pièces' offers a passionate defence of the Protestant churches in the face of ongoing Catholic persecution. Both pastors also appreciated the structure of Tessereau's history, which essentially took the form of a miscellany: rather than writing a narrative history of the persecutions, Tessereau presented his readers with a varied collection of primary documents, interspersed with commentaries and preceded by a short preface.[40] Delaizement thus praised 'the pieces one can find in their entirety, such as our general petitions and *placets*, and some even by our principal enemies'.[41] Du Bosc shared this opinion, writing that 'what I like most is that each piece is accompanied by [your] response and remarks, which will forever serve as a defence of our communities'.[42]

In presenting his history in the form of a miscellany, Tessereau drew on an older tradition of Huguenot history-writing that first emerged during the Wars of Religion, and which blended documentary evidence with polemical narrative. In 1563 the Orléans printer Éloi Gibier, who served as the official publisher of the Huguenot leader Condé, decided to clear his stock of Protestant memoranda and pamphlets by selling them in sets. These *receuils* clearly struck a chord with readers interested in compiling an archive of recent events, because throughout the wars many more miscellanies appeared that either offered an anthology of previously printed texts (following the example of Gibier), or that combined

---

Henri Delaizement to Abraham Tessereau, Leiden, 25 December 1688.   37 Delaizement is recorded as the pastor administering the baptism in ADCM, I 179, Baptism of Abraham Tessereau, 25 October 1667, fo. 47.   38 Marsh's Library, MS Z2.2.10, Pierre Du Bosc to Abraham Tessereau, Rotterdam, 21 June 1689.   39 Marie Léoutre, Jane McKee, Jean-Paul Pittion, and Amy Prendergast (eds), *The diary (1689–1719) and accounts (1704–1717) of Élie Bouhéreau: Marsh's Library Z2.2.2* (Dublin, 2019), p. 7.   40 On the genre of the miscellany, see: Angus Vine, *Miscellaneous order: manuscript culture and the early modern organization of knowledge* (Oxford, 2019).   41 Marsh's Library, MS Z2.2.10, Daniel Henri Delaizement to Abraham Tessereau, Leiden, 9 January 1689.   42 Marsh's Library, MS Z2.2.10, Pierre Du Bosc to Abraham Tessereau, Rotterdam, 21 June 1689.

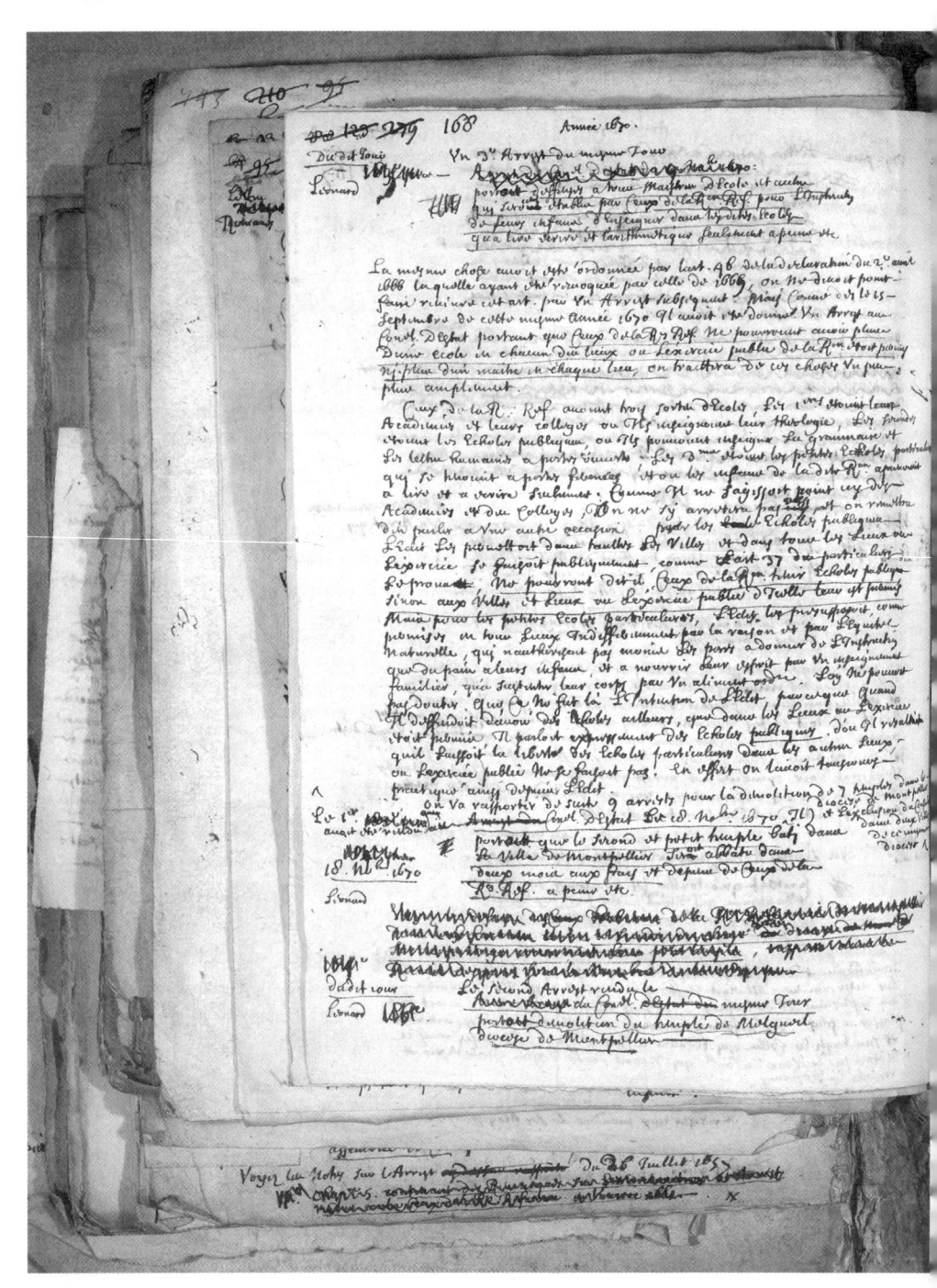

5.1. Image from the first volume of the 'Mémoires et pièces'. On the left, written narrative by Tessereau (fo. 168), on the right, a printed document with marginal comments in his hand (fo. 182); at the centre, an inserted slip of paper (fo. 169).

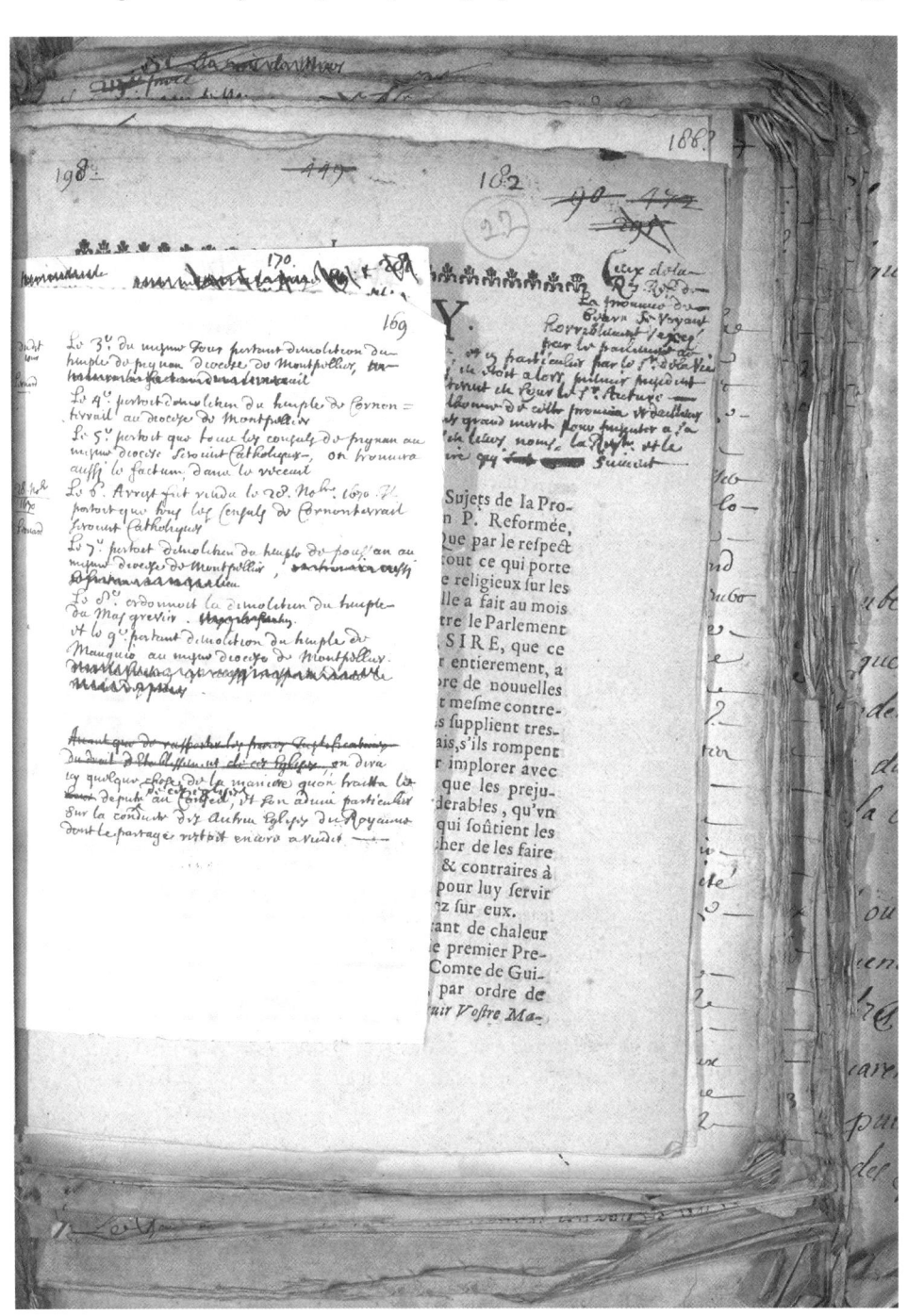

Huguenot history-writing during the reign of Louis XIV

narrative history with extensive documentation. The Huguenot pastor Simon Goulart, for example, published the *Mémoires de l'estat de France* and the *Mémoires de la Ligue*; both were essentially a collection of primary documents joined together by a polemical narrative that decried the Catholics' murderous hatred of the Protestants.[43]

Tessereau's history clearly followed this pattern of publishing and commenting on primary documents, as also suggested by the title of his history, 'Mémoires et pièces'. The documents in his miscellany fall into roughly three categories. By far the largest category consists of edicts, ordinances, declarations, and *arrêts* issued against the Huguenots since 1656, which Tessereau either copied out verbatim or summarized – although he also inserted some printed copies. To string these documents together he added brief commentaries, usually directly below the cited document, but sometimes also scribbled in the margins or on separate slips of paper (see fig. 5.1). In addition, he included Protestant petitions and memoirs presented to the king and his ministers to defend particular churches or privileges, either by provincial deputies like Tessereau himself, or by the deputy-general of the Protestant churches, Henri de Massue, marquis de Ruvigny. The third and final cluster of texts comprised personal testimonies of persecution, in particular those regarding the 1681 dragonnade in the Poitou.

Although Tessereau claimed that his own confession played no part in his history, like Goulart and other Protestant historians before him he was not an impartial collector. As he admitted in the preface to his miscellany, he had consciously selected and annotated these documents in order to prove 'the injustice and illusion of all these devious tactics that have served, step by step, to arrive at the ultimate goal that the enemies of the Protestants had devised: the extinction of the public exercise of the Reformed Religion'.[44] In particular the legal documents produced by the French state were to serve as irrefutable evidence that the Huguenots had been unjustly persecuted from the moment Louis XIV took power. Condemning religious intolerance by citing written evidence produced by one's enemy – what Alain Dufour has called 'the damning document' (*le document accablant*) – was a common Protestant strategy, which dated back to the era of the religious wars. Goulart, for instance, had included in his *Mémoires de l'estat* a letter by the Duke of Guise, in order to demonstrate that Catholics had orchestrated the Saint Bartholomew's Day massacre.[45]

---

43 Amy Graves-Monroe, 'La méthode pragmatique: la pratique de l'histoire dans les *Mémoires de Condé* et leurs prolongations' in Danièle Bohler and Catherine Magnien-Simonin (eds), *Écritures de l'histoire, XIVe–XVIe siècle* (Geneva, 2005), pp 455–69; Amy Graves-Monroe, *Post tenebras lex: preuves et propagande dans l'historiographie engagée de Simon Goulart (1543–1628)* (Geneva, 2012). **44** Marsh's Library, MS Z2.2.9, fo. 1. **45** Alain Dufour, 'Une particularité de l'historiographie protestante au XVIe siècle: le document accablant', *Protestantesimo*, 54:3 (1999), 285–91; Alain Dufour, *Théodore de Bèze: poète et théologien* (Geneva, 2009), p. 151.

By citing royal legislation, Tessereau likewise aimed to demonstrate the concerted attack on French Protestants. He noted for instance that Catholics had begun their campaign by excluding Protestants from urban government. Especially in Languedoc, many cities were governed by a *consulat mi-parti*, a town council composed of equal numbers of Catholic and Protestant councillors. In August 1656, however, Catholics from Montpellier persuaded the royal council to issue an *arrêt* that forever excluded Huguenots from the *consulat*. Tessereau commented that the ruling was 'unjust and dishonest', because article twenty-seven of the Edict of Nantes unequivocally allowed Protestants to hold public office, just as royal decrees in 1631 and 1652 had confirmed their right to sit on Montpellier's *consulat*. Additional anti-Protestant *arrêts* discussed by Tessereau include a ban on Protestant worship in episcopal cities, a prohibition on sermons that defamed the Catholic faith, and a ban on singing psalms in public. As he wryly concluded, 'once the time of the civil wars [i.e., the Fronde] had passed, the Reformed were no longer needed, and Catholics regarded them as people that they wished to destroy'.[46]

In his history, Tessereau also struggled with a question that has occupied many historians ever since: why did Louis XIV revoke the Edict of Nantes? The standard response has been that the edict was never designed as a lasting solution to the problem of religious diversity. The ultimate aim of the monarchy, scholars have argued, was to reconcile Protestants with the Church of Rome, not to install permanent religious co-existence. They often cite as evidence the preamble to the Edict of Nantes, which had expressed hope that religious pluralism was a temporary measure, 'until it would please God to have all French men and women worship him in the same religion'.[47] It is important to note, however, that this teleological perspective on the edict's supposed weakness has been inherited from Huguenot historians writing in the 1680s. Shaped by the experience of persecution and flight, they created what we might call a 'Black Legend' of the Revocation, accusing the French monarchy and Catholic clergy of a premeditated plot to destroy their communities. The reign of Louis XIV played a pivotal role in this story, as authors argued that it was the king's personal reign that had inaugurated the anti-Protestant campaign. When in 1681 the Huguenot pastor Pierre Jurieu published his polemical treatise *La politique du clergé de France*, he argued that 'the design to ruin the Protestant party in France was only born in the year 1660', following the Peace of the Pyrenees concluded between France and Spain the year before.[48] Jean Claude, writing from exile in 1686, also

---

[46] Marsh's Library, MS Z2.2.9, Avant propos servant d'introduction, unfoliated. On the *consulats mi-partis*, see Olivier Christin, *La paix de religion: l'autonomisation de la raison politique au XVIe siècle* (Paris, 1997), pp 86–97.   [47] Jean Orcibal, 'Louis XIV and the Edict of Nantes' in Ragnhild Hatton (ed.), *Louis XIV and absolutism* (London, 1976), pp 154–76; Labrousse, *Une foi, une loi, un roi?*, p. 28; Holt, *The French Wars of Religion*, pp 166–7; Cabanel, *Histoire des protestants en France*, pp 335–6.   [48] Pierre Jurieu, *La politique du clergé de France, ou entretiens curieux de deux Catholiques romains, l'un parisien & l'autre provincial,*

claimed that 'this is a project they have devised for a long time', noting that from once peace had been signed with Spain, 'the plan was settled to destroy the Protestants'.[49]

Tessereau contributed to this Black Legend of the Revocation more than any other author of his generation. His miscellany mostly points the finger at the Catholic clergy, whom he accused of having hatched a plot to eradicate Protestantism, which they had ruthlessly carried out by poisoning the king's mind. 'The misfortunes the Protestants have suffered can be attributed to the constant maxim of the Catholic Church not to tolerate the faith of those they call heretics and to extirpate them by all the unjust means that force and violence can invent', Tessereau wrote.[50] Unlike Jurieu, he situated the origins of this plot in 1656, when Louis XIV had first decided to send out *commissaires de l'édit* into the provinces, allegedly to ensure the Edict of Nantes was observed by both Catholics and Protestants. Drawing on his own experiences as a deputy for the Aunis, however, Tessereau argued the commissions 'were only invented to serve as a pretext for ruining all the Protestant churches'.[51] After all, he noted, previous bipartisan commissions – sent out by the monarchy in 1599, 1611, and 1620 – had already settled disputes arising from the civil wars. The new commissions merely opened the door to new Catholic demands, including the exclusion of Protestants from government and the closure of their temples. Regarding the first commission, dispatched to Languedoc in April 1661, Tessereau claimed that the Catholic commissioner had been instructed to oppose all Protestant demands, thus resulting in a *partage* that would surely be decided in favour of the Catholics. He concluded, therefore, that this commission 'was the beginning of the ruin of all public exercise of the Reformed religion in France'.[52] Subsequent documents included in the miscellany supported Tessereau's assertion that Protestants had been the victim of a sinister plot, as he presented a series of royal *arrêts* issued against Huguenot communities in Languedoc and the Poitou, especially the closure of their churches.

Because Tessereau's history was never published, his impact on subsequent historians of the Revocation has long gone unnoticed. Both prior and following his death, however, Huguenot exiles generously borrowed from his papers to denounce the politics of the French monarchy and clergy, and in doing so further disseminated Tessereau's Black Legend. Jurieu, for example, must have had access to the eyewitness testimonies Tessereau had collected on the Poitou dragonnade, because in 1682 he included several of these horror stories in a damning sequel to *La politique du clergé*, titled *Les derniers efforts de l'innocence*

sur les moyens dont on se sert aujourd'huy, pour destruire la religion protestante dans ce royaume, s.l. (1681), p. 21. **49** Jean Claude, *Les plaintes des Protestans, cruellement opprimez dans le royaume de France* (Cologne, 1686), pp 4 and 9. **50** Marsh's Library, MS Z2.2.9, Inventaire de touttes les pieces et memoires contenues dans ce receuil, unfoliated. **51** Marsh's Library, MS Z2.2.9, Avant-propos, fo. 7. **52** Marsh's Library, MS Z2.2.9, Notice on the commission of 15 April 1661, fo. 178.

affligée.[53] Following Tessereau's death in 1689, his miscellany ended up in the hands of the refugee savant Henri Basnage de Beauval, who in May 1691 proposed to the Walloon synod meeting in Leiden to publish the finished history, as had been Tessereau's intention. Yet the assembled delegates recalled that Élie Benoist, a refugee pastor at Delft, had for several years been working on a history of the persecutions, which was almost ready for publication. The papers were thus handed over to Benoist, who integrated them into his five-volume *Histoire de l'édit de Nantes* (1693–95). In the preface to the third volume, Benoist explicitly acknowledged that he had drawn on Tessereau's miscellany to write his chapters on the Protestant deputies at court and the Poitou *dragonnade*, but a closer analysis reveals that Benoist went much further. The tone and argument of the *Histoire de l'édit de Nantes* are strikingly similar to Tessereau's: Benoist, too, argued that crown and clergy had worked in tandem to destroy the Protestant churches by means of legislation.[54] The Black Legend of the Revocation thus lived on in print well beyond Tessereau's death.

CONCLUSION

Abraham Tessereau's miscellany has largely escaped the attention of historians. This unwieldy mass of legal documents, petitions, and eyewitness testimonies, interspersed with commentary scribbled in the margins or inserted on scraps of paper, does not make for leisurely reading. The fact that his 'Mémoires et pièces' was never published because of Tessereau's untimely death – at the moment his manuscript was ready to go to press – has also contributed to its relative obscurity. As this essay has demonstrated, however, Tessereau's background as a lawyer and Protestant deputy at court, as well as his legal perspective on the downfall of the Protestant churches, has had a tremendous impact on Huguenot history-writing in the Revocation era. The documents he included and annotated in his miscellany were not only intended as an irrefutable record of the persecutions, they also served to support his claim that the Huguenots had fallen victim to a sinister plot that had been long in the making, at least since the beginning of Louis XIV's reign. When authors such as Pierre Jurieu and Élie Benoist borrowed from Tessereau's papers, then, they contributed to this Black Legend; it was a seductive narrative that gave sense and purpose to the Revocation.

---

53 Le Fanu, 'Mémoires inédits d'Abraham Tessereau', pp 577–8; Van der Linden, *Experiencing exile*, pp 180–2.   54 Émile Bourlier, *Livre synodal contenant les articles résolus dans les synodes des Églises wallonnes des Pays-Bas*, 2 vols (The Hague, 1904), ii, pp 99–100; Élie Benoist, *Histoire de l'édit de Nantes, contenant les choses les plus remarquables qui se sont passées en France avant & après sa publication* 5 vols (Delft, 1693–1695), iii, preface, sig. ***2. On Benoist's history and sources, see: Van der Linden, *Experiencing exile*, pp 194–207.

Interestingly, the miscellany continued to exert influence within the Huguenot diaspora even after the publication of the *Histoire de l'édit de Nantes*. The fact that Tessereau's papers ended up at Marsh's Library suggests that a wider network of Huguenot intellectuals was interested in preserving a record of the recent past. The key figure here was Tessereau's friend Élie Bouhéreau, who secured the papers from Benoist after the latter had finished his history, and eventually stored them in Marsh's Library when he became its first keeper. Already in 1683, Tessereau had told his friend about a secret testament he had drawn up: in the event of his death, Bouhéreau was to inherit and preserve his most important papers. As he wrote from exile in London,

> after my death certain manuscripts, which you know I possess, will be handed over to you by my executor, on the condition that from now on you will look after them on the same conditions as I received them, namely to never allow copies to be taken and never to relinquish them during your lifetime, either by loan or otherwise. This is what my true inheritance consists of.[55]

Exactly which manuscripts Tessereau was bequeathing to Bouhéreau remains unclear, but it seems probable that they included the priceless documents regarding the persecutions in France. Tessereau's choice to appoint Bouhéreau as guardian of his archive was not without reason either, because his friend had already shown an interest in safeguarding key documents on Huguenot history. Prior to the Revocation, Bouhéreau served as secretary to the Protestant church of La Rochelle, and as such supposedly managed to smuggle out part of the consistory archives in 1683 through a deal with the English ambassador in Paris.[56] Perhaps Bouhéreau acquired the papers left by Tessereau in January 1697, when he passed through the Dutch Republic and visited the Rochelais pastor Delaizement in Leiden.[57] In any event, the many lives of Tessereau's miscellany remind us that record-keeping and history-writing were crucial to Huguenot identity in the Revocation era. Refugee authors not only sought to preserve a record of the recent past, they also knowingly created a narrative of premeditated persecution that has long shaped the narrative of Huguenot suffering – even until the present day.

---

55 BPF, MS 713/2, Abraham Tessereau to Élie Bouhéreau, London, 1 February 1683 (translation is the author's own). See also Marsh's Library, MS Z2.2.15 (1.3), Abraham Tessereau to Élie Bouhéreau, London, 4 May 1684.   56 Jean-Paul Pittion, 'Un médecin protestant du dix-septième siècle et ses livres: anatomie de la collection Élie Bouhéreau à la bibliothèque Marsh', *Irish Journal of French Studies*, 16 (2016), 37.   57 Léoutre et al., *Diary and accounts*, p. 295.

Psalms and sonnets in the correspondence between Élie Bouhéreau and Laurent Drelincourt

JANE McKEE

INTRODUCTION

Nineteen letters written by Laurent Drelincourt (1625–80), pastor of Niort in the Deux-Sèvres, to Élie Bouhéreau in La Rochelle, between 6 August 1674 and 14 January 1679 are included in the Bouhéreau correspondence in Marsh's Library.[1] Nearly twenty years older than Élie Bouhéreau, Laurent Drelincourt was the eldest son of the influential pastor of Charenton, Charles Drelincourt, and had strong links to the Reformed community in Paris and to literary circles there. He was pastor of La Rochelle for ten years from 1651 and had worked alongside Bouhéreau's father until the latter's death in 1653. Expelled from La Rochelle in 1661, he was appointed to Niort in 1663.[2] With a few excursions into medical and other matters, the correspondence between these two men is primarily focused on two topics. The first is the revision of the 1562 psalter of Marot and Bèze carried out in the 1670s by Valentin Conrart, a prominent member of the Charenton church and permanent secretary of the *Académie française* from its foundation in 1635; the second is discussion of Laurent Drelincourt's *Sonnets chrétiens*, before and after their publication in 1677.[3]

CONRART'S REVISION OF THE PSALMS

Before looking at what the correspondence tells us about Conrart's revision project, some background on the history of the psalms in Calvinist and Reformed worship and on the genesis of Conrart's project may be helpful.

The psalms in French in the Reformed tradition
Reformed worship was built primarily around the exposition of the word of God as contained in the Bible. This was done through the sermons of a well-educated

---

1 Marsh's Library, MS Z2.2.14 (13), 1–19. Letters from Laurent Drelincourt to Élie Bouhéreau (1674–9). They have recently been published in Charles Drelincourt, *Correspondance de Charles Drelincourt et de ses enfants, 1620–1703*, ed. Jane McKee (Paris, 2021), pp 409–44. References in this paper will use the published edition. All letters cited are from Laurent Drelincourt to Élie Bouhéreau. 2 Drelincourt, *Correspondance*, pp 409–15. 3 Laurent Drelincourt, *Sonnets chrétiens sur divers sujets. Divisez en quatre livres* (Niort, 1677).

clergy, but communal singing of translated and versified psalms in church soon became another essential element of Calvinist worship.

In a liturgy which allowed for few responses by the congregation, the communal singing of the psalms permitted active participation by everyone present. The decision to sing psalms, rather than hymns, also respected the central position of the text of the Bible.

Poets were paraphrasing psalms from the Bible in French and putting them into verse well before any official psalter existed. Clément Marot (1496–1544) composed his first paraphrase in around 1531 and in 1537 it was suggested to the council of Geneva that hymn-singing would make a good addition to worship.[4] In Strasbourg in 1539, John Calvin published a collection of psalms and hymns accompanied by melodies, some written by Marot and others by himself. When he returned to Geneva in 1541, Calvin focused on psalms, encouraging the work of Marot, who completed forty-nine psalms before leaving the city in 1543. He made them easy to sing by creating metrical paraphrases with verses of identical length. Using the same method, the theologian and poet, Théodore de Bèze, who was to be Calvin's successor in Geneva, took up the work again during the 1550s.[5] The melodies which accompanied the psalms were composed primarily by Guillaume Franc, Louis Bourgeois and Pierre Davantès.[6] All 150 psalms were completed and published in 1562, as the *Pseaumes de David, mis en rime Françoise par Clément Marot et Théodore de Bèze*.

This version of the psalms rapidly became embedded in Reformed worship. The paraphrases were in rhyme, therefore easy to remember, and the fact that they were divided into verses of equal length made them easy to set to music so that they allowed the worshippers to express their faith publicly and together. Calvin discouraged other efforts to paraphrase them in French and the *Pseaumes de David* by Marot and Bèze became 'the' Reformed version of the psalms. Indeed, apart from minor revisions in 1587, they remained untouched until the late 1600s, assuming a definitive value, on much the same terms as the King James Bible in England. As Jacques Pineaux put it: 'Le psautier finit par avoir une existence propre, indépendante de toute considération littéraire: il "est", au même titre que la Bible.'[7] Protestant poets stopped paraphrasing the psalms and turned their attention to other poetic or lyrical elements of the Bible.

In the 1670s, however, Valentin Conrart (1603–75) undertook a revision of the language of the psalms. He was neither a theologian nor a scholar and, famously,

---

4 Jean Michel Noailly, 'Le psautier des églises réformées au XVIe s.', *Chrétiens et Sociétés*, Numéro spécial, I (2011), http://journals.openedition.org/chretienssocietes/2728, paragraph 4, accessed 24 March 2024.   5 Julien Goeury, *La muse du consistoire: une histoire des pasteurs poètes des origines de la Réforme jusqu'à la révocation de l'édit de Nantes* (Geneva, 2016), pp 85–9.   6 Noailly, 'Psautier,' paragraphs 8–20.   7 Translation: In the end the psalter takes on a life of its own, independent of any literary considerations: like the Bible, it just is. Jacques Pineaux, *La poésie des protestants de langue française (1559–98)* (Paris, 1971), p. 236. All translations are the author's own.

did not know Latin. His authority came from the fact that he was a figure of considerable importance in the literary world of the time. As a *secrétaire du roi*, working under the chancellor, Pierre Séguier, he had the job of handing out letters of privilege,[8] a task which brought him into literary circles. He frequented the salons, rubbed shoulders with many significant literary figures of the time and set up his own literary group which became the *Académie française* in 1635. He was the first perpetual secretary of the *Académie*, to which Cardinal Richelieu entrusted the task of regularizing and purifying the French language. This mission reflected earlier efforts to impose order on the French language and its aims were shared by many writers of the time. Its work involved modernizing and simplifying spelling and linguistic usage and resulted in the publication of a first dictionary in 1694.

Conrart was a man with a keen interest in the French language, but he was also a faithful and respected member of the Reformed Church at Charenton which served the city of Paris. He gave his co-religionists the benefit of his contacts and, importantly, of his advice. Nicolas Schapira has traced his efforts to bring the writings of Reformed clergymen, such as Jean Daillé, to the attention of his friends from the *Académie*, and noted the advice he gave his co-religionists on preparing books for publication, particularly in relation to matters of language and style.[9]

According to Orentin Douen, Conrart's interest in the revision of the language of the psalms was sparked by the reaction of a member of the *Académie* who heard him singing psalms in his study and reproached him with the old-fashioned language in which they were written. He took the matter to the church of Charenton which adopted and promoted the project.[10] Laurent Drelincourt notes, in this correspondence, that Conrart was entrusted with the task of modernizing the language of the psalms by the consistory of the church at Charenton: 'le Consistoire de Charenton, de qui étoit dérivée la prémière vocation qu'avoit l'illustre Défunt à ce grand et pieus ouvrage qu'il avoit si noblement entrepris. Cela paroit assez dans l'acte du Synode de l'Ile de France.'[11]

In fact, the texts of both the Geneva Bible and the psalter had become a matter of serious concern in the second half of the seventeenth century. Both had been produced in the 1560s and the language in which they were written was

---

8 Licences which enabled a book to be printed and the printer to hold a monopoly on publication, after the censor had approved them. For discussion of the range and nature of Conrart's activity, see Nicolas Schapira, *Un professionnel des lettres au XVIIe siècle: Valentin Conrart: une histoire sociale* (Seyssel, 2003), pp 98–224.   9 Schapira, *Un professionnel des lettres*, pp 306–13.   10 Orentin Douen, *La révocation de l'édit de Nantes à Paris d'après des documents inédits*, 3 vols (Paris, 1894), i, pp 300–1.   11 Tr: the consistory of Charenton from which had come the first calling of our famous late hero to that great and pious task which he had so nobly undertaken. This is clear from the proceedings of the [provincial] synod of the Île-de-France. Drelincourt, *Correspondance*, 14/19 November 1675, pp 433–4.

becoming increasingly remote from that spoken a hundred years later. This was important, since the faithful, at all levels of society, were expected to read and understand the Bible and sing the psalms. There was also increasing concern, particularly among the clergy at Charenton, about the number of printers' errors that had crept into the Geneva Bible. But others treasured the text of the 1560 Bible and were resistant to change, especially if it did not come with the blessing of Geneva.[12]

The national synod of Loudun in 1659 had attempted to deal with the problem of printers' errors in the most important religious works by asking all provinces to note errors in editions and forward them to the consistory of Paris, at Charenton, which was ordered to present the most significant errors to the provincial synod of the Île-de-France which would then give the necessary order for a new and more accurate version of these works: the Bible, the psalms, the liturgy and the catechism.[13] Nothing significant happened at an official level, although there were a number of approaches to Geneva about the need for a revised French version of the Bible, including one by Conrart, after the publication of Lemaistre de Sacy's translation into French of the New Testament in 1667.[14] His efforts were unsuccessful, but he was already working quietly on his own new version of the New Testament, with Jean [Adrien] Daillé, a pastor at Charenton and son of Conrart's great friend, Jean Daillé. Their version appeared in 1669, but was condemned by the provincial synod, officially on the grounds that it had not been formally commissioned by the previous synod, but unofficially because Charenton seemed to be acting unilaterally. The upshot was that the 1669 revision was suppressed.[15]

Conrart did not give up on his modernization project, but he changed direction, turning his attention to the psalter in the early 1670s. This time, anxious to avoid the previous problems with the New Testament, he did not work in secret and present the book as a *fait accompli*. Rather, he sought support and involvement from across the Reformed Churches. His manuscripts include drafts of letters written in 1675 to various provincial synods taking place that year, and we know that he sent an actual copy of his manuscript revision to the synod of the Île-de-France in Vitry in April 1675.[16]

An idea of Conrart's revision technique can be gained from a comparison of a 1675 manuscript version of Psalm 33:2, as reproduced by Jean-Michel Noailly, with that of Marot and Bèze:[17]

12 Schapira, *Un professionnel des lettres*, pp 313–14.   13 Jean Aymon, *Tous les synodes nationaux des églises réformées de France*, II (The Hague, 1710), pp 775–6.   14 *Le Nouveau Testament de Nostre Seigneur Jesus Christ: traduit en françois selon l'édition vulgate avec les differences du grec*, (Mons, 1667). The translation was the work of the Jansenist Louis-Isaac Lemaistre de Sacy, assisted by other prominent Jansenists. Its existence made the need for modernization of the Calvinist Bible much more compelling.   15 Douen, *La révocation*, I, pp 297–300.   16 Schapira, *Un professionnel des lettres*, p. 317.   17 Noailly, 'Psautier,' Annexe 5; Clément Marot; Théodore de Bèze, *Les psaumes en vers français avec leurs mélodies: fac-similé de l'édition genevoise de Michel Blanchier, 1562* (Geneva, 1986), 99.

Fig. 1: Psalm 33:2

Marot & Bèze, *Pseaumes de David*, 33:2	Ms Conrart	Authorized version of the Bible [Psalms 33:3-4]
Chantez de luy par melodie Noueaux vers, nouuelle chanson: Et que bien on la psalmodie A haute voix, & plaisant son. Car ce que Dieu mande, Qu'il dit & commande, Est iuste & parfait. Tout ce qu'il propose, Qu'il fait & dispose, A fiance est fait.	Loüez son nom, par l'harmonie, De vos Cantiques mesurez, Ajoûtez-y la Symphonie, De tous les instrumens sacrez. Ce que Dieu demande, Qu'il fait, qu'il commande, [Var: Qu'il fait, ou commande,] Est juste, et parfait, Et de toute chose, C'est luy qui dispose, [Var: Il voit et dispose, Il sayt et dispose,] La cause et l'effet.	Sing unto him a new song; play skilfully with a loud noise. For the word of the Lord is right; and all his works are done in truth.

Conrart retained the metre of Marot and Bèze and the length of the verses, to allow the psalms to be sung to the same melodies as before. He also tried to respect the original rhyme scheme, as far as possible. What he changed was primarily the wording, to make the language more elegant and the meaning more readily comprehensible to a seventeenth-century worshipper.

Drelincourt and Bouhéreau: reasons for their involvement in the revision project
This then is the project that brought Laurent Drelincourt and Élie Bouhéreau together in 1674 and in which they continued to be involved after Conrart's death in 1675. Why were they chosen and what did they contribute to the project?

Both men were well known to Conrart. Drelincourt had grown up in Paris, the son of a pastor of Charenton. He shared Conrart's desire for revision of the French of the Geneva Bible and had raised the problem with Ésaïe Colladon, first magistrate of Geneva, in 1664, before Conrart's approach on the same subject to the Genevan theologian, François Turrettini. The first communication between Laurent Drelincourt and Colladon, probably in 1663, has not survived, but the letters sent by Drelincourt and dated 7 January and 9 February 1664, some 49 pages in total, are in the Tronchin archives in Geneva.[18] They contain a detailed analysis of the linguistic and other problems posed by contemporary editions of the Geneva Bible, from the inclusion of words and phrases having a different meaning or no longer used in the seventeenth century, and of expressions abusive of the Catholic Church and therefore illegal in France, to printers' errors and the use of poor quality paper, fonts and ink.[19] Drelincourt also offered a large number of possible emendations to existing editions and urged Geneva to produce a new corrected version. As Guillaume Peureux has pointed out, he displays a considerable concern for linguistic purity which reflects the interests of the *Académie*[20] and he may even have consulted Conrart on the matter, for the appendix to the proposals of 7 January contains some information about the latest ideas on spelling.

Bouhéreau, for his part, was an intellectual and a protégé of Conrart. He had paid a prolonged visit to Paris from late 1663 to June 1664 and spent another two months there in 1667 after a trip to Italy. In Paris, he moved in literary circles and became acquainted with Conrart who suggested that he undertake a translation from the Greek of one of the most important works of early Christian apologetics, Origen's *Contra Celsum*. Written in AD 248, this work was a refutation of *On the true doctrine* by the Greek philosopher Celsus, one of the earliest critical attacks on the Jews and Christianity. Ruth Whelan notes an allusion to the translation in a letter from Turon de Beyrie to Bouhéreau on 5 July 1669[21] and it appears at intervals in the correspondence under consideration here. It is first mentioned in the seventh letter (27 July 1675), where Drelincourt seems only recently to have become aware of it and offers encouragement. On 28 October 1675 he insists that work on it should continue after the death of Conrart, and he enquires again about progress on 22 June 1676.[22] In fact, the translation was not published until 1700, when it was printed in Amsterdam.[23]

Both men, then, were well known to Conrart and both had a definite interest in language. Drelincourt's concern about the language of the Bible was perhaps more immediately pertinent to the revision of the psalms, but Bouhéreau's work as a translator was also very relevant to the revision project. They seem to have become involved early, even before the contacts with provincial synods in 1675, noted by Schapira.

---

18 Institut de l'histoire de la Réformation-Musée historique de la Réformation (IHR-MHR), Geneva, Archives Tronchin, 100. Mémoires de Laurent Drelincourt à Ésaïe Colladon, 7 January and 9 February 1664.   19 For a detailed examination of this material, see Guillaume Peureux, 'Le mémoire de 1664 ou le psautier face au "tyran des langues"', *Revue d'histoire du protestantisme*, 5 (2020), 401–11.   20 Ibid., 404–8.   21 Ruth Whelan, 'La correspondance d'Élie Bouhéreau (1643–1719): les années folâtres,' *Littératures classiques*, 71:1 (2010), 91–5, 98–9.   22 Drelincourt, *Correspondance*, 27 July and 28 October 1675, 22 June 1676, pp 427, 431, 437.   23 *Traité d'Origéne contre Celse; ou, Défence de la religion chrétienne contre les accusations des païens*. Traduit du grec par Élie Bouhéreau (Amsterdam, 1700).

The revision project in the correspondence

The correspondence examined here includes only letters from Laurent Drelincourt to Bouhéreau, twelve of the nineteen written in 1674 and 1675 and four in 1678. The first, dated 6 August 1674, is a response to a letter from Bouhéreau which seems to have accompanied a manuscript from Conrart, containing draft revisions of a number of psalms. We do not have any of this draft material. What survives is only the accompanying correspondence, dealing with the way in which the project was carried out rather than with the textual revisions to the psalms. This letter seems to be Drelincourt's first contact with the adult Bouhéreau. It contains the standard protestations of friendship and respect, but it also establishes Drelincourt's status: a colleague of Bouhéreau's late father, an acquaintance of his grandfather and independently in contact with Conrart, from whom he expects instructions on the destination of the manuscript.[24]

Following letters deal with discussion of the project by the provincial synod of Saintonge, Aunis, Angoumois in the autumn of 1674. Drelincourt asks for information in the letter of 15 October 1674 and belatedly thanks Bouhéreau for news of a positive result in the letter of 16 March 1675.[25] Conrart, then, was seeking support for his project from provincial synods as early as 1674, to avoid the problems experienced with his translation of the New Testament. He also needed validation by those who understood the Bible better than himself, since he was neither a scholar nor a theologian.

In the same letter, Drelincourt describes how the revision system functions: He, Drelincourt, has read and made comments on the sixteen revised psalms he received from Bouhéreau and returned both psalms and comments to Conrart. Conrart, in turn, re-edited and returned fourteen of them to Drelincourt, along with six new ones. Drelincourt reviewed this material before sending all twenty draft psalms, as instructed by Conrart, to Abraham Gilbert, pastor of the nearby church in Melle, but has had no instruction to send them to Bouhéreau. So, the process is one of repeated revision by Conrart, with the aid of suggestions from multiple consultees who are sufficiently respected to be consulted on further edits to the same psalms.

This complex methodology could be adversely affected by delays in reading and returning comments and manuscripts. This was the case with the psalms sent to Abraham Gilbert, for Drelincourt is obliged to apologize to Bouhéreau, in the letter of 1 May 1657, for not being able to obey Conrart's instruction to transmit another set of revised psalms to him, together with the 20 sent to Gilbert, because these have not yet been returned, despite repeated requests. A

---

24 Drelincourt, *Correspondance*, 6 August 1674, pp 419–20.   25 Drelincourt, *Correspondance*, 15 October 1674 and 16 March 1675, pp 420–2. The second letter mentions a decision, without further clarification. The nature of that decision is clarified in the reference to 'le nouvel aplaudissement' [the renewed approval], in the letter of 14 November 1675.

6. Aoust 74.

Monsieur,

L'esperance que j'avois d'un prompt retour de Mr votre beaupère, pour vous écrire par luy, m'a fait différer jusqu'icy la réponse que je devois à la Lettre obligeante dont vous m'avez honoré. Je vous en rens très humbles graces, Monsieur, & vous suplie de croire que j'ay beaucoup d'estime & beaucoup d'amitié pour vous, & dans la considération de votre propre mérite, & dans le souvenir de l'honneur de l'afection de feu Mr votre père. J'aurois bien de la joye de vous pouvoir témoigner cette vérité par des éfets plutôt que par des paroles: & j'en embrasseray toûjours avec empressement les occasions. J'ay fait savoir à l'excellent Mr C.

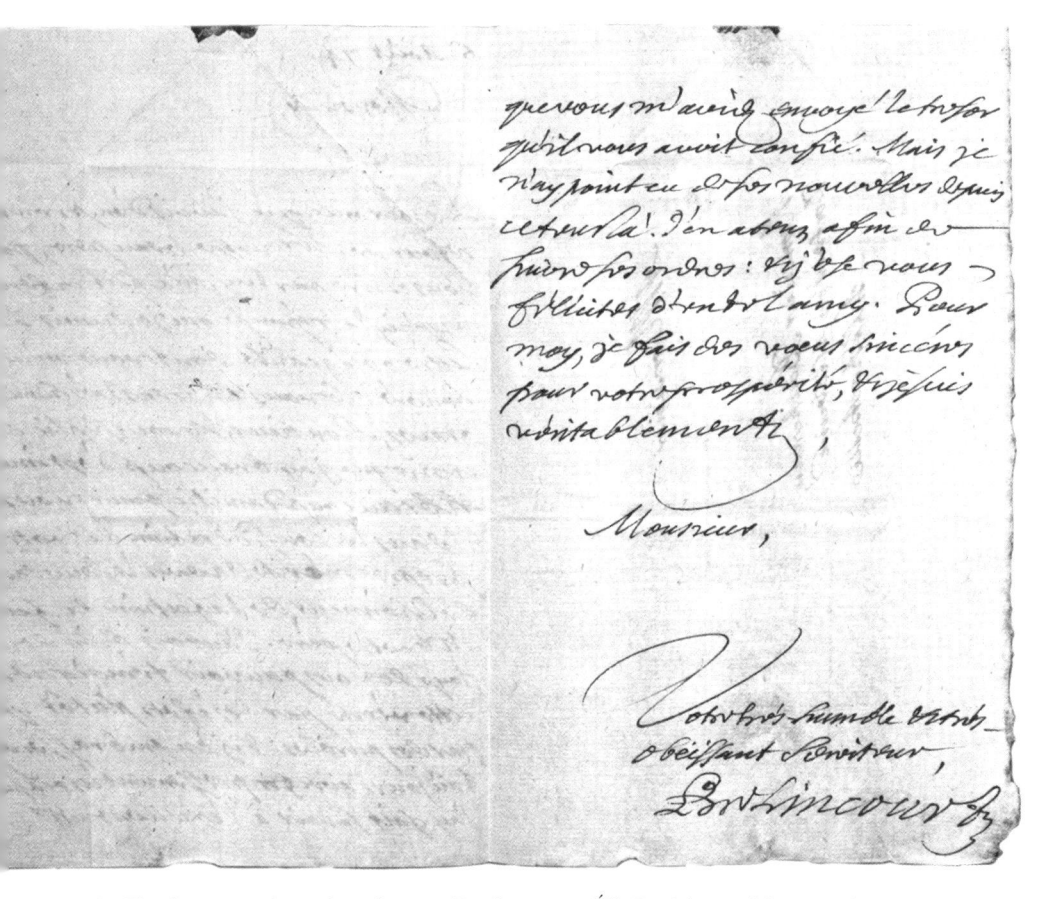

que vous m'aviez envoyé le trésor
qu'il vous avoit confié. Mais je
n'ay point eu de ses nouvelles depuis
ce tems la! J'en attens, afin de
suivre ses ordres: et j'ay b[ie]n vous
felicités d'entre l'amy. Pour
moy, je fais des vœux sincères
pour votre prosperité, et je suis
veritablement,

Monsieur,

Votre tres humble et tres
obeissant Serviteur,
Drelincourt

6.1 The first extant letter from Laurent Drelincourt to Élie Bouhéreau, 6 August 1674. Marsh's Library, MS Z2.2.14 (13.2), pp 1 and 3 (p. 2 is blank). By permission of the Governors and Guardians of Marsh's Library.

week later, on 8 May, he writes that the psalms sent to Gilbert have just been returned and are being sent on to Bouhéreau.[26] No further mention of Gilbert is made in the correspondence.

Conrart's health was mentioned as a concern as early as March 1675[27] and his demise on 23 September 1675, mentioned in the letter of 28 October, marks a delay in work on the revision, although Drelincourt assumes that work will continue. He already knows that Conrart has appointed Marc-Antoine de La Bastide[28] as his replacement and so he arranges for the mail he had sent to Bouhéreau for forwarding to Conrart, to be returned to Niort so that he can remove material irrelevant to the revision project and send it back to Bouhéreau for onward transmission to Paris when instructed.[29]

By 14 November, Bouhéreau's provincial synod has again approved the project, urged its continuation, and officially appointed Bouhéreau to the task of helping to complete it on behalf of his province. This represents a strengthening of his position as a consultee and, as Julien Goeury suggests, it seems to reflect an ambition on his part to occupy a more central role in the project. Goeury also detects some ambiguity in Drelincourt's reaction to this news: he greets the synod's decision with approval and assures Bouhéreau of general support for his work, but in response to a probable request for letters of introduction, he goes on to tell him that he does not know either La Bastide or Conrart's nephew and heir, although he has written to the latter and sent him, through Bouhéreau, the last '*cayres*',[30] that he had intended to return to Conrart. He will write to his former colleague Jean Daillé to urge him to action, but claims not to know other people sufficiently well to recommend Bouhéreau to them and urges Bouhéreau to write, enclosing the decision of the synod of Saintonge, to Conrart's nephew, to La Bastide and to the consistory of Charenton, the body which entrusted the task of revision to Conrart.[31] It should be noted that the raising of the topic at the provincial synod does not seem to be an exceptional move on the part of Bouhéreau, for Drelincourt had also been asked by Conrart to raise it at the synod of Poitou and had been sent copies of decisions made at other synods to help him do so. The synod was prevented from convening between 1673 and 1677, so he had been unable to comply and, without the official approval granted to Bouhéreau, he seems content to leave the younger man to maintain contact with the revision project:

26 Drelincourt, *Correspondance*, 1 and 8 May 1675, pp 422–4. 27 Drelincourt, *Correspondance*, 16 March 1675, p. 421. 28 Marc-Antoine Crozat, sieur de La Bastide (1624–1704), a lawyer, diplomat and highly regarded lay theologian. 29 Drelincourt, *Correspondance*, 28 October 1675, pp 431–2. 30 *Cahier*. Term used by Drelincourt to describe a manuscript plus suggestions for improvements. 31 Julien Goeury, 'Laurent Drelincourt, Élie Bouhéreau et l' "illustre ami": un éclairage épistolaire sur la révision du Psautier de Genève (1674–1679)', *Revue d'histoire du Protestantisme*, 5 (2020), 423–4.

Je m'étois chargé positivement de représenter cette afaire au notre. Et notre Incomparable amy m'avoit envoyé pour cela des copies d'actes de quelques autres Synodes. Si Dieu nous fait la grace de tenir enfin notre Synode ... je ne manqueray pas d'y exposer l'état où la chose se trouvera dans ce tems là, et que j'espère alors pouvoir aprandre de vous exactement.[32]

Drelincourt seems to have had little further direct involvement in the project until 1678. His health, which had always been fragile, becomes worse.[33] He describes his symptoms to Bouhéreau in some detail and seeks his medical advice on the use of *polychreste*, in the letter of 15–16 August 1676.[34] He was losing his sight and was completely blind by late 1679.[35] He also becomes increasingly preoccupied with work on his own sonnets which he published in 1677.

He mentions the revision project in letters during 1676, but is not directly involved. On 22 June he is distressed by a rumour that La Bastide is too busy with other things to continue work on the psalms, but is delighted, on 15–16 August, with news from Bouhéreau that they will be published after all. We have no letters for 1677, the year in which Drelincourt's *Sonnets chrétiens* and the first fifty psalms were published, but on 13 September 1678, Drelincourt is back at work on the new edition of the psalms. He has read the, as yet unpublished, second batch of fifty psalms revised by Conrart and is sending them on to Bouhéreau for him to offer his suggestions. They are better than the first batch, in Drelincourt's opinion. He is now in direct contact with La Bastide and passes on his request for Bouhéreau to suggest revisions and return them and the manuscript directly to La Bastide in Paris. When this batch of psalms is returned to him, La Bastide will send the final fifty psalms to the two men and he hopes to publish the complete edition early in the new year. A further letter on 17 September passes on an injunction to Bouhéreau not to let the manuscript out of his hands.[36] The last letter that we have is dated 14 January 1679. In it Drelincourt notes that it accompanies the final fifty psalms sent, at La Bastide's request, for Bouhéreau's comments. Bouhéreau is also asked for any revisions he

---

[32] Tr: I had volunteered to raise the matter at our synod. And, to help with that, our incomparable friend had sent me copies of decisions of some other synods. If God grants us the grace of holding our synod ... I will surely explain how things stand with the project at that time, which I hope to learn from you. Drelincourt, *Correspondance*, 14 November 1675, p. 434.   [33] Drelincourt, *Correspondance*, 27 July 1675, 22 June and 15–16 August 1676, 8 February and 13 September 1678, pp 427, 437–40, 441–3.   [34] A tartar salt developed in La Rochelle in the mid-seventeenth century by Jean Seignette and his sons. *Correspondance*, p. 439.   [35] Paris, Bibliothèque de la SHPF, MS 87. Registre du consistoire de Niort, meeting of 10 December 1679. He uses a scribe for the letters of 13 and 17 September 1678 and 14 January 1679, *Correspondance*, pp 442–4.   [36] Drelincourt, *Correspondance*, 13 and 17 September 1678, pp 442–3. For discussion of the extent of La Bastide's revisions to Conrart's manuscript, see Orentin Douen, 'La Bastide, ancien de Charenton et la révision des *Psaumes* de Conrart,' *Bulletin de la Société de l'Histoire du Protestantisme Français*, 38 (1889), 506–23.

might like to suggest to the fifty psalms published in 1677 and is asked to work quickly, because La Bastide needs the revisions urgently.[37] In fact, the first complete edition appeared in February–April 1679, under the same title as the 1677 edition, and a revised second edition of the complete psalter was published in June–August of the same year.[38]

Both Bouhéreau and Drelincourt were therefore among those who were significantly involved in Conrart's revision of the psalms. Bouhéreau had an official function, appointed to the completion of the project by his own provincial synod in 1675. Drelincourt, for his part, seems to have been working primarily in a personal capacity. The value of their input can be gauged by the fact that although they had had no contact with La Bastide before he took on the completion of the project and may not have been involved in the actual publication of the first batch of fifty psalms, they were asked to offer their assistance with preparation of the publication of the complete edition in 1679.

DRELINCOURT'S *SONNETS CHRÉTIENS*

Conrart's revision of the psalter brought the two men together, but it was not long before Drelincourt introduced his own poetry into the correspondence, in the third letter on 16 March 1675, where he asks permission to send his correspondent some '*Vers pieux*' or religious verses. Writing poetry was a relatively unusual activity for a Reformed clergyman whose primary activity was expected to involve preaching and expounding the scriptures. Some of the clergy wrote poems as young men, but few continued to write after ordination. The poetry of those who did was often didactic, harnessed to the fulfilment of their vocation.[39] Drelincourt seems to need to justify his literary activity, explaining in the letter of 8 May 1675 that his poems had an almost therapeutic function, helping him through difficult nights of insomnia:

> tous ces petits tableaus de la nature et de la grace, ont été formez peu à peu, Depuis quelques années, pendant de mauvaises heures d'insomnie, pour divertir et fixer inocemment mon imagination triste et vagabonde[40]

His poems are all profoundly religious, the 160 sonnets divided into four books of which the central two are retellings of, or reflections on, stories of the Old and

---

37 Drelincourt, *Correspondance*, 14 January 1679, p. 444.   38 *Les Psaumes en vers françois, retouchez sur l'ancienne version de Cl[ément]. Marot et Th[éodore]. de Bèze par feu M[onsieur]. V[alentin]. Conrart* (Paris, 1679).   39 For a detailed study of the poetry of the French Reformed clergy of the seventeenth century, see Goeury, *La muse du consistoire*.   40 Tr: all these little pictures of nature and grace have gradually been created, over several years, during difficult hours of insomnia, to distract my sad and wandering imagination and give it a good direction. Drelincourt, *Correspondance* 8 May 1675, p. 424.

New Testaments. The anthology begins with a book of poems on nature and its Creator and ends with a series of sonnets on aspects of the Christian experience.

Drelincourt chose the sonnet form for his poems, rather than the epic which had been the vehicle for such powerful and influential Reformation religious poems as *La Sepmaine* by Guillaume du Bartas or *Les Tragiques* by Agrippa d'Aubigné. Although it had previously been used by French Protestant poets, it was, in the seventeenth century, associated with the elegant love poetry of the Paris salons. Indeed, Drelincourt's justification for using the sonnet in the foreword to the book compares the anthology to a bouquet of flowers,[41] reminiscent of the famous *Guirlande de Julie* of the salon of Madame de Rambouillet, some thirty years earlier.[42] But for someone as concerned with propriety of expression as Drelincourt had shown himself to be, the brevity of the sonnet form, and the formal constraints it imposed, presented perhaps a more interesting linguistic challenge than the traditional epic. His comment on the poem praising his father by James Pontadius and sent to him by Bouhéreau certainly indicates a preference for complexity: 'Cette manière de louër est ingénieuse. Mais les vers ne sont composés que d'une pensée qui est fort étenduë.'[43]

In the same letter of 1 May 1675, Drelincourt asks Bouhéreau to read the sonnets with a critical eye and tells him that they have already been read with approval by Conrart and the Chevalier de Méré, another habitué of the salons.[44] In the letter of 8 May 1675 which accompanies the manuscript of the sonnets, he insists that Bouhéreau set aside the approval given by Conrart and Méré who have each read the poems twice, and that he give his own opinion with total freedom. This double mention of important sponsors seems a little disingenuous, but Bouhéreau takes him at his word and on 10 September 1675 Drelincourt responds to a detailed examination of the poems by Bouhéreau, thanking him for the excellence of his comments, and giving some detail of the type of examination carried out:

> Vous m'avez fait voir des négligences qui sans vous n'eussent pas été corrigées. Et vous ne vous êtes pas contenté de marquer les fautes : vous y avez de votre grace ajouté de riches corrections ; ce qui y comble la

---

41 'C'est icy comme un Bouquet de diverses Fleurs …' Laurent Drelincourt, 'Avertissement,' *Sonnets chrétiens sur divers sujets. Divisez quatre livres* (La Rochelle, 1678).   42 An illustrated manuscript book of madrigals, written by *habitués* of the salon of Madame de Rambouillet, including Conrart, in honour of her daughter, Julie d'Angennes. Each poem evokes a different flower.   43 Tr. This way of praising is ingenious. But the lines are made up of only one idea which is very extended. Drelincourt, *Correspondance*, 1 May 1675, p. 423.   44 Antoine Gombaud, 1607–84, who adopted the title chevalier de Méré, was an important theorist of the qualities of a gentleman [*honnête homme*] and a significant figure in the salons. He was friendly with Pascal and may have inspired the latter's work on probability theory. He was not a member of the *Académie française*.

mesure. A peine ay-je rien trouvé à balancer dans de si justes et judicieuses remarques : et si j'ay hésité quelque part, j'ay pris la liberté de vous le marquer sur le cayre que je vay renfermer dans cette Lettre.[45]

Bouhéreau's contribution to the sonnets has involved picking up problems and offering suggestions for improvements. Drelincourt has accepted nearly all of these and is returning the manuscript to Bouhéreau with the places where he disagreed clearly marked. The same method of repeated examination and revision is being used for the sonnets as for the psalms.

Drelincourt also follows Conrart's method in consulting widely. In addition to Bouhéreau, Conrart and Méré,[46] he has involved a number of other people in the process, among them André Lortie (1637–post 1720), a theologian and pastor of the church in La Rochelle, Paul Colomiès (1638–92), a writer and scholar in La Rochelle and Philippe Le Valois (1632–1707), Marquis de Villette-Mursay, a naval officer with an estate near Niort and a descendant of Agrippa d'Aubigné.[47] He asks, however, that the poems not be shown to anyone else, although he probably asked Lortie to show them to the marquis de Loire, a major figure in the church of La Rochelle (10 September and 9 December 1675).[48]

The correspondence offers no concrete examples of changes proposed to the text of the psalms, but it does with the sonnets where queries about wording are occasionally included at the end of letters. On 4 June 1675,[49] for example, Drelincourt includes three queries or '*doutes*':

- he is concerned about avoiding repetition in the sonnet *Sur le soleil*. The line is: 'Comme un superbe Roy qui brille dans sa Cour,' and he comments 'Mais remarquez qu'il y a brillant au premier vers.'[50]
- a second query, relating to the sonnet *Sur Saint-Jean Batiste décapité*, is about clarity. The line is: 'Aus dépens de ta vie une Danseuse infame' and his query is about replacing '*Courtisane*' with '*Danseuse*': 'De peur que la Courtisane ne

---

[45] Tr. You have pointed out careless expressions which would not have been corrected without you. And you have not just marked the errors, you have gone much further and kindly added a wealth of corrections. I found very little to query in such apposite and judicious remarks. And I have taken the liberty of marking the places where I was not persuaded on the manuscript which I will enclose in this letter. Drelincourt, *Correspondance*, 10 September 1675, p. 429. [46] Méré is still actively involved in helping polish the sonnets. Correspondence sent to him and received from him on the subject is mentioned on 19 November and 9 December 1675, *Correspondance*, p. 435. [47] Drelincourt, *Correspondance*, 8 May, 4 June and 10 September 1675, pp 424–5, 430. [48] Isaac Isle, marquis de Loire, was an important member of the Reformed community in La Rochelle. Louis Delmas, *L'Église réformée de La Rochelle. Étude historique* (Toulouse, 1870), pp 268, 277, 39. [49] Drelincourt, *Correspondance*, 4 June 1675, pp 425–7. [50] Tr. Like a magnificent king who dazzles in his court ... but remember that I have already used '*dazzling*' in the first line. In the first edition of the sonnets, Drelincourt kept the line proposed here, but modified the first line of the sonnet to avoid repetition. Drelincourt, *Sonnets chrétiens*, book 1, sonnet 17, *Sur le soleil* [*On the sun*],

semble la même personne qu'au premier quatrain ; quoy que Courtisane soit plus noble'[51]

- finally, in the sonnet *Sur la Paix*, he raises the question of the use of classical references in his poetry. The line on which he consults Bouhéreau reads: 'Le commerce au marchand, à Thémis la puissance.' He remarks: 'Je n'aime pourtant guère ces mots Payens : et j'ay déja Bellone au premier quatrain.' He dislikes pagan words, like *Thémis*, and has already used a classical reference to '*Bellone*' in the first quatrain. By the time the poem is published both references have been suppressed and the line reads: 'Le commerce aux marchands; à nos lois la puissance.'[52] This dislike of classical or pagan references is reflected in the foreword to the 1678 edition of the anthology where he objects to the dominance of the classical tradition in poetry in a Christian society and says that he prefers to seek inspiration in the Christian tradition and in the language of the Bible.[53]

The examples above cover a range of areas, from language (elegance of style and clarity of expression) to Christian content (avoidance of pagan references). Additions and alterations continue up to publication in 1677 and beyond. A new sonnet is announced on 10 September 1675; he sends a further query about a change to a line on 22 June 1676; notes another change on 13 September 1678, and ends the final letter, on 14 January 1679, with a query about the appropriateness of a change suggested to him by someone else.[54]

Another point raised with Bouhéreau was the use of notes with the poems. In the letter of 8 May 1675, Drelincourt consulted him on the value of adding historical and moral notes to his poems. In the first edition there are on average two notes per sonnet, referring to the Bible, classical history, mythology and the teachings of the Church Fathers, in a display of erudition, rather than as a device to stress moral messages to the reader as one might perhaps expect from a clergyman.[55] Drelincourt clearly likes the notes, but Bouhéreau advises restraint

---

line 5   **51** Tr. At the cost of your life, an infamous dancer ... courtesan or dancer ... For fear that the courtesan should seem to be the same person mentioned in the first quatrain; although courtesan is nobler. Here, he kept the line he suggests, but altered the first line of the sonnet. Drelincourt, *Sonnets chrétiens*, book 3, sonnet 11, *Sur Saint-Jean-Baptiste décapité* [On Saint John the Baptist decapitated], line 5.   **52** Tr: commerce to the merchant, power to Thémis ... I do not like these pagan words and I already have Bellone in the first line ... commerce to the merchant, power to our laws. Drelincourt, *Sonnets chrétiens*, book 4, sonnet 10. *Sur la Paix* [On Peace], line 7.   **53** Drelincourt, 'Avertissement,' *Sonnets chrétiens*. Drelincourt displays some ambivalence here. He removes Thémis from the poem, but retains Thémis in the notes, where he explains that Peace was the daughter of *Thémis*, goddess of justice.   **54** Drelincourt, *Correspondance*, pp 429, 438, 443–4.   **55** It is in the poems themselves, in the tercets and particularly the final tercet, that he comments on the content of the poem, although he rarely addresses direct moral recommendations to his readers. For a discussion of the use of notes in religious poetry see Florent Libral, 'La note d'autorité dans la poësie religieuse du XVIIe siècle', *Littératures classiques*, 64:3 (2007), 147–68.

and on 10 September 1675 the poet reluctantly accepts his advice on keeping the notes simple rather than developing them more fully. They remain short in the first edition of the sonnets in 1677, but by 13 September 1678 he has abandoned brevity and tells his correspondent that he has developed the notes for the Dutch edition, unobtrusively, to an average of six lines.[56]

Drelincourt also seeks Bouhéreau's help with the publication of his sonnets. On 4 June 1675, he asks Bouhéreau to sound out booksellers in La Rochelle about the possibility of publishing the poems in cooperation with booksellers in Niort, Saint-Jean-d'Angély and Saumur, who have already been approached on the matter. On 19 November 1675, he says he is nearly ready to send the book to the printer; on 22 June 1676, he writes that the sonnets are soon to be printed in Saumur. He is ill and asks Bouhéreau for medical advice, but he is still revising, asking Bouhéreau's opinion on a line from sonnet 22 of book 3: *Sur l'agonie de Notre-Seigneur au Jardin des Olives* (On the agony of Our Lord in the Garden of Olives). He alludes to the sonnets again on 22 January 1678, when he thanks Bouhéreau for his favourable remarks on the sonnets sent to him and for his work on the edition, in fact two editions, to be published in La Rochelle by Jacob Mancel and which appeared in 1678. A duodecimo edition is also to be printed in Saumur and the book has been well received. By 8 February 1678, he is asking for a copy of the second edition printed in La Rochelle and on 13 September 1678 he mentions editions in Geneva and Holland.[57] He has developed the notes for the Dutch edition, but has altered the text of the poems themselves only in very few places. Yet in the last letter on 14 January 1679, which is focused primarily on the edition of the psalms, he seeks Bouhéreau's opinion once again, this time on a possible revision to a sonnet suggested by someone in Paris.[58]

The *Sonnets chrétiens* were to find considerable success both before the Revocation of the Edict of Nantes and in the Refuge, where they were sometimes used in schools. Julien Gœury cites forty-six extant editions before the end of the eighteenth century, with one edition in the twentieth century and his own in 2004.[59] The correspondence between Drelincourt and Bouhéreau offers considerable insight into the final stages of their preparation for publication and the role of trusted advisors in their production.

---

56 Drelincourt, *Correspondance*, pp 430, 440–1, 443.   57 Ibid., pp 425–6, 435, 437, 440 and 442–3. Mancel published both an octavo and a duodecimo edition of the *Sonnets chrétiens* in 1678. See Julien Goeury, 'Bibliographie des *Sonnets chrétiens* de Laurent Drelincourt: l'histoire éditoriale d'un livre réformé,' *Bulletin de la Société de l'Histoire du Protestantisme Français*, 147 (2001), 412.   58 Drelincourt, *Correspondance*, p. 444.   59 Goeury, 'Bibliographie', 410–11; Laurent Drelincourt, *Sonnets chrétiens sur divers sujets. Divisez en quatre livres*, ed. Albert-Marie Schmidt (Paris, 1948); Laurent Drelincourt, *Sonnets chrétiens sur divers sujets*, ed. Julien Goeury (Paris, 2004).

CONCLUSION

This correspondence traces the continuing contribution of Laurent Drelincourt and the much younger Élie Bouhéreau to the first significant revision of the language of the psalms in French since the publication of the 1562 edition of the *Pseaumes de David* by Clément Marot and Théodore de Bèze. The two men seem to have been more important members of the network than some of the other consultees mentioned in the correspondence. Bouhéreau was officially appointed to represent the ecclesiastical province of Saintonge and Aunis, while Drelincourt was chosen to seek approval for it from the province of Poitou, a task he was prevented from carrying out by local ecclesiastical difficulties. With his efforts to secure the modernization of the text of the Bible, Drelincourt was an obvious choice as a collaborator on the project, but the choice of the much younger Bouhéreau provides clear evidence of the respect in which he was held in Reformed literary circles. Drelincourt was also sufficiently impressed with Bouhéreau's contribution to the revision of the psalms to enlist his help, alongside a few other eminent advisors, with the final revision for publication of his *Sonnets chrétiens*. In the case of both projects, the correspondence bears witness to a process which is a serious pursuit of linguistic and literary quality. Bouhéreau emerges, not just as an educated man, but as a person whose judgment is respected by other intellectuals and whose opinion, in literary matters, is worthy of serious consideration.

Religion and the singing of psalms: Huguenot worship music in eighteenth-century Dublin

ELEANOR JONES-McAULEY

Dublin in the eighteenth century was a thriving centre of trade and culture which was undergoing rapid expansion. Between 1700 and 1800 the population of the city increased from around 50,000 to almost 200,000 people, commerce and industry considerably expanded, and the city developed a strong elite culture of leisure visible in its many public gardens and musical entertainments.[1] It was also a multi-denominational city: while the majority of its inhabitants were either Catholic or Anglican, many other religious groups were active in Dublin, including the Presbyterians, Methodists, Baptists, Quakers, Moravians and Lutherans. One of the larger and most influential of these communities was that of the French Calvinists, or Huguenots, which at its height numbered around 4,000 and whose members were drawn from every part of society, from humble traders and labourers to some of the most powerful men and women in Dublin.[2] This diverse community came together for worship at the city's French Huguenot churches and meeting houses.[3] Among them was Élie Bouhéreau, the first librarian of Marsh's Library and a regular congregant at the Huguenot church in the Lady Chapel of St Patrick's Cathedral, where he was buried alongside several generations of family members upon his death in 1719.[4]

This chapter builds upon research carried out as part of my doctoral studies and detailed in my thesis: Eleanor Jones-McAuley, 'The worship music of Dublin's Church of Ireland parishes and other Protestant denominations in the long eighteenth century: sources, repertoire and cultural context' (PhD, TCD, 2022). This research has also been supported by a 2023/4 Maddock fellowship at Marsh's Library, Dublin.   1 Patrick Fagan, 'The population of Dublin in the eighteenth century with particular reference to the proportions of Protestants and Catholics', *Eighteenth-Century Ireland / Iris an dá chultúr*, 6 (1991), 121–56 at 148. Colm Lennon, 'Dublin in 1756' in Colm Lennon and John Montague, *John Rocque's Dublin: a guide to the Georgian city* (Dublin, 2010), pp xvii–xxi.   2 Raymond Hylton, 'Dublin's Huguenot refuge: 1662–1817', *Dublin Historical Record*, 40:1 (December 1986), 15–25.   3 The term 'church' is frequently used to refer to meeting houses in this chapter, following common eighteenth-century practice.   4 J.J. Digges La Touche (ed.), *Registers of the French Conformed churches of St Patrick and St Mary, Dublin* (Dublin, 1893), p. 219. A plaque in the Lady Chapel of St Patrick's Cathedral, Dublin records the burials of Élie Bouhéreau, his mother, wife, daughter, son-in-law and two young granddaughters. It was erected by Jerome Cecil Tierney in 1985. Bouhéreau's strong connection to St Patrick's is also evidenced by his appointment to the position of precentor there in 1709; see Marie Léoutre, Jane McKee, Jean-Paul Pittion and Amy Prendergast (eds), *The diary (1689–1719) and accounts (1704–1717) of Élie Bouhéreau: Marsh's Library MS Z2.2.2* (Dublin, 2019), p. 360, and note 54 below.

This chapter examines the music that Bouhéreau and the wider Huguenot community would have listened to and performed at their religious services. It focuses in particular on the central role of the Genevan psalms, detailing surviving printed sources, performance practice, and the role played by the organ and the Huguenot schoolchildren in the provision of service music. Despite the centrality of music to Huguenot worship, this topic has to date been somewhat under-researched, primarily due to the scarcity of surviving sources. Though almost ubiquitous in the churches and meeting houses of eighteenth-century Dublin, music is rarely discussed at length in contemporary accounts and church records, and so reconstructions of musical worship practices must necessarily extrapolate from scattered references in account books, vestry books, consistory records, and personal material such as letters and diaries. Much music at the parish or meeting house level was performed and transmitted orally, without the use of any printed music or even texts. Additionally, and tragically, a great number of primary sources from this period were destroyed in the fire at the Public Records Office in 1922 at the start of the Irish civil war. Nevertheless, as this chapter demonstrates, enough has survived to provide considerable insight into this rather neglected area of Irish Huguenot cultural history.[5]

HUGUENOT PLACES OF WORSHIP

It will be useful at the outset to provide a brief overview of the Dublin Huguenot churches active in the eighteenth century. The oldest and probably best known was Bouhéreau's own congregation, which met in the Lady Chapel of St Patrick's Cathedral. This congregation had been established in 1666 through the efforts of the duke of Ormonde, James Butler, and followed a 'conforming' form of worship that represented a compromise between the Established Church and their own Reformed traditions.[6] While the Anglican archbishop had granted them permission to retain their Calvinist polity of a consistory of elders, and allowed them to worship in French, they were still required to use the Book of Common Prayer in their services.[7] This 'conforming' style of Huguenot worship was not unique to Dublin but closely resembled the forms of worship practised

---

[5] Records relating to the Dublin Huguenot school and the organ of the Lady Chapel, in particular, have proved highly informative, and, to my knowledge, have not previously been incorporated into any overview of the musical culture of Dublin Huguenots (see relevant sections below for details). Various constraints prevented extensive research into private correspondence, memoirs or diaries (aside from that of Bouhéreau himself) for the purposes of this chapter, and as such these remain potentially fruitful sources of information on Huguenot music for the attention of future scholarship. [6] The term 'Established Church' (with a capital 'E') here refers to what is now commonly known as the Anglican Church or the Church of Ireland. While both latter terms are mildly anachronistic, the term 'Anglican' has occasionally been used in this chapter for reasons of clarity. [7] Hylton, 'Dublin's Huguenot refuge', 16–17.

by many Huguenot churches in London. The Lady Chapel Huguenots made use of the same Book of Common Prayer translation as the English conforming churches, a translation by Jean Durel produced in 1665; two copies of this were printed in Dublin and subtitled 'according to the use of the church of Ireland' in the early eighteenth century.[8] As well as being the earliest to be established, the Lady Chapel congregation was also the last to be dissolved, remaining active until the early nineteenth century.[9]

The end of the seventeenth century marked the high point of Huguenot immigration into Dublin. This was the result of several factors, including the Revocation of the Edict of Nantes in France and the conclusion of the Williamite wars, which saw many Huguenot soldiers in William's army being pensioned in Ireland. As a result of these increasing numbers, the Lady Chapel became overcrowded, with the congregation growing to over 400 communicants by 1700. A second 'conforming' church was established north of the river Liffey in 1701, known as St Mary's for its location within the ruins of St Mary's Abbey. This 'overflow' church remained open until 1740.[10]

In addition to these two 'conforming' meeting houses, which used the Book of Common Prayer, there were also a number of Huguenot congregations in Dublin that remained independent of the Established Church. In 1662, as an incentive to encourage Huguenot immigration and spearheaded by the duke of Ormonde, an act had been passed 'for encouraging Protestant strangers […] to inhabit and plant in the Kingdom of Ireland'. The act granted sweeping benefits to Protestant immigrants, including tax breaks and reduced fees for membership of city guilds.[11] A second act was passed in 1692, this time granting full freedom of worship to foreign Protestants.[12] Although the Lady Chapel congregation and later that of St Mary's continued to worship according to their conforming compromise, some Huguenots took advantage of their new legal freedoms to establish an independent, non-conforming French church on Bride Street in 1692.[13] Five years later, this congregation relocated to a former Jesuit chapel in Lucy Lane (now Chancery Place), where it remained active until 1773. A schism

---

8 T.P. Le Fanu, 'The Huguenot churches of Dublin and their ministers', *Proceedings of the Huguenot Society of London*, 8:1 (1905), 87–139 at 91 and 97. Copies of these two books are stored in Marsh's Library: *La liturgie c'est à dire, le formulaire des prières publiques … selon l'usage de l'Eglise d'Irlande* (Dublin, 1704) and *La liturgie ou formulaire des prières publiques … selon l'Usage de l'Eglise d'Irlande* (Dublin, 1715).   9 Hylton, 'Dublin's Huguenot refuge', 24.   10 Ibid., 24. Steven Smyrl, *Dictionary of Dublin dissent: Dublin's Protestant dissenting meeting houses, 1660–1920* (Dublin, 2009), pp 168–9.   11 *An act for incouraging Protestant-strangers and others to inhabit and plant in the kingdom of Ireland* (Dublin, 1662). Early English Books Online Text Creation Partnership (EEBO-TCP) reproduction of original in the Bodleian Library, Oxford: http://name.umdl.umich.edu/A45967.0001.001, accessed 30 September 2023.   12 Hylton, 'Dublin's Huguenot refuge', 21.   13 Ruth Whelan, 'Sanctified by the Word: the Huguenots and Anglican liturgy' in K. Herlihy (ed.), *Propagating the word of Irish dissent, 1650–1800* (Dublin, 1998), pp 74–94.

within the Lucy Lane congregation resulted in the establishment of a second non-conforming congregation on Wood Street in 1701; ten years later this group relocated to nearby Peter Street, where they remained until the nineteenth century.[14]

Although there were many non-conforming Huguenots who were highly resistant to any union with the Established Church, which struck them as too close to Catholicism for comfort, relationships between the city's different Huguenot churches appear nonetheless to have been relatively amicable.[15] The conforming and non-conforming communities collaborated on charitable matters such as the provision of charity and the running of the Huguenot school. The late nineteenth-/early twentieth-century Huguenot scholar Thomas Philip Le Fanu, who had access to many sources that have subsequently been lost, estimated that the combined communities of St Patrick's Lady Chapel and St Mary's numbered around 800 in the early eighteenth century, and those of Peter Street and Lucy Lane around 900; while there were slightly more non-conforming than conforming Huguenots, therefore, the communities were still approximately equal in strength.[16] Ruth Whelan's analysis of the forms of worship practised at the different Huguenot churches also reveals surprisingly few differences in the format of services, with both conforming and non-conforming services consisting largely of scripture-reading and sermons, and incorporating psalm-singing and prayers.[17] This general similarity facilitated the 'denominational peregrinations' of many Huguenots during this period, such as Isaac Dumont de Bostaquet, who was an elder at the Lady Chapel in the 1690s but later appears on the registers of the French Reformed Church in Portarlington, or the minister of Peter Street, Caufredon, who in 1767 announced that he intended to take Anglican orders but still continue in his ministry to the non-conformists.[18]

---

14 Smyrl, *Dictionary of Dublin dissent*, pp 171–3.   15 Ruth Whelan has written at length on this complex topic, arguing that relationships between different Huguenot communities were not quite as friendly as portrayed in traditional scholarship; see, for example, Whelan, 'Sanctified by the Word', and the address given by the same author at St Patrick's Cathedral on 3 November 1996, 'The Huguenots, the crown and the clergy: Ireland 1704', published in the *Proceedings of the Huguenot Society*, 26:5 (1997), 601–10. Nonetheless, in musical matters there does seem to have been considerable co-operation and overlap between the conforming and non-conforming communities.   16 Le Fanu, 'Huguenot churches of Dublin', 109. Notes taken by Le Fanu on these sources survive in Marsh's Library, Dublin, MS Y3.5.16 (2). Copy documents relating to the French churches of Dublin. As these were working notes intended for his own use, they are often incomplete or illegible; they are certainly not comprehensive. As a result, it is often difficult, or even impossible, to verify claims made in his writings upon these archival sources, many of which were destroyed in the fire at the Public Records Office in 1922.   17 Whelan, 'Sanctified by the Word', p. 86.   18 Ibid., pp 74–9; Marsh's Library, Dublin, Y3.5.16(2)/FHF.II.1.iv. Extracts from the consistory books of the nonconformist churches, 1703–1801, entry for 13 December 1767. These are transcribed by T.P. Le Fanu from original sources which have since been destroyed.

THE GENEVAN PSALMS

One unifying feature of Huguenot worship at this time was the music, which for both conforming and non-conforming Huguenots was firmly centred upon the congregational singing of psalms.[19] John Calvin wrote that music was a divine gift and so care had to be taken to avoid 'soiling and contaminating it'.[20] Because music had the ability to 'move hearts' and 'bend this way and that the morals of men', it had the potential to be a powerful force for both praising God and edifying congregations, but it was also important that such a force be used wisely.[21] To Calvin, this meant using only texts that had been directly provided to humanity by God – in other words, the words of the Book of Psalms, along with a small number of other biblical passages which were believed to have originally been sung, such as the *Nunc dimittis* (Song of Simeon). The Book of Psalms, in particular, was highly praised by Calvin for its eloquent expression of the highs and lows of human experience.[22] To ensure that the texts came across clearly in performance, they ought to be sung metrically (i.e. texts set in poetic metre rather than in prose), in unison, by the whole congregation, using simple, unadorned tunes without any instrumental accompaniment.[23] This was in contrast with the Catholic and Lutheran traditions, where choirs, instruments and singing in multiple parts were common elements of worship music.[24]

Calvin's philosophy of church music found expression in the Genevan psalter, a monumental publication that first appeared in its complete form in 1562 and consisted of all 150 psalms in metrical French versifications by Clément Marot and Théodore de Bèze, as well as two canticles. All of these were set to music for use in public and private worship. The Genevan psalter became the central text of Calvinist worship across Europe and beyond, as well as strongly influencing the Anglican psalm-singing tradition.[25] The psalms were sung as part of worship,

---

[19] The use of the French language in services, including when singing psalms, was a further unifying feature, although there is some uncertainty about whether the psalms were still sung in French towards the end of the eighteenth century, as by then English had become the primary language of Dublin's Huguenot community. T.P. Le Fanu, 'The Huguenot churches of Dublin', p. 126.   [20] John Calvin, preface to the 1542 Genevan psalter, quoted in Jonathan Willis, *Church music and Protestantism in post-Reformation England: discourses, sites and identities* (Farnham, 2010), p. 49.   [21] Calvin, quoted in Charles Garside Jr, 'Calvin's preface to the psalter: a reappraisal', *The Musical Quarterly*, 37:4 (October 1951), 566–77 at 570.   [22] John Calvin, *A commentary on the psalms*, trans. Arthur Golding, quoted in J.R. Watson, *The English hymn: a critical and historical study* (Oxford, 1999), p. 44.   [23] Paul Westermayer, 'Theology and music for Luther and Calvin' in R. Ward Holder (ed.), *Calvin and Luther: the continuing relationship* (Gottingen, 2013), p. 52.   [24] For an introductory overview of Catholic and Lutheran church music traditions in the early modern period, see the relevant sections of Joseph Dyer, 'Roman Catholic church music', and Robin A. Leaver, 'Lutheran church music', Oxford Music Online, 20 January 2011: https://doi-org.elib.tcd.ie/10.1093/gmo/9781561 592630.article.46758 and https://doi-org.elib.tcd.ie/10.1093/gmo/9781561592630.article. 46760, accessed 26 April 2024.   [25] Robert Weeda, 'Le psautier a conquis l'Europe', *Bulletin de la Société de l'Histoire du Protestantisme Français*, 158 (2012), 283–382. Nicholas Temperley

in the home and in public; singing them was a community exercise and a profession of religious identity.[26] In worship services, they replaced all other music: at least three psalms were usually sung, and longer services could include far more.[27] The origins of the melodies used to sing the Genevan psalms are various and contested, but a substantial number were either newly composed or adapted from older tunes by the musician Louis Bourgeois; other contributors included Guillaume Franc and a 'Maître Pierre le chantre' (probably Pierre Davantès). Many of the tunes are adaptations of pre-existing Lutheran tunes, while others were adapted from secular melodies, or from Gregorian chant.[28]

One significant difference between the psalm-singing traditions of the Huguenots and contemporary English-speaking Protestants was in their attitude towards tunes. Psalm-singing was similarly prominent in anglophone worship during this period, having been introduced to Britain by Protestants returning from exile in Europe. While heavily influenced by European Calvinist psalmody, however, the English and Scottish psalm traditions developed in their own distinct directions. One notable feature of the anglophone tradition was the use of a relatively limited number of poetic metres in the psalm texts. A typical example is the *Whole booke of psalms*, a central text of English psalmody first published in the same year as the Genevan psalter, in which 131 of the psalms were set in 'common metre' (four-line stanzas of alternating eight- and six-syllable lines).[29] These texts could then be sung to any tune which suited the metre, allowing congregations to sing the vast majority of psalms even if they only had knowledge of a small number of tunes. At the end of the sixteenth century, Thomas East wrote that in most churches in England just four psalm tunes were in common use.[30] In contrast, the Genevan psalter contains a staggering 125 unique tunes, with very few tunes used to accompany more than one text. One reason for this great number is that unlike English-language psalters, the texts of the Genevan psalter are written in a wide variety of poetic metres – around 120 different metres.[31] The result is a close association of specific texts with specific unique tunes that is largely absent in the anglophone tradition during this period. Genevan tunes, unlike those in the anglophone

---

et al., 'Psalms, metrical', Oxford Music Online, 16 October 2013: https://doi-org.elib.tcd.ie/10.1093/gmo/9781561592630.article.22479, accessed 30 September 2023. **26** See Roger Zuber, 'Les psaumes dans l'histoire des Huguenots', *Bulletin de la Société de l'Histoire du Protestantisme Français*, 123 (1977), 350–61. **27** Ibid., 353. **28** G.R. Woodward, 'The Genevan psalter of 1562; set in four-part harmony by Claude Goudimel, in 1565', *Proceedings of the Musical Association*, 44th session (1917–18), 167–92 at 171. Temperley et al., 'Psalms, metrical'. For a detailed account, with examples, of how the tune of psalm 118 was adapted from an existing tune by Matthias Greiter, see Édith Weber, 'The French Huguenot psalter: its historical and musical background yesterday and today', *Proceedings of the Huguenot Society of London*, 22:4 (1974), 318–29. **29** Temperley et al., 'Psalms, metrical'. **30** Nicholas Temperley, 'The old way of singing: its origins and development', *Journal of the American Musicological Society*, 34:3 (Autumn 1981), 511–44 at 520. **31** Woodward, 'The Genevan psalter of 1562', 171.

tradition, were rarely given names but were instead referred to by the number of the psalm with which they were associated (such as 'tune of psalm 130'). They were also retained unchanged when the texts of the Genevan psalter were 'modernized' in the late seventeenth century by Valentin Conrart and the consistory of Geneva, a feat that would have necessitated tailoring the new texts to fit the existing tunes, and which demonstrates the high regard in which these tunes were still held more than a century later.[32]

The psalms and the Genevan tunes that accompanied them also held particular historical and cultural significance for Huguenots due to their close association with the foundational events through which Huguenot community identity was formed. The texts of the psalms deal extensively with the experience of faith in exile, and even before the Revocation of the Edict of Nantes and subsequent diaspora Huguenot preachers frequently drew parallels between the experiences of the Israelites in exile and the persecution experienced by loyal Huguenot believers.[33] Psalm-singing played a central role in the fifteenth-century French Wars of Religion, a key part of Huguenot history, as well as in the later Camisard War of the early eighteenth century. Stories abound of Huguenot battalions singing psalms during decisive battles to intimidate the enemy, celebrate victories, and demonstrate their continued commitment to their faith in the face of violent opposition. Psalm 118, for example, was said to have been sung during the battle of Coutras in 1587 to boost morale and intimidate the Catholic forces.[34] Agrippa d'Aubigné wrote that Henry of Navarre had his troops sing psalm 118 before battles and psalm 124 afterwards, and that he himself sang psalm 88 when in prison.[35] In the seventeenth century, psalm-singing was highly restricted, particularly singing at home or in public, outside of church services; many arrests were made.[36] Psalm 68, the 'battle psalm', was sung during the Camisard War, and later became known as 'the Huguenot Marseillaise'.[37] Stories like these associated the psalms with strength, faith, resistance to persecution and community solidarity. By singing the psalms,

---

32 For an example of the Conrart edition of the psalter, see the *Pseaumes de David* described below. For more on Conrart's 1679 edition of the Genevan psalter and Élie Bouhéreau's contribution to it as editor, see Jane McKee's chapter in this volume.   33 Nicholas Must, *Preaching a dual identity: Huguenot sermons and the shaping of confessional identity, 1629–1685* (Boston, 2017), pp 87–90.   34 Émile Doumergue, 'Music in the work of Calvin', *The Princeton Theological Review*, 8:4 (October 1909), 529–52 at 542–3.   35 Zuber, 'Les psaumes dans l'histoire des Huguenots', 356–7.   36 Ibid., 354.   37 Gilbert Dahan, 'L'exégèse protestante des psaumes et son influence dans les usages militaires des réformés', *Revue d'histoire du protestantisme* 5:2/3 (April–September 2020), 339–56 at 349. Beat Föllmi, 'Du bûcher au champ de bataille: Le chant des psaumes pendant les conflits confessionnels au XVIe siècle', *Revue d'histoire du protestantisme*, 5:2/3 (April–September 2020), 357–77 at 359. Föllmi also provides interesting context regarding the later historiography of Huguenot 'battle psalms', and in particular the role played by the nineteenth-century historian Orentin Douen; among other rhetorical flourishes, Douen noted that both the melody of psalm 68 and the composer of the 'Marseillaise', Rouget de Lisle, originated in Strasbourg.

therefore, Huguenots could forge a connection with the historical events and narratives upon which their identity was based.

DUBLIN HUGUENOT MUSIC BOOKS: *LES PSEAUMES DE DAVID* (1731) AND *CANTIQUES SACREZ* (1748)

The centrality of the Genevan tunes to Huguenot worship music can be seen in the two books of music published in Dublin in the eighteenth century for the use of the Huguenot community. The first of these was an edition of the Genevan psalter in its seventeenth-century 'Conrart' form, published by Samuel Powell, one of the city's foremost music printers, in 1731 (see plate 9).[38] It is a small but incredibly dense volume containing all 150 psalms fitted with individually printed tunes, as well as a catechism, orders of service for baptisms, communions and weddings, prayers, and a prologue giving the history of the Conrart edition. At the front is an elaborate engraving by Dublin engraver Philip Simms depicting King David, traditionally the composer of the psalms, seated at his harp.[39] The contents of the book strongly resemble, but are not identical to, those of two similar Huguenot psalters printed in Amsterdam in 1729, one of which was financed by the French Church of London.[40] At least two formats of the Dublin psalter, an octavo and a duodecimo size, were produced, and at least twenty-eight copies have survived to the present day, of which fifteen are held in Irish libraries.[41] This suggests that despite being quite a substantial, and therefore potentially expensive, volume, the book sold well. Its title page lists four booksellers from whom copies could be procured, all based on Dame Street in Dublin's city centre: George Risk, George Ewing, Guillaume (William) Smith and Abraham Bradley. One of the copies held in the British Library is inscribed with the name 'Jane Blosset'; this may be the Jane Blosset who was a member of the Lady Chapel congregation in the eighteenth century, and who died in 1783 at the age of 82.[42] This evidence supports T.P. Le Fanu's statement that the

---

[38] *Les pseaumes de David mis en vers francois, avec la liturgie, le catechisme, & la confession de foi des eglises reformées* (Dublin, 1731), Trinity College Dublin, OLS B-9-650 and OLS 192.p.83. For more information on Samuel Powell, see 'Powell, Samuel' in the Dublin Music Trade database: http://dublinmusictrade.ie/node/376, accessed 30 September 2023.   [39] 'Philip Simms, engraver' in W.G. Strickland, *A dictionary of Irish artists* (Dublin, 1913). Library Ireland online edition: https://www.libraryireland.com/irishartists/index.php, accessed 30 September 2023. The engraving is signed 'P. Simms'.   [40] *Les pseaumes de David, mis en vers francois* (Amsterdam, 1729), Bodleian Library Oxford Ps.Fr.1729 f.1 and Ps.Fr.1729 f.2, both accessed via Eighteenth-Century Collections Online (ECCO).   [41] Information on surviving editions derived from the English Short Title Catalogue: estc.bl.uk. TCD OLS 192.p.83 is a copy of the octavo version, and TCD OLS B-9-650 the duodecimo version. Although both books are dated 1731, this may be the source of W.H. Grattan Flood's claim that a second edition of the *Pseaumes* was published by Powell in 1735: see W.H. Grattan Flood, 'Music-printing in Dublin from 1700 to 1750', *The Journal of the Royal Society of Antiquaries of Ireland*, 5th series, 38:3 (30 September 1908), 236–40 at 238.   [42] Digges La Touche, *Registers*

congregation of the Lady Chapel used the Conrart version of the Genevan psalter in their worship.

The second Huguenot book published in eighteenth-century Dublin, also by Samuel Powell, is a much slimmer volume dating from 1748 containing twenty-three metrical *cantiques sacrez*, or sacred songs, set to psalm tunes from the Genevan psalter.[43] Each of the *cantiques* is intended for use on a specific day of the church year, such as Christmas, Pentecost, or Communion days. A table at the back of the volume gives detailed instructions for choosing appropriate *cantiques*, and even appropriate verses of each *cantique*, for use on various feast days. This table indicates that *cantiques* could be sung before or after sermons – the usual position of the psalm in Huguenot services – and suggests that a *cantique* might be used in place of a psalm on special occasions. For most feast days, the table recommends splitting an appropriate *cantique* in half, and singing one half before the sermon and one half after. As with the *Pseaumes*, evidence suggests that the *Cantiques* did circulate among Dublin Huguenots. The copy held in the library of Trinity College Dublin once belonged to an 'Andrew de la Maziere', likely the André de la Maziere who appears in the registers of St Patrick's French church in the early eighteenth century, and whose family were associated with the Lady Chapel from at least 1702.[44] At some point, the family also appears to have become associated with Peter Street, as a 'Mr Maziere' was a member of the Peter Street consistory in the nineteenth century.[45]

The small selection of tunes chosen for inclusion in the *Cantiques* offers potential insight into which of the many Genevan tunes were particularly well known or well-liked by Dublin Huguenots, particularly as the tunes differ from those used in a similar book of *cantiques* published in London in 1707, suggesting variations in local preference.[46] Eleven tunes are used in the Dublin *Cantiques*, identified by their psalm number from the Genevan psalter (i.e., 'l'air du Ps. CXVII').[47] Six of these tunes appear alongside more than one *cantique* text. The most frequently appearing tune is that of psalm 89, which appears five times. This tune is still one of the best known from the Genevan psalter today.[48] Another tune which appears frequently is the tune of psalm 118, which accompanies four different *cantique* texts. Notably, it was closely linked to the French Wars of Religion, as was psalm 68, which also appears in the *Cantiques*, albeit only once. It would be unsurprising if such associations contributed to the popularity of these tunes and resulted in their being more frequently sung than others.

of the French Conformed churches, p. 250. British Library, Music C.16.0: accessed via ECCO. 43 *Cantiques sacrez pour les principales solemnitez Chrétiennes* (Dublin, 1748), TCD, Starkey 128. 44 Ibid.; Digges La Touche, *Registers of the French Conformed churches*, pp 65 and 106. 45 Le Fanu, 'Huguenot churches of Dublin', 88. 46 *Cantiques sacrez pour les principales solennitez des Chretiens* (London, 1707), British Library 3438.ee.65. 47 The tunes are those of psalms 8, 18, 24, 45, 68, 89, 13, 110, 116, 118, and the Ten Commandments. 48 Hymnary.org entry for 'Genevan 89': https://hymnary.org/tune/genevan_89, accessed 30 September 2023.

PERFORMANCE PRACTICE

Although very little direct evidence remains of worship music practices at the Dublin Huguenot churches, it is certain that they continued to sing the Genevan psalms as part of their services. T.P. Le Fanu wrote that the form of worship at the Lady Chapel 'remained unchanged' from standard French practice, and that for the psalms 'the version of Marot and de Bèze, and later that of Conrart' were used.[49] The copy of Durel's *Liturgie* published in Dublin in 1715 includes the texts of the Genevan psalms (Marot/de Bèze versions) at the back, supporting the first part of Le Fanu's claim; the fact that the Conrart psalms were later printed and sold in Dublin, as discussed above, supports the second.[50] The 1694 'Discipline' of the Lady Chapel indicates that psalms were sung before and after the sermon, a practice which was also followed by the non-conforming congregations.[51]

At least two of the Huguenot churches, the Lady Chapel and Peter Street, employed a *chantre*, or cantor, presumably to chant the psalms as an aid to congregational singing as was standard practice in the Established Church at the time.[52] The parish clerks of Established Churches, who were expected to perform this duty, often had little formal musical training, and this may also have been the case among the Huguenots: Henry Pascal, who was elected cantor at the Lady Chapel in 1759, had previously served as the organ bellows-blower.[53] The first cantor named in the consistory records of the Lady Chapel is a man named Durga, who was replaced by a Mr Tourmie in 1728.[54] Later in the century the Lady Chapel also employed a *sous-chantre* in addition to the cantor, who could substitute for the cantor in case of illness or other incapacity.[55] A man named André Grant was serving as the cantor at Peter Street in 1762, and had enough knowledge of the psalms that he was able to teach them to the children of the charity school.[56]

---

49 Le Fanu, 'Huguenot churches of Dublin', 97.   50 *La liturgie ou formulaire des prières publiques* (Dublin, 1715).   51 Representative Church Body Library (RCB), Dublin, IHA MS 90. Discipline pour l'eglise françoise de Dublin qui s'assemble à St Patrick (1694) (photocopy of original manuscript); Whelan, 'Sanctified by the Word', p. 83.   52 For a detailed contemporary description of the musical responsibilities of the Established Church parish clerks, see Benjamin Payne, *The parish-clerk's guide* (London, 1731), British Library 1412.c.17. 53 Marsh's Library, Dublin, MS Y3.5.20. Livre des actes consistoriaux de l'eglise francoise unie de Dublin, 1716–1901, entry for 1759. Before the invention of electric bellows, organs required a bellows-blower to keep air flowing through the pipes while they were being played. This was a physically, rather than a musically, demanding task.   54 Marsh's Library, MS Y3.5.20, entry for 1728. Although Bouhéreau was appointed '*chantre*' of St Patrick's in 1709, this appears to have been a precentor role connected with the main Anglican establishment and not directly concerned with the provision of music at the Lady Chapel. See Léoutre et al., *Diary and accounts*, pp 356 and 360.   55 Marsh's Library, MS Y3.5.20, from the entry for 8 June 1777 onwards.   56 Marsh's Library, MS Y3.5.16 (2)/FHF.II.1.ii. Extracts of the minute books of the *Société Charitable des Réfugiés Francois*, 1722–99, transcribed by T.P. from records now lost, entry for 1766.

HUGUENOT ORGAN MUSIC

One interesting quality of Huguenot service music in Dublin was that it often included accompaniments on the organ. As we have seen, Calvin was opposed to the use of musical instruments as part of worship, and the original Genevan psalms were intended to be sung unaccompanied. This remained standard practice among anglophone Reformed congregations in Britain and Ireland, where organs were only sporadically introduced from the eighteenth century onward. On the Continent, however, attitudes towards organ music were somewhat more varied. From the mid-seventeenth century, Dutch Reformed congregations began to use organs to accompany their psalm-singing, and in the eighteenth century, organs were introduced to churches in Switzerland. As these instruments were intended primarily to accompany psalms, rather than, as in the Lutheran tradition, for performing complex solo pieces, they were generally modest.[57] The Huguenot church at Erlangen in Germany still boasts its eighteenth-century organ, built by Johann Nikolaus Ritter.[58] The use of organs in the Established Church in Britain and Ireland was standard practice where finances allowed, and in London, the conforming Huguenot church at the Trinity Hospital possessed an organ in 1720, which, according to a contemporary writer, was played 'when they sing their Psalms'.[59]

Details of organ music in Dublin's Huguenot churches are hard to establish, but it is certain that at least two Huguenot places of worship had organs: the Lady Chapel and the Lucy Lane nonconformist meeting house. The Lady Chapel organ was acquired some time in the mid-eighteenth century. In 1726, the consistory were approached by a musician named Loiseau, who claimed he could secure them an organ worth £250 for only £100, and serve as their organist for a year.[60] This offer is particularly impressive given that the organ which was installed in St Michan's parish church in Dublin in the same year cost more than £400 to build.[61] Loiseau's offer was rejected by the consistory, who

---

[57] Andreas Marti and Bert Polman, 'Reformed and Presbyterian church music', Oxford Music Online, 20 January 2001: https://doi-org.elib.tcd.ie/10.1093/gmo/9781561592630. article.48535, accessed 26 April 2024. The Dutch organ music tradition was a notable exception to the general rule of Reformed organs being modest, and primarily used for accompaniments; a strong non-liturgical tradition of organ music developed in the Netherlands after the Reformation, with organists performing solo pieces before and after services and on official state occasions. [58] Entry for Erlangen church in Piet Bron's Orgeldatabase: http://orgbase.nl/scripts/ogb.exe?database=ob2&%250=2026226&LGE=NL&LIJST=lang, accessed 30 September 2023. [59] John Strype, *A survey of the cities of London and Westminster*, 2 vols (1720), i, p. 212. Established Church organs during this period were also typically modest instruments, without pedals. See Barbara Owen, 'Organ music from c.1750' in John Caldwell et al., 'Keyboard music', Oxford Music Online, 20 January 2001: https://doi-org.elib.tcd.ie/10.1093/gmo/9781561592630.article.14945, accessed 26 April 2024. [60] Marsh's Library, MS Y3.5.20, entry for 21 June 1726. [61] RCB Library Dublin, MS P.0376.28/3. St Michan's Memorial Book, 1724–89, p. 84.

wrote that it was 'neither convenient nor possible' to purchase an organ at that time.[62] At some point in the following thirty years, however, an organ was evidently acquired, as it is clearly referred to in the consistory acts of 1759.[63] The curious lack of reference to the purchase and installation of the organ in the records may simply be due to a general laxity of record-keeping among the consistory in the mid-eighteenth century, as there are very few entries in the consistory book for this period compared to earlier and later parts of the century.

The first mention of the organ in the records of the Lady Chapel is in fact a tangential one: the above-mentioned 1759 reference to Henry Pascal's work as the organ blower. It is not until 1760 that the organ itself or its player is mentioned, in a terse resolution that the organist should not allow people access to the organ console during services.[64] The first person to actually be named as the organist is a man named Grand, who was serving as the organist at the time of his death in 1773 and whose son William also served briefly as a *sous-chantre*.[65] As the spellings 'Grand' and 'Grant' are frequently used interchangeably in the consistory records, this could be the same person as André Grant, who became the organ blower in 1759 and is likely the same André Grant who was cantor at Peter Street in 1762 as mentioned above.[66] After the death of Grand in 1773 the post was held by Samuel Murphy; this is probably not the same Samuel Murphy who was organist at St Bride's and St Patrick's Cathedral in the mid-eighteenth century, as the dates do not fully align, but may have been a relative.[67] Despite the care of the organ-builder Henry Millar, who was hired to maintain the instrument in 1773, the organ appears to have fallen into disrepair at some point in the 1770s, as in 1781 Murphy was re-engaged as organist and played upon the organ 'for the first time since its re-establishment'.[68] Murphy left the Lady Chapel in 1785 to become organist of the Established Church of St Andrew, and was replaced briefly by Jeremy Boucher; Boucher in turn left to become a parish organist at St Mary's five months later and was succeeded by a Mr Mathew.[69] This quick turnover of organists at the Lady Chapel may have been due to the relatively low salary on offer of £12 per year – less than half of what was available at St Andrew's.[70]

---

62 Marsh's Library, MS Y3.5.20, entry for 21 June 1726.   63 Ibid., entry for 1759.   64 Ibid., entry for 1760.   65 Ibid., entry for 1771.   66 Ibid., entries for 1759 and 1764. Marsh's Library, MS Y3.5.16 (2)/FHF.II.1.ii, entry for 1766. The Consistory acts book states that André Grant left his organ blower position to become a 'reader' at Peter Street some time prior to 1764.   67 Marsh's Library, MS Y3.5.20, entry for 25 April 1773. Brian Boydell, *A Dublin musical calendar, 1700–1760* (Dublin, 1988), p. 285.   68 Marsh's Library, MS Y3.5.20, entry for 29 April 1781. Millar also built the organ for St Werburgh's church in 1754, at a cost of £470. W.H.Grattan Flood, 'Irish organ-builders from the eighth to the close of the eighteenth century', *Journal of the Royal Society of Antiquaries of Ireland*, 5th series, 40:3 (September 1910), 229–34 at 233.   69 Marsh's Library, MS Y3.5.20, entries for 16 February and 22 May 1785.   70 Ibid., entry for 16 February 1785. RCB Library, Dublin, MS P.0059.05/1.Vestry book of St Andrew's parish church, Dublin, 1757–1817, 14 January 1785 (detailing the election of Murphy as organist).

In 1787, the *sous-chantre*, Pierre Brunel, proposed to the consistory that he be appointed organist in addition to his *sous-chantre* position, on the condition that he took lessons and achieved a satisfactory standard. The consistory were favourably disposed towards this suggestion, and Brunel was appointed organist six months later, despite the fact that the position was still being occupied by Mr Mathew.[71] It is possible, however, that Mathew had not actually been able to play upon the instrument for some time; the consistory records for 1787 state that repairs were carried out on the organ in that year as its condition had once again declined.[72] Brunel remained as the organist throughout the 1790s and into the 1800s, and is last named in connection with the role in 1809.[73]

Brunel appears to have been the last organist of the Lady Chapel congregation. French services were no longer held there after 1817, and Brunel himself appears to have died in 1828.[74] Le Fanu writes that the French Church 'surrendered ... their organ and fixtures to the Dean and Chapter' of the cathedral in 1816.[75] It is possible that for a few years, the organ was used by the congregation of the parish church of St Nicholas Without, who held services in the Lady Chapel from 1805 onwards.[76] The eventual fate of the Lady Chapel organ is unknown; the last identifiable trace of it is found in an advertisement in *Saunders's News-Letter* from 1826, which lists for sale 'A fine-toned church organ, made by Snetzler, formerly belonging to the French Church, St Patrick's'.[77]

The organ of Lucy Lane remains even more of a mystery; its very existence is now only known from a few brief mentions in T.P. Le Fanu's notes on now-lost archival material. It was present at Lucy Lane in 1762, when it was repaired at a cost of half a guinea; the fact that money was spent on repairs suggests that the instrument was actually in use. Le Fanu notes in addition that when the Lucy Lane meeting house was sold to a Presbyterian congregation in 1773, its organ was also sold, for £22 10s. (though not necessarily to the Presbyterians).[78] Where this instrument originally came from, what was played upon it, and what became of it after this sale is unknown. The very low sale price may indicate that by 1773 it was not in a fit state to be played.

The surviving records do not provide any specific details about the music played upon these organs as part of Huguenot services. It is likely that their

71 Marsh's Library, MS Y3.5.20, entries for 24 June and 11 December 1787.   72 Ibid., entry for 24 June 1787.   73 Marsh's Library, Dublin, MS Y3.5.1. Account book of the *Société Charitable des Francais Refugiés* (SCFR), 1780–1822, entry for 14 May 1809. Entries in this book throughout the 1790s and 1800s continually refer to Brunel as the organist of the church. 74 Hylton, 'Dublin's Huguenot refuge', 24. Marsh's Library, Dublin, MS Y3.5.2. Account book of the *Societé des Francais Réfugies*, beginning in 1823. Mentions of Brunel, regular until 1828, cease after that point. An anonymous and undated note at the back of the volume states that 'Peter Brunelle died in 1828'.   75 T.P. Le Fanu, 'Appendix: The French church in the Lady Chapel of St Patrick's Cathedral, 1666–1816' in H.J. Lawlor, *The fasti of St Patrick's Dublin* (Dundalk, 1930), pp 277–84 at 281.   76 Marsh's Library, MS Y3.5.20, entry for January 1806.   77 'Organs and Piano Forte For Sale', *Saunders's News-Letter*, 22 June 1826, p. 3. British Newspaper Archive.   78 Marsh's Library, MS Y3.5.16 (2)/FHF.II.1.iv, entries

primary use, as in the parish churches at the time and in Continental Reformed worship, was to accompany the singing of the psalms. It is also possible that, as in the parish churches, the organist would be expected to play a short 'voluntary', or improvised solo piece, at the beginning and the end of services, although as these were very rarely written down it is impossible to be certain.[79] That Murphy and Boucher were both able to make the transition from the Huguenot church to Established parish churches suggests that the duties of the organist in the conforming Lady Chapel, at least, were similar to those of a parish church organist. General opinion among Established Church critics during the eighteenth century was that organ music ought to be serious and seek to create a tranquil, contemplative mood; it was also regularly commented, with some exasperation, that organists were prone to indulge instead in melodious, technically challenging pieces of a 'theatrical', 'Italianate' style.[80] Whether or not the organists of the Huguenot churches favoured a similar style of music, we can only speculate.

THE HUGUENOT SCHOOL

One strong musical resource at the disposal of Dublin's Huguenot congregations was the studentry of the Huguenot school, who were trained to sing psalms as part of their education. The Huguenot school was established in 1723 by the *Société Charitable des Françoises Refugiés*, a Huguenot charitable organization.[81] It was a joint endeavour between the conforming and non-conforming communities, and sermons were regularly preached in both the Lady Chapel and Peter Street to raise money to keep the school running.[82] The school was explicitly modelled after the charity schools that were common in anglophone parishes at the time, which aimed to provide poor children with a basic education (usually comprising reading, writing, basic arithmetic and religious knowledge) with the goal of raising them out of poverty and improving their prospects later in life.[83] Some charity schools, especially later in the eighteenth century, also provided training in basic skills and crafts such as weaving and knitting.

for 28 March 1762, 18 July 1762 and 23 May 1773. **79** A detailed description of the duties of an organist in one of Dublin's eighteenth-century parish churches can be found in RCB Library, MS P.0376.28/3, pp 106–8. **80** Nicholas Temperley, *The music of the English parish church* (New York, 1979), pp 102 and 137. The organist's duties laid out in the St Michan's 'Memorial book' show a similar insistence that the organist should play in a solemn, serious style; the word 'solemn' appears three times in connection with the service music. RCB Library, MS P.0376.28/3, pp 106–7. **81** Marsh's Library, MS Y3.5.16 (2)/FHF.II.1.ii, entry for 2 September 1723. **82** See, for example, ibid., entry for 1 December 1729. **83** 'Resolved to make Rules for the Society's school similar to those of the Charity Schools of the Kingdom'. Ibid., entry for September 1725. For a detailed exploration of the charity school phenomenon, see M.G. Jones, *The charity school movement: a study of eighteenth-century*

Children were usually admitted to the schools at between eight and twelve years of age, and after a few years of instruction finished their schooling by completing an apprenticeship with a local tradesman or entering service.[84] The Huguenot school followed this model closely, providing its students with the fundamentals of education and some training in manual work, and finding them a suitable apprenticeship at the end of their schooling.[85] The school took in both boys and girls, and at its height could boast thirty students, though numbers often fell as low as five or six. From 1732 until its closure in the early nineteenth century, the school was run out of a building on Myler's Alley, a street adjoining the north close of St Patrick's Cathedral (now the site of St Patrick's Park).[86]

Music was a central part of the Huguenot school's curriculum from the beginning. T.P. Le Fanu's notes on the early records of the school, the originals of which have regrettably been lost, record that on 2 September 1723 it was resolved 'to establish a school for a certain number of poor children pour leur enseigner à lire, écrire, la religion et le chant des pseaumes'.[87] This was in line with the practice in contemporary Anglican charity schools, where it was usual for the children to be taught to sing psalms so that they could serve as a makeshift choir at Sunday services.[88] The students at the Huguenot school were initially expected to attend each of the four Huguenot places of worship in turn on Sundays, but by 1733 they were attending only the Lady Chapel in the morning and Peter Street in the afternoon. In 1738 they were divided into different classes 'for the different churches', and from then on were only expected to attend 'one of the churches' each Sunday.[89] Midweek trips for the purpose of reciting the catechism were also made to Peter Street on Wednesdays and to the Lady Chapel on Thursdays.[90] Of the approximately eight to thirty children enrolled on average in the school at any given time, it is unclear how many would have belonged to (and therefore attended) each church; Le Fanu

---

Puritanism in action (Cambridge, 1938). 84 Edward Synge, *Methods of erecting, supporting & governing charity-schools, with an account of the charity-schools in Ireland, and some observations thereon*, 2nd ed. (Dublin, 1719), Bodleian Library Oxford G. Pamph. 1466(1). 85 These general statements about the operation of the school are derived from the records of the school held at Marsh's Library: MS Y3.5.16 (2)/FHF.II.1.ii. Extracts of the minute books of the SCFR; MS Y3.5.1. Account book of the SC*FR*. 86 Marsh's Library, MS Y3.5.16 (2)/FHF.II.1.ii, entry for 11 September 1732. Le Fanu, 'Huguenot churches of Dublin', 125–6. Myler's Alley is visible on John Rocque's 1756 map of Dublin. See John Rocque, *An exact survey of the city and suburbs of Dublin* (1756), Bibliothèque nationale de France, available online through Gallica: https://gallica.bnf.fr/ark:/12148/btv1b530571173, accessed 30 September 2023. 87 Author's translation: '... to teach them to read, write, religion and the singing of psalms'. Marsh's Library, MS Y3.5.16 (2)/FHF.II.1.ii, entry for 2 September 1723. As with all Le Fanu's notes on now-lost sources, which were largely made for his personal use, it is difficult to tell what parts of this quotation, if any, are taken directly from the source, but it seems likely the abrupt switch into French (the language of the school records at this time) marks the beginning of the source quotation. 88 Temperley, *Music of the English parish church*, p. 129. 89 Le Fanu, 'Huguenot churches of Dublin', 125. Marsh's Library, MS Y3.5.16 (2)/FHF.II.1.ii, entry for 10 December 1752. 90 Ibid., entry for 21 March 1735/6.

estimated perhaps three quarters of the students attended Peter Street, but this cannot be confirmed without corroborating records.[91]

The usual practice in the parish charity schools was for the organist at the local parish church to instruct the children in singing.[92] When the Huguenot school was founded, however, none of the Huguenot churches were in possession of organs or organists. They overcame this difficulty by hiring a musician named Loiseau (the same man who proposed the acquisition of a reasonably priced organ) to teach the schoolmaster, Lautal, enough music that he would be able to instruct the children.[93] When Lautal was fired for poor conduct in 1727, his replacement was examined in 'the psalms' as well as religion, arithmetic, and French before being offered the job.[94] This demonstrates the importance which was placed upon the teaching of the psalms at the school, as well as the extent to which 'music' and 'the psalms' were functionally interchangeable. Also around this time, Major Bouhéreau, Élie Bouhéreau's son, donated eighteen 'books of psalms' to the school which were bound for the children's use.[95] As this donation predates the publication of the 1731 *Pseaumes*, it is unclear what edition, or indeed what translation, the children were using. It was almost certainly in French, however; on the same day the accounts also record that an English Bible was bought 'to teach the children to read in that language'.[96] This suggests that their command of English, or at least their ability to read English, was relatively poor. Major Bouhéreau made an even more generous donation in 1730, giving forty psalm books to the school.[97] The final mention of psalm books in the school records occurs in 1748, when it was resolved that Louis Ostervald, the minister of Peter Street, would obtain 'psalms' for the children.[98]

The status of music at the charity school in the mid-eighteenth century is uncertain, as the information that has survived concerning this period is very sparse. In 1766, the cantor of Peter Street, André Grant, was engaged to teach the children 'the music of our psalms' – presumably meaning the Genevan tunes.[99] In 1770, the schoolmaster, Isaac Dufour, died, and the school board were

---

91 Marsh's Library, MS Y3.5.16 (2)/FHF.II.1.ii, comment apparently by T.P. Le Fanu without a clear source.   92 See, for example, RCB Library, Dublin, MS P.0276.13/2. St Michan's school minute book, 1777–1825; RCB Library, Dublin, MS P.0059.05/1. Vestry book of St Andrew's, entry for 21 April 1784; RCB Library, Dublin MS P.0045.05/3, Vestry minute book of St Peter's, 1774–1807, entries for 1774 and 1775.   93 Marsh's Library, MS Y3.5.16 (2)/FHF.II.1.ii, entry for 5 December 1725. One of the schoolboys, Charles Grant, was also apprenticed to Loiseau in June 1726 'to learn music'.   94 Ibid., entry for 5 March 1726/7.   95 Ibid., entry for 4 March 1725/6. This is Bouhéreau's son Richard Des Herbiers who was appointed a Dublin Major on 16 December 1719. Léoutre et al., *Diary and accounts*, p. 387.   96 Marsh's Library, MS Y3.5.16 (2)/FHF.II.1.ii, entry for 4 March 1725/6.   97 Marsh's Library, MS Y3.5.16 (2)/FHF.II.1.ii, entry for 28 May 1730.   98 Ibid., entry for 5 June 1748. Le Fanu, 'Huguenot churches of Dublin', 136.   99 Marsh's Library, MS Y3.5.16 (2)/FHF.II.1.ii, entry for 1766. Le Fanu's note reads, 'Mr André Grant Lecteur & Chantre de St Pierre to teach the Children music de nos Pseaumes'. Again, it is unclear which parts of this quote are directly taken from the source and which are Le Fanu's paraphrasing.

unable to find another teacher for the salary offered who could instruct the students in both English and French. By this time, English was the children's first language; a visitor to the school in 1760 noted that French was 'not familiar to them'.[100] Le Fanu writes that at this point, having no knowledge of French and being 'incorporated into and unified with English families', the students were unable to participate in the French-language services and so stopped attending the Huguenot churches, instead attending morning services at St Nicholas Without and afternoon service at St Patrick's Cathedral proper.[101]

This did not, however, mark the end of music education at the Huguenot school. After Pierre Brunel, the *sous-chantre*, was appointed organist in 1787, he received regular payments every year for almost a decade for teaching the children to sing psalms.[102] He was even granted two guineas by the school administrators to buy a spinet (a small keyboard instrument) to use in his instruction of the children.[103] It is unknown whether the students were at this point putting their musical training into practice by singing during services; if they were, it is possible that they did so at the services of St Nicholas Without, and that the psalms they were being taught were English-language psalms derived from the Anglican tradition. As Brunel was the organist of the French church, however, there is a tantalizing possibility that he revived the tradition of schoolchildren singing Genevan psalms at French services that had lapsed decades previously.

CONCLUSION

The worship music of Dublin's eighteenth-century Huguenots is often a challenging subject to research, with little extant scholarship on the topic and few substantial extant sources. Despite this, an examination of those sources that have survived has been able to provide extensive insight into a Huguenot musical culture that has not previously been the focus of much scholarly attention. The two surviving printed musical sources, the records of the Huguenot school and the consistory books of the French churches, in particular, have proved to be particularly valuable sources. There are still significant gaps in the historical record, and much work remains to be done; this chapter is intended both to augment existing scholarship and to encourage further study into this fascinating aspect of Huguenot culture in eighteenth-century Dublin.

The term 'St Pierre' was commonly used in the French-language records to refer to Peter Street. **100** Ibid., entry for 1760. **101** Ibid., entry for 1770. **102** Marsh's Library, MS Y3.5.1, entries from 1792 to 1797. The entry for 1792 records that at that point Brunel had already been teaching psalms to the schoolchildren for three years. **103** Marsh's Library, MS Y3.5.20, entry for 27 July 1788.

What does emerge very clearly from this research, however, is that music, and in particular the performance of the psalms, was a core part of Huguenot worship in Dublin as it was elsewhere in the diaspora. Psalms were sung by the *chantre* and congregation in services, played upon the organ, published in books and taught to the children at the Huguenot school. Dublin's Huguenots continued to use the Genevan psalms in their services, as they and their predecessors had done in France and as their coreligionists did in other countries. Closely associated with the Huguenot worship tradition and with defining events from the community's history, these psalms functioned not only as expressions of faith but also as markers of Huguenot identity. By surrounding themselves with this culture, Dublin's Huguenots were able to participate in a tradition that connected them both with their community's history and with the wider Huguenot diaspora in Europe and beyond.

The envoy's wife: diplomatic sociability, family, and loss in the diary (1689–1719) of Élie Bouhéreau

AMY PRENDERGAST

Prior to recording his involvement in the military campaign of 1694–6 in Piedmont, or noting details of his final years in Dublin as keeper of Marsh's Library, Élie Bouhéreau employed his diary to record his experiences as personal secretary to Thomas Coxe, envoy extraordinary for William III to the Swiss cantons, from August 1689 to September 1692. Those diary entries that chart Bouhéreau's experiences in the cantons afford us remarkable insight into diplomatic sociability during the late seventeenth century. Included among Bouhéreau's meticulous recordings of diplomatic life – the letters sent and received, the passports issued, the attempts to raise troops or to negotiate agreements – are meetings between Thomas Coxe and various local dignitaries. It is these entries in particular, combined with later diary entries charting the Coxes' familial circumstances, that afford us unexpected glimpses of the significant roles played by women in late seventeenth-century associational life, complicating and disrupting assumptions about public and private lives, diplomacy, and women's history generally.

Early modern diplomatic exchanges can be seen as a component in a series of broader cross-cultural exchanges and interactions, with both an official or formal dimension, as well as an array of informal elements, in what would now be termed 'track two diplomacy', implying 'unofficial, informal interaction'.[1] Diplomats at this time had three main daily functions: 'representation and the maintenance of good relations between the two sovereigns concerned; negotiation; and the gathering and transmission of intelligence.'[2] In addition to securing recognition of William III's rule, Thomas Coxe was also attempting to persuade the Swiss into the alliance against France, and there are meticulous recordings of the various diets and meetings held in relation to such missions throughout this early section of the diary.[3] However, this chapter adheres to the

---

Content warning: The second part of this chapter focuses on many difficult issues, including miscarriage and infant and child mortality. 1 Joseph Montville, 'The arrow and the olive branch: a case for track two diplomacy' in Vamik Volkan, Joseph Montville, and Demetrios Julius (eds), *The psychodynamics of international relationships: vol. 2, unofficial diplomacy at work* (Massachusetts, 1991), pp 161–76, at p. 162. 2 Christopher Storrs, 'British diplomacy in Switzerland (1689–1789) and eighteenth-century diplomatic culture', *Études de Lettres*, 3 (2010), 181–216; online pagination, http://edl.revues.org/266: 1–21. 3 Christopher Storrs, 'Thomas Coxe and the Lindau project' in Albert de Lange (ed.), *Dall'Europa alle Valli Valdesi*:

tenets of 'new diplomatic history', examining the cultural and social aspects of diplomacy and the 'multiple identities, behaviours, rituals and belief systems of diplomats', rather than prioritizing the specific unfolding of various political events, or analysing the treaties under negotiation.[4] The social component of diplomacy, incorporating balls, dinners, and public celebrations, was a key element of diplomatic activity and was an obligatory part of the diplomatic project. By privileging the cultural and social dimensions of diplomatic life we reposition women within diplomacy, allowing us to map connections with other forms of associational life, recognizing parallels and overlaps, as well as departures.[5]

Polite sociability at this time was based on the principle of *honnêteté*: 'the new secular ethic that would regulate behaviour in polite society,' a principle preconditioned on a variety of ostensibly feminine attributes – seduction, ease, and light heartedness – which required women to be treated with civilized attention as they taught men how to refine their behaviour.[6] The value awarded to this new social behaviour, a concept bound up with ideas of nobility which continued to evolve in the salons, elevated women to new positions within society.[7] Women were positioned at the centre of the literary salons in their role as *salonnière* – a position filled by women who 'subscribed to an ethos of sociability, not domesticity'.[8] It was the *salonnière* who organized the salons as well as committing herself to structuring the dialogue, inviting the guests, and of course providing the actual physical site for discussion. In the seventeenth-century salon the *salonnière* acted as both hostess and avid participant, contributing to the debate with her own interjections, as well as offering her own written material for conversation and formal improvement.[9] Of course, as Joan

Atti del convegno Il Glorioso Rimpatrio, 1689–1989 (Turin, 1990), pp 199–214.   **4** See the journal *Diplomatica: A Journal of Diplomacy and Society*, founded in 2019 by the Network for New Diplomatic History: newdiplomatichistory.org/journal and Giacoma Giudici, 'From new diplomatic history to new political history: the rise of the holistic approach', *European History Quarterly*, 48:2 (2018), 314–24.   **5** See Glenda Sluga, *The invention of international order: remaking Europe after Napoleon* (Princeton, 2021), which reimagines the role of women in diplomacy; Glenda Sluga and Carolyn James (eds), *Women, diplomacy and international politics since 1500* (London, 2015); Jennifer Mori, 'How women make diplomacy. The British embassy in Paris, 1815–1841', *Journal of Women's History*, 27:4 (2015), 137–59.   **6** It is described as combining both ethics and aesthetics. Rather than translating *honnêteté* into the English 'honesty' it should instead be understood as referring to the principle of honour that emerged from Italian Renaissance court culture. See Nicole Pohl, 'Perfect reciprocity: salon culture and epistolary conversations', *Women's Writing*, 13:1 (2006), 139–59, and Benedetta Craveri, *The age of conversation*. Trans. Teresa Waugh (New York, 2005). See also Antoine Lilti, *The world of the salons* (Oxford, 2015), which highlights the resemblance between salons and early modern courts.   **7** For the development of *honnêteté*, see Emmanuel Bury, *Littérature et politesse: l'invention de l'honnête homme* (Paris, 1996).   **8** Joan Landes, *Women and the public sphere in the age of the French Revolution* (Ithaca, 1988).   **9** Carolyn Lougee, *Le paradis des femmes: women, salons, and social stratification in seventeenth-century France* (Princeton, 1976); Faith E. Beasley, *Salons, history and the creation of seventeenth-century*

Landes and others have pointed out, women had previously also played an important role in the 'spectacle of royalty' or the royal court, providing heirs as well as facilitating access for aspiring courtiers.[10] However, the salon was an institution that gave even greater exposure to the important roles that could be embraced by women, which expanded into other aspects of public life, namely the diplomatic sphere.[11]

Diplomatic sociability involved extensive communication at a cross-European level, with officials often working across linguistic boundaries and encountering obstacles. However, their knowledge of the rules of polite social behaviour meant that the different nobles and various members of the diplomatic network were able to adhere to these rules as part of a pan-European cosmopolitan elite. Literary salons played a major role in transmitting these rules of sociability during the seventeenth century, allowing homogenization of manners and attitudes to take place within a secure environment, thereby acting not only as schools of sociability and politeness but as 'schools for assimilation into aristocratic manners'.[12] Madame de Stael's *De l'Allemagne, On Germany* (1810; trans. 1813) later 'underscore[s] the symbolic and practical significance of the salon in the story of modern diplomacy, both as the site of international politics and as the model of diplomatic methods.'[13] We have myriad records of men and women from Britain and Ireland frequenting the French salons, disseminating their modes of polite conversation and sociability, and indeed later emulating their practices.[14] Clearly, diplomatic sociability, by its very nature, was built upon cultural transfers and exchanges, and echoed the practices of the literary salons, and the incorporation of the central role of the harmonizing female hostess.

Diplomacy is often seen as a largely masculine world, and indeed it was and still is largely masculine, and certainly officially so: 'until 1946, no British woman could officially represent her nation abroad', for example, and we know that 85% of the world's ambassadors were men in 2014, and 'constitute an even higher share of negotiators and chief mediators in peace negotiations'.[15] During the period in which Bouhéreau served as secretary, diplomacy was not yet a full-time, formal profession, which gave a greater space for elite women in high-level negotiations.[16] Many of the envoys in the late seventeenth and eighteenth

---

France (Aldershot, 2006).   10 Landes, *Women and the public sphere*, p. 31.   11 Dena Goodman, *The republic of letters: a cultural history of the French Enlightenment* (Ithaca, 1995). 12 Marianne D'Ezio, 'Literary and cultural intersections between British and Italian women writers and *salonnières* during the eighteenth century' in Hilary Brown and Gillian Dow (eds), *Readers, writers, salonnières, female networks in Europe, 1700–1900* (Oxford, 2011), p. 15. 13 Glenda Sluga and Carolyn James, *Women, diplomacy and international politics, before and after the Congress of Vienna*, in Sluga and James, *Women, diplomacy and international politics*, pp 120–36, at p. 125.   14 Amy Prendergast, *Literary salons across Britain and Ireland in the long eighteenth century* (Basingstoke, 2015).   15 Karin Aggestam, 'The gender turn in diplomacy: a new research agenda', *International Feminist Journal of Politics*, 21:1 (2018), 9–28, at 10; Helen McCarthy, *Women of the world: the rise of the female diplomat* (London, 2015). 16 Lucien Bély, *L'art de la paix en Europe: naissance de la diplomatie moderne, XVI–XVIIIe*

centuries evidently travelled with their wives, and these women often had a significant role to play in the development of international friendships and in maintaining successful diplomatic relations. This was particularly apparent in relation to diplomatic sociability and the construction and maintenance of diplomatic networks connected to that. In addition to their formal role, the presence of diplomats in a town or city would have had a significant implication for the area's associational life, as Christopher Storrs has made clear: 'Diplomatic communities in the cantons could enrich elite social life *and* facilitate diplomacy.'[17] The envoys' wives frequently performed a role similar to that of the *salonnière*, proffering invitations and accepting visits, facilitating discussions and harmonizing conversation, either in the company of their husbands, or alone, but always within the sphere of the diplomatic role currently embodied, ensuring polite communication could take place.

The surviving diary of Élie Bouhéreau affords us a glimpse into this underexplored aspect of mixed-gender associational life in the late seventeenth century. In the towns and cities of the (Protestant) Swiss cantons, particularly those of the canton of Bern, the envoys' wives frequently interacted with the full cast of officials at mixed-gender events and had an important role to play in such meetings. This reinsertion of women into our discussions of diplomatic life via Bouhéreau's diary entries enhances our understanding of both diplomacy and sociability at this time, as well of course as assisting our broadening understanding of women's lives and roles during the period of the diary's composition.[18] This latter aspect is particularly to the fore in terms of the realities of childbearing, child rearing, and infant mortality, which did not cease during diplomatic missions, with children themselves often playing a role as diplomatic actors. Life writing offers us a particularly useful source for exploring such details, as well as providing a platform for men and women to record difficult episodes in their lives, to acknowledge the losses experienced, and to better cope with their grief. This chapter combines analysis of the public and private dimensions of the role of an envoy's wife, thereby expanding our understanding of sociability, diplomacy, and family life more generally in the period in question through engagement with the extraordinarily useful source that is the diary of Élie Bouhéreau.

THE ENVOY'S WIFE AND DIPLOMATIC SOCIABILITY

The wife of an envoy had a considerable role to play overseas, within the domestic sphere where she frequently organized and furnished the physical

---

siècle (Paris, 2007). 17 Storrs, 'British diplomacy', 193. 18 https://warwick.ac.uk/fac/arts/history/students/modules/hi2b2/programme/week9/) Christian Windler, 'Diplomatic history as a field for cultural analysis: Muslim–Christian relations in Tunis, 1700–1840', *The*

space, as well as in 'supporting their spouse's work and contributing to the efficacy of the embassy'.[19] Women such as Lady Mary, née Seymour (1628–73), countess of Winchilsea, the second wife of Heneage Finch, ambassador of Charles II to the Ottoman Empire, outside Constantinople, or Lady Ann, née Howard (1650–1707), wife of Richard Graham, Viscount Preston, the English envoy to France, at Paris, acted as diplomatic hostesses and were at the centre of diplomatic life and activity, entertaining the wider diplomatic community and cultivating significant friendships across Europe.[20] Élie Bouhéreau's diary includes mention of the wives of various envoys to Switzerland, who recur throughout this early part of the diary and perform the role of hostess, for example, Madame Valkenier, wife of the Dutch envoy, and Countess Govon, wife of the envoy from the duke of Savoy. At the centre of the diary's portrayal of this mixed-gender associational life is Englishwoman Mary Coxe, née Peachell/Pechill (identified as Marie Péchel by Bouhéreau), who accompanied her husband to the Swiss cantons, setting out as part of his travelling party in September 1689.[21] Bouhéreau's references to Mary Coxe and her children provide us with an insight into the co-existence of family life and diplomacy; of the role of the household in the diplomatic mission; and how the role of the diplomatic wife echoed the more widely-celebrated position of the French *salonnière*.

Largely absent from the first few months of the diplomatic mission, Mary Coxe makes numerous appearances later in 1690. Bouhéreau's diary entries from that period record how the envoy extraordinary's wife accompanied him on numerous official occasions. In July, for example, while travelling to Bern, the party stopped in Lenzburg, 'a Protestant town, three hours from Baden'. There Mrs Coxe accompanied the envoy in order to demonstrate their thanks to the bailiff, Mr Steiguer, who was also joined by his spouse:

> The envoy directed his secretary to go to thank the bailiff, and he then went up to the castle himself, along with his wife and all his suite. The bailiff and his wife received them there with all manner of politeness (10/20 July 1690).[22]

Again, a few days later in the same month, now in Burgdorf, Bouhéreau records how, following a spirited display from the townspeople,

---

Historical Journal, 44:1 (2001), 79–106. 19 Helen Jacobsen, *Luxury and power: the material world of the Stuart diplomat, 1660–1714* (Oxford, 2012), p. 56. 20 Ibid., p. 57. 21 With thanks to Geoff Kemp who shared details regarding the identity of this Lincolnshire heiress with me. Kemp has identified 22 July 1678 as the date on which Thomas Coxe junior married Mary Peachell. He estimates Mary as having been no more than ten when her father Thomas's will was made on 1 September 1665, The UK National Archives, PROB 11/322/2. See also Geoff Kemp's chapter in this volume. 22 Marie Léoutre, Jane McKee, Jean-Paul Pittion and Amy Prendergast (eds), *The diary (1689–1719) and accounts (1704–1717) of Élie Bouhéreau:*

The *avoyer* and his wife, along with the French minister, Mr Cabrit, came to dine with the envoy. During the meal, he was presented with six flagons of local wine, and the *avoyer* added to this two of his own. Then we went to the promenade to see some residents, who were firing blanks, and to whom the envoy gave tokens of his generosity. The envoy and his wife, with their suite, went up to the castle, to see the commander and his wife (15/25 July 1690).[23]

Such displays of solidarity and welcome across both towns clearly included the wives of those involved, and the mention of politeness gestures to the social behaviour necessary for these occasions to function. *Politesse* and *honnêteté* are generally seen as fundamental to salon life, but, clearly, they also formed part of the requirements of polite, diplomatic sociability, offering a model for respectful interaction and social exchange.

In addition to accompanying her husband on various occasions, Mary Coxe was also responsible for arranging certain meetings. In the winter of 1691, for example, Mrs Coxe made specific appointments with the princess of Baden-Durlach, to arrange a meeting while in Bern:

The envoy then had his secretary present his respects to the prince and princess, and the envoy's wife asked Her Serene Highness if she could have the honour of seeing her after dinner. The princess responded that she would await her, at five o'clock in the afternoon; and the envoy's wife went there, in her coach, with the envoy, the marquise d'Arselliers, and Madame Frisching, daughter wife of the eldest son of the colonel. On his first visit, the envoy had also taken the marquis d'Arselliers and a number of others, in his coach. All the company was treated to supper with Their Serene Highnesses by the gentlemen of the city of Bern, at the Falcon (23 November/3 December 1691).[24]

Again, this is a markedly mixed-gender gathering, with a preponderance of women, and allowed for royalty and diplomatic figures to socialize together when the situation permitted. Diary entries such as these generally record the person who established the connection (very often a woman); the intermediary involved – generally a secretary such as Bouhéreau; those present at the gathering; and the time and date of its occurrence. In this way we get a sense of the networks forming and the frequency of gatherings, though generally not of their content or the conversations that occurred. Both husband and wife would have been expected to understand and observe the particulars of diplomatic etiquette, and to not bring embarrassment or dishonour to their official capacity. The

Marsh's Library Z2.2.2 (Dublin, 2019), p. 71.   23 Ibid., p. 75.   24 Ibid., p. 139.

negotiations inherent in the diplomat's role were episodic in nature, but we should note that the diplomat was intended to represent the sovereign on a daily basis. This quotidian element of their role was certainly assisted by the wives of the envoys, whose activities can be read as strategic interventions with the potential to curry favour, gain influence, reinforce networks, and participate in informal dialogue with high-profile and influential figures.

More specific, celebratory events in the Swiss cantons also involved the various diplomats' wives, pointing to their important role in ceremonial diplomatic sociability as well as the various day-to-day diplomatic interactions. It has been noted how 'successive British ministers were expected to maintain good relations with the states to which they were sent (and that) this sometimes involved them in more or less overtly propagandistic activity, including the celebration of British successes.'[25] The celebration of the siege of Limerick in November 1691, on William III's birthday, for example, was an event recorded in Bouhéreau's diary as being hosted by both the envoy and his wife, with Bouhéreau recording that:

> At midday, the envoy, with those from his household, went to collect Mr Daxelhoffer from his home ... At the same time, the envoy's wife entertained several of the principal ladies and several gentlemen of the town in her apartments, the same [men and women] who had offered her company at the feast that had been given in her honour, upon her arrival. She had had them invited in a similar fashion, by the secretary (4/14 November 1691).[26]

The diary demonstrates that Mary Coxe had a specific hosting role to embody on this occasion, and seems to have done so successfully. Bouhéreau provides details of the celebrations, including the illumination of the envoy's residence by 'an infinite number of candles', as well as a fountain that substituted wine for water. The celebrations concluded with a ball, as he notes: 'It all ended with a ball that the envoy gave for Madame Graffenried, the wife of the councillor, who had invited all the ladies of the town there ...'. The *Calendar of State Papers* from the period echoes Bouhéreau's account precisely and explains the additional expenses incurred by the celebratory bonfires; wines offered to the people; and 'a ball at night to the ladies'.[27] Additional expenses were of necessity incurred, but the importance of such occasions is clearly underlined.

In addition to ceremonial celebrations for sovereigns' birthdays or dynastic marriages, military victories were often celebrated by diplomats in their residence, which itself was a symbol of the sovereign the diplomat represented,

---

25 Storrs, 'British diplomacy', 189. **26** Léoutre et al., *Diary and accounts*, p. 135. **27** William John Hardy (ed.), *Calendar of State Papers, domestic, William and Mary (1693–1693)* (London, 2012–13, e-book), p. 42.

with early eighteenth-century Venice particularly given to such rejoicing.[28] Not all the elements of such ceremonial diplomatic sociability and celebration of military success were mixed-gender, and a year earlier, while celebrating the Williamite victory in Ireland, Bouhéreau records that:

> At the same time, the envoy's wife was served in her apartment, where the most important ladies of the city kept her company ... It was the day chosen to celebrate the good news that had just reached us regarding the great victory obtained by the king, on the 1/11 of July, over the army of King James in Ireland ... Various other fireworks, both on the ground and in the water, and several cannon salvoes. The celebration ended with a ball ... (24 July/3 Aug. 1690).[29]

The status of the envoy's wife is apparent from this entry, where she is accorded the presence of those women judged the most important within the environs, though the celebrations are divided along gender lines, and remind us of the divisions of space within the residence itself.

The example of Madame Valkenier further illustrates the role women could play in diplomatic exchanges. In May 1692, in the absence of her husband, the envoy of Holland, Madame Valkenier, attended in his stead:

> The town secretary came immediately, to enquire if Mr Coxe would be able to receive the magistrates' visit. Madame Valkenier, in the absence of her husband, the envoy of Holland, made the same enquiry. Then she came in person with mademoiselle her daughter (21/31 May 1692).[30]

Though a *de facto* male role, we see here that a woman could temporarily assume some of her husband's responsibilities during his absence. The following day, 22 May, the English envoy arranged a visit to the same woman and her daughter, accompanied by his own wife, after having requested an audience. Although not noted in Bouhéreau's diary, there are examples extant to show that, 'If a husband was ill and incapable, a wife might write his regular report home, cf marchesa Desmarches to comte de Saint Laurent, Geneva, September 1745.'[31] The memoirs and correspondence of Lady Anne Fanshawe, the wife of the English ambassador to the Madrid court (1664–6), also shows that Fanshawe oversaw embassy business while her husband was in Lisbon hoping to obtain a truce between Spain and Portugal.[32] Thus, in addition to their roles in entertaining

---

28 Nina Lamal and Klaas Van Gelder, 'Addressing audiences abroad: cultural and public diplomacy in seventeenth-century Europe', *The Seventeenth Century*, 36:3 (2021), 367–87, at p. 374.   29 Léoutre et al., *Diary and accounts*, p. 79.   30 Ibid., p 157.   31 Storrs, 'British diplomacy', 193 footnote 66.   32 Laura Oliván Santaliestra, 'Lady Anne Fanshawe, ambassadress of England at the Court of Madrid (1664–1666), in Sluga and James, *Women, diplomacy and international politics*, pp 68–85.

and arranging gatherings, there were instances where a woman could in fact temporarily intervene into the more formal aspects of diplomatic life.

The envoys' departure from the Swiss cantons entailed further pageantry, and, as part of the myriad compliments of farewell that made up the displays upon their departure, 'Mary Coxe, Madame Valkenier, Mesdemoiselles their daughters, and five other ladies', attended a 'magnificent' feast in their honour, with both men and women in Zurich the same week. Mary Coxe and Madame Valkenier are described by Bouhéreau as having been placed at the top of the table, indicating their status, and as a note of respect:

> There, the burgomasters, and various other members of the council, awaited both the envoy and his company, for the feast that had been prepared, on two tables, magnificently served, by young people of the foremost quality. Mrs Coxe, Madame Valkenier, Mesdemoiselles their daughters, and five other ladies, were also at the feast, and Mrs Coxe and Madame Valkenier were placed at the top of the table. The principal healths were toasted to the fanfare of trumpets, and to the salvoes of six cannons, placed on the bastion of the lake (23 May/2 June).[33]

The women are again part of the theatre of diplomacy, here positioned centre stage, amid the fanfare. Recent work has explored modern concepts of cultural diplomacy from the fields of international relations in historical context, examining symbolic communication and detailing how 'diplomats were both participants and spectators with their own part to play.'[34] In this example it is the diplomats and their entourage who are represented as receiving the largesse of the hosts, but they nevertheless remain as part of a larger performance and pageantry in which all were engaged, each with an explicit role.

The envoys' wives all had a specific function to enact, and certain clear duties and roles to perform. Those who appeared as different, or not quite fitting in to their expected roles, are also recorded by Bouhéreau. He is particularly struck by the appearance of Countess Govon, wife of the envoy extraordinary of the duke of Savoy for the Swiss, who dined with him in Aarau on several occasions:

> The Count and Countess Govon have come from Lucerne, which is eight hours from Aarau, to see the envoy and his wife. The countess is a young Italian lady, dark haired, but very pleasant. She arrived in riding dress, a *juste-au-corps*, a cravat with a ribbon the colour of fire, a wig, and a grey hat with a white feather (10/20 August 1690).[35]

---

[33] Léoutre et al., *Diary and accounts*, p. 159.   [34] Lamal and Van Gelder, 'Addressing audiences abroad', 372.   [35] 'The count, countess, and the lady-in-waiting, dined with the envoy in his lodgings. They also dined there on the days that followed'. Léoutre et al., *Diary and accounts*, p. 85.

She clearly made an impression on Bouhéreau, although this is not the only time in the diary that he remarks on clothing, and indeed there are repeated mentions of women's attire throughout.[36] A particularly striking example of the importance and significance of dress at the time in relation to diplomacy is recorded by Bouhéreau in November 1691, where he notes that several women were fined for dressing in the French style. Bouhéreau states that:

> Several ladies from Bern have been fined for having attended the envoy's ball, dressed and coiffed à la *Française,* contrary to the law of this state; however, those who had not appeared in the streets were exempted from this, having dressed and undressed in his residence, as in a privileged space (19/29 November 1691).[36a]

While those who appear 'in the streets' are fined and reprehended, the envoy's residence is explicitly recognized as 'a privileged space' and those within, thus immune from culpability. The entry reminds us of the significance of such events and the attention they receive more broadly, albeit in a negative capacity here. Distinctions between venues designated as public and private, or a combination of the two, as with the literary salon, or the diplomatic residence here, focus our minds on the porosity between the features of what we might consider public and private, and our expectations for behaviour and performance within both.

FAMILY AND LOSS: LIFE WRITING AND PUBLIC EXPRESSIONS OF SORROW

Indeed, Bouhéreau's own diary is a useful textual counterpart to illustrate such interstices, in that he incorporates details of his official role as secretary and the contingent roles this required, as an official chronicle, alongside and within entries recording his own family life and that of the Coxes, blurring any clear distinction between the different roles he held. This practice of providing details of one's life and one's loved ones alongside household expenditure and wages, continues right through the eighteenth century, with both men and women embracing the diary form owing to its plurality of functions.[37] A later Irish

---

36 For example, while in Ulm, a Lutheran imperial city, Bouhéreau describes how, 'We were surprised by the various styles of clothing of the women there, which all appeared very strange to a foreign eye.' 3/13 November 1689, Léoutre et al., *Diary and accounts*, p. 19.   36a Ibid., p. 137.   37 Christina Sjöbald, 'From family notes to diary: the development of a genre', *Eighteenth-Century Studies*, 31:4 (1998), 517–21. Amy Prendergast, *Mere bagatelles: women's diaries from Ireland, 1760–1810* (Liverpool, 2024). The multifunctionality of the form is immediately apparent from a quick survey of the surviving diaries from eighteenth-century Ireland. These reveal the full spectrum of possibilities the diary form afforded, whether for better mental health, negotiation of national identity, assistance in the transition to adulthood,

Huguenot diarist in Dublin, Meliora Bermingham Adlercron (d. 1797), for example, kept a meticulous record of her children's births, illnesses, and deaths, alongside household expenditure from 1782 to 1794.[38] Bouhéreau's own diary was commenced too late in his life to record the birth of his own offspring, but it does record the births, baptisms, and deaths of his various grandchildren. Bouhéreau's daughter Blandine, who married Jean Jourdan, in April 1699, for example, safely delivered eight children over the course of fourteen years. Upon the birth of his granddaughter Marguerite on 27 January 1714, Bouhéreau announces: 'She is her eighth child: three boys and five girls; all living.'[39] Bouhéreau's eldest daughter Marguerite, meanwhile, had an extremely sorrowful litany of infant mortality. She married Louis Quartier, minister of the French church of Saint Patrick, in July 1703, and upon the birth of her second child, Marguérite-Marie, Bouhéreau records that, 'She is her second child. Her first daughter died, a little over a month ago' (26 March 1706).[40] The infant Marguérite-Marie is then recorded as having died in September of that year. A third child, Jeanne, was then born in April 1707, but her mother subsequently died several days later: 'April 21 1707 – Death of my dear eldest daughter, at six o'clock in the morning, precisely at the end of the thirteenth day after she delivered her child.' Bouhéreau's son Richard and his wife also experienced personal tragedies, with four of their children dying during the course of the diary, the birth of baby Jeanne recorded, for example, as: 'She is the fifth of their children; the third of the surviving ones' (10 June 1712).[41]

Bouhéreau was recording these details for posterity. The inclusion of paratextual apparatus within a diary generally (as occurs throughout Bouhéreau's with his extensive emendations and marginalia), alongside attention to presentation and historical contextualization, makes it clear that an audience for a diary was frequently to the fore in the long eighteenth century, whether a future or posthumous audience, or an immediate familial one.[42] Ruth Whelan has identified a common pattern amongst Huguenot life writers, wherein their 'writing was composed with the children of the writer in mind' with these men and women writing their lives 'in order to hand on traditions, family lore and an identity.'[43] Bouhéreau's diary is certainly written with such an audience in mind,

---

coping with bereavement, dealing with assault, or establishing a literary voice.   38 National Library of Ireland, MS 3846 and MS 4481. Adlercron account books. Household expenses and wages book of Mrs. Meliora Adlercron of Dawson St., Dublin, including some notes on births and deaths of members of her family, and references to small-pox epidemics in Dublin, 1782–94.   39 Léoutre et al., *Diary and accounts*, p. 375.   40 Ibid., p. 341.   41 Ibid., p. 371. 42 Amy Prendergast, 'Glossing the diary: women writing for posterity, the case of Elizabeth Edgeworth (1781–1800)', *Life Writing*, 19:2 (2020), 277–94.   43 Ruth Whelan, 'Marsh's Library and the French Calvinist tradition: the manuscript diary of Élie Bouhéreau (1643–1719)' in Muriel McCarthy and Ann Simmons (eds), *The making of Marsh's Library: learning, politics and religion in Ireland, 1650–1750* (Dublin, 2004), pp 209–24, at 222.

and the inclusion of details of the various Bouhéreau and Coxe family members' births and baptisms serves to acknowledge their short existence as well as to strengthen a sense of the families' lineages and interconnections. Details of the Coxe family's composition and demographics co-exist with and are awarded equal attention to the official meetings and negotiations mentioned in the early portion of Bouhéreau's diary. Details regarding the changing household of Thomas Coxe are meticulously noted by Bouhéreau, and the contemporary reader is reminded that the difficulties of pregnancy, childbirth, and infant and child mortality were not suspended during diplomatic missions.

The earlier example of the ambassador to the Ottoman Empire, Heneage Finch (1628–89), who had four wives, and twenty-seven children, 'of which 16 lived to some maturity', brings such issues to the fore.[44] The Earl had eleven surviving children with his second wife, Lady Mary, née Seymour (m. 1649), the woman he was married to during his role as ambassador-extraordinary (1660–7). The couple travelled to Constantinople in October 1660 with their baby, leaving five older children at home, until Lady Mary returned in late 1667 'on account of her illness', with her husband following in 1669.[45] Lady Mary suffered five miscarriages in one year,[46] and the couple's third daughter, also named Mary, is recorded as having 'died in Turkey of the plague, during her father's ambassy'.[47] It is highly unlikely that these losses did not have a great impact upon the parents, and this is generally borne out by the array of life writing that survives. Mirroring wider global trends, the historical experience of pregnancy, miscarriage, and infant mortality in an Irish context has received earnest scholarly attention over the past two decades, particularly from social historians.[48] Diaries can offer the historian a useful source for data acquisition on the topic, as well as closer access to the emotional effects of such events on the individuals involved, though still very much mediated for an audience. Mourning journals from the later eighteenth and early nineteenth centuries, such as that of Dublin-born Huguenot poet and diarist Melesina Chenevix St

---

44 Arthur Collins, *The peerage of England* ... 5 vols (London, 1756), ii, p. 310.   45 Sonia P. Anderson, 'Finch, Heneage, third earl of Winchilsea' in *ODNB*, https://www.oxforddnb.com, accessed 14 July 2024. Account of journey available in Paul Rycaut, *A narrative of the success of the voyage of the right honourable Heaneage Finch* (1661); Thomas H. Fuhimura 'Etherage at Constantinople', *Publications of the Modern Language Association (PMLA)*, 71:3 (1956), 465–84, at 468.   46 Jacobsen *Luxury and power*, p. 55.   47 Collins, *The peerage of England*, ii, p. 310. Constantinople was particularly badly affected by plagues, and experienced 'almost annual visits' so that by 1778, 'possibly a third of the population died of plague'. Philip Mansel, *Constantinople: city of the world's desire, 1453–1925* (New York, 1998), p. 225.   48 Rosemary Raughter. '"A time of trial being near at hand": pregnancy, childbirth and parenting in the spiritual journal of Elizabeth Bennis, 1749–79' in Elaine Farrell (ed.), '*She said she was in the family way': pregnancy and infancy in modern Ireland* (London, 2012); Gabrielle Ashford, 'Childhood: studies in the history of children in eighteenth-century Ireland' (PhD, DCU, 2012); Sarah Anne Buckley, 'Women, men and the family, *c.*1730–*c.*1880' in James Kelly (ed.), *The Cambridge history of Ireland, vol. 3, 1730–1880* (Cambridge,

George Trench (1768–1827), offer harrowing accounts of the trauma experienced after the loss of a child, and while these are not replicated as frequently in the period during which Bouhéreau was writing, individual entries confronting infant mortality survive within larger diaries and make it clear that the lived experience of loss was a painful one then as it is now, in spite of earlier expectations regarding child mortality.[49] Academic research on sorrow and child loss had historically discussed the lack of emotion displayed, but life writing frequently affords us glimpses into the grief experienced by the diarist in a myriad of unexpected ways, and more recent scholarship reflects a shift in perspective.[50] While the joint topics of loss and grief are often visible in the omissions, silences, and euphemisms discernible across life writing, particularly in diary entries, they are also addressed explicitly, as in the writings of Mary Rich, née Boyle, countess of Warwick (1624/5–78). Mary Rich and her husband Charles were devoted to their two children Elizabeth (1642–3) and Charles (1643–64), both of whom died very young, at fifteen months and twenty years old respectively. The distress, grief, and trauma experienced by both mother and father is evident in the memoirs of the former, wherein it is recorded that upon the death of his son, Mary's husband Charles 'cryed out so terably that his cry was herd a great way.'[51]

Where women's bodies and bodily functions are involved, both men and women's diaries from the long eighteenth century are frequently full of euphemisms and silences, with pregnancy in particular shrouded in a variety of oblique, polite expressions. However, information can again be gleaned from omissions and absences, by reading in between what is actually committed to the page. Many of the diaries written by women themselves hint at the lived experience of both pregnancy and miscarriage in the lengthy gaps between certain entries, the mention of illnesses, and the low spirits reported. In the diary of Anne Weldon, née Cooke (1726–1809), for example, references to various

2018), pp 231–54. **49** Katharine Kittredge, 'A long-forgotten sorrow: the mourning journal of Melesina Trench', *Eighteenth-Century Fiction*, 21:1 (2008), 153–77. One of the first people to estimate infant/child mortality rates was London-born John Graunt in his *Natural and political observations made upon the London bills of mortality* (1662). For contemporary analysis of such data see Lucia Pozzi and Diego Ramiro Farinas, 'Infant and child mortality in the past', *Annales de Démographie Historique*, 129 (2015), 555–75; and Andrea Rusnock, 'Quantifying infant mortality in eighteenth-century England and France' in Gérard Jorland, Annick Opinel, George Weisz (eds), *Body counts: medical quantification in historical and sociological perspectives-/La quantification médicale, perspectives historiques et sociologiques* (Montreal, 2005). **50** See Paige Donaghy's work, which incorporates non-foetal gestations into her considerations of pregnancy loss, 'Miscarriage, false conceptions, and other lumps: women's pregnancy loss in seventeenth- and eighteenth-century England', *Social History of Medicine*, 34:4 (2021), 1138–60. **51** British Library, Add. MS 27357. Autobiography of Mary Rich, 1625–74, followed by other writing on her death dated 21 March 1691/2, and other notes up to 20 January 1715. Some specialities in the life of M. Warwick, fo. 31v; Sara H. Mendelson, 'Rich [née Boyle], Mary, countess of Warwick' *ODNB*:

1. Map of La Rochelle in 1620, by Matthäus Merian, seventeenth century, 4 PL 194. Courtesy of La Médiathèque d'agglomération Michel-Crépeau, La Rochelle.

2. Isaac Baulot, *Mutus liber* (La Rochelle, 1677), title page. The famous work of alchemy is almost entirely pictorial, and thus only the initiated could follow its instructions. By permission of the Governors and Guardians of Marsh's Library.

3. The Reformed temple in Villeneuve, La Rochelle, built *c*.1630 and demolished on 1 March 1685 by royal decree. By permission of Musée Rochelais d'Histoire Protestante.

Les Oeuvres de Balzac, de Sarrazin, et de Voiture. Les Entretiens de Voiture et de Costar. Toute la dispute de Costar et de Girac. Toutes les Traductions de Mr. d'Ablancourt; Son Minutius Felix, Son César, Son Tacite, Son Lucien, Son Thucydide, Son Marmol, &c. Le Quinte-Curce de Vangelas. Les Ouvrages de Mr. de la Chambre, ou, du-moins, les principaux; Sur-tout, les Caractéres des Passions. L'histoire de l'Académie Françoise, par Mr. Pellisson. La Vie de Socrate, par Mr. Charpentier; et tout ce qu'il a traduit de Xénophon. Quelques Ouvrages de Mrs. de Port-royal; comme les Lettres Provinciales, contre les Jésuites; les Essays de Morale; &c. Quelques Relations choisies; comme celles que Mr. Thévenot a fait imprimer.

Bouhéreau, Docteur en Médecine, Ruë des Augustins. A La Rochelle.

5. Portrait of John Locke by John Greenhill, oil on canvas, 1672.
© National Portrait Gallery, London.

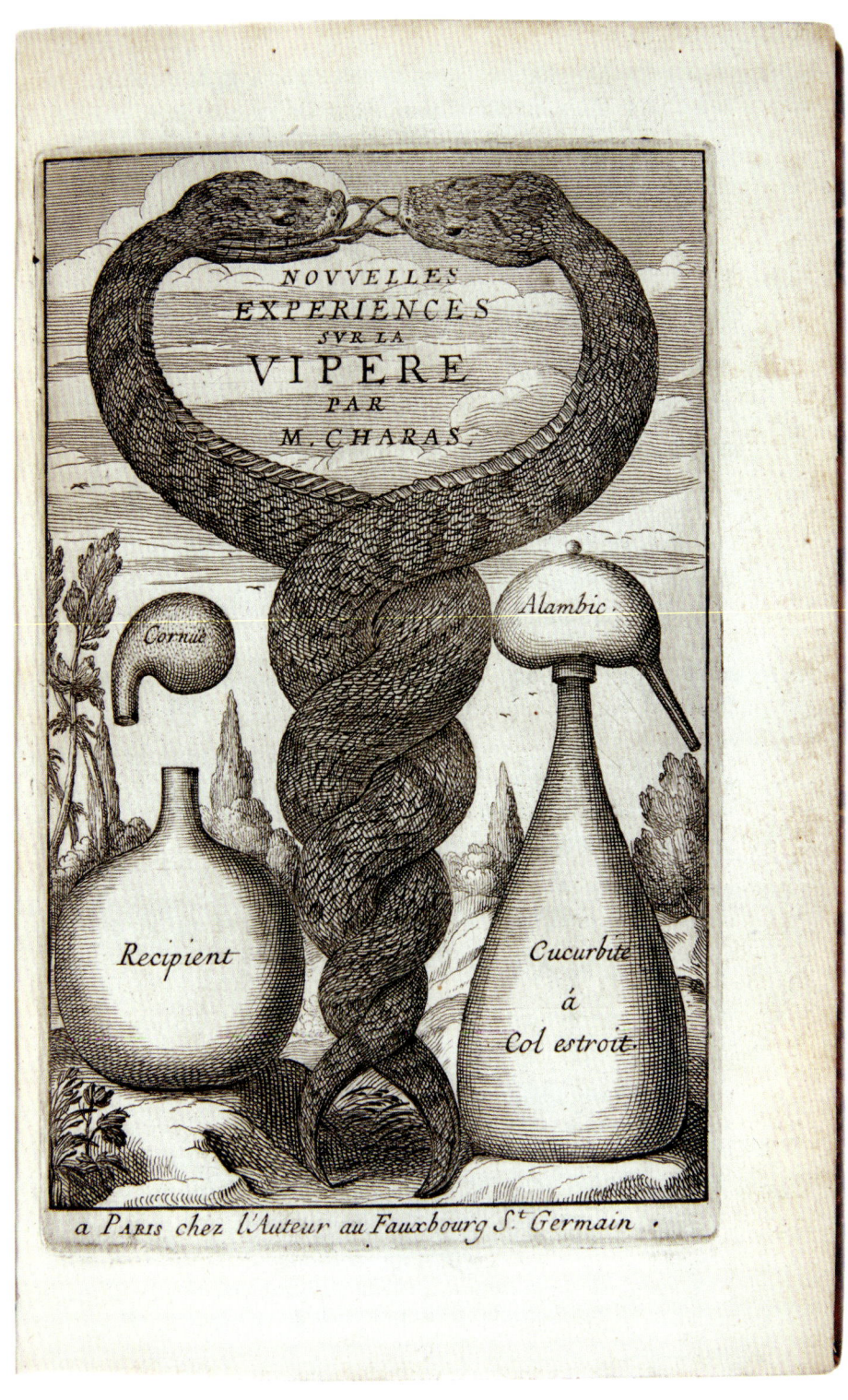

6. Moyse Charas, *Nouvelles expériences sur la vipere* (Paris, 1672), engraved title page.
© By permission of the Governors and Guardians of Marsh's Library.

7. Portrait of Laurent Drelincourt, artist unknown, oil on canvas, seventeenth century. Photograph © February 2025 Museum of Fine Arts, Boston.

LES
PSAUMES
DE DAVID.

Retouchez sur la Version

De MAROT & de BEZE;
par. Mar. Ant. de la Bastide.
Approuvez par les PASTEURS
de l'Eglise de PARIS.
et par valenE T Conrart
Par les Synodes de FRANCE,
Revûs a *Geneve* & à *Berlin*:

AVEC
La LITURGIE, le CATECHISME,
& la Confession de Foi.

Nouvelle EDITION,
Corrigée sur les precedentes.

A LONDRES,
Pour Jean Cailloué, & Jaques Levi, Libraires François. MDCCI.

8. *Les Psaumes de David: retouchéz sur la version de Marot et de Bèze* (Paris, 1701), title page. This is Élie Bouhéreau's copy of a new edition of the 1679 Genevan psalter, in which he has added the names of the editors, Valentin Conrart and Marc-Antoine, Sieur de la Bastide. By permission of the Governors and Guardians of Marsh's Library.

9. *Les pseaumes de David mis en vers françois* (Dublin, 1731), frontispiece of King David playing the harp. NLI, Dublin Dix 1731 (21). Courtesy of the National Library of Ireland.

10. The Lady Chapel, St Patrick's Cathedral, Dublin. By permission of the Dean and Chapter of St Patrick's Cathedral.

11. Portrait of Henri de Massue, marquis de Ruvigny, earl of Galway, (1648–1720). Irish Linen Centre & Lisburn Museum, no. 2008.163.

12. Tanneguy Le Fèvre, *On the sublime* (Saumur, 1663), front pastedown and endleaf. Élie Bouhéreau's copy was a gift from the author. The first flyleaf is covered in Bouhéreau's distinctive system of note-taking.

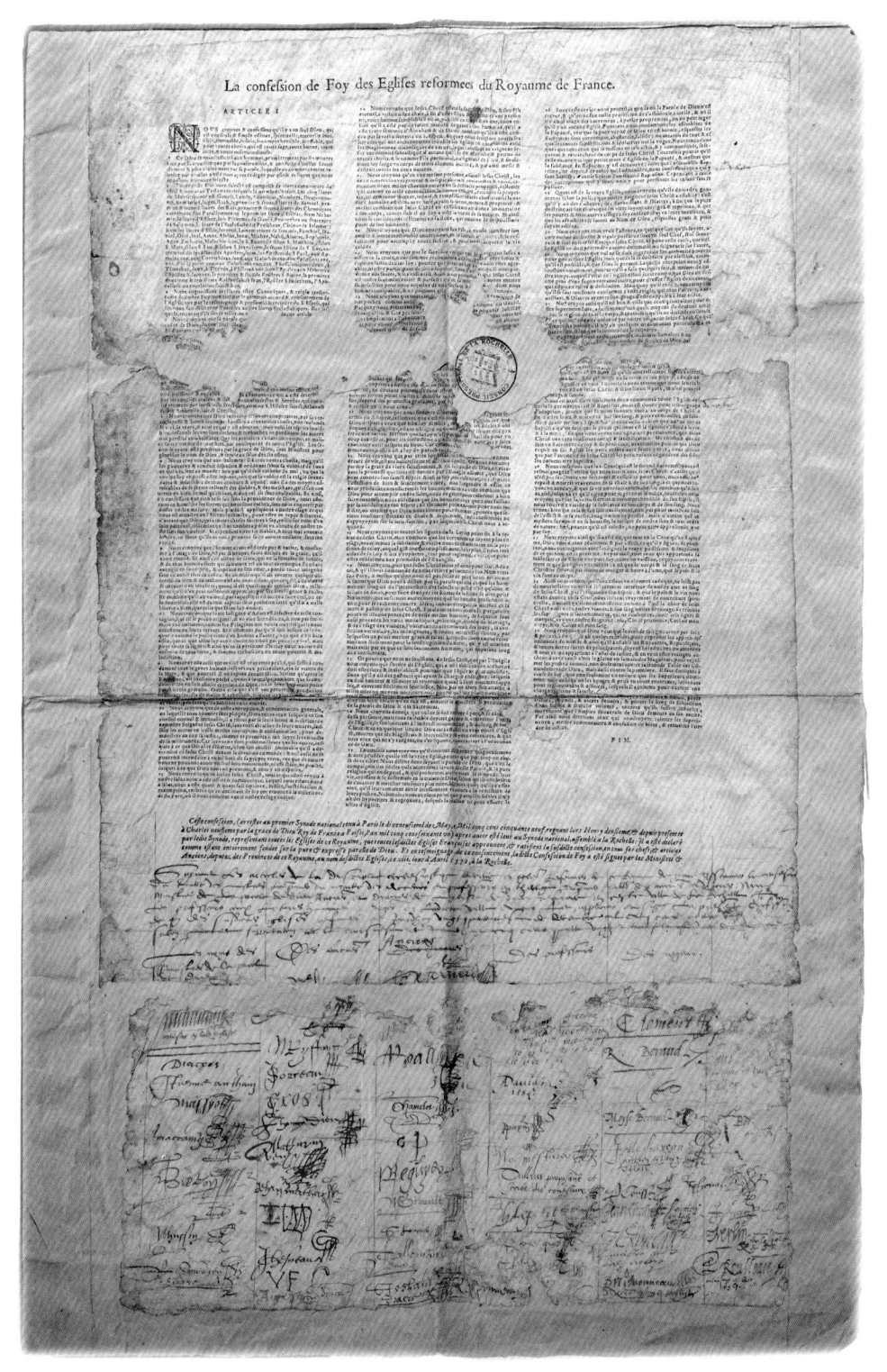

13. Confession of Faith of the Reformed Church of La Rochelle, 1571 (printed 1572) signed by Jeanne d'Albret, Henry of Navarre, and the ministers of the Reformed Churches of France. By permission of Musée Rochelais d'Histoire Protestante.

14. Élie Bouhéreau's books in the old reading room of Marsh's Library.

15. 'List of missing books, 1828', Marsh's Library, MS ML 36, pp 86–7. These pages list Élie Bouhéreau's books recorded missing from shelves R2.9 to R3.4 of Marsh's Library in 1828, among them the 1515 edition of Pindar (R3.4.8). By permission of the Governors and Guardians of Marsh's Library.

TRAITÉ D'ORIGÉNE CONTRE CELSE.

OU

Défence de la Religion Chrétienne contre les accusations des Païens.

Traduit du Grec
Par ELIE BOUHÉREAU.

A AMSTERDAM,
Chez HENRY DESBORDES, Marchand Libraire, dans le Kalver-straat.

M. D. CC.

16. Élie Bouhéreau, *Traité d'Origéne contre Celse: ou défence de la religion chrétienne contre les accusations des païens* (Amsterdam, 1700). By permission of the Governors and Guardians of Marsh's Library.

preparations for her lying-in in Dublin, in both January 1767 and December 1768, are not followed by the mention of any subsequent children.[52] The realities of pregnancy, particularly the discomforts of the third trimester, could disrupt regular life, and certainly intruded upon the full embracing of the diplomatic role of the English envoy's wife. In Bouhéreau's diary we are never told that Mary Coxe is pregnant, but her pregnancy is notable in her absence from meetings and the wider sphere of diplomatic relations. There are no references to her lying-in or preparations for this as in later diaries, but the birth and early days of the couple's two infants are themselves carefully charted.

The initial presentation of Thomas Coxe's family within the diary, introduced as part of Bouhéreau's travelling retinue, includes two children, later identified by Bouhéreau as one son, and one daughter, named Marie. This unit was augmented for a short period by the birth of two further children, a baby girl followed by a little boy. The Coxes' daughter Marie Jeanne Violante was born 11/21 November 1689, while on 5/15 May 1691 between seven and eight p.m. a son, Philibert, was born. The dates of their baptisms, the chaplain who baptized them, and those who acted as godparents are subsequently entered into the diary and recorded for posterity.

This chapter has previously detailed the celebration of official achievements and joyous occasions, with the various displays to mark William III's birthday, or the anniversary of the coronation of the king and queen. Bouhéreau's diary also contains mentions of the public dimension of this small diplomatic family unit, connected to the birth and death of their children. French refugees in Bern arrive to 'present their compliments to the envoy upon the birth of his new son' on 13/23 May, for example. One month after the birth of Marie Jeanne, on December 10/1, Bouhéreau records that both mother and daughter are in good health. However, the child's death is recorded the following summer, on 23 June/3 July 1690. Philibert suffered from ill health and difficulties breathing from birth, and died on 14/24 December 1691, 'after having languished for several days'. A medical examination of his body was conducted two days later, including investigation of the spleen, liver, diaphragm, chest, and brain, before the body was carefully embalmed and prepared for burial. The personal loss of these two children also contained a public element, with official marks of commiseration and respects paid upon the deaths of the two children:

> Six representatives of the council of this city of Zurich came to pay their respects to the envoy and his wife, on the death of their daughter. Mr Landolt, the bursar, spoke for them in German, and the envoy replied in French (25 June/5 July 1690).[53]

https://www.oxforddnb.com, accessed 14 July 2024. **52** Anne Cooke Weldon, 'Anne Cooke diary', *Journal of the County Kildare Archaeological Society*, 8 (1915–17), 104–32, 205–19 and 447–63. **53** Léoutre et al., *Diary and accounts*, p. 67.

> Four representatives from the clergy of the city came to pay their respects also, Mr Schadlerus speaking for them, in Latin. The envoy responded in like fashion (26 June/6 July 1690).[54]
>
> A minister and an elder, representatives of the French refugees, came to pay their respects to the envoy on the death of his son (23 December/ 2 Jan. 1692; and again 24 Dec./3 Jan. 1692).[55]

We see in these entries that respects were extended to include the envoy's wife in the first instance, though condolences on the second loss were more explicitly paid to the envoy, or at least recorded thus by Bouhéreau. The pan-European nature of the diplomatic sphere is again in evidence through the myriad of languages employed in these dialogues of sympathy and respect, encompassing French, German and Latin.

Bouhéreau was also careful to record precise details of the two children's funerals. Both occasions communicate to the reader that the Coxes eschewed pomp, in preference for smaller, more intimate ceremonies:

> The funeral ceremony took place without pomp, although the whole city had offered to come there together. The body was placed in a coach and six, covered with black drapes, accompanied by the chaplain and the lady-in-waiting. The secretary and all the servants followed on foot, dressed in mourning (5/15 July 1690).[56]

Here, the Coxes clearly declined the offer extended by 'the whole city', to instead mark their personal sorrows in a more private fashion. Recent work by Rachel Wilson engages with the universal public mourning in Ireland for members of royalty over the age of 14, and here we see this mourning echoed at a much smaller level within the diplomatic sphere, for those under that age.[57] The Coxe family are described as having departed from Zurich to go to the diet of Aarau four days after this funeral, by 9/19 July, and it is difficult to assess the impact of this loss upon the family unit. The diplomatic mission continues, and unlike eighteenth-century diaries that were used as a platform to explore and address loss and grief, here Bouhéreau's diary instead simply records their loss and hints at their pain. Yet it serves to offer a sense of the varifold experiences of late seventeenth-century life and diplomacy, and the fusion of the public with the private, as well as to record the evolving details of the family's composition for future generations.

---

54 Ibid., p. 69. 55 Léoutre et al., *Diary and accounts*, p. 143. 56 Ibid., pp 69 and 71. 57 Rachel Wilson, '"All Dublin is as black as black can be": the material culture of Irish mourning for the Stuarts and Hanoverians, 1694–1801'. Paper presented at *Eighteenth-Century Ireland Society Conference*, June 2021.

CONCLUSIONS

This chapter makes clear that distinctions between the ostensibly public and private worlds of this diplomatic interlude in Bouhéreau's diary are porous, with boundaries between public and private generally obfuscated and instead replaced by a sense of the numerous interstices at play across all aspects of diplomatic life. Bouhéreau's diary in this period moves between chronicling Thomas Coxe's activities in the manner of an entering book, into more private areas as in the personal, domestic sorrows encountered by Coxe and his family while in the Swiss cantons, frequently allowing us insight into both the quotidian aspects of diplomatic life as well as the ceremonial interludes. It also adds to our understanding of the diary form as one that affords a platform for recording changing family composition, which frequently incorporated deaths as much as births, anticipating later forms of life writing that foregrounded the emotional responses to such losses. The diary form's flexibility and textual fluidity permits Bouhéreau to record the contours of the short lives of his own grandchildren and the Coxe children, acknowledging their place in the families' history and legacy, and demonstrating the deep interconnections of the various families involved.

As a remarkable social document, the diary of Élie Bouhéreau also repeatedly draws our attention to both the presence and interventions of the envoy's wife, Mary Coxe. In addition to accompanying her husband to various locales not examined in this chapter, such as theatrical performances, to sites of significance, and to church to worship, the diary entries repeatedly demonstrate that Mary Coxe clearly participated in the available diplomatic social gatherings, both in single-sex and mixed-gender settings, contributing to multiple aspects of European associational life available to her. She is explicitly depicted as inviting local guests via Bouhéreau, as well as initiating meetings and visits with local or visiting dignitaries, thereby indicating her own role in establishing connections during her husband's and her residence in the cantons, as well as participating via the various other avenues noted throughout the chapter.

Though unequivocally a masculine world in its official capacity, the informal but obligatory elements of the diplomatic expedition clearly benefited from the presence of women such as Mary Coxe, women who could play an unofficial role in creating and strengthening relations with representatives from other countries, ensuring the performance and observation of the rules of polite society, and employing social diplomacy to advance political objectives. Engaging with Élie Bouhéreau's diary in this way places women at the centre of this social diplomacy rather than as peripheral actors, and pushes us to think more seriously about their participation in diplomatic culture. The micro social analysis performed on Bouhéreau's diary enables us to gain a better understanding of multiple dimensions of women's lives in the late seventeenth century, and underlines the need for further research on the topic in other courts, regions, and (inter)national contexts.

Managing money in early modern Ireland: the financial accounting of Élie Bouhéreau, 1689–1717

CHARLES IVAR McGRATH

This chapter seeks to address the day-to-day management of money in Ireland in the late seventeenth and early eighteenth centuries. It will do so by examining the diary and account book of Élie Bouhéreau, which provides detailed information on his financial activity from 1689 through 1717. As a French Protestant exile living in Ireland and working as keeper of Marsh's Library, Bouhéreau first and foremost looked to provide for his refugee family, yet he also acted as an international financial manager for a number of his fellow exiles in Ireland, England, Holland, and elsewhere. Thus it was that from the local, personal and private to the world of international money exchange, people's lives were itemized in these day-to-day financial transactions recorded by Bouhéreau, including the experiences of those who were religious exiles and who were trying to survive in foreign lands. Bouhéreau's diary and account book therefore lays bare the complexities of how early modern financial practices including domestic economy, church economics, and international financial exchange rates impacted directly upon private individuals who first and foremost were occupied in looking to negotiate their own financial survival.

I

Bouhéreau commenced his diary in 1689, and over the ensuing years up to 1704 he recorded a great deal of his financial activity within his diary entries. However, as stated in the introduction to the account book section in the Irish Manuscripts Commission's 2019 edition of the diary and accounts, he only started his system of accounting in his account book on 25 March 1704. The evidence from the diary indicates that prior to that time he kept records of his financial transactions on 'loose sheets' and a 'separate book' for his 'personal accounts'.[1]

The extant account book follows a simple system, with receipts on the left-hand page and payments on the right-hand page. The notebook itself was lined in five columns of varying width, for accounting purposes. Each entry provides

[1] Marie Léoutre, Jane McKee, Jean-Paul Pittion and Amy Prendergast (eds), *The diary (1689–1719) and accounts (1704–1717) of Élie Bouhéreau: Marsh's Library Z2.2.2* (Dublin,

the date in the left-hand column, a description of the source of income or purpose of expenditure in the second and widest column, and then the amount of money received or spent in the three right-hand columns, with pounds, shillings and pence each in a column of their own.[2] As is usual, and is evident in other similar accounts books in the early modern period, receipts accounted for a lot fewer entries than payments, which could leave a significant blank space on the bottom half of the left-hand page.[3]

For Bouhéreau, this physical constraint of paper-size resulted in the accounting periods being of varied durations rather than annual, half-yearly or quarterly. Instead, his accounting periods were payment-volume orientated, delineated by the number of payments that could be recorded on the right-hand page. Hence the first full accounting period was from 1 September 1704 to 12 February 1705.[4] Then, in a paper-saving exercise, from the accounting period for 1 August 1705 to 1 January 1706 onwards, Bouhéreau started to carry over his subtotal from the bottom of the right-hand page of payments and thereafter enter any remaining payments for the latter part of each accounting period beneath the final receipt and payment balances for that period on the left-hand page. For the unsuspecting reader, it could result in significant confusion with later receipt dates being followed by earlier payment dates.[5] A further complicating factor arose from the fact that a number of pages are missing from the original manuscript, which has resulted in two consecutive accounting periods, from 4 November 1708 to 28 February 1709 and from 28 February 1709 to 11 November 1709, being rendered incomplete. The same issue arises from 25 March 1716 to an unknown date before Bouhéreau's death.[6]

It is also the case that the first one or two pages of the account book are missing. Hence the first, though incomplete, period of accounts covers 1 June 1704 to 1 September 1704. We only have the payments for this period, though it

---

2019), pp 331 and 391. 2 With regard to the lined pages, it is of note that Bouhéreau actually was using the notebook upside-down for the diary section and the right way up for the accounts, given the requirement for three narrower columns on the right-hand side of each page for recording old-style pounds, shillings and pence. 3 Marsh's Library, Dublin, MS Z2.2.2. The diary (1689–1729) and accounts (1704–14) of Élie Bouhéreau, 'Accounts', 1 Sept. 1704–12 Feb. 1705, pp 2–3; Léoutre et al., *Diary and accounts*, pp xii and 391. [Editors' note: the author has elected to cite both the manuscript accounts and the print edition thereof, in different places throughout this chapter. The manuscript will hereafter be referred to as Marsh's Library, MS Z2.2.2, and the print edition as Léoutre et al., *Diary and accounts*.] For similar accounting practices in the early modern period see Fiona Pogson, 'Financial accounts of Thomas Wentworth, earl of Strafford, and Sir George Radcliffe, 1639–40', *Analecta Hibernica*, 48 (2017), 93 and 98–100; Brian Mac Cuarta, 'Sir Barnaby O'Brien's Irish revenues for 1629–31, Thomond rent, 1629, and Carlow tenants 1639', *Analecta Hibernica*, 48 (2017), 41–2 and 45; Brigid Clesham, Edward King and John Bergin, 'Cong Abbey estate papers (1608–1756) and the Catholic families of Tasburgh, Lynch and Macnamara', *Archivium Hibernicum*, 73 (2020), 187–211. 4 Marsh's Library, MS Z2.2.2, pp 2–3; Léoutre et al., *Diary and accounts*, pp 396–9. 5 Marsh's Library, MS Z2.2.2, pp 6–7. 6 Léoutre et al., *Diary and accounts*, p. 393.

is still very revealing of two themes relating to early modern financial practices that emerge from the account book and diary.

The first theme is to do with domestic life and the running of the household, while the second is with regard to personal financial management transactions. With regard to the former, it is of course the most obvious or expected theme to emerge in a private diary and account book, but the detailing of household expenses provides a window into the realities of daily life for the family of a well-educated man of professional status in early modern Dublin.

The second theme however is less expected, as it involved Bouhéreau acting as a financial manager or proto-banker for a range of people. At a time when private banks were only beginning to emerge in Ireland, the services associated with such institutions tended to be provided by other professionals with sufficient financial resources and international networks, such as goldsmiths and merchants. It was more unusual to find other individuals acting in that capacity, but it was possible for Bouhéreau to do so because of the existence of the Protestant exile network to which he belonged.[7]

The discussion hereafter of both themes aims to gives a sense of the financial content of the diary and account book, while also looking to highlight some aspects of the second theme which take us beyond the more traditional domestic concerns of a private individual in his financial accounting, most particularly with regard to the methods for the movement of money internationally at that time.

II

Matters of classical economy – of running the household – loom large from the outset in Bouhéreau's account book. The figures recorded, the money expended, and the items purchased tell us the story of a closely-knit exile family of moderate but comfortable means, with an income sufficient to allow them to live with some degree of luxury and refinement while also indulging in occasional charitable giving.[8] The very first entry on 2 June 1704 was for £5 paid to Bouhéreau's eldest daughter, Marguérite, for a month's household expenditure. Soon after, on 9 June, he provided a further £3 12s. to his daughter for coal, but the amount was to be deducted in instalments from the ensuing monthly household allowances. Accordingly, at the beginning of July 8s. was deducted

---

7 In that regard see Marie Léoutre, 'Financial networks and the payment of military pensions, 1692–1720' in Vivienne Larminie (ed.), *Huguenot networks, 1560–1780: the interactions and impact of a Protestant minority in Europe* (New York, 2017), pp 173–85.   8 As detailed in the final section of this chapter, Bouhéreau's annual income as keeper was *c.*£200, which was equivalent to that of one of the more lucrative or valuable Church of Ireland clerical livings or benefices. See Toby Barnard, *A new anatomy of Ireland: the Irish Protestants, 1649–1770* (London, 2003), pp 83–7. For examples of Bouhéreau's charitable giving, see Léoutre et al.,

from the monthly £5 allowance to Marguérite, with a view to paying off the cost of the coal over the following nine months. However, the accounts were balanced slightly sooner, with the remaining £1 4s. deducted out of the January 1705 allowance.[9]

Bouhéreau had explained the commencement of the monthly payment of £5 for household expenses on the grounds that 'My eldest daughter and I stopped accounting our past expenditure, as we were obliged to cover extraordinary expenses due to circumstances. I take responsibility for dealing with what was owed up to the end of May'.[10] The extraordinary expenses seem to have been related to the death of Bouhéreau's wife, Marguérite, on 22 May 'after a long and painful illness'. The following day, her body 'was laid in the French church of St Patrick's', in the same place where Bouhéreau's mother, Blandine, was laid in 1700 'beneath the communion table'. This was in reference to the Lady Chapel in St Patrick's Cathedral, where the French conformist community in Dublin worshiped.[11] The various extraordinary expenses related to the costs of the funeral. On 17 June Bouhéreau paid £3 14s. to his eldest son, Richard, 'towards funeral expenses'. A further £4 6s. was paid on 20 June to his son-in-law, Jean Jourdan – a refugee clergyman married to Bouhéreau's second daughter, Blandine – in the form of 'four *Louis d'or*, towards funeral expenses, and twelve shillings to clothe Henry', Jourdan's son, who had been named after his godfather, Henri de Massue de Ruvigny, earl of Galway.[12] From the evidence available, it would seem that these funeral expenses were not excessive. Nor was it unusual for the head of the family to cover these costs from their own financial resources.[13]

Almost a month on from the funeral, Bouhéreau and 'most of my family' travelled to the house of Blandine and Jean Jourdan in Dunshauglin to stay for a week. The cost of the travel, by coach, came to 10s. The return journey was made in the company of Louis Quartier, minister of the French church of St. Patrick's, and his wife, Marguérite, Bouhéreau's eldest daughter.[14]

Other one-off or occasional additional personal or family costs made at that time included £4 10s. on 7 June to Mr Bradshaw 'pour du Drap' (for some cloth) and a further £1 5s. 10d. to the tailor and dyer 'to settle outstanding bills' as well as 18s. 6d. on 10 June to Mr Forcade, 'for some wine'.[15] It is not evident if these costs also related to the funeral, or whether they were just part of wider domestic activity. Either way, we can start to build a picture very quickly of the

---

Diary and accounts, pp 405, 449, 451, and 485 and Marie Léoutre's chapter in this volume. **9** Léoutre et al., *Diary and accounts*, pp 395 and 401. **10** Ibid., p. 395. **11** Ibid., pp 321 and 333. **12** Ibid., p. 395. **13** See, for example, Barnard, *New anatomy*, pp 135 and 298; Raymond Gillespie, 'Funerals and society in early seventeenth-century Ireland', *Journal of the Royal Society of Antiquaries of Ireland*, 115 (1985), 86–91; Patricia Lysaght, 'Hospitality at wakes and funerals in Ireland from the seventeenth to the nineteenth century: some evidence from the written record', *Folklore*, 114:3 (Dec. 2003), 403–26. **14** Léoutre et al., *Diary and accounts*, pp 332–3 and 395. **15** Ibid., pp 394–5.

9.1 The first extant page of Elie Bouhéreau's accounts, listing personal payments, as well as management of funds on behalf of his wide Huguenot network. Marsh's Library, Dublin, MS Z2.2.2. The diary (1689–1719) and accounts (1704–14) of Élie Bouhéreau, 'Accounts', fo. 1. By permission of the Governors and Guardians of Marsh's Library.

domestic or home life of the first keeper of Marsh's Library and his family, living in Augustan Dublin, and we can start to analyse the nature of the early modern economy of the household.

In that regard, it is of note that Marguérite, the eldest daughter, although married herself and soon to be a mother, was responsible for running Bouhéreau's home. Appointed as keeper in May 1701, in December 1703 Bouhéreau had moved his family into the newly constructed and spacious lodgings provided on St Patrick's Close for the holder of that office. The fact that Marguérite's husband, Louis Quartier, was the minister of the French church in St Patrick's Cathedral beside the family residence presumably lent itself either to the concept of the household-family living in the same quarters or to Marguérite managing two households close to each other.[16] Whichever the circumstance, Marguérite clearly was performing the traditional role of the female housekeeper, which for a widower could readily be undertaken by a 'kinswoman', who in this instance happened to be Bouhéreau's eldest daughter.[17]

III

Interspersed with the day-to-day expenses of running the Bouhéreau household are the transactions of Bouhéreau the financial manager or proto-banker. The second entry for 2 June 1704 was for '£400 to my Lord Galway, in the form of bills of exchange payable in London. It is at a rate of 7 per cent', and accounted for a total of £428.[18] Bouhéreau had been closely connected with Galway since 1693, when he was employed as the latter's secretary when Galway was sent by William III to command the British forces in Piedmont serving on behalf of William's ally, the duke of Savoy.[19]

In arranging the June 1704 payment for Galway, Bouhéreau was acting as a financial manager, a role he fulfilled more generally in support of the wide network of the French Protestant exile community. In that same month alone we can see further examples of Bouhéreau's financial management for that network.

On 3 June, Bouhéreau paid £3 10s. 'of England to Mr de La Bouchetiére, by order of Mr Boyer', which amounted to £3 15s. 10d. This was Paul De la Roque Boyer, another refugee minister who had received his passport to go to Holland and then England in May 1691 from Bouhéreau in his capacity as secretary to the English envoy to the Swiss cantons, Thomas Coxe, stationed at that time in Bern.[20]

---

16 Ibid., pp xv, 327, 329, 333 and 401. 17 Naomi Tadmor, 'The concept of the household-family in eighteenth-century England', *Past & Present*, 151 (May 1996), 117–18, and 138.
18 Léoutre et al., *Diary and accounts*, pp 394–5. 19 Léoutre, 'Financial networks', p. 175.
20 Léoutre et al., *Diary and accounts*, p. 395.

Then on 15 June Bouhéreau paid 'to Mr Delpy, for the benefit of the marquis d'Arselliers', £7 2s. 3d. This was Gaspar Perrinet, marquis d'Arsellières, who appears on several occasions in Bouhéreau's diary as part of the group travelling on the Continent in 1689–90 as part of Coxe's entourage.[21]

All of these names can be found among the lists of French pensioners on the Irish Establishment – the formal or official documentation detailing the annual cost or charge of government in Ireland. The French pensioners were exiled Huguenots who had served William III during the war of the Grand Alliance in various theatres of war, including Ireland. After the Irish war of 1689–91, the first cohort of demobilized and invalided Huguenot soldiers were given pensions on the Irish Military Establishment, paid for out of the Irish treasury.[22] In 1692 the total amount for that purpose was £6,120,[23] and by 1698 it had risen with occasional additions of more men to £7,770.[24] Then, following the end of the war of the Grand Alliance in 1697, five Huguenot regiments were transported to Ireland as part of William's plan to maintain as much of his standing army as he could in preparedness for renewal of war with France. The Westminster parliament had other plans, however, and as part of the drive of English MPs to reduce William's forces to a bare minimum, the Huguenot regiments were ordered to disband in late 1698. As a result, these men, set adrift in Ireland, were added to the Irish Establishment of French Pensions. Thus in August 1699 when a revised establishment was implemented, it included the significantly increased sum of £25,830 for more than 600 French pensioners, whom had all been moved to what was termed the Civil List, the transfer occurring in part because the Military List had already been inflated by the addition of £21,572 for other half-pay disbanded officers. William III's sense of obligation to the Huguenot regiments was a significant factor in this provision made for them from Irish tax revenue.[25]

IV

The brief excursion above into two themes arising during the first accounting period in the account book from June to September 1704 demonstrates the variety of payments being made by Bouhéreau and the fact that his financial activities were not solely those of the average private individual. Bouhéreau's total payments for this first period of accounting was the sum of £513 8s. He also had a carry-over balance on his receipts for the period of £309 1s. 6d. These were

21 Ibid., p. 395.   22 Marie Léoutre, *Serving France, Ireland and England: Ruvigny, earl of Galway, 1648–1720* (London, 2018), pp 131–4.   23 British Library, Add. MS 4761. An account of the money due to the Civil and Military Lists according to the Establishment for Ireland from 1 Jan. 1691[2] to 25 March 1694, fo. 246.   24 *Calendar of State Papers, Domestic, 1698*, p. 440; *Calendar of Treasury Books, 1698*, pp 141–3.   25 Charles Ivar McGrath, *The making of the eighteenth-century Irish constitution: government, parliament and the revenue,*

substantial sums. So where did the money come from? In looking to answer that question, the most fruitful avenue of exploration is the second theme regarding Bouhéreau's management of the financial affairs of the Protestant exile community.

For the period 1 September 1704 to 12 February 1705, the two most substantial receipts were each for £238 4s. on 12 October 1704 and 31 January 1705.[26] These were both paid from the Irish treasury, and were quarterly instalments of Galway's £1,000 per annum pension on the Irish Establishment.[27]

The next largest sum received by Bouhéreau in the period September 1704 to February 1705 was £100 received from a Mr Gallet. In total, Bouhéreau's receipts for this period were £1,029 16s. 5d., inclusive of the carried over balance, in a period of just over five months.[28]

But clearly this money was not at Bouhéreau's personal disposal. With Galway's pension, the money was soon transmitted overseas to Galway himself or dispersed in other ways to meet his various financial commitments. On 1 September £268 was given to Gallet for Galway – the very same day Gallet had given £100 to Bouhéreau. This latter sum would appear to have been a loan, on which Bouhéreau paid interest of 8 per cent, as evidenced by an entry on 10 September 1705, one year later, when he recorded that he paid Gallet 'for the interest of a hundred *pièces*' or pounds sterling. The same amount of interest was paid again in November 1706, and again on 5 September 1707 which was the last time such interest, or any payments of any kind, were made to Gallet.[29]

Bouhéreau also acted for other Huguenot exiles in similar fashion. In the same September 1704 to February 1705 accounting period, he received two payments from 'Mr Des Brisay' totalling £32 15s. 11d. for d'Arsellières, who was in receipt of a French pension of £109 10s. per annum on the Irish Civil List.[30] Captain Theophilus Desbrisay was a French pensioner himself,[31] but also acted for the other pensioners as an agent – a financial go-between or middle-man with the treasury. Hence the vast majority of d'Arsellières financial transactions in Bouhéreau's accounts were handled by Desbrisay.[32] Like a number of other exiled Huguenot families, the Desbrisays became significant players in Dublin life and Irish financial circles in the first half of the eighteenth century. Theophilus died in 1722, but his son and namesake went on to be one of the leading army regimental agents in the country, looking after the financial affairs

---

1692–1714 (Dublin, 2000), p. 66.   **26** Léoutre et al., *Diary and accounts*, p. 399.   **27** *The journals of the House of Commons of the kingdom of Ireland*, 3rd ed., 21 vols (Dublin, 1796–1800), ii, appendix, p. cxx. The quarterly amounts received by Bouhéreau with regard to all pension payments from the Irish treasury were always net amounts, having already had treasury fees deducted.   **28** Léoutre et al., *Diary and accounts*, pp 397–9.   **29** Ibid., pp 397, 411, 427 and 435.   **30** *Calendar of Treasury Books, 1700–1*, p. 437.   **31** *Calendar of Treasury Books, 1699*, p. 144.   **32** National Archives of Ireland, Dublin, Frazer MSS 10. Minute book of the committee of public accounts, 1703–17, Capt. Theo[philus]. Desbrisay, agent to the French

of as many as ten regiments stationed in Ireland in the 1740s, though he eventually went bankrupt in 1767.[33]

As before, the money received by Bouhéreau for d'Arsellières was transferred quickly. On 2 September 1704 he paid £60, 14*s*. 8*d*. to the Dublin-based Huguenot merchant, Pierre Vatable, 'for the benefit of' d'Arsellières.[34]

While continuing to receive the payments outlined above for Galway, d'Arsellières and others, later receipts show other sources of income for a variety of people. On 27 April 1705 Bouhéreau 'received from the customs, for my Lord Galway' £11 9*s*. The same amount was received from the same source on 14 January 1706 and on 4 January and 31 December 1707. This was an ongoing payment for Galway, and was later described as a wine licence, which appears to have been granted on an order of the Irish Privy Council in December 1705, for the same amount as the existing income from unspecified customs duties paid since April 1705.[35]

V

As highlighted at the outset, all of this movement of money begs a further question regarding how and in what forms did the money move about. What were the various media of exchange?

Ireland, like many other countries at the time, suffered from a scarcity of coinage or ready specie because of the fact that the creation of, and access to, gold and silver coin had very evident, real and obviously finite limitations. But as a subordinate and dependent sister kingdom of England, the shortage of coin in Ireland appeared to be more acute than elsewhere, not least because it was deemed inappropriate, for constitutional reasons, for the country to have its own mint or coinage. Therefore Ireland was dependent upon export trade for bringing new coin into the kingdom, but this was counter-balanced by a sizable import trade which resulted in much of that coin leaving the country again, alongside that going out for absentee rents, salaries and pensions.[36]

The most significant shortages were in the area of small silver coin, though problems existed for gold and copper as well. The coinage in circulation in Ireland was made up from English silver coins and guineas, and continental gold coin as follows: *Louis d'ors*, pistoles, double pistoles, doubloons, and moidores. There was little or no continental silver, and the English silver that existed was

pensioners, 1717 [unfoliated]). **33** A.P.W. Malcomson, *Nathaniel Clements: government and the governing elite in Ireland, 1725–75* (Dublin, 2005), pp 125, and 144–6. **34** Léoutre et al., *Diary and accounts*, p. 399; Léoutre, 'Financial networks', p. 180. **35** Léoutre et al., *Diary and accounts*, pp 403, 415, 423, 437 and 455. **36** C.I. McGrath, 'Banks, paper currency and the fiscal state: the case of Ireland, stated, 1660–1783' in Aaron Graham and Patrick Walsh (eds), *The British fiscal-military states, 1660–c.1783* (Abingdon, 2016), pp 38–9.

constantly taken out of the country by bankers and merchants because of the favourable exchange they received in England for silver over gold. The crux of the exchange problem lay in the fact that in Ireland the value of all coins had over time been raised above their intrinsic value, with gold and silver ceasing to bear an equal proportion to each other.[37]

So when people talked of Irish pounds, shillings and pence, they meant a money of account, which in fact was made up of a hotch-potch of coins from various countries. The rate of exchange with English sterling was set by statute and proclamation, and from 1701 onwards for the rest of the eighteenth century it was officially set at £108 6s. 6d. Irish to £100 English. In reality, fluctuations occurred depending on the demands of overseas trade.[38]

Not surprisingly, therefore, alternative forms of currency were not new to Ireland in the late seventeenth century, as, like elsewhere, shortage of specie saw innovations among local entrepreneurs, be it the issuing of tokens[39] or the long-standing merchant practice of using letters or bills of exchange.[40] During the Restoration period in the 1660s and 1670s, goldsmith bankers and their paper receipts became a new and more user-friendly credit alternative to the medieval statute-staple. Merchants also entered the private banker market, providing much needed credit for remittance of rents, exchange with London, and other transactions. But the real explosion in private banking occurred following the Glorious Revolution of 1689, best exemplified by the establishment in the later 1690s of Dublin's first major private bank by Benjamin Burton and Francis Harrison, merchants from a landed background who were at the heart of the rapid escalation in the circulation of private bankers' notes throughout Ireland in the 1690s and thereafter. It is notable however that their bank only appears for three transactions in Bouhéreau's account book, all in June 1705, perhaps demonstrating that private banks were still in their infancy in Ireland and that merchants still dominated exchange activities.[41]

All of these concerns can be seen in Bouhéreau's various financial transactions in the diary and account book. In the summer of 1697 he moved from England to Ireland, taking up the role of secretary to Galway, who had been appointed to the commission of the lords justices for the government of Ireland. Bouhéreau's diary thereafter details his activities on behalf of other exiles who were in receipt of French pensions on the Irish Establishment.

---

37 C.I. McGrath, 'The Irish experience of "financial revolution" 1660–1760' in Chris Fauske and C.I. McGrath (eds), *Money, power and print: interdisciplinary studies on the financial revolution in the British Isles* (Newark, 2008), pp 171–3.   38 Thomas M. Truxes, *Irish-American trade, 1660–1783* (New York, 1989), p. 297.   39 Sir William Petty, *A treatise of taxes and contributions* (London, 1662), p. 65.   40 L.M. Cullen, *Anglo-Irish trade 1660–1800* (New York, 1968), pp 98–101 and 170–3; Mac Cuarta, 'Barnaby O'Brien', pp 39–40.   41 See in general Patrick Walsh, *The South Sea bubble and Ireland: money, banking and investment, 1690–1721* (Woodbridge, 2014), pp 46–53. See also Rowena Dudley, 'The failure of Burton's Bank and its aftermath', *Irish Economic and Social History*, 40 (2013), 2–4; Stephen Quinn,

One of the first to be encountered was Phillipe de La Basoge, a brother-in-law of Bouhéreau's old friend, Jacques Richier de Cerisy.[42] La Basoge had served as a cornet in Galway's regiment in Ireland during the war of 1689–91 and, having been wounded, was granted an Irish pension in January 1692. Later that year he moved to Holland, thereby instigating the need for a more complex process for payment of his pension.[43]

Marie Léoutre has detailed the complex process by which Bouhéreau managed La Basoge's pension on the basis of the multiple entries in the diary and account book in that regard. In summary, during November–December 1697 Bouhéreau worked with a Dublin-based Huguenot merchant, Paul Augier, to calculate what was owed to La Basoge on his pension which, as was common in the 1690s, was in serious arrears. In total, Augier paid £85 17s. to Bouhéreau for La Basoge. This was a net amount, after deduction of the not insignificant sum of £16 19s. 10d. in agent's and exchequer fees and licences for making payments to pensioners living outside Ireland. Bouhéreau then arranged for payment of a debt of £8 owed by La Basoge to Isaac Sigart, a Rotterdam merchant, by giving that sum to a Dublin-based Huguenot merchant, Jean Haÿs, who in turn passed it on to Sigart. Then, when a favourable exchange rate arose in April 1698, Bouhéreau organized for the remaining £77 17s. Irish currency to be sent to La Basoge. Bouhéreau did so by getting a letter of exchange for £66 16s. 6d. English sterling from Sir John Rogerson, a former mayor of Dublin, Irish MP, merchant and property developer. On instructions from Richier de Cerisy, Bouhéreau then gave the letter of exchange to a Captain de Coulombiére, who in turn sent it to London to his cousin Madame de Dobrzensky, the wife of the envoy of Brandenburg. She in turn was to take the letter of exchange to John Ward, a London merchant, to receive the actual sterling sum in ready specie.[44]

So it was that La Basoge's pension payment relied upon a chain of people to get the money to him in Holland: an army captain in Dublin took possession of a Dublin merchant's letter of exchange payable by a business associate in London; the army captain delivered the letter of exchange to an envoy's wife in London; and the envoy's wife redeemed it with the London merchant and then delivered the money to La Basoge. It is only this last step that we have no record of. But as is evident, a network of merchants, family members and Protestant refugees all made the complex process possible, and at its centre was Bouhéreau acting as an international financial manager for his fellow religious exiles.

And what did Bouhéreau get from it all? It is not evident in the diary or account book as to whether or not Bouhéreau took or was paid any fee for his role

---

'Balances and gold-smith bankers: the co-ordination and control of inter-banker debt clearing in seventeenth-century London' in David Mitchell (ed.), *Goldsmiths, silversmiths and bankers: innovation and the transfer of skill, 1550 to 1750* (London, 1995), pp 53–76.   42 Léoutre et al., *Diary and accounts*, p. 177.   43 Léoutre, 'Financial networks', pp 175–6.   44 Ibid., pp 176–81. See also *Diary and accounts*, pp 307–11; Daniel Beaumont, 'Rogerson, Sir John I' in

in the transaction process. Instead, there seems to have been a reciprocity offered within the Protestant exile community. Most immediately, in October 1698 La Basoge acted on Bouhéreau's behalf in collecting 146 florins and 6 sols owed to Bouhéreau from Rotterdam lottery tickets he and his wife had previously bought. Amounting in total to £14 12s. 8d. in Irish currency, when combined with another debt for three barrels of butter Bouhéreau had sent to Richier de Cerisy's wife, in total Bouhéreau was owed £20 7s. 7d. The simplest solution therefore was for Bouhéreau to deduct that amount from a further £26 he had received from La Basoge's pension. An added attraction of this process was that no money actually had to change hands or be moved anywhere for the debt to be settled, thereby avoiding possible theft as well as any additional charges, fees or rates of exchange.[45]

What can we learn from these transactions? The very significant pay arrears on the Irish Establishment in the 1690s, and recurring periods of serious arrears thereafter, provided money-making opportunities for regimental and other agents to advance cash to those whose pay was in arrears, but at a price, even if that price was negotiable.[46] The cost of exchange from Ireland to elsewhere further reduced people's incomes and made money for others, and was dependent upon merchant or banker networks where bills or letters of exchange could be honoured in hard currency in London or elsewhere. But like agents' fees, better rates could be found if you shopped around. Also, living outside of Ireland came at a cost in terms of licences for Irish pension payments to be sent abroad. And money could be moved in a variety of ways, including agents, go-betweens, relatives, friends, and family – or accounts could be balanced without money moving at all, as with the debt to Bouhéreau.

In light of such matters, it is not surprising that exchange rates and varied methods of paper transmission arose with great regularity in Bouhéreau's diary and accounts. From early in the accounts up to 1707, Thomas Putland, a Dublin merchant and landowner, was a primary source of bills of exchange for London. The rates he charged varied: in October 1705 a bill of exchange of £205 6s. was charged at a rate of eight-and-a-half per cent, costing £222 15s.; nine months later, in July 1706, Putland's rate had dropped to seven-and-a-half per cent, thereby costing £271 16s. for two bills of exchange for a total of £252 17s. In both instances the money was ultimately payable in London to Boyer for the benefit of Galway and d'Arsellières and, in 1706, of La Basoge also.[47]

On other occasions, money was transmitted by '*billets*' or 'notes' – in some form or other a promissory or non-legal-tender bank note. Certainly it appeared to be a less formal or official promissory note that was referred to on 24 April

---

Dictionary of Irish biography, https://www.dib.ie, accessed 5 July 2024.   45 Léoutre, 'Financial networks', p. 178; Léoutre et al., *Diary and accounts*, pp 313–15.   46 For pay arrears see McGrath, *Irish constitution*, pp 49–72.   47 Léoutre et al., *Diary and accounts*, pp 412–13 and 421.

1707 when Bouhéreau's son-in-law, Quartier, asked him to collect on his behalf 'un billet de' £12 6*d*. However, when Bouhéreau received £233 in May 1711 for Galway in '*billets*' or 'notes' from the Dublin-based Huguenot merchant Théodore Raboteau, who had in turn received them from the Irish treasury, it was more likely that the money came in some form of bank or treasury note or tallies.[48]

Raboteau appears in the account book early on, but became a more regular feature from early 1709 onwards, with his name turning up regularly thereafter as a primary provider of various means of transmitting money. In July 1709 Bouhéreau sent a bill of exchange for £106 15*s*. 8*d*. to London, provided by Raboteau for £115 13*s*. 8*d*.; in November 1710 he sent another for £168 18*s*. purchased for £182 19*s*. 5*d*.; and in March 1711 he sent another for 1,100 écus, valued at £275 sterling, and bought for £297 18*s*. 4*d*. Irish. In the interim, Raboteau had also provided Bouhéreau with a more modest letter of credit for his eldest son, Richard, for £20 in September 1710.[49]

Raboteau's network for facilitating such movement of money included his cousin, Jean Raboteau in London, who purchased for Bouhéreau £200 worth of English government lottery tickets in December 1712. The tickets were sold at £10 each, plus 2*s*. commission per ticket. As has already been seen, Bouhéreau was not averse to investing in government debt, and in March 1713 he received £9 12*s*. from Jean Raboteau for a year's interest on £160 worth of tickets he had bought in the 1711 royal lottery.[50]

VI

The various sums Bouhéreau earned from all of his transactions as a financial manager were not however sufficient in themselves to sustain himself and his family. So, as a final consideration, the question also arises as to what money in the accounts actually belonged to Bouhéreau?

On 17 October 1704 and 27 January 1705 Bouhéreau received two quarterly instalments of a pension payable to him from the Irish treasury, amounting on both occasions to £48 10*s*.[51] These payments were quarterly instalments of an annual pension of £200 on the Irish Civil List granted in June 1701 in order to cover his salary as keeper of Marsh's Library. The pension was to cease once the position of either treasurer or precentor of St Patrick's Cathedral became vacant, a situation which did not occur until November 1708 following the death of the incumbent of the latter office, Samuel Synge, dean of Kildare.[52] The income

---

48 Ibid., pp 431 and 471. For Raboteau, see Léoutre, 'Financial networks', p. 180.
49 Léoutre et al., *Diary and accounts*, pp 453, 463, 469 and 471.   50 Ibid., pp 495–7, 499. For Jean Raboteau, see Léoutre, 'Financial networks', p. 180.   51 Léoutre et al., *Diary and accounts*, p. 399.   52 *Calendar of Treasury Books, 1700–1*, pp 282–3; David Hayton, 'Clerical opposition

from the precentorship was therefore likewise intended to cover Bouhéreau's salary as keeper, a provision which had been officially formalized in the 1707 Act of the Irish parliament for the establishment of the library.[53]

Bouhéreau was installed in the office of precentor in March 1709, and on 16 May recorded that he 'took the oaths again, at the queen's bench, further to my appointment as precentor of St Patrick's'.[54] As often happens in the diary, on this occasion Bouhéreau referenced other times upon which he had been required to take such oaths. As he explained, with reference to having taken the oaths on 19 May 1704, he was required to do so by an act of the Irish parliament: 'I took the oath requested by the latest parliament of Ireland at the court of common pleas, and I showed, and left there, a certificate that I received communion on Sunday, the 14th instant, in the parish church of St Nicolas Without Dublin.'[55] The legislation to which he was referring was the 1704 Act to Prevent the Further Growth of Popery, which had introduced to Ireland the 1702 Oath of Abjuration of the Stuart Pretender, which also included acknowledgment of the succession in the House of Hanover. All office holders were now required to take this new oath along with the Oath of Allegiance, New Oath of Supremacy and the Declaration against Transubstantiation. The 1704 act also introduced to Ireland the sacramental test as a requirement for all public office holders, whereby such individuals had to provide a certificate proving they had received the sacrament in accordance with the rites of the Church of Ireland – just as Bouhéreau had done in 1704.[56]

It was because he continued to conform in such a manner that Bouhéreau could receive the incomes of his new office from March 1709 onwards. However, the new source of income is not immediately evident in the account book, owing to the fact that the receipts for September 1708 to February 1709 are incomplete, while those for March to October 1709 are not extant. However, in the next fully extant set of receipts for 11 November 1709 to 4 September 1710 there is a notable alteration in terms of Bouhéreau's income. One of the first receipts, on 24 November 1709, was £15 from Marmaduke Coghill, 'for the half year [rent] due on last St Michaelmas day'. This was followed by further rent payments, as follows: of £18 on 25 November from 'Mr. Brand ... for a year ... on houses'; of £21 5s. on 9 December from Mr Pooley for a half year; of £35 on 10 January 1710 and of £20 on 13 March for a year's rent, both from Mr Thornton; of £9

---

to the statutory establishment of Marsh's Library in 1707: a case-study in Irish ecclesiastical politics in the reign of Queen Anne' in Muriel McCarthy and Ann Simmons (eds), *The making of Marsh's Library: learning, politics and religion in Ireland, 1650–1750* (Dublin, 2004), pp 164–6; Léoutre et al., *Diary and accounts*, p. 357.   53 Muriel McCarthy, *Marsh's Library, Dublin: all graduates and gentlemen* (2nd ed., Dublin, 2003), pp 43–5 and fn. 11.   54 Léoutre et al., *Diary and accounts*, p. 361.   55 Ibid., p. 331. The church of St Nicholas of Myra is on Francis Street in the Dublin Liberties, hence it was referred to as 'Without' the medieval city limits.   56 *The statutes at large passed in the parliaments held in Ireland*, 21 vols (Dublin, 1765–1804), iv, 21–2.

on 10 June from Mr Brand; of £12 on 13 June from Mr Parry 'for a year and a half ... on houses'; of £18 on 15 June from 'Mr Higgins, for Ardree, a year and a half'; of £10 on 24 June from Mr Brand for a half year's rent; of £21 5s. on 30 June from Mr Pooley for a half year's rent; of £14 on 11 July from Coghill, 'for the half year'; and a further £35 from Thornton on 12 August. In total, these payments amount to £228 10s. It is possible that £70 from Brand was for other unspecified reasons other than rent, so the rental income may have been £158 10s.[57] All of these rents appear to derive from the position of precentor of St Patrick's, which included the prebend of Lusk and the patronage of, and presumably income from, two Dublin churches.[58] In that latter regard, other receipts in the same accounting period included on 6 December 1709 and 21 April 1710 the payments of £2 'for a half year' on each occasion from the dean of St Patrick's and on 16 March 1710 of £10 from 'Dr Travers, for a year of the returns from ten pieces ... which he pays by half years, as minister of St Andrew's'.[59]

However, as Nial Osborough has pointed out, the precentorship had come to Bouhéreau with a debt obligation of about £240 owed for building work undertaken by Synge when he was precentor. As a consequence, and with the assistance once again of Galway, Bouhéreau successfully petitioned to have his pension on the Irish Civil List continued for a further two years in order to be able to meet these debts.[60] Thus in the account book his quarterly payments from the pension continued until March 1711.[61]

As was evident, the precentorship was not just a source of income – it also came with overheads. Nor surprisingly, these costs were also detailed in the account book. On 7 July 1710 Bouhéreau paid £10 15s. 11d. 'for the second term of the first fruits'.[62] There is no evidence of when the first term was paid, but the final payment was made on 8 June 1711, for the amount of £19 11s. 9d. We do not know what the full cost was to Bouhéreau, but the first fruits were a once-off tax to be paid by the appointee for the full value of the first year's income of any clerical office. On 6 June 1711 he also recorded that he paid £1 19s. 4d. 'for the twentieth parts', which was an annual tax on clerical offices to the value of 5 per cent of the annual income of any such post. The payment made by Bouhéreau could therefore not have been the full tax owed. The smallness of the amount was tied in with the fact that it coincided with the governmental decision to remit payment of twentieth parts, and to grant the income from first fruits back to the Church of Ireland for its own use.[63] Hence the twentieth parts do not re-appear in Bouhéreau's account book thereafter.

---

57 Léoutre et al., *Diary and accounts*, pp 455 and 457.   58 W.N. Osborough, 'Anne, chapter 19: "settling and preserving a public library forever"' in M. McCarthy and A. Simmons (eds), *Marsh's Library: a mirror on the world: law, learning and libraries* (Dublin, 2009), p. 56.   59 Léoutre et al., *Diary and accounts*, pp 455 and 457.   60 Osborough, 'Anne, chapter 19', pp 53–7.   61 Léoutre et al., *Diary and accounts*, p. 465.   62 Ibid., p. 461.   63 McGrath, *Irish*

Such tax-relief did not remove all the costs of office, however. In March 1709 Bouhéreau had paid two guineas (or £2 6s.) to the choir of St Patrick's, 'upon entering into my employ', and in April a further £2 2s. 6d. 'for some expenses regarding my installation'. In August 1709 he had to pay £112 10s. to 'Mr Wilson, and Mr Vauteau, as precentor of St Patrick's', and on 5 April 1710 £4 10s. to 'Mr Worrall, for my vicar, as precentor of St Patrick's'. The following month he 'entrusted to the chief remembrancer' of the court of exchequer the sum of £80.[64] These larger amounts may have been tied in with the legacy debt the office came with.

However, despite the legacy debt, it is evident that the ongoing income from the precentorship was sufficient to maintain Bouhéreau and his family in the manner to which they had become accustomed. Given that his earlier government pension had been for £200 per annum and had been granted in order to replicate the intended income of the keeper of the library, it is safe to state that the annual income from the precentorship was of a similar amount. In that regard, it was equivalent to one of the better clerical livings and benefices of the Protestant clergy in Ireland.[65]

VII

This brief excursion into the Bouhéreau diary and account book hopefully helps to demonstrate the great value on a whole range of levels of this source for our understanding of the day-to-day management of money in Ireland in the late seventeenth and early eighteenth centuries – and of being a religious exile trying to survive in foreign lands. From the local to the international, people's lives were itemized in these quotidian financial transactions recorded by Bouhéreau, while the world of early modern financial practices was laid bare in the complex ways in which people had to negotiate their financial survival.

As Ruth Whelan has argued, 'there is nothing unusual' from an early modern perspective in Bouhéreau's account book being kept in the same book as his diary. As is evident, from the outset Bouhéreau had included much detail in the diary with regards to his finances, especially before 1704 and his decision to start working from the back in recording his financial accounts in a more formal fashion. As Whelan states, 'in the early modern period, diaries and *livres de raison* were often little more than account books, where to the daily reckoning of expenditure were added a few notes about the things or events that brought about that expenditure.' In that regard, she points out that Bouhéreau was 'saving experiences, events, good stories and family records in order to ensure

---

constitution, pp 33 and 250–1. **64** Léoutre et al., *Diary and accounts*, pp 451, 453, 459 and 461. **65** See Barnard, *New anatomy*, pp 83–7. For the keeper's salary, see Léoutre et al., *Diary and accounts*, p. xv.

they were not worn out of memory. It is also clear that his diary is a form of accounting, the adding up of life through incremental daily fragments until the summation of the whole becomes visible at the end.' In this he was accounting to himself, to his family, to all those present in the diary, and ultimately to God.[66] But he was also accounting to us in the here and now.

---

66 Ruth Whelan, 'Marsh's Library and the French Calvinist tradition: the manuscript diary of Élie Bouhéreau (1643–79)' in McCarthy and Simmons (eds), *The making of Marsh's Library*, pp 230–1.

Financial agent, secretary, protégé: Bouhéreau and the earl of Galway

MARIE LÉOUTRE

This chapter examines the relationship, spanning three decades, between two influential Huguenots who settled in Ireland at the end of the seventeenth century, Élie Bouhéreau and Henri de Massue de Ruvigny. Ruvigny had been the last *Député Général de la Religion Prétendue Réformée* – the representative of the Protestant minority at court – in France until the Revocation of the Edict of Nantes in 1685. He later became earl of Galway in the Irish peerage and a lord justice of Ireland, while his protégé, Élie Bouhéreau, had had a medical career in La Rochelle, and later became the first librarian of Marsh's Library in Dublin.

From 1693 Bouhéreau was secretary to Lord Galway, initially following him on the Continent during the war of the Grand Alliance, and from 1697 in Ireland. While Lord Galway was Bouhéreau's patron, Bouhéreau was more than just a secretary – he was Galway's financial agent, conducting personal and official business on his behalf. Piecing together the evidence scattered in several archives for the first time, this chapter allows a glimpse into eighteenth-century accountancy and transactions, a pan-European Huguenot network, and confirms the place of Lord Galway – with the help of Bouhéreau – as a leading figure of the Protestant International.

It explains some of the financial transactions Bouhéreau conducted on behalf of Galway, the significance of these within the Refuge, and the wider network they reveal. Of particular interest are the transactions that Bouhéreau undertook as part of Galway's philanthropic endeavours, supporting Huguenot refugee veterans, widows and orphans, in Ireland and beyond. Looking at how Bouhéreau and Galway ensured that refugees who had served in the armies of William III, and their dependants, received their pensions, provides a concrete example of how solidarity translated into a high level of transnational organization. Furthermore, through Bouhéreau's and Galway's papers, the human side of impoverished or vulnerable exiles appears – with some details of names, circumstances, cost of survival, as well as empathy and solidarity in the Refuge.

BOUHÉREAU AND GALWAY: THEIR RELATIONSHIP

The Ruvignies were originally from Picardie, but lived in Paris. This is where Henri, the future earl of Galway, was born in 1648.[1] Both he and his father, also called Henri, served Louis XIV in the military, as courtiers, as diplomats and as *Députés Généraux de la Religion Prétendue Réformée*, a post created in 1603 shortly after the Edict of Nantes was signed.[2] At the Revocation the Ruvignies were among the very few who were allowed to remain in France without having to convert, but they nonetheless chose exile to England in 1686.[3] The family had obtained letters of naturalization in 1681. This English connection had originated in 1634 when Rachel de Ruvigny married Thomas Wriothesley, fourth earl of Southampton, later Lord High Treasurer.[4]

The Bouhéreaus were from the Protestant stronghold of La Rochelle. The first marquis de Ruvigny had been present at the siege of La Rochelle in 1627, during the French Wars of Religion, but on the royalist side.[5] The port city is where Élie was born in 1643. After his studies at the *académie* of Saumur, Élie spent a few years in Paris in the early 1660s.[6] Both the first and second marquis de Ruvigny held the position of *Député Général* in the capital, and references from multiple correspondents going back to the early 1670s attest of connections between Ruvigny and Bouhéreau prior to the Refuge.[7]

Following the Revocation, both the Ruvignies and the Bouhéreaus settled in Greenwich, near London, in early 1686.[8] A refugee community formed around the Ruvignies in Greenwich. There has been a lot of controversy over the Ruvignies' role as *Députés Généraux* – with some accusations of their having relinquished their duty to protect their coreligionists – but it is clear that for many exiles the family was still their representative and leader.[9] Soon Bouhéreau was naturalized in England (in 1687) and became tutor to the children of the duchess of Monmouth, a post he held until 1689.[10] His next post was as secretary to Thomas Coxe, envoy extraordinary to the Swiss cantons during the war of the Grand Alliance.[11] He did not return to England until September 1692.

---

1 See Solange Deyon, *Du loyalisme au refus: les Protestants français et leur député général entre la Fronde et la Révocation* (Villeneuve-d'Ascq, 1976); Marie Léoutre, *Serving France, Ireland and England: Ruvigny, earl of Galway, 1648–1720* (New York, 2018).   2 Deyon, *Du loyalisme au refus*, chapter 1.   3 Ibid.   4 Léoutre, *Serving France, Ireland and England*, chapter 1. 5 Ibid.   6 Newport J.D. White and M. Léopold Delayant, 'Elias Bouhéreau of La Rochelle, first public librarian in Ireland', *Proceedings of the Royal Irish Academy*, 27C (1908–9), 126– 58.   7 Bouhéreau's correspondence makes it clear that some of his friends, including Guybert and Abraham Tessereau, were in direct contact with Ruvigny in the 1670s. See Marsh's Library, Dublin, Solon Baudouin (MS Z2.2.16 (8.11–13)), Louis de la Forest (MS Z2.2.12 (3.64)), and Louis Benion (MS Z2.2.14 (10.1)).   8 Léoutre, *Serving France, Ireland and England*, pp 36–9.   9 Ibid., pp 25–8.   10 Marie Léoutre, Jane McKee, Jean-Paul Pittion and Amy Prendergast (eds), *The diary (1689–1719) and accounts (1704–1717) of Élie Bouhéreau: Marsh's Library Z2.2.2* (Dublin, 2019), p. 2.   11 For this period see Léoutre, 'La Politique extérieure de Guillaume III: l'ambassade de Lord Galway à Turin et les Vaudois', *Riforma e*

Meanwhile, in early 1691, Ruvigny joined the forces of the new king of England, William III, on the Irish front of the war of the Grand Alliance. The following year he spent time at sea and in Flanders.[12]

It was not before late November 1693 that the two men started working closely. Bouhéreau became secretary to Ruvigny, now Viscount Galway, who was sent to the front in Savoy-Piedmont as military commander of the British troops and envoy extraordinary to the duke of Savoy, Victor Amadeus II.[13] There is very little evidence of how Galway and Bouhéreau interacted or got on during the three-year period they spent in northern Italy, or what they talked about in their leisure time, if they conversed for pleasure at all: did they discuss the idea of a Protestant International? Did they reminisce about their former lives in Paris, or mention the people they missed? Did they discuss the difficult question of conformity?

One thing is abundantly clear from the surviving records for this period. Jean-Paul Pittion was the first to notice that Bouhéreau was already functioning as Galway's agent in Piedmont-Savoy, 'providing, on Galway's behalf, money and passports to the refugees he met during his embassies, and recruiting them' for William III.[14] Bouhéreau was handling money on Galway's behalf in a private capacity as early as 1694, if not earlier.[15] Since Pittion's initial breakthrough however, the inherent difficulty in bringing together the complex extant sources – scattered in several repositories and written in different languages – as well as the near impossibility to understand the account book, without prior and intimate knowledge of the Huguenot community in exile, means that until now no significant or in-depth work has been carried out.

With the war coming to an end, Bouhéreau and Galway travelled again from Piedmont to England in late 1696. In January 1697, Galway, who was already commander of the forces in Ireland since 1692, was appointed as part of a commission of the lords justices to govern the country – he was *de facto* governor of Ireland. Galway arranged that Bouhéreau would remain his secretary, at first as his private secretary and then as second secretary to the lords justices.[16] In essence, Galway took advantage of the fact that the first secretary to the lords justices, Matthew Prior, was away on the Continent for the peace negotiations to

---

movimenti religiosi, 10 (Dec. 2021), 139–70; 'Seventeenth-century Protestant *entraide*: brokering an edict of toleration for the Vaudois', *Huguenot Society Journal*, 36 (2023), 32–43. 12 Léoutre, *Serving France, Ireland and England*, chapter 2. 13 Léoutre, 'L'ambassade de Lord Galway à Turin'. 14 C.E.J. Caldicott, Hugh Gough and J-P. Pittion (eds), *The Huguenots and Ireland: anatomy of an emigration* (Dún Laoghaire, 1987), p. 61. 15 Léoutre et al., *Diary and accounts*, 4/14 Dec., p. 219; Marie Léoutre, 'Financial networks and the payment of military pensions, 1692–1720' in Vivienne Larminie (ed.), *Huguenot networks, 1560–1780: the interactions and impact of a Protestant minority in Europe* (New York, 2017), pp 173–86. 16 Longleat, Prior Papers, Bouhéreau to Prior, 8/18 June 1697, fo. 30; J.C. Sainty, 'The secretariat of the chief governors of Ireland, 1690–1800', *Proceedings of the Royal Irish Academy*, 77C (1977), 1–33. There is however nothing in the diary confirming payment for

promote the second secretary, Humphrey May, thereby opening up the post of second secretary to Bouhéreau.[17] He remained in this post until 1701.

Bouhéreau accompanied Galway on a few of his trips across Ireland, for example in June 1698 when they went to Portarlington.[18] The exact nature of this visit to Galway's estate is not divulged, but the presence of Jacques de Belrieu, baron de Virasel, another of Galway's agents who dealt specifically with the Huguenot settlement at Portarlington on behalf of Galway implies that it was more than a pleasure trip.[19] At the end of the war of the Grand Alliance in 1697, the number of troops had been reduced and the Huguenot regiments were disbanded, with officers pensioned on the military and on the civil lists of the Irish Establishment.[20] Many veterans settled in Portarlington, and it is likely that the trip was to take count of who was there and entitled to what. Much of Galway's time as lord justice was dedicated to the disbanding of the army and he drew and redrew many pensions' lists. Bouhéreau played a central role in his endeavours to ensure provision for the disbanded Huguenot officers. Pittion pointed out that at that time Bouhéreau added to his 'official duties the role of private banker. His diary records the payments of pensions in Ireland and England, the granting of loans and the purchase of stock, and shares in tontines and lotteries', which are discussed below.[21] Within a fortnight of the trip to Portarlington Galway and his fellow lord justice Winchester departed Dublin again, to review the troops across the kingdom, a four-week tour. Bouhéreau noted that Galway left him to take care of correspondence as his 'services ne sont pas necéssaires dans ce voyage' (services are not necessary [...] during this trip). Galway also entrusted Bouhéreau with £3 for Madame Pickard and eighteen shillings for Madame de Montigny.[22] Mr de Montigny was a captain in de la Melonière's Huguenot regiment of Foot, while Madame Pickard has not yet been identified with complete certainty.[23]

In 1697 Galway had no doubt he could be 'de quelque utilité en Irlande à nos pauvres réfugiés' (of some utility in Ireland to our poor refugees), and he proposed a settlement in the western province of Connacht.[24] In a *Mémoire* he

---

the post of secretary, while there was such a reference in 1693. **17** Léoutre, 'Life of a Huguenot exile: Henri de Ruvigny, earl of Galway, 1648–1720' (PhD, University College Dublin, 2011), pp 182–3, and forthcoming article; Raymond Pierre Hylton was the first to suggest it in his *Dictionary of Irish biography* entry for Bouhéreau, https://www.dib.ie/biography/massue-de-ruvigny-henri-a5505, accessed 7 March 2024. **18** Léoutre et al., *Diary and accounts*, 28 June/8 July 1698, p. 310. **19** See Hylton, 'The Huguenot settlement at Portarlington, 1692–1771' in Caldicott et al., *The Huguenots and Ireland*, pp 297–32, at 305–6; Hylton, 'Huguenot settlement at Portarlington' (MA, University College Dublin, 1982), pp 15 and 23. **20** Léoutre, *Serving France, Ireland and England*, chapter 6. **21** Jean-Paul Pittion, 'French Protestants and the Edict of Nantes' in Caldicott et al., *The Huguenots and Ireland*, p. 60. **22** Léoutre et al., *Diary and accounts*, 15/25 July 1698, pp 310–11. **23** David C.A. Agnew, 'Historical introduction', *Protestant exiles from France*, ii, section VIII, p. 86. **24** Galway, Zurich, to Pieter Valkenier, 9/19 March 1697, in Marie de Chambrier, 'Projet de colonisation en Irlande par les réfugiés français, 1692–1699', *Proceedings of Huguenot Society*

recommended twenty-six prominent French refugees for leases of land 'confiscated in the province', in order to 'promote the settlement of French Protestants in Ireland', and set the conditions for their resettlement, including the following directives which he hoped would encourage others to come settle there. They should be granted confiscated land through an act of parliament, and, in return, the Huguenots would pay a quit-rent (a land tax) of half the value of the revenue; they should lease to other Protestants for three lifetimes; they should develop wool production by having a number of sheep proportional to the acreage, and reserve a certain amount of land to grow flax and hemp, as well as plant a certain number of trees.[25] Among the names listed were officers from the Huguenot regiments, including Armand de Bourbon, marquis de Miremont (Horse), Isaac Monceau de la Melonière (Foot), Pierre Belcastel (Foot); and Jean de Jocour, marquis de Villarnou, whom Galway would send to England to plead for the naturalization of disbanded Huguenots in early 1699.[26] Also on the list were the names of Galway's closest associates and some long-standing friends, with whom Galway worked closely on a resettlement project of French refugees from the Swiss cantons to Ireland from 1692 onwards: Gaspard Perrinet, marquis d'Arsellières, the baron de Virasel, Philibert d'Hervart, and Henri de Mirmand; family members, including Jacques Muysson in Holland; and the name of his own secretary and financial agent, Élie Bouhéreau.[27] The inclusion of Bouhéreau is significant: land was highly valued. The land redistribution that took place from 1692 was a direct consequence of the Williamite victory – many Jacobites were dispossessed and their estates redistributed as grants to reward Williamites.

Bouhéreau's correspondence to the English undersecretary of state during the years 1700–1 provides some rare insights into Galway's life beyond his work in Dublin Castle and as commander of the forces. He recorded Galway's health declining, and accompanied him to Lutrellstown, an area near Lucan in west County Dublin, for a period of rest when his gout was debilitating. He later reported the return of Galway's health, commenting on his hunting in what is now Phoenix Park.[28] On a more personal note, in April 1700 Galway stood as godfather to Bouhéreau's grandson, the son of his daughter Blandine and her husband, the Church of Ireland minister Jean Jourdan: the child was named Henri after him.[29] In mid-March 1701, Bouhéreau records that 'My Lord Gallway a diné avec moi, et ma famille' (My Lord Galway dined with me and my family) and three other prestigious guests – the master general of the ordnance

Great Britain & Ireland (henceforth *PHSGBI*), 6:4 (1898–1901), 414. **25** Léoutre, *Serving France, Ireland and England*, p. 50; 'A proposed Connaught settlement', *PHSGBI*, 25:1 (1989), 96. **26** Léoutre, *Serving France, Ireland and England*, p. 138. **27** Léoutre, *Serving France, Ireland and England*, pp 45–51; 'A proposed Connaught settlement', 96. **28** See British Library, MS 28885. Letter from Élie Bouhéreau to John Ellis, 8 July 1700, fo. 271. **29** Léoutre et al., *Diary and accounts*, 21 April / 2 May, 1700, pp 320–1.

of Ireland, the bishop of Meath, and a judge – as a farewell dinner. Indeed, in April 1701 Galway was replaced in the government of Ireland and returned to England to enjoy retirement, with a pension of £1,250 a year.[30]

However, Galway's departure did not signify the end of his patronage of Bouhéreau, as the correspondence of Narcissus Marsh, archbishop of Dublin and former lord justice of Ireland who had served on the same commission as Galway, reveals. Galway was present in the chain of acquaintances that led to Bouhéreau's introduction to Marsh in 1697. Marsh wrote to the incoming lord lieutenant of Ireland, the earl of Rochester, in early May 1701, inquiring 'whether Lord Galway had acquainted his Excellency with a design of erecting a library at Dublin for public use'. Marsh informed Rochester that 'a very learned gentleman, a refugee, one Mr. Bonhereau [Bouhéreau], who held great correspondence in foreign parts', was in 'every way qualified to be a library keeper', and laid out how Bouhéreau, who had 'moreover a collection of books worth between 500*l*. and 600*l*.', could be paid:

> This gentleman, being ancient, would give his books (which were in a manner all his substance) to this library (when erected) and become library keeper himself, if he might have 200*l*. a year settled on him for life. Were the treasurership or chancellorship of their cathedral of St. Patrick void, he (the Bishop) would bestow it on him who was well qualified for such a dignity and would endeavour to make it a preferment for a library keeper for ever, there being no duty belonging thereto besides preaching three or four times in a year. But it being uncertain when either of these might become void, the only expedient that could be thought of was, that the King would graciously bestow a salary of 200*l. per ann.* on Mr. Bonhereau as library keeper, either during life or until otherwise provided for, which might be paid out of the first fruits, and then the work would go on. The library would at first opening be pretty well stocked with those books ... Lord Galway was fully apprised of the matter.[31]

The matter was discussed three weeks later in Kensington between William III and the lords of the Treasury, when it was resolved that 'Monsieur Buckerow [Bouhéreau] as Library Keeper is to have 200*l*. a year from Midsummer during pleasure provided that if the Treasurership or Chancellorship of the Cathedral Church of St Patrick becomes void this pension to cease or so soon as any other preferment is found for him'.[32] In June, Bouhéreau noted, in his very factual style, that he was appointed first librarian of Marsh's Library, besides St Patrick's Cathedral, with a pension of £200 sterling per year attached to the post.[33]

30 *Calendar of Treasury Books* (*CTB*), vol. 16, 28 May 1701, p. 70.   31 *CTP*, vol. 2, 6 May 1701, pp 488–9.   32 *CTB*, vol. 16, 28 May 1701, p. 70.   33 Léoutre et al., *Diary and*

At that stage Bouhéreau had been Galway's secretary for seven years, in times of war and in times of peace, and had travelled with him across Europe. As they were eighteenth-century men of different social strata it would be inaccurate to qualify their relationship as 'friendship', but nonetheless they had established a strong relationship based on trust. Galway had left for England, but Bouhéreau continued as Galway's financial agent in Ireland long after 1701, conducting monetary transactions of all sorts on his behalf, mostly distributing sums to Huguenot refugees in Ireland, Holland and Switzerland. There is no extant correspondence between Bouhéreau and Galway for the years when Galway was in England, until 1704, or after that, but in late May 1704, Galway wrote a petition to the Lord Lieutenant of Ireland, James Butler, second duke of Ormond, on behalf of Bouhéreau, probably seeking protection for him as he was about to go to the continent.[34] Indeed, the war of the Spanish Succession had begun in 1702, and in July 1704 the earl was appointed commander of the troops by Queen Anne and sent to Portugal. While the number of entries in his diary decreases, Bouhéreau does record the departure of Galway for the continent, and the fact that his own son-in-law, Jean Jourdan, accompanied him as his chaplain.[35]

While Galway was on the Iberian Peninsula, fighting and suffering great bodily injuries – he lost an arm to a cannon ball and an eye to a sabre cut – Bouhéreau was collecting Galway's pension from the Treasury every quarter and sending it to him through bills of exchange within a fortnight. This pattern continued like clockwork from October 1704 until October 1715.[36]

While no correspondence between Bouhéreau and Galway has been found to date for the period of the war of Spanish Succession, Bouhéreau did on at least one occasion seek the protection of his patron. In November 1708 Bouhéreau recorded the 'mort du Doyen Synge, à qui je dois succéder, dans la dignité de Chantre de l'église cathédrale de St Patrick: ce qui me tiendra lieu de ma pension' (Death of Dean Synge, to whom I shall succeed, in the [illegible word] dignity of precentor of St Patrick's Cathedral, which will be a substitute for my pension).[37] As seen above this had been planned since Bouhéreau took the post of library keeper, but an unexpected complication prompted Bouhéreau to write up a petition. In February 1709 (New Style), Galway was still in Lisbon when he wrote to the Lord High Treasurer to testify 'to the great merit and learning of, and to his particular esteem for Doctor Bouhéreau, who had been his secretary in Piedmont'. Galway forwarded the petition of Bouhéreau, 'Keeper of the Public Library near St Sepulchres, Dublin', explaining that he 'was allowed 200*l*.

accounts, 8/19 June 1701, p. 322.   **34** HMC, *Calendar of the manuscripts of the marquess of Ormonde*, 8 vols (London, 1902–20), viii, pp 75–6.   **35** Léoutre et al., *Diary and accounts*, 31 August 1704, p. 332.   **36** For Galway in the war of the Spanish Succession, see Léoutre, *Serving France, Ireland and England*, chapter 7; for the transactions during this period, see Léoutre et al., *Diary and accounts*.   **37** Léoutre et al., *Diary and accounts*, 30 November 1708, pp 356–7.

a year by the beneficence of her Majesty until the chantership of the Cathedral Church of St Patrick fell vacant by the death of Dean Synge', but was now 'required to pay two third parts of 360 odd pounds expended in buildings to the executors of the Dean', and asked for 'the continuance of his pension for two years'.[38] The account book indicates that the pension was continued – Galway's patronage had been successful.[39]

Later in 1709 Galway returned from the war, once again settling in England. Owing to a change of political leaders in the later part of the reign of Queen Anne, he faced a show trial in 1710 and was censured.[40] However he managed to recover from it, and at the death of the Queen in 1714 the new monarch, George I, was prompt to capitalize on Galway's previous experience of Ireland. His knowledge of the army, parliamentary procedure and administration were invaluable, especially in the volatile context of a potential Jacobite rising. Galway was sent back to Ireland, being appointed a lord justice once again in September 1715, and arriving there on 1 November. Galway was then in very poor physical health, but still oversaw a parliament that would have long lasting consequences in Ireland for a number of reasons, one of them being the creation of a national debt.[41]

There is no extant trace of a personal relationship between Bouhéreau and Galway during the years of his second lords justiceship, but given the close proximity of Dublin Castle and Marsh's Library it is possible that they paid each other an occasional visit, which would explain the lack of correspondence. During these years Bouhéreau was still distributing money on behalf of Galway and the latter did not forget his godson: in February 1717, the earl advanced £50 for the apprenticeship of Henri Jourdan, to the relief of Bouhéreau.[42] On 12 March of that year, Galway dined at Bouhéreau's apartments in the library with Bouhéreau, his sons, the archbishop of Tuam, one bishop and two lords – a dinner that cost Bouhéreau the considerable sum of £4, 17 shillings and 6 pence. In this case again it was a farewell dinner as Galway was replaced and left Ireland for England on 21 March. This dinner is the last time Galway is mentioned in Bouhéreau's diary. The last entry extant in the accounts is dated just a few days later, on 25 March 1717, and the last recorded transaction Bouhéreau conducted for Galway was 18 March.

Bouhéreau continued to live a relatively quiet life in Ireland until his death in 1719, and Galway finally enjoyed his retirement, living at Rookley House in Hampshire, regularly visiting his relative, Rachel Russell, at nearby Stratton

---

38 *CTP*, vol. 112, 22 January 1709, p. 92.   39 See, for example, Léoutre et al., *Diary and accounts*, 18 November 1710, p. 462.   40 Léoutre, *Serving France, Ireland and England*, chapter 8.   41 For Galway's second term as lord justice, see Léoutre, *Serving France, Ireland and England*, chapter 9; For details on the national debt, see Charles Ivar McGrath, *The making of the eighteenth-century Irish constitution: government, parliament and the revenue, 1692–1714* (Dublin, 2000).   42 Léoutre et al., *Diary and accounts*, 14 February 1717, p. 383.

Park. There is evidence that Galway continued to assist Huguenots settled in Ireland. For instance, in 1717 when François Duroure, a former officer of Foot, informed him that he and several others were reaching the end of their military pensions and sought his intervention on their behalf, he answered: 'j'escris dès aujourd'huy en Irlande pour tâcher de vous ayder dans le rétablissement d'une pension' (I will write starting today to Ireland to try and help you in the reinstatement of a pension).[43] In March 1718, Galway and leading members of the Huguenot community petitioned George I to grant a royal charter of incorporation for the Hospital for poor French Protestants in London. It was granted and Galway was made first governor of *La Providence* in July. He later bequeathed £1,000 to the hospital, and did not forget his godson Henri Jourdan, to whom he left £100.[44] Galway died on 3 September 1720 in his cousin Rachel's Stratton home and was buried at nearby Micheldever churchyard.[45]

ACCOUNTS

Bouhéreau's financial transactions need to be contextualized before focusing on those he completed on behalf of Galway. Bouhéreau did have a separate notebook for his own accounts with various people, now lost.[46] However in the account book still extant there are transactions that are personal and/or of a day-to-day nature, which allow us a glimpse of the life and interactions of Huguenot settlers in the Irish capital. Among these personal transactions are: purchasing a hat from Mr Nobileau, a Huguenot hat maker settled in Dublin; using the services of the Huguenot merchant Pierre Poey of Dublin to send cider to La Rochelle, and to import eaux de vie from there; buying his paper from Mr Pipiat, a Huguenot stationer.[47] He also collected rent money for property leased, seemingly on behalf of the dean of St Patrick's Cathedral – for example from Thomas Pooley, on what is ostensibly 'cathedral property'.[48] Bouhéreau pocketed £21 5s. twice a year from him, as he was entitled to collect part of the income from the properties leased.[49]

43 Huguenot Society Library, London. MS F/DV3 Galway, Stratton, to Francois Duroure, London, Duroure Family Papers, 16 August 1717; see also Léoutre, 'Député Général in France and in exile: Henri de Ruvigny, Earl of Galway' in Jane McKee and Randolph Vigne (eds), *The Huguenots, France, exile and diaspora* (Brighton, 2013), pp 145–54. 44 Randolphe Vigne, 'The good lord Galway', *PHSGBI*, 24:6 (1987–8), 532–50, at pp 546–7. 45 Harman Murtagh, 'Massue de Ruvigny, Henri de, earl of Galway, and marquess of Ruvigny in the French nobility (1648–1720)', *ODNB*, Oxford, 2004; http://www.oxforddnb.com, accessed 7 July 2024. 46 Léoutre et al., *Diary and accounts*, 25 March 1704, p. 330. 47 Léoutre et al., *Diary and accounts*, 7 March 1708/9 pp 448, 460, 518, 524, and 530 respectively. 48 David Hayton, 'Opposition to the statutory establishment of Marsh's Library' in Muriel McCarthy, *The making of Marsh's Library: learning, politics, and religion in Ireland, 1650–1750*, p. 170. Maybe the brother of Bishop John Poley. 49 See Léoutre et al., *Diary and accounts*, 26 July 1716: 'pour mes droits sur trois leases renouvellées' (for my rights on the renewal of three leases), pp 548–9.

A noteworthy aspect is Bouhéreau's investments. The seminal work of Alice Carter in the 1950s showed the importance and scale of Huguenot investment in the English national debt.[50] Alongside the establishment of the Bank of England, state-controlled lotteries first started in 1694, in an effort to raise revenue for the state to continue fighting Louis XIV. In the eighteenth century a lottery ticket was an investment, a form of speculation, rather than gambling, as it 'posed no risk for the purchaser'; in fact in 1694 'each £10 ticket guaranteed its purchaser an annual prize, ranging from £1 to £1,000 for 16 years'.[51] The first mention of Bouhéreau – actually, his wife, Marguerite – investing in a lottery is in 1698 in Rotterdam.[52] Bouhéreau was among the 10 per cent of Huguenot investors in the English lotteries of 1711 and 1712, having purchased tickets to the tune of £160 in the Royal Lottery of 1711. The interest for a year he pocketed in March 1713 amounted, after a 'deduction of half a percent ... for the commission' taken by his correspondent in England, to £9 12s.[53] In December 1712 he had invested £200 (Irish) for the purchase of 20 lottery tickets. In May 1714, he received £15 for six months' interest on his London tickets. He sold five of them in September for £39. In November, he pocketed another £30 for a year's interest.[54] For the year 1714 alone, it is a net gain of £74. In January 1715 Bouhéreau invested again, this time over £200, in lottery tickets.[55] It is also noteworthy that while there were private bankers in Dublin, Burton and Harrison, specializing in the sale of English lottery tickets to Irish customers,[56] Bouhéreau consistently used his Huguenot network instead of them. Interestingly, Bouhéreau does not seem to have subscribed to the Irish national debt in 1716.[57]

According to Randolph Vigne, Galway invested in the South Sea Company, an investment likely to have been made through Theophile Desbrisay, which would explain why his name does not appear, and perhaps why it took one of his heirs six years to recover the investment.[58] Given the volume of financial interactions between Bouhéreau and Desbrisay recorded in the account book, Galway's South Sea investments might have been recommended by Bouhéreau.

Bouhéreau recorded the state of the income and expenditure of the money that passed through his hands. This includes his immediate and extended family; for example between his son-in-law Mr Jourdan and his relative the officer Mr de Crosat, or between Mr Jourdan and his clock maker, Mr Adam Soret, probably the son of Joseph, a native of France who settled in Dublin before the

---

50 Alice Carter, 'The Huguenot contribution to the early years of the funded debt, 1697–1714', *PHSGBI*, 29:3 (1954–5), 21–41.   51 Patrick Walsh, *The South Sea bubble and Ireland: money, banking and investment, 1690–1721* (Woodbridge, 2014), pp 99 and 36.   52 Léoutre et al., *Diary and accounts*, 28 October/7 November, 1698, p. 314. She made just over £14. See Léoutre, 'Financial networks', pp 173–86.   53 Léoutre et al., *Diary and accounts*, 26 January/8 August 1713, p. 498.   54 Ibid., p. 32.   55 Ibid.   56 Walsh, *South Sea bubble and Ireland*, pp 50, 57 and 64.   57 See Charles Ivar McGrath, *Ireland and empire, 1692–1770* (London, 2012), pp 198–9.   58 Vigne, 'The good lord Galway', p. 548. Walsh does not mention it in his *South Sea bubble*.

Revocation. On these thirteen occasions it is Bouhéreau who conducts the transactions on behalf of his son-in-law.

Many transactions were conducted on behalf of Galway, in fact well over 300, for the most part while Galway was away from Ireland. There are two types of transactions: official ones, such as the payment of pensions to Huguenot veterans and their families in accordance with the Establishment (for instance cornet La Basoge);[59] and the more personal ones, payments made by Galway through Bouhéreau to friends, associates, and people in need.

While he himself conformed, Bouhéreau noted giving ten shillings quarterly to the French non-conformist church of Lucy Lane. Perhaps somewhat controversially, given his insistence on conformity in 1693, Galway also supported non-conformist congregations: for instance both subscribed to the building of the second French nonconformist church, St Peter's. Bouhéreau gave £12 for both churches.[60] It is also through Bouhéreau that Galway supported the French nonconformist minister Benjamin de Daillon, and his family after his death.[61] The money was taken directly from Galway's pension.

Of particular interest are the recurring payments that Bouhéreau makes for Galway. Among the recipients are the unmarried daughters of Huguenot officers. On ten occasions, between February 1712 and January 1717, Bouhéreau notes giving sums ranging from £1 to £10 to Mesdemoiselles de Champlaurier, by order of Galway. The total given over seven years is £23. Mesdemoiselles de Champlaurier were Ester, Mary and Susanne, who were to receive £24 per year from 1702 according to a list of yearly pensions (in England) granted by Queen Anne.[62] Ester de Champlaurier died unmarried in Portarlington in April 1712.[63] In the Establishment of annual pensions granted by George I starting in 1715, Mary and Susanna de Champlaurier were to receive £30 per annum.[64] They appear on two other lists in 1723 and 1726 at the same rate, but at this stage both Bouhéreau and Galway were dead, and so was Mary, who was buried in August 1725 in Portarlington. There was also a Demoiselle Anne de Champlaurier in Portarlington, who may well have been included in the Galway payment. She was in Portarlington in 1703 and still alive in 1735.

There were two men named Champlaurier who were pensioners in Ireland: Pierre Thibaut, Sieur de Champlaurier, a captain of infantry who was pensioned in 1692, naturalized in 1697 and who died in Portarlington in March 1701.[65] The second was Marc Thibaut de Champlaurier, who had been an ensign in the

---

59 For details of international payments to La Basoge, see Léoutre, 'Financial networks'. 60 Léoutre et al., *Diary and accounts*, pp 423 and 473. 61 See Léoutre, *Serving France, Ireland and England*, chapter 2. 62 W.A. Shaw, 'The English government and the relief of Protestant refugees', *PHSGBI*, 5:4 (1895), 343–423, at 386. 63 T.P. Le Fanu, 'Registers of the French church of Portarlington, Ireland', *PHSGBI*, 29 (1908), 72. 64 Shaw, 'The English government and the relief of Protestant refugees', 397. 65 He appears in The UK National Archives (TNA), T14/6 1692. The two of them appear in TNA, 14/7 1698, and TNA, T14/8 99.

Huguenot regiment of Belcastel,[66] 'who had been wounded under the shoulder by a grenade at the first siege of Limerick' and whose wife kept a school by 1714.[67] Marc was likely pensioned in 1692. In all cases where the brothers appear on pensions lists, it is without a first name, and the only way to tell them apart is by the amount they receive. Marc de Champlaurier and Galway were both at the second siege of Limerick.

It is difficult to say whose daughters the demoiselles de Champlaurier were – but Galway was either supplementing their pensions out of his own pocket or paying part of what was due to them. In any case he was providing for unmarried women who were from a noble background and who had settled on his estate.

Among the recipients are also a number of widows: Grant, Magnan, Foullon, Salomon, Des Champs, Nau, and La Chapelle, the latter receiving £10 in 1709, £49 in 1710, and £3 in 1713. Some are the widows of officers, some are yet to be identified.

CONCLUSION

This thorough examination of the Galway–Bouhéreau relationship demonstrates that steady financial and philanthropic networks existed and functioned within the Refuge over several decades. It demonstrates that the Huguenots who settled in Ireland were very much active in the financial side of state-building from the mid-1690s onwards.[68] It further shows that to understand the transactions, it is fundamental to know the network of people who were instrumental in moving money across the channel.

The Galway–Bouhéreau partnership lasted over twenty-five years. They had witnessed the world they had grown up in disintegrate, and had gone into exile. The times were uncertain, and Europe was at war more often than at peace. They were part and parcel of the 1688 revolution, part of the Williamite settlement, and part of the financial revolution. Both threw their lot wholeheartedly in the Williamite cause and the wider Protestant International. They were connected to a network of refugees all over Europe, with their main correspondents based in England and Holland. And finally, the transactions Bouhéreau conducted on behalf of Galway demonstrate that the earl endeavoured to be the *Député Général de la Religion Prétendue Réformée* he could never have been in France.[69]

---

66 T.P Le Fanu and W.H. Manchee, 'Dublin and Portarlington veterans: King William III's Huguenot army', *PHSGBI*, 41 (1946), 27. 67 Le Fanu, 'Registers of the French church of Portarlington', xvii. 68 For confidence in state see McGrath, *Ireland and Empire*, p. 202. 69 Léoutre, 'Député Général in France and in exile', pp 145–54.

The lost notebooks of Élie Bouhéreau: reading, recording, and retrieving in the seventeenth century

NOREEN HUMBLE

Information management is a perpetual problem, no more so now than in Bouhéreau's day. Scholars have always made notes on their readings in a variety of ways and already in the early modern period there was a range of practices, from the school-learnt practice of keeping a commonplace book (which generally consisted of passages copied from ancient authors organized under prescribed, usually moral, headings), to marking up the margins of the books being read, to keeping notes in other forms such as diaries and journals, or, indeed, some combination of the above.[1] In all these varied practices there is a concern not just to record passages and thoughts but also to have a useful way of retrieving the information. The headings, for example, in commonplace books, were thus as important for retrieval as for initial organization. The constraints posed by standard commonplace books for more serious scholarly endeavours, however, soon led to wider experimentation with methods of notetaking that were more flexible and allowed for the recording of thoughts on reading and other personal observations as they occurred. These types of collections of notes were generally termed *adversaria* and were coming into vogue in the mid-seventeenth century just as Bouhéreau would have been embarking on his note-taking practice. The political philosopher John Locke (1632–1704), for example, was a regular and enthusiastic compiler of notebooks of *adversaria* who thought long and hard

---

This research would not have been possible with the generosity and help of all the staff at Marsh's Library where I have been fortunate to have held two Muriel McCarthy research fellowships (in 2013 and 2014), which resulted in an article on Bouhéreau's notetaking in the one extant notebook (Noreen Humble, 'Élie Bouhéreau (1643–1719): a scholar at work in his libraries', *Lias*, 44:2 (2017), 143–98). A subsequent Maddock research fellowship in 2018 allowed me to collect the material which made this article possible, a task facilitated with patience, good humour and hard labour by the then librarian, Maria O'Shea. Conversations with Jean-Paul Pittion, Geoff Kemp and Keith Sidwell have saved me from too many infelicities, as have the keen eyes of the editors. Any shortcomings that remain are due to me alone.   1 Especially useful on this topic are the following: Élisabeth Décultot, 'Introduction' in É. Décultot (ed.), *Lire, copier, écrire* (Paris, 2003); the special edition of *Intellectual History Review*, 20:3 (2010) edited by Richard Yeo, which includes in it Ann Blair, 'The rise of note-taking in early modern Europe', *Intellectual History Review*, 20:3 (2010), 303–16; also A. Blair, *Too much to know: managing scholarly information before the modern age* (New Haven, 2010), particularly pp 62–116, and R. Yeo, *Notebooks, English virtuosi, and early modern science* (Chicago, 2014).

about how best to organize his notes so as to be able to retrieve them with as much ease as possible. Indeed, in 1686 he published, anonymously and first in French, his 'Méthode nouvelle' ('new method') on this very topic.² Briefly stated, the system advocated using carefully chosen Heads (or, as he called them, Titles) in combination with an indexing system that comprised an alphabetical code for each heading (commonly the initial letter and vowel of the headword), which would be listed at the front of each notebook.³

Locke's well-known views on the matter of recording and retrieving information in notebooks provide an interesting point of contrast with the little-known method employed by Élie Bouhéreau, not least because the two men knew each other, meeting in La Rochelle in September 1678, only a few years before Locke published his 'Méthode nouvelle'.⁴ But whereas we have forty-five extant notebooks of Locke's left to peruse to judge the effectiveness and the rigour (or lack thereof) with which he applied his method,⁵ we have but one notebook belonging to Élie Bouhéreau, which was only recovered by Marsh's Library by chance in the twentieth century.⁶

Examining Bouhéreau's method of taking notes is of interest obviously for anyone studying Bouhéreau himself, but it is also of interest for wider socio-cultural reasons. Less attention has been paid to the more randomly surviving notebooks of those men and women not regarded as the foremost intellectuals of their time. Yet whether they are *sui generis*, as Bouhéreau's appears to be, or of a more standard type, they can substantially broaden our understanding about the ways in which knowledge was ordered, managed and transmitted at different levels of society and among different groups.⁷ As I will show, when we examine this data in combination with what we know about Bouhéreau's collection as a whole and what we know about the broad outlines of his life story, we can refine our understanding of both.

In Bouhéreau's notebook can be found the following: a Latin chronology, which fills the first sixty pages, followed by four pages of dense notes on various subjects (though these are, paradoxically, often ignored in descriptions of the

---

2 John Locke, 'Méthode nouvelle de dresser des recueils', *Bibliothèque universelle et historique*, 2 (1686), 315–40.   3 Again there is much bibliography on this, but useful are M. Stolberg, 'John Locke's "New method of making commonplace books": tradition, innovation and epistemic effects', *Early Science and Medicine*, 19 (2014), 448–70; Yeo, *Notebooks*, pp 175–215; and R. Yeo, 'Thinking with excerpts: John Locke (1632–1704) and his notebooks', *History of Science and Humanities*, 43:2 (2020), 180–202.   4 See Geoff Kemp's essay in this volume for the intricate web of connections between these two men.   5 See Yeo, *Notebooks*, pp 182–4, for an overview.   6 A bookseller in Tunbridge Wells, England, found it in 1915. Jason McElligott, 'Introduction' in Marie Léoutre, Jane McKee, Jean-Paul Pittion and Amy Prendergast (eds), *The diary (1689–1719) and accounts (1704–1717) of Élie Bouhéreau: Marsh's Library Z2.2.2* (Dublin, 2019), p xi.   7 See, for example, K. Sharpe, *Reading authority and representing rule in early modern England* (London, 2013), pp 51–3 on the commonplace books of parliamentarian Sir William Drake (1606–69).

notebook); next can be found 125 pages of diary entries starting from 1689 to the year of his death, and, finally, forty pages of accounts.[8] An examination of the four pages of dense notes allows us to assert with confidence that Bouhéreau employed a notetaking style that can be categorized as *adversaria*, that is, he recorded random things deemed important as and when they struck him. So, for example, we find, in addition to notes of varying degrees of detail on his reading, also a summary of a manuscript and some copied out correspondence.[9] Though there are few dates and though these were not recorded in any systematic fashion, they are enough to show that the recording is chronological. There are, however, no headings of the sort which might be found in a commonplace book or of the more extended type of titles recommended by and employed by Locke, and indeed by many others.[10]

The pages in the notebook were numbered by Bouhéreau and start at C.V, which hitherto was understood to mean p. 105, and that, therefore, 104 pages were missing (possibly with one hundred of these being in a prior notebook since the physical nature of the extant notebook suggests only a few pages could be missing at the start). But a closer look at the four pages of notes themselves and at the flyleaves of the books to which they refer reveals that there must have been three notebooks originally, labelled A, B and C, and that C.V is actually the fifth page of a third notebook, labelled C.[11] So, for example, in the third note on the page labelled C.LXX, the last of the four pages of notes in the existing notebook, Bouhéreau wrote: 'Quae addenda habeam iis quae scripsi A.II.4. et B.LXXXV.' ('Which things let me have added to those which I wrote in A.II.4 and B.LXXXV'). This note demonstrates that C in the existing notebook is not to be read as the Roman numeral representing one hundred, but as the third letter of the alphabet, and that C.LXX refers to page seventy of this third notebook.

Further confirmation can be found in reverse, as it were. In note five on page seventy of notebook C, Bouhéreau wrote: 'Sur le mot de <u>Coqueluche</u>, dans Les <u>Origines</u> de Ménage, Voyez, dans le Journal qui suit, le 6e. de Juin 1711.' ('On the word Coqueluche in *The Origines* of Ménage, see in the Journal which follows, 6 June 1711').[12] When Bouhéreau's own copy of Gilles Ménage's *Les*

---

8 The latter two portions of the notebook – the diary entries and the accounts – are now published in a handsome edition by the Irish Manuscripts Commission: Léoutre et al., *Diary and accounts*. Yeo, *Notebooks*, pp 182–8, notes how diary/journal entries and accounts, among other things, also featured in some of Locke's notebooks.   9 See Humble, 'Élie Bouhéreau (1643–1719): a scholar at work', for an in-depth analysis of these notes and his method.
10 Numerous different examples can be extracted from the bibliography in n. 1 above.
11 For a thorough account of how the system works, see Humble, 'Élie Bouhéreau (1643–1719): a scholar at work', 149–53. What follows here is a summary for purposes of contextualization.   12 The 'Journal' refers to the diary that follows and in which he made reference again to this work by Ménage in an entry on this date. See Léoutre et al., *Diary and accounts*, pp 366–9.

origines de la langue françoise (Paris, 1650) is examined, on the flyleaf in Bouhéreau's hand is the following:

>   Pag.481.l.ult./A.X.6.
>   Pag.595.l.25/A.X.10.
>   Pag.182.l.4/A.XI.3.
>   Pag.391.l.14./B.VI.3.
>   Pag.301.l.3./B.VII.1.
>   Pag.313.l.25./B.LXVIII.4.
>   Pag.435.l.15./B.LXVIII.5.
>   Pag.512.l.26./B.VI.3.
>   Pag.228.l.28./C.LXX.5.

Note in particular that the last of these entries corresponds directly to note five on page seventy of notebook C. Further, by turning to page 228 and locating line twenty-eight (helped by the fact that Bouhéreau put a pencil mark beside the line), it is possible to locate the precise passage of interest, that is, the entry on the word 'Coqueluche'.

This precise and novel method of cross-referencing, therefore, clearly reveals that there were originally three notebooks – A, B and C – in which Bouhéreau recorded his thoughts. The method also presents a distinctive and effective means of retrieving notes that does not rely on either titles or elaborate indices of the sort Locke proposed: by looking at the flyleaf of a book, Bouhéreau could locate instantly where he had made notes on prior readings and on what passages.

Notebooks A and B are lost, but there is one way in which at least some idea of their contents and of which books Bouhéreau thought worth recording some comment on can be gleaned. Because his collection of books is almost completely intact – its preservation resting on his fulfilled promise to leave his collection to Archbishop Marsh's new public library in exchange for being granted the post of its first librarian – we can work backwards using his own retrieval system, that is, the cross-references noted on the flyleaves of the books themselves, to see what works he took notes on. Already, for example, it is clear from the list of cross-references on the flyleaf of Ménage's work that *Les origines de la langue françoise* was a work to which Bouhéreau kept returning and on which he kept making observations and/or notes over the course of the lifetime of his three notebooks, for the earliest reference here 'Pag.481.l.ult./A.X.6.' is to page ten of the first notebook (A) and the latest 'Pag.228.l.28./C.LXX.5.', as we have seen, is to the third last note on the last page of notes, page seventy, in the third notebook (C). Thus by collating the cross-references we can get a glimpse into what works interested him over the period of time he kept these notebooks.

Before looking at what the data yields, it is worth summarizing some of the observations Philip Benedict and Pierre-Olivier Léchot made about the general character of Bouhéreau's collection based on Bouhéreau's own catalogue.[13] Bouhéreau's was a fairly large collection for one who was not one of the literary giants of the day, comprising as it does 2,022 titles in 1,741 volumes.[14] The broad categories of subject matter break down roughly as follows: religious (36%), belles-lettres (19%), history (16%), medicine (9%), philosophy (7%), science (6%), and law (3%). The median date of the books in the collection, however, is 1619, which observation reflects the fact that he inherited books both from his father and from his great-uncle, making the collection more a 'palimpsest of its owner's family history',[15] than a snapshot of his individual preferences. Books which were published between 1650 and 1685, that is, the period of his prime before he went into exile, and so which can be put down to his own purchasing habits, amount to roughly 28% of the total, and only sixty-four books date from 1685 or later, a fact which undoubtedly reflects his reduced circumstances and the fact that he was often on the move.

Yet his individual stamp is present on the collection too and stems from his period of time in Saumur, with a striking number of imprints from there among the collection: one hundred in total.[16] These books reflect not just his scholarly interests but also his religious outlook. Protestant authors in the collection certainly reflect works popular in other Huguenot collections, such as those by Pierre Du Moulin, Charles Drelincourt and Jean Daillé, but Bouhéreau also shows a preference for more controversial authors, such as Moses Amyraut, who was one of his tutors in Saumur.[17]

Benedict and Léchot's survey, therefore, tells us enormous amounts about this collection in its time. But its broad sweep and reliance on Bouhéreau's own catalogue for information means it misses some of the granularity which looking at the actual books themselves can provide. For example, while the figure for books dating to the period of his exile is stark – sixty-four – it does not take into account how many of these later acquisitions were gifts to Bouhéreau, rendering the figure starker still. I have counted at least nineteen, that is, c.30 per cent of his acquisitions at this time. This data is not recorded in his catalogue but can be seen on the flyleaves of his books. For example, his old college friend, and a former pastor in La Rochelle, Daniel Henri Delaizement, whom he visits in Leiden in 1692, 1693 and 1696 (during the period when Bouhéreau is in the employment first of Thomas Coxe and then of Henri de Ruvigny),[18] gifts him

---

13 Philip Benedict and Pierre-Olivier Léchot, 'The library of Élie Bouhéreau: the intellectual universe of a Huguenot refugee and his family' in Muriel McCarthy and Ann Simmons (eds), *Marsh's Library – a mirror on the world: law, learning and libraries, 1650–1750* (Dublin, 2003), pp 165–84. 14 For an explanation of the discrepancy between the act of 1707 count of Bouhéreau's books (2,057) and that of Benedict and Léchot see the introduction to this volume. 15 Benedict and Léchot, 'The library of Élie Bouhéreau', p. 165. 16 Benedict and Léchot, 'The library of Élie Bouhéreau', p. 171. 17 See Benedict and Léchot, 'The library of Élie Bouhéreau', pp 175–8. 18 Léoutre et al., *Diary and accounts*, pp 174–5, 176–7, 182–3, and 294–5.

three books post-exile: two of his own – *Histoire des Réforméz de La Rochelle depuis l'année 1660, jusqu'à l'année 1685, en laquelle l'édit de Nantes a été révoqué* (Amsterdam, 1689) and *Sermon sur ces paroles de l'evangile selon S. Matthieu* (Amsterdam, 1686) – the other *Recherches sur les commencemens et les premier progrès de la Réformation en la ville de La Rochelle* by Philippe Vincent (Rotterdam, 1693), who was Bouhéreau's godfather.[19]

Further, the broader data on the collection cannot really tell us which books were of greatest importance to Bouhéreau and which he actually read closely – for as we all know, having a book in one's library, though it certainly tells us what the owner thought she ought to possess, does not automatically translate to knowledge of the contents of that book. And considering how great a proportion of the collection Bouhéreau inherited, which books were important to him – his father's, his great-uncle's, his teachers', his own purchases – is not an insignificant enquiry, if we want to examine more broadly contemporary reading and note-taking practices, of Huguenots, of Protestants more generally, and/or of just the general educated population of the time.

There are limitations, of course, to what such a search can reveal, the most obvious of which is that from a cross-reference and a pencil mark it is not possible to gauge the tenor of the note precisely – though in some cases, as I will show, it is possible to make an educated guess about what might be going on, based on the type of notes he makes in notebook C. Further, it is clear from the four pages in notebook C that Bouhéreau is not only recording thoughts on his reading of his own books in these notebooks: for example, the first note, which covers all of page sixty-seven and the first half of page sixty-eight, is primarily a précis of a manuscript letter which was loaned to him, with a reasonably lengthy verbatim quotation from it at the end. The remainder of page sixty-eight and all of page sixty-nine record some correspondence between Bouhéreau and his friend Isaac Sarrau from the years 1682 and 1683, correspondence which is nowhere else preserved (and in fact most of which is earlier than any other extant correspondence between them).[20] Therefore, collecting the remaining cross-references on the flyleaves will not result in a complete outline of what is recorded in the missing notebooks, but it will be a start.[21] Conversely, an

---

19 On the flyleaf of the Delaizement volumes (bound together): 'Don de l'auteur Mr Delaizement' and on the vincent: 'Don de Mr Delaizement'. 20 On C.LXVIII are two letters: the first is from Sarrau to Bouhéreau dated 11 March 1682, followed by Bouhéreau's response of 19 March 1682; on C. LXIX is a letter from Bouhéreau dated 15 April 1682, followed by Sarrau's response of 23 January 1683 and a further reply from Bouhéreau dated 28 January 1683 (on these see Humble, 'Élie Bouhéreau (1643–1719): a scholar at work', 156–8). In the Bibliothèque du protestantisme français (BPF), MS 713.7 (4) 1–3 are three letters from Sarrau to Bouhéreau from 1683 (1 January, 8 December, and 25 December); and MS 713.7 (4) 4–35 contains another 32 letters from Sarrau to Bouhéreau from the years 1684–5. An additional 21 letters from Sarrau to Bouhéreau are preserved in Marsh's Library (the earliest dating to 12 January 1684 and the last to 30 June 1685), Z2.2.14 (16) 1–20. 21 For example, an interesting marginal note on C.LXVIII reveals further complexity in the filing

examination of his books shows that he also wrote notes in the margins of some of them,[22] and so not all his notes on his reading ended up in the notebooks.

Further, the system works when Bouhéreau uses it with the precision noted above. But, as we can see also in the case of Locke,[23] this was not always the case, as the four pages in notebook C show. Sometimes in his note he gives insufficient bibliographical detail of the work he is referring to, sometimes he gives sufficient detail but inexplicably there is no cross-reference on the flyleaf of the book in question, and sometimes the book in question will have gone missing.[24] But these shortcomings are more of an issue when working back from the notes to the books in the collection than for the exercise being carried out in this paper. What follows, therefore, presents what we can learn specifically about the two lost notebooks, A and B, as well as about Bouhéreau's note-taking practices more generally, by following the trail left on the flyleaves of all the remaining books.

First, some general observations can be made.

(1) Not all his books have cross-references to notebooks on the flyleaves. Indeed, the number which does is only 151 volumes or roughly 8.7 per cent of Bouhéreau's whole collection (twenty-six of which are referred to in notebook A, 138 in notebook B). Still, these editions span the whole collection. So they include not just books Bouhéreau acquired of his own accord, though there are some interesting examples on that front which I will come back to.

(2) We already know that four consecutive pages of notebook C were dedicated to *adversaria*, pages sixty-seven to seventy. We also know why there are no earlier entries of this type: it is because of the extensive chronology found up to that point in the notebook.[25] Likewise, we know why they end at page seventy: it is because Bouhéreau shifted to a diary format on page seventy-one, a practice he himself links clearly to his changed circumstances in 1689, though it should

---

system: 'J'ay gardé, Sur une fueïlle volante, copie d'une autre Lettre, que j'ay ecrite à Mr. Sarrau, le 20.e d'Août, 1682. Et je l'ay mise, avec quelques autres copies de Lettres, dans mon premier Livre de Remarques, à l'endroit marqué, A.V.' ('I kept, on a separate sheet, a copy of another letter, which I had written to Mr. Sarrau, 20 August 1682, and I put it, with some other copies of letters, in my first book of remarks, marked on the right, A.V'). For further details, see Humble, 'Élie Bouhéreau (1643–1719): a scholar at work', 157. 22 Examining these marginalia is a separate exercise from the one I have undertaken here. There are many editions that contain marginalia in Bouhéreau's hand and it will not be clear, without a rigorous and systematic investigation, what the proportion of notes in the notebooks is compared to notes in the books themselves. For some examples during his period in Dublin, in books that are definitely not mentioned in notebook C, see Humble, 'Élie Bouhéreau (1643–1719): a scholar at work', 176–7. 23 Yeo, *Notebooks*, p. 200, notes that the sheer range of topics defeated Locke sometimes. 24 For examples of where the system breaks down, see Humble, 'Élie Bouhéreau (1643–1719): a scholar at work', 160–1 and 165–6. 25 I have not found any evidence yet of when he might have started the chronology. It is possible there is material in the extant letters which might help. See, for example, David C.A. Agnew, *Protestant exiles from France in the reign of Louis XIV*, 2nd ed. (London, 1871), pp 140–1, who quotes (without giving its provenance) from a letter Bouhéreau wrote on 7 April 1672 to Jean Rou upon receipt of his *Tables chronologiques* which he says he will use often in his 'serious study'.

be noted that reading notes appear in a number of much later diary entries too.[26] A search of the flyleaves for cross-references to notebooks A and B reveals different distribution patterns: cross-references exist only for pages one to twenty-one in notebook A, but for pages one to 150 in notebook B. Without the physical copies of the notebooks it is hard to know for certain what is happening and so there are a number of ways we can interpret this data. But if the notebooks were similar in size and format to notebook C, which had roughly speaking *c*.240 pages, then the space devoted to scholarly notes of one kind or another in notebook A would be 8.75 per cent of the whole, in notebook B 62.5 per cent of the whole. It is safe to assume that these pages were filled with at least some of the same sorts of materials also found in notebook C which do not fit the cross-reference system (that is, letters, summaries of reading from borrowed books, etc.). We cannot be sure, of course, that the notebooks physically resembled one another. In both cases, however, whatever else they included, the two lost notebooks began their life as repositories for Bouhéreau's thoughts on his reading, whereas, by contrast, we can see that the opening pages of notebook C were used for a specific but different type of enquiry, being dedicated to working out a historical chronology.

(3) Though we do not have the complete picture, we can see that the number of notes on each page of the two lost notebooks varies significantly. Page two of notebook A, for example, has at least twelve separate notes, whereas page 115 of notebook B has no further subdivisions. And there is every permutation in between these two. This mirrors what we see in notebook C, where page sixty-seven is wholly taken up with one note which actually spills over onto page sixty-eight, but page seventy has seven separate notes. Also mirroring notebook C is the overall randomness of the length of the individual notes. For example, there are 107 entries spread over twenty-one pages for notebook A and 281 spread over 150 pages in notebook B. While this amounts roughly to an average of 5.1 notes per page for notebook A and 1.87 notes per page for notebook B, the calculation does not take into account the number of pages to which no cross-references have been found (three in notebook A and sixty-one in notebook B, which closes the gap between the averages to 5.9 to 3.2).[27] These observations, in conjunction with the fact that the cross-referencing system extends across the three notebooks, enables us to assume with a high degree of confidence that all three notebooks presented chronologically recorded *adversaria*.

(4) A number of books, such as the example cited above of Ménage's *Les origines de la langue françoise*, have multiple cross-references on the flyleaves, and so give some indication of the frequency and relative time frame of Bouhéreau's

---

26 For these reading notes in the diary entries, see Léoutre et al., *Diary and accounts*, pp 336–9, 342–7, 352–7, 360–1, 362–5, 366–9, and 376–7; and for analysis of the same, see Humble, 'Élie Bouhéreau (1643–1719): a scholar at work', especially 158–73 and 190–8.   **27** The gaps range usually from one to three pages, but two of them in notebook B are very lengthy:

use of and interest in these works. Usually, the books which have multiple cross-references to a wide range of pages in notebooks A and B are reference works. For example, the forty cross-references listed on the flyleaves of the two volumes of the *Suda*, a *c.* tenth-century CE Greek encyclopaedia, which like Ménage's work, is an alphabetically-ordered reference work, show that he returned to the work repeatedly: the earliest reference is to A.X, the latest to B.CXLI. By contrast, there are other books which have multiple cross-references all bunched together. So, for example, Le Fèvre's 1663 edition of Longinus *On the sublime*, has the most cross-references – sixty-six – of any book (see plate 12). While the last reference is to B.CVII, the first sixty-three are confined to pages one to eight of notebook A. This bunching suggests a level of intense reading of this work, and so represents a different sort of intellectual activity from that painted by the *Suda* cross-references.

(5) Rarer in number than the cross-references to the notebooks, but still important for considering his notetaking and how he read his books, are other things which he recorded on flyleaves such as (a) cross-references either to pages in the same book, or to other books,[28] but not to a notebook; and (b) more extensive notes of the kind we might have expected to be recorded in the actual notebooks but which do not seem to have been, though I will come back to an interesting example in this category below. These types of notes somewhat disrupt – happily I think – the picture of the systematic and precise notetaker the cross-referencing system implies, revealing, as they do, more spontaneous responses to his reading.

(6) Finally, it is worth noting as well that the overall examination of the pastedowns and flyleaves showed evidence of other types of record keeping or thoughts provoked by the material in the volume, or of the circumstances of their acquisition (for example, sometimes where the book was purchased and for how much is noted), both in hands other than Bouhéreau's but also in Bouhéreau's own hand. The latter examples range from a simple signature, and/or a noting of when the book was gifted to him, to an insertion of the name of the author of the work on the title page if it is missing (something that happened with surprising frequency), to brief tables of contents or summaries of the volume at hand, and to other miscellanea, such as poems. These all give us important information about what he considered important and how his mind worked.

If we zero in more closely on the results from each of the two missing notebooks, further observations can be made. We can, for a start, make a stab at dating them. Since it does not look as though Bouhéreau was trying to do something different with his notetaking in notebook B, we can with some degree

---

fourteen (pages 38–51) and thirteen (pages 53–65) pages respectively.   28 For example, the 1663 Longinus also contains, as the third last reference, 'Pag.314.v.5./V. Euripid. Iphigen.Aulid.v.220.' Bouhéreau has a 1562 edition of Euripides, but there is no corresponding reference on the flyleaf of that volume back to this volume.

of certainty assume that he did not start notebook B until he ran out of room in notebook, A, and likewise that the notes in notebook C postdate those in notebook B. Further, it seems reasonably secure to propose a date of around 1680 or slightly earlier for the transition from notebook B to notebook C since the latest publication referred to in notebook B (B.CXXXII.5) was published in 1680 (*De la guérison des fièvres par le quinquina*)[29] and the first note in notebook C summarizes and quotes from a manuscript dating to 1680. Fortuitously, also, the cross-reference to the very first note in notebook A (A.I.1) exists. It refers to Le Fèvre's 1664 edition of Phaedrus' *Fabulae*. Notebook A, therefore, could not have been begun before this book was published. The transition between notebooks A and B is more challenging to work out. I would tentatively propose *c.*1668 on the following grounds. In notebook A, the latest publications referred to are: (a) on page two, Le Fèvre's 1671 edition of Justin's *Epitome of Pompeius Trogus*; (b) on pages seventeen and twenty, two different books published in 1667, and (c) on page nineteen, a book published in 1668. Conversely, in notebook B, on page five we have the first of a number of references to the 1669 *Perroniana et Thuana*. If we ignore (a) above for a moment, the proposed date of *c.*1668 looks reasonable enough.

The early reference on page two of notebook A to a volume not published until 1671, however, needs some explanation, since it seems inherently unlikely that a mere page and a half represented six years of notetaking, particularly when it is bookended by what is almost a line-by-line commentary on Longinus' *On the sublime* extending from pages one to eight. We do know from the brief four pages in notebook C that Bouhéreau went back and added things later in the margins beside earlier notes and I would suggest that this is precisely what has happened also in this instance. For a start the cross-reference is one of a few we have which comes not from the flyleaf of the book (where all Bouhéreau had actually written was 'Page 26 Notae'), but from the third note on page seventy of notebook C (see above). But there is more to be said.

In 1714 Bouhéreau published a conjecture on Justin's *Epitome* (2.10) in *Bibliothèque ancienne et moderne*.[30] This conjecture had been the work, or perhaps, rather, the obsession of a lifetime. The note in notebook C is not particularly forthcoming but does refer back to A.II.4 and B.LXXXV, as well as forward to the diary entry of 4 October 1705. In the diary entry we find an earlier draft of

---

29 It should be noted though that the cross-reference to this book, which was gifted to Bouhéreau by A. Du Verney, might have been a later addition to the same note, since there is another cross-reference to B.CXXXII.5 referring to the second latest book referred to in notebook B, i.e. *De L'Ame des bétes*, which was published in Lyon in 1676. Though the author on the title page is listed as A. Du *****, Bouhéreau has added 'Verney' so it is Verney who connects the two entries (something that would not be possible to tell if Bouhéreau had not noted by whom he was gifted the 1680 volume on the pastedown of that book).   30 'Article II: Lettre de Mr. Bouhéreau, sur un passage de Justin, Liv. II.C.10', *Bibliothèque ancienne et moderne*, 2 (1714), 299–308. See Humble, 'Élie Bouhéreau (1643–1719): a scholar at work',

The lost notebooks of Élie Bouhéreau

the conjecture published in 1714, a draft which had itself been well worked over at least once after it was written down in 1705. In this diary entry Bouhéreau notes that Le Fèvre and Johann Graevius are at odds over the point he is at pains to make and that Le Fèvre agrees with him and Graevius does not. Both Le Fèvre's (1671) and Graevius' (1683) editions of Justin can be found among Bouhéreau's books. What we can tell by looking at these copies is that Le Fèvre accepted Bouhéreau's conjecture in his 1671 edition, on page twenty-six of the *Notae* (the very internal cross-reference Bouhéreau made on the flyleaf). When Graevius' edition came out in 1683 with its refutation of Bouhéreau's conjecture, Bouhéreau immediately – one presumes – wrote a response on the flyleaf of that volume (though with no cross-reference to anywhere else). It is this response which eventually ends up in the diary entry in 1705, slightly modified. So the earliest *extant* evidence we have of Bouhéreau's conjecture is what Le Fèvre included in his 1671 edition. The two men, however, must have been discussing the point prior to this and I suspect that the note at A.II.4 was concerned with the early stages of the discussion and that Bouhéreau added a cross-reference back to that entry when he was working on the note again in 1705.

Though I argued above that the nature and distribution of the cross-references do nothing to undermine the suggestion based on notebook C that Bouhéreau's style of note-taking is other than that of *adversaria*, within the random chronological recording of thoughts, there are some patterns of interest worth commenting upon.

(1) Not only do the bulk of the notes on the first eight pages of notebook A refer to Le Fèvre's 1663 edition of Longinus' *On the sublime*, the majority of the cross-references to notebook A deal with classical authors, three of them (Longinus, Phaedrus and Aelian) in editions by Le Fèvre. Biblical passages receive only five entries. Exegesis of one kind or another and theologically oriented texts more broadly only come in for four entries. These are surpassed, though not by much, by notes on contemporary material of a different sort: the letter collections (three notes) of Isaac Casaubon (1559–1614),[31] works by Jean-Louis Guez de Balzac (1597–1654) (four notes),[32] and a few other odds and ends.

(2) While the range of material in notebook B is broader than in notebook A – partially unsurprising given the greater number of pages devoted to the *adversaria* there – notes on ancient Greek and Latin authors do not dominate overall in the way they did in notebook A, accounting for roughly thirty-seven per cent of the total cross-references (a figure based solely on book titles). Further, they are more prominent in the first half of notebook B, whereas works falling into the broad remit of religion dominate more in the last third of the entries in particular.

162–3.   31 Isaac Casaubon, *Epistolae* (Magdeburg, 1656).   32 Jean-Louis Guez de Balzac, *Lettres familieres de M. de Balzac a M. Chapelain* (Leiden, 1656); *Les œuvres de M. Balzac* (Rouen, 1657).

(3) Of contemporary authors and works, Gilles Ménage (1613–92) and Jean-Louis Guez de Balzac garner the most references for individual contemporary authors. The former was close to Le Fèvre and both were friends of Valentin Conrart (1603–75), one of the founders of the *Académie française* who had been the very one to encourage Bouhéreau in his work on a French translation of Origen's *Against Celsus* which was published eventually in 1700.[33]

(4) Legal and scientific texts barely appear at all (a few notes on Galileo being a rare exception in the latter category) and popular literary classics even less so (for example, Tasso garners just one note).

(5) Medical texts, which do not, anyway, make up a significant portion of his collection, are likewise almost absent, appearing only on four occasions and in each case connected with specific plant substances: ephemerum, quinine and, in the very last entry in notebook B (B.CL.5), aloe vera (recorded in two different books).[34] It is possible of course that Bouhéreau kept notes on medical matters in a different place,[35] but if he did, evidence of this is not forthcoming from the medical books in his collection.

(6) Also not immediately evident on this superficial sweep are references to books which would reflect his work on his one major publication, his French translation of Origen's *Against Celsus*. It is tempting, however, to wonder whether or not the two big gaps in notebook B (B.XXXVIII–LI and LIII–LXV), which bookend a cross-reference on page fifty-two to a book in which conjectures on texts of Origen were discussed,[36] mark the real beginning of his work on Origen in *c*.1672. Because Celsus' work contains many references to pagan philosophical works as well, any number of the cross-references could well by feeding into this undertaking. It is detail of this type which is much harder to pick out from the basic data the retrieval system on the flyleaves provides.

(7) A number of notes (A.II.2; A.XIII.1 and 2; A.XVIIII.2; B.XCVII.1; B.CX.2; B.CXXIII.2) have cross-references from both the first (1638) and second (1656) editions of Isaac Casaubon's *Epistolae*. Indeed, there is no occasion on which one edition is mentioned alone in a note without the other, a pattern which collating the cross-references throws into stark relief. The pencil marks in each volume refer to the same letters, so it seems reasonable to assume that we

---

33 Newport J.D. White, 'Elias Bouhéreau of La Rochelle, first public librarian in Ireland', *Proceedings of the Royal Irish Academy*, 27C (1908–9), 139, records 1672 as the first extant mention by Conrart that Bouhéreau undertake this task. M. Marcovich (ed.), *Origines. Contra Celsum libri VIII* (Leiden, 2001), p. xiii, notably refers to Bouhéreau's *Notae* which follow his translation as containing 'brilliant emendations'.   34 Some medical books have brief notes on the flyleaves but most remain unmarked. Jean-Paul Pittion, 'Medicine and religion in seventeenth-century France: La Rochelle, 1676–83' in S.A. Stacey and V. Desnain (eds), *Culture and conflict in seventeenth-century France and Ireland* (Dublin, 2004), p. 54, notes that Bouhéreau's collection held many current medical texts, but a comparison with the collection of the roughly contemporary Huguenot doctor, Josias Floris, reveals that, overall, medical books were not Bouhéreau's focus (see Benedict and Léchot, 'The library of Élie Bouhéreau', pp 173–4).   35 As Locke in fact did; see Yeo, *Notebooks*, p. 185.   36 *Ioannis Croii specimen*

see here, starting very early on, a practice which manifests itself in some late diary entries. There we can see that when he had recorded an error while reading an entry in the first edition of Pierre Bayle's *Dictionnaire historique et critique*, he goes back to the same entry once he has access to the second edition to record whether or not Bayle has self-corrected.[37] Without these notes in the diary entries we would not be able to understand what he is doing because the editions he accesses of Bayle's work are not ones he owns personally so he does not mark them up on the flyleaves.[38]

(8) Finally, when looking at notes with references to multiple different works, while the collation of the cross-references on its own does not always immediately reveal what the possible connection could be,[39] sometimes a quick glance at the pages referred to gets the investigator a little closer. For example, note three on page 107 of notebook B makes reference to page 541 of *Petri Moninaei Hyperaspistes sive Defensor veritatis adversus calumnias* (Geneva, 1636) and page 300 of *Les Oeuvres de Mr de Balzac derniere edition, premiere partie* (Rouen, 1657). When those pages are examined it turns out that Bouhéreau's characteristic pencil mark in the former marks the start of a letter 'Response de Monsieur Du Moulin à la lettre de Monsieur de Balzac' (Response by Mr Du Moulin to Mr Balzac's letter) and in the former marks the start of 'A Monsieur du Moulin' (To Mr Moulin). The connection is clear, even if the detail being discussed cannot be reconstructed.

Although we do not know the actual content of the notes and must always keep in mind the fact that these cross-references do not represent everything Bouhéreau thought worth recording, nevertheless, we can see broad patterns that slot interestingly into, and enhance, what we already know about his life trajectory. For example, the fact that notebook A, which starts sometime in 1664, is dominated by classical material, especially editions of classical authors by Bouhéreau's old tutor Le Fèvre, attests to Bouhéreau's close and continuing connection with him after leaving Saumur in 1662. Indeed, in the publication in 1665 of his second volume of letters, Le Fèvre included twenty-one (out of seventy-two) which he had written to Bouhéreau.[40] In them he often solicits Bouhéreau's scholarly opinion on ancient Greek and Latin texts, both pagan and

---

coniecturarum et observationum in quaedam loca Origenis, Irenaei, Tertulliani, & Epiphanij (Cabala, 1632). A second cross-reference to this work occurs at B.CXLIII.2.   37 See, for example, Léoutre et al., *Diary and accounts*, pp 352–3 (the entry for 9 February 1708). The same type of thing seems to be going on in the note at B.XXIV.2, where the 1619 Italian *Historia del Concilio Tridentino* appears to be being compared with the 1621 translation of the same into French, *Historie du Concile de Trente*.   38 See Humble, 'Élie Bouhéreau (1643–1719): a scholar at work', 166–73, for a detailed examination of Bouhéreau's method here.   39 Except in some cases, for example, B.XCVII.2 has references to four different works of Mr de Balzac, the author himself clearly being the linking factor, whatever the specific point of discussion was.   40 Tanaquil Faber (Tanneguy Le Fèvre), *Epistolae, pars altera* (Saumur, 1665).

Christian. Many of the discussions deal with proposed conjectures for emendations to ancient texts, an activity Le Fèvre was famous for,[41] and a passion for which he passed on also to his pupil, accepting, as noted above, one of Bouhéreau's conjectures in his 1671 edition of Justin. Le Fèvre also dedicated his own 1668 French translation of Diogenes Laertius' *Life of Aristippus* to Bouhéreau.[42] But more than this, this new data provided by the cross-references fits nicely into what we know about his change in career direction at this time too. For, prior to a six-month stay in Paris (December 1663 to June 1664) with his friend Paul Bauldry, Bouhéreau was on track to pursue a career as a pastor, yet after the trip to Paris, he decided on a career in medicine, a pursuit which he clearly viewed as one which would allow him to spend significantly more time on his scholarly interests.[43] We can easily imagine him starting notebook A upon his return from Paris. And the continuing wide variety of material and emphasis on ancient authors until well into notebook B, along with the fact that he was able to accomplish a translation of Origen while engaging in this scholarly reading, to keep connected with other men of letters, to participate in the life and politics of his local consistory, and to practise medicine (which he did from 1668 until 1683 when, as a Protestant, he was forbidden from continuing this profession), attests to the success of the way in which he organized and balanced his interests and responsibilities during these years. The general shift, later in notebook B, of the notes to privileging material on religious controversies then surely reflects the broader political situation and the growing concern in the Huguenot community in the 1670s that their rights were coming under threat.[44]

One of Bouhéreau's cross-references also meshes tantalizingly with the story of Bouhéreau, the apothecary Moyse Charas, Locke, and the eminent London physician, Thomas Sydenham and their shared interest in intermittent fevers and the quinine trail which has been uncovered by Geoff Kemp in this volume. As noted, there are very few cross-references to medical works in Bouhéreau's collection. This does not of course mean that he was not making extensive notes of a medical nature, simply that if he was, we cannot see evidence of it in his regular recording and retrieval system. But of the four cross-references to medical books, one (at B.CXXXII.5) is to the anonymous *De la guérison des*

---

41 See Jean-Paul Pittion, 'Tanneguy Le Fèvre (1615–1672)', Archives de la ville de Saumur, http://archives.ville-saumur.fr/_depot_amsaumur/_depot_arko/articles/815/tanneguy-le-fevre-1615-1672-_doc.pdf), accessed 4 July 2024.   42 *La Vie D'Aristippe, écrite en grec par Diogène, et mise en français par Mr. Le Fèvre* (Paris, 1668).   43 Early letters from Bauldry show the two friends debating and analyzing New Testament texts and how they are interpreted by protestant theologians, but they also attest to a lively interest in classical texts. Ruth Whelan, 'West coast connections: the correspondence network of Élie Bouhéreau of La Rochelle' in V. Larminie (ed.), *Huguenot networks, 1560–1780: the interactions and impact of a Protestant minority in Europe* (New York, 2017), pp 155–71, is the most recent, clearest exposition of the path Bouhéreau's life took in this period (though without precise references to individual letters).   44 See Pittion, 'Medicine and religion', especially 56–62, for a good overview.

fièvres par le quinquina published in Paris in 1680; the reference on the flyleaf is simply 'au titre' ('at the title') and accordingly we find a pencil mark against the first line on the title page.[45] While we cannot know what the note was about, the short volume holds another note of interest. On page nine, next to the beginning of the sentence 'un habile Medecin de Londres, dans un traité qu'il a fait des maladies aiguës, allegue de tres-bonnes raisons de cette methode' ('a skilled doctor from London, in a treatise he wrote on acute illnesses alleges very good reasons for this method'), Bouhéreau has written 'Sydenham'. Further, this is one of two books on quinine in Bouhéreau's collection, the other is Nicolas de Blégny's *Le remède anglois pour la guérison des fièvres publié par ordre du Roy* (Paris, 1682).[46] On the flyleaf of de Blégny's volume is the following note: 'Voyez le 6.e Journal des Scavans de 1683' (see the sixth ed. of the *Journal des Scavans* from 1683). This leads us to the opening article in volume six of this journal which is entitled 'L'Usage du quinquina ou remède contre toutes sortes de fièvres, imprimé par l'ordre du Roy. 1683' (The use of quinquina, or remedy against all types of fever, printed by the order of the King. 1683). This concentrated interest in publications on the use of quinine, illuminated briefly through the cross-references, makes perfect sense in light of Geoff Kemp's reconstruction of Bouhéreau's role in sustaining Moyse Charas' supply of quinine and in keeping secret Charas' knowledge of how to use it.[47]

To conclude, Bouhéreau's method of recording and retrieving is, as far as we can tell, *sui generis*, and it is only the happy coincidence of the discovery of notebook C and the preservation of his library which allows us to gain a deeper understanding of his reading and interests over the course of the keeping of the

---

45 *De la guérison des fièvres par la quinquina* (Paris, 1680). The title page names no author but it is said to be François de Monginot; see Justin Rivest, 'Secret remedies and the rise of pharmaceutical monopolies in France during the first global age' (PhD, Johns Hopkins, 2016), pp 110, 112, and 122.   46 *Le remède anglois pour la guérison des fièvres* (Paris, 1682). De Blégny, as Rivest, *Secret remedies*, p. 122 points out, directly responds to the earlier anonymous treatise on pp 42–3.   47 One further possible connection in the history of the use of quinine and Bouhéreau's part in it can be made, though it does not come from the cross-referencing system. Wouter Klein and Toine Pieters, 'The hidden history of a famous drug: tracing the medical and public acculturation of Peruvian Bark in early modern western Europe (*c*.1650–1720)', *Journal of the History of Medicine and Allied Sciences*, 71:4 (2016), 418, make mention of a court physician, Antoine Menjot, who was interested in treating fevers though who only ever published more traditional remedies. They speculate, however, that his presence in salons of the day makes it likely that he knew well what was going on with the use of the substance. I would add another piece of evidence in support of their speculation and Kemp's arguments. Bouhéreau was in correspondence with Antoine Menjot (publishing a letter to him about textual matters in Plato dated May 1679 on pp 413–16 of his French translation of Origin's *Against Celsus* and subsequently copying Menjot's response on the flyleaf of the same book). Further Menjot gifted a copy of the second edition of his *Febrium malignarum historia et curatio* (Paris, 1674) to Bouhéreau. While none of this points directly to them discussing quinine and its use, given what Geoff Kemp has uncovered, it is hard to rule out the possibility that Menjot was more deeply embedded in the quinine network, as Klein and Pieters speculate.

three notebooks, from 1664 to his death in 1719. We have no evidence that Bouhéreau and Locke debated the pros and cons of their very different methods of recording and retrieving information when they met in La Rochelle in September 1678.[48] Both their methods have their merits and their shortcomings. For Locke subject matter was of prime importance as clearly indicated by his use of titles and his elaborate method of indexing by means of these titles, but it was a difficult system to manage if the range of topics became unwieldy. Bouhéreau used no titles but devised an effective means of cross-referencing notes to books he owned; this, however, means that only a portion of his notes, which were by no means all connected to his reading of his own books, are retrievable through this method. The collation of the cross-references on the flyleaves of his own books is, therefore, only a small glimpse from one perspective into the way Bouhéreau read, recorded and retrieved his thoughts and what books he felt especially compelled to record thoughts on. But the examples above show that even without having the actual notebooks A and B, and so knowing precisely what was catching his attention, collating them nonetheless still deepens and enriches our understanding and appreciation not just of Bouhéreau's own personal world but the wider scholarly world in which he was a committed and engaging participant.

---

48 Locke did own a copy of Bouhéreau's translation of Origen but Bouhéreau did not own any of Locke's works, though this may be explained by his reduced circumstances during the period when Locke was publishing prolifically.

The peregrinations of the archives of the Reformed Church of La Rochelle

DIDIER POTON

In 1862, Robert Travers, assistant librarian at Marsh's Library, composed a 'Catalogue of French Protestant documents' containing the documents deposited there in 1714 by Élie Bouhéreau.[1] This catalogue was compiled following the decision of his Grace Richard Whately, archbishop of Dublin, to return the archives of the Reformed Church of La Rochelle to its consistory, in accordance with the wishes of Élie Bouhéreau, who had expressed the hope that they would be repatriated when Protestant worship was re-established in France. This occurred in 1862, as Napoleon III did not challenge the entry into force of the Organic Articles of 1802. These articles permitted Protestants to practise their faith, to organize worship, and to convene regional synods under conditions imposed by the state, but which nevertheless granted Protestants equal political recognition to Catholics.[2]

On 23 September 1862, these archives were carefully packaged and entrusted to Henry Sandis, the agent appointed by the consistory of La Rochelle to transfer them.[3] In his history of Rochelais Protestants published in 1870, the pastor of the Reformed Church of La Rochelle, Louis Delmas, included in the appendices a 'Chronological inventory of the archives of the La Rochelle consistory brought by pastor Élie Bouhéreau, who was exiled in Scotland after the Edict of Nantes was revoked, and deposited at Marsh's Library, in Dublin, and returned to the presbyterian council of La Rochelle on 24 November 1862 in accordance with Bouhéreau's final wishes.'[4] This appendix is not just a list of the documents received; it describes the contents of some of them. Louis Delmas was the first to have been able to make use of this corpus of sources in a book. These sources are essential to the political and religious history of the

---

Translated from the French by DCU Translation Services.   1 Muriel McCarthy, 'Élie Bouhéreau, first public librarian in Ireland', *Proceedings of the Huguenot Society* 27:4 (2001), 543–60; Newport John Davis White, 'Elias Bouhéreau of La Rochelle, first public librarian in Ireland', *Proceedings of the Royal Irish Academy*, 27 (1908/19), 126–58.   2 Didier Poton and Patrick Cabanel, *Les protestants français du XVIe au XXe siècle* (Paris, 1996), pp 68–71.   3 Marsh's Library, Dublin, MS Z2.2.11, Correspondence between Marsh's Library and the Reverend Louis Delmas, president of the consistory of the Protestant church [La Rochelle], 1858–60.   4 Louis Delmas, *L'Église réformée de La Rochelle: étude historique* (Toulouse, 1870), pp 416–33. The author commits two errors: naming Élie Bouhéreau as a pastor by profession, he was a doctor; and stating Scotland was his country of exile, it was Ireland.

Reformed Church of La Rochelle and more broadly, of the Protestant ecclesiastical province of Saintonge, Aunis and Angoumois, which became progressively more organized after the 1560s.[5]

This chapter will provide an overview of this corpus of documents first brought to England, then brought to Ireland and finally conserved at Marsh's Library by Élie Bouhéreau, who had acted as his consistory's secretary since 1674. It will then consider the conditions under which the person most familiar with the documents of the Reformed Church of La Rochelle was entrusted to take a selection of them out of France to protect them from judicial action under the Counter-Reformation policies initiated by Louis XIV in 1661 at the request of the Catholic Church. Why was this done?

AN IMPORTANT ARCHIVAL SOURCE FOR THE HISTORY OF THE REFORMED CHURCH OF LA ROCHELLE

The catalogue compiled by Robert Travers contains forty-nine pages. The documents are presented as a numbered list from 1 to 372. Each reference corresponds either to an individual document ('Petition from Reformed of La Rochelle complaining of being unfairly assessed to the King's taxes, signed Ph[ilippe]. Vincent') or several documents grouped together in a file under the same topic (nos. 144 to 214 inclusive, 'Printed statements & cases on behalf of the Reformed in various parts of France in the reign of Louis XIV. Among which are some duplicates. In all seventy-one distinct pieces and five duplicates'). Sometimes, comments on the condition of certain documents are included after the title. Let us take some examples: 'Acquittance for one year rent of the Temple due at St Louis's day, 1637, signed Berchaud. Paper, one sheet, wormed & injured by damp' (no. two); 'Confession of Faith with autograph signatures of the Ministers of La Rochelle – Printed broadside, much injured by damp and much of it wholly lost' (no. twenty-one). The majority of documents are dated from the seventeenth century (338 documents, 90 per cent) compared to those from the sixteenth century (33 documents, 10 per cent).

The sixteenth-century collection begins with a document of great importance, the royal order to authorize Protestant worship in two houses in La Rochelle, an outcome of the peace that ended the first French war of religion (1562–63).[6] Eighty-two per cent of the sixteenth-century documents are dated

---

5 Muriel Hoareau, Louis-Gilles Pairault and Didier Poton (eds), *Huguenots d'Aunis et de Saintonge, XVIe–XVIIIe siècles* (Paris, 2017); Jean-Claude Bonnin, 'Les synodes des Eglises réformées de Saintonge, Aunis et Angoumois (1560–1683)', *Revue de la Saintonge et de l'Aunis*, 43 (2017/18), 29–40.   6 Marsh's Library, Dublin, MS Z2.2.8, Catalogue of French Protestant documents (CFD), deposited in Marsh's Library by Dr Élie Bouhéreau in 1714,

from the years 1590–98, the period during which Henry of Navarre, 'Protector of the Reformed Churches in the kingdom of France', became Henry IV, king of France. At the time, Henry also had to confront both the armies of the Catholic League and the King of Spain, while facing pressure from Protestants who, in their political assemblies and synods, demanded that he uphold his promise to impose a statute on the 'papists' enforcing civil and religious tolerance for the Protestant minority. The documents from this period clearly communicate this political climate:

- extracts from documents of the political assemblies of Montauban (1579, 1580–1581, 1584, 1591), Sainte-Foy (1594) and Châtellerault (1597–1598).[7]
- the oaths taken by Henry of Navarre as protector of the Reformed Churches of France (Alliance between the Prince of Navarre, the Prince of Condé and the Reformed Churches of France, no date;[8] Act of union between the Reformed Churches of France and their protector: the king of Navarre, 1588).[9]
- documents attesting to the tensions between the Reformed Churches and Henry who had become King of Navarre.[10]
- documents taken from debates and decisions from the Protestant provinces of Saintonge, Aunis and Angoumois.[11]

It is worth highlighting one other document from this collection: 'Confession of Faith with autograph signatures of the Ministers of La Rochelle – Printed broadside, much injured by damp and much of it wholly lost.'[12] It is the Confession of Faith of the Reformed Churches of France, approved in 1571 during the national synod in La Rochelle, which was held at the request of Jeanne d'Albret, queen of Navarre, and chaired by Théodore de Bèze.[13] The

---

and restored to La Rochelle in 1862, no. 86.   7 Léonce Anquez, *Histoire des assemblées politiques des réformés de France (1573–1622)* (Paris, 1859); Hugues Daussy, *Le parti huguenot. Chronique d'une désillusion (1557–1572)* (Geneva, 2014).   8 Marsh's Library, CFD, no. 105. 'Formulaire du serment d'union des membres des églises adopté par l'assemblée de Montauban de 1581'; Léonce Anquez, *Histoire des assemblées politiques*, pp 30–3 and 452–3. 9 Marsh's Library, CFD, no. 108. This act of union was agreed between Henry of Navarre and the delegates of the Protestant ecclesiastical provinces during a political assembly held in La Rochelle. Léonce Anquez, *Histoire des assemblées politiques*, pp 39–51.   10 Marsh's Library, CFD, nos., 109, 110 and 117.   11 Synod of the province of Saintonge, Aunis and Angoumois, Saint-Jean-d'Angély (29 June 1593), Jean-Claude Bonnin, 'Les synodes des Eglises réformées', p. 38.   12 Marsh's Library, CFD, no. 21.   13 A first edition of the *Confession de foi des Eglises réformées de France* was drafted in Paris in 1559 during an assembly that was considered to be the first national synod of these churches. The problem of deciding on a text and ensuring that it was received by each of the churches in 1571 was reflected in the observation made by Théodore de Bèze that inexact copies of the 1559 text were being circulated. Olga de Saint-Affrique, 'La confession de foi de La Rochelle' in Pierre Gisel (ed.), *Encyclopédie du protestantisme* (Paris, 1995), p. 257; Emile et Eugène Haag, *La France*

secretaries of the synod drafted three copies, one for Jeanne d'Albret, one for Théodore de Bèze and one for the consistory of the church of La Rochelle. The copy brought to Geneva by Théodore de Bèze is the only one that has been preserved.[14] Because the synod had demanded that each Reformed Church of France had to possess a copy of this French Confession of Faith, the so-called Confession of Faith 'of La Rochelle', were hundreds of copies printed in La Rochelle by the workshop of Guillaume Berton in 1572, then sent to each province so that the provincial synod could distribute it to each church? It is impossible to answer this question. Particularly as the Confession of Faith printed and brought by Élie Bouhéreau to Dublin and returned to La Rochelle in 1862, which is currently on display at the Protestant History Museum of La Rochelle, is the only known copy in France to this day (see plate 13).[15] What happened to the handwritten copy kept by the church of La Rochelle?

The 338 references from the seventeenth century can be categorized into the following four chronological series: The first is composed of documents dated from the period 1598–1628, from the Edict of Nantes to the tragic siege of La Rochelle in 1628 which caused between 15,000 and 18,000 recorded deaths, which was approximately eighty per cent of the population.[16] This collection of seventeen references (five per cent) is similar in nature to that of the sixteenth century: documentation from national (La Rochelle, 1607) and provincial (Jarnac, 1621 and 1623) synods, political assemblies (Sainte-Foy, 1601; Jargeau, 1608; La Rochelle, 1613) complemented by supplementary documentation from these meetings (Guidelines for convening provinces, 1611; Guidelines of the Sainte-Foy synod for general deputies of the Reformed Churches of France and of the King, 1601; Jarnac: Copy of complaints of the churches of the provinces of Saintonge, Aunis and Angoumois, 1623; Adoption of the theological decisions of the synod of Dordrecht, 1623). It also includes a letter from the consistory of La Rochelle to the colloquy of Aunis about the La Rochelle Assembly, 1613; notebooks of complaints from Protestants in the province (1609, 1623); and a list of pastors of the Reformed Churches of the kingdom of France (1603).

The second series comprises thirty-five references dated between 1629 and 1662 (ten per cent) and is only focused on one topic: the construction of a temple on a plot of land and the opening of a cemetery in the La Villeneuve area (1630–57). This project was a result of the large temple of the Reformed Church of La Rochelle, which opened for worship in 1606, being confiscated by the king in 1628 to turn it into a Catholic church. But after the religious clauses of the Edict of Nantes were reaffirmed in 1630, the monarchy was obliged to permit the survivors of the siege to have a place of worship and a cemetery. This construction could not be completed as the town had to be allocated a bishop,

---

protestante (Paris, 1859), ix, p. 99.   14 Geneva State Archives, Geneva, MS Parchment, 1571, P. H. 1005.   15 Protestant History Museum of La Rochelle, C 4.1.   16 Hoareau et al., *Huguenots d'Aunis et de Saintonge*, pp 50–9.

and the Edict of Nantes did not authorize Protestant worship in episcopal towns.[17] The area of La Villeneuve is indeed surrounded by ramparts but this is not the heart of the *intra muros* city, it was founded at the start of the seventeenth century with the extension of the defensive walls to the east of the town. This collection of documents is made up of merchant bills and receipts for work carried out in the temple, cemetery and library (twenty-one documents), rent payments owed to the landowners (eight documents), in addition to royal declarations confirming the temple and the cemetery (not dated), prohibiting Rochelais Protestants from being buried in a Catholic cemetery (1630), the mandate of pastors of La Rochelle, a letter from the king to Mr d'Argenson in favour of Protestants (1645), a petition from Protestants against paying a tax, and the obligation to decorate the streets and house fronts when a Catholic procession was passing (not dated).

The third series includes, under one single reference, thirty-three letters from the pastor of La Rochelle, Philippe Vincent, to his colleague Élie Bouhéreau, the father of the doctor/librarian of Marsh's Library, and five 'minutes' of responses (1635–40). This correspondence has never been transcribed and merits its own edition because it is an essential corpus for studying the survival conditions of 5,000 to 6,000 Rochelais Protestants as they became a minority in their own town, as after 1629 Protestants who were not born in La Rochelle were prohibited from residing there. This clause prevented any demographic recovery of the community via Protestants arriving from the province of Saintonge or other provinces. Meanwhile, the monarchy and religious congregations were actively undertaking a vigorous Catholic re-population policy. Under this policy, Catholics were able to occupy land and buildings that were vacated by the death of owners or that were confiscated by the officials responsible for the terms of demolishing the ramparts and the authoritarian purging of the town, ultimately recreating the urban fabric.[18]

The fourth series is the largest in volume (302 references, eighty-five per cent of the total). It comprises documents testifying to the offensive of Louis XIV against the Reformed Churches of his kingdom from 1663 until it ended in 1685 with the Revocation of the Edict of Nantes:

- anti-Protestant legislation (printed royal judgements and declarations against Protestants, 271 documents, ninety per cent);
- various documents about the violent measures, decided by the intendant of the province, imposed against Protestants in Poitou known as the '*dragonnades*' (Response to affairs in Poitou, not dated; Factum on the Reformed Churches of Poitou, not dated; A brief on affairs in Poitou, 1681;

17 Ibid., p. 62. The first bishop only took up residence in La Rochelle in 1648. Louis Pérouas, *Le diocèse de La Rochelle de 1648 à 1724: sociologie et pastorale* (Paris, 1964) (re-ed. EHESS-Mouton, 2008).   18 Ibid.

Defence statement of the minister and the former elders of Fontenay-le-Comte imprisoned in Angoulême, 1681).
- judgements and orders against the churches of La Rochelle and other provinces (Montpellier, Caen, Quevilly, Castres) and documents testifying to their reaction (A brief on the many examples of harassment committed against the Protestants of Aunis, 1680–1682; documents related to the violence carried out against the Reformed Churches of Aunis, 1681; letter from the consistory of La Rochelle about some victims of persecution, 1680).
- judgements and orders prohibiting Protestants from practising certain professions (Judgement of the council of the king on the exclusion of Protestants from certain professions, 1664; order of the council of the king on occupational prohibitions in La Rochelle, 1669; sentence on occupational prohibitions, not dated).
- four documents on the initial departures of the Refuge (papers related to the troubles of 1681 encouraging Protestants to flee; an unsigned letter on the flight of Protestants by boat, La Rochelle, 1681; letter on persecution and exile, Marennes, 1681; letter on the exiled in Delft, not dated).
- four documents on theology.

This final series of papers testifies to the pressure exerted on Protestants from La Rochelle and to the pains they took to communicate with other churches to find out what they were enduring and what measures they were taking to defend themselves. There is no doubt that after 1674 these written exchanges and copies of edicts, judgements and ordinances were carried out by Élie Bouhéreau, the secretary of the consistory, as part of his duties.

THE ARCHIVES REQUIRED FOR DEFENDING PROTESTANT WORSHIP IN LA ROCHELLE

After a tour of Italy, Élie Bouhéreau returned to La Rochelle in 1667. The 'coltish years' were over.[19] He married Marguerite Massiot; a union with the world of big business and finance.[20] As the future head of the family, he had to forge a career. He practised medicine in the municipal health service of La Rochelle. He was held in high regard for his work by his colleagues, both Protestant and Catholic.[21] The contents of his library, however, are a testament to the fact that he did not abandon his love of literature.[22] In 1674 he was elected

---

19 Ruth Whelan, 'La correspondance d'Élie Bouhéreau (1643–1719): les années folâtres', *Littératures classiques*, 1:71 (2010). 20 Denis Vatinel, *Dictionnaire des familles protestantes d'Aunis, Saintonge et Angoumois*, Musée du protestantisme de l'Ouest, Record no. 01592 (2018), pp 4– 5. 21 Jean Flouret, 'L'émigration pour la foi du Rochelais Élie Bouhéreau: une réussite?', *Colloque du Centre des Travaux Historiques et Scientifiques* (1995), 17–25, at 18. 22 Ibid., p. 20.

to the consistory of the Reformed Church of La Rochelle. It was a significant appointment. Was he elected because he was a pastor's son, a scholar, or because he was a man renowned for his action within the community, particularly among the poor, who were afflicted with different diseases, and the elderly? Undoubtedly, he was appointed for all three of these qualities. He joined his cousin Élie Richard who, we know, was a member of the consistory at the time, since he represented the church of La Rochelle, with pastor Daniel Henri Delaizement, at the provincial synod that was held in Marennes from 9–18 of October 1674.[23] The representative at these synods was always one of the members of the consistory from each of the provincial churches. In the rare documents preserved from the colloquia of Aunis and the synods of Saintonge, Aunis and Angoumois, there is no trace of Élie Bouhéreau being present as the delegate of his church.[24] His correspondence demonstrates that he maintained ongoing relations with several pastors in his province and in Poitou.[25] Some of them contacted him to ask him to edit and help publish their manuscripts, if he considered them interesting after sharing any potential comments or corrections. From the years 1679–80, the written correspondence with the pastors veered towards legal advice in the wake of the administrative burden both they and their churches had to endure. The exile of pastor Élie Merlat from Saintes, one of Élie Bouhéreau's correspondents, was a severe warning for all of the province's pastoral bodies.[26]

The purpose of the consistory derives from Calvin's thesis on the visible church. According to the Genevan reformer, the Reformed Churches should have a daily mission to establish provisional order on earth, 'a prelude to the impeccable order of the Kingdom of God'.[27] In France, the reformer expected each of the congregations to have established a consistory, an action via which he acknowledged that the Church was 'readied' to be sent pastors. The first

23 French National Archives, Paris, MS TT251, file XV, Provincial synod of Marennes (October 1674). The documentation of this synod contains lists of the provincial synods of the province of Saintonge, Aunis and Angoumois following the National synod of Loudun of 1659–60: Saint-Savinien (1660), Marans (1661), Jonzac (1662), Jarnac (1663), La Tremblade (1664), Taillebourg (1665), Mauzé (1666), Pons (1667), Verteuil (1668), Saint-Just (1669) Soubise (1670), Marans (1671), Barbezieux (1672), La Rochefoucauld (1673). Only the documentation of the synods of Jonzac and Marennes has been preserved. It is therefore impossible to know if Élie Bouhéreau represented the church of La Rochelle at one or several of these synods. 24 French National Archives, Paris, Documents from the synods of Marennes (1674), Jonzac (1678) and Barbezieux (1674), MS TT 233–246–251; Simon Balloud, 'Les synodes provinciaux protestants en Aunis, Saintonge et Angoumois au XVII^{e}siècle' (Master's thesis, University of La Rochelle, 2010). 25 Jean Flouret, 'La correspondance du médecin rochelais, Élie Bouhéreau (1643–1719)', *Correspondre: actes du 120e Congrès national des sociétés historiques et scientifiques* (Aix-en-Provence, 1995), pp 670–1. 26 Didier Poton, 'Le pasteur saintongeais Élie Merlat (1634–1705)' in Hoareau et al., *Huguenots d'Aunis et de Saintonge*, pp 223–5; Élie Merlat, 'Réponse à l'avis aux Réfugiés' in Didier Poton (ed.), *De Saintes à Lausanne: Élie Merlat (1634–1705)* (Paris, forthcoming). 27 Janine Garrisson, *Les Protestants au XVIe siècle* (Paris, 1998), p. 194; Didier Poton, 'Le pasteur saintongeais Élie Merlat (1634–1705), in Hoareau et al., *Huguenots d'Aunis et de*

consistorial election is perceived as a key event in the foundation of the Reformed Churches of France. After 1559, the *Discipline ecclésiastique des Eglises réformées du royaume de France* (Ecclesiastical discipline of the Reformed Churches of the kingdom of France) established the election procedure for each of the hundreds of Protestant churches that emerged in the years 1550–1560: 'Where the order of the Discipline has not yet been established, the Elections of both the Elders and the Deacons will be decided by the common voice of the people with the Pastors, praying for divine intervention to make the right choice. And the nomination will be spoken aloud in the aforementioned consistory, before those who have been chosen, and their duties will be read to the consistory, so that they are informed of the role to which we wish to elect them. If they give their consent, we will then nominate them to the people over two or three Sundays, so that the people also give their consent.'[28] The consistorial roles were defined in detail: 'The duty of the elders is to monitor the flock with the pastors, to ensure that the people gather and each of them attends the Holy Congregations. It is to report scandals and wrongdoing, by informing and judging with the pastor and more generally, taking care of all things concerning the order, maintenance and governance of the Church'.[29] The discipline then defines the conditions for the functioning of the consistory: a meeting every fortnight after Sunday worship or prayer gatherings, generally on Wednesdays and Fridays, presided over by a pastor. The minutes of the deliberations were taken by a clerk called the 'scribe' in La Rochelle, and were signed by the attendees. These are an essential source of the history of the Reformed Churches even though they do not outline the internal deliberations, only the decisions taken. There is, however, a clear difference in how these were taken in the Languedoc churches compared to other provinces. The former are a lot more detailed, especially in the case of convening one or more faithful believers for reprehensible behaviour. The investigation, questioning and the suspects' responses are often noted.

Saintonge, pp 223–5; Poton, *De Saintes à Lausanne.* 28 Isaac d'Huisseau, *Discipline des Eglises réformées du royaume de France* (Saumur, 1665), pp 69–71. The author, a professor at the *académie* of Saumur, which had been entrusted the mission of drafting and publishing the current state of the ecclesiastical discipline by the national synod of Loudun (1659), states that the basis of this article was drafted by the national synod of Paris in 1559. He then recounts the precisions and modifications implemented by the national synods. It is worth noting that the churches that wanted to elect elders directly by popular vote were met with strong disapproval. As were those that allowed the outgoing elder to appoint his successor even though the proposition came under the competency of the consistory, and those that sent the pastor(s) to 'gather the vote of the people one after another'. In practice, a co-option process was imposed. It was also stated that one had to reside in the church's area in order to be elected. 29 Ibid., p. 73. An article which barely acknowledges the notable amendments and additions made by the national synods. Didier Poton, 'Les institutions consistoriales: les exemples des XVIe et XVIIe siècles', *Bulletin de la Société de l'Histoire du Protestantisme Français*, special no. 1852–2002 (October–December 2022), 953–64.

The Reformed Churches of La Rochelle elected the elders of its first consistory in 1558. In his history of the Reformed Church up to 1628, Etienne Trocmé could only present little information about the Rochelais consistory and only from other sources.[30] In 1561, the consistory had twenty-seven elders. It had fourteen in 1582 but the presence of five deacons is noted. Their functions and role are not clearly defined: in some churches, the deacons are members of the consistory, while in others they do not participate in meetings unless the mission that has been entrusted to them is on the agenda. These missions were most commonly linked to financial and management duties. In 1615, a document mentions nineteen names. The number is likely to have increased quickly to about twenty elders. Analysis of some of the names enabled Etienne Trocmé to assert that the majority of the elders were chosen from the 'middle class, neither very poor nor very rich' Rochelais.[31] It therefore seems that this so-called 'bourgeoisie' social group dominated the municipal organization of La Rochelle and comprised merchants, specialized artisans, and members of the liberal professions who were very engaged in the political life of the city. Like the *corps de ville* (the central body for municipal government), the consistory was the stage for lively, sometimes even violent, debates when La Rochelle was under threat, and opinions were shared about policy to be implemented, or about the military strategy to be deployed in times of open war. The pastoral body tried to maintain harmony, to contain passions … but it was also divided.

Each elder was responsible for a *quartier* of La Rochelle, where they had to ensure harmony among the faithful believers, visit homes afflicted by illness, identify the 'shameful poor' who asked for nothing, and ensure that the obligation to attend worship, certain prayer gatherings and catechism classes was followed. It is worth noting that due to the lack of preserved records, it is currently impossible to write the history of the internal workings of the Reformed Church of La Rochelle from 1560 to 1685. It is likewise impossible to create a list of the elders and deacons. It is also impossible to study the activities of the consistory even over a period of a few years and to draw any interesting conclusions on the evolution of this ecclesiastical organization from the 1560s to the Revocation of the Edict of Nantes.[32] This loss of archival resources is not particular to La Rochelle. The inventory of consistorial records compiled by Raymond Mentzer on archival collections in France and in Refuge countries reports that there are 285 preserved registers which is, according to estimates, less than ten per cent of those drafted by the secretaries of the consistories, based on the number of churches and therefore the number of consistories. Thirty

---

30 Etienne Trocmé, 'L'Eglise réformée de La Rochelle jusqu'en 1628', *Bulletin de la Société de l'Histoire du Protestantisme Français*, 99 (1952), 133–99.   31 Ibid., p. 182.   32 Didier Poton, 'Les institutions consistoriales …', *Bulletin de la Société de l'Histoire du Protestantisme Français* (2002), 953–64.

percent of these records date from the sixteenth century, seventy per cent are from the seventeenth century.[33] In an article, Mentzer investigates the causes of this archival loss.[34] First, he points to the systematic destruction of the archives of the churches in France by officers of Louis XIV at the end of the seventeenth century. This campaign actually began in the 1660s when the commissions sent by the monarchy required churches to provide proof that they were legally permitted to exist in accordance with the Edict of Nantes (1598–1600) and the Edict of Alès (1629). To defend their freedom, the consistories handed over the records. They were collected in the provinces and then sent to Paris, to the council of the king to be processed by lawyers working for stakeholders in the Catholic Counter-Reformation, as part of an investigation into contested places of worship. Some of these documents are today part of the TT series of the French National Archives. There are few consistorial records in this collection: fifty-two in total. Taking the example of Montauban, one of the most important Reformed Churches in the kingdom, Raymond Mentzer shows that the royal officers sorted the Protestant archives after the Revocation of the Edict of Nantes. The records of baptisms-marriages-burials were handed over to the administrative office of the *sénéchaussée* (a court of the *Ancien Régime*) because they were considered to be of 'public interest' for family life, and it should be added that they are a precious basis for compiling a list of families who had to renounce their faith and become the 'New Converts' or the 'New Catholics' (NC). All the other 'entirely useless' paperwork, including twenty-one records of consistorial deliberations, were burned. The only paperwork kept was financial documentation that could be used to initiate procedures to confiscate assets of the consistory. These assets came from donations and legacies from faithful believers, mainly to support activities aimed at helping the poor in the community. This systematic destruction of 'heretical' archives of the 'false religion' was widespread. In Saintes, the *lieutenant général* (deputy to the governor of the province), an officer of the *présidial* (court of appeal in the bailiff's jurisdiction), forced the consistory to hand over its records. Included in the latter, there is a record of a book being handed over to the *parlement* of Guyenne (provincial appellate court) in Bordeaux, as Saintonge fell under the jurisdiction of this royal court.[35] What became of these records that were confiscated by the *justice royale* (central authority of the monarchy)? Were they destroyed like in Montauban? There is no mention of them in the archives of the *présidial* of Saintes nor in the collection of the *parlement* of Guyenne.

33 Raymond Mentzer, *La construction de l'identité réformée aux XVIᵉ et XVIIᵉ siècles* (Paris, 2006). 34 Raymond Mentzer, 'La mémoire d'une "fausse religion": les registres de consistoire des Églises réformées de France (XVIᵉ–XVIIᵉ siècles)' in Philippe Chareyre and Raymond Mentzer (eds), *La mesure du fait religieux: l'approche méthodologique des registres consistoriaux dans l'espace calvinien XVIe–XVIIIe siècles*, Actes du colloque de Pau (2005), *Bulletin de la Société de l'Histoire du Protestantisme Français*, special no., 153 (October–December, 2007), 461–75. 35 *Portrait de la conduite des consistoires et de la Religion P. R. tirés*

What about in La Rochelle? The church was brought before the court at the end of 1684 for having welcomed a woman to the temple who had renounced her faith. This was one of the many legal proceedings initiated by Catholic lawyers for cases of 'relapsing'. The consistory, conscious of not welcoming men and women to avoid being accused of this crime, was caught off guard, according to Élie Benoist's account. At the beginning of 1685, a dual lawsuit was undertaken: one against the pastors and one against the church, which led to the consistory being summoned. The case was brought before the *parlement* of Paris (the highest court of justice under the *Ancien Régime*) as Aunis appealed to this chamber. Aside from the temple bell being confiscated and pastors leaving, we do not have sources that describe what happened after the consistory was summoned.[36] Were the records seized by the judiciary under the framework of these proceedings against the church? Were they sent to Paris?

As secretary of the consistory, Élie Bouhéreau was responsible for maintaining the archives of his church and for keeping the minutes of meetings. At a time when legal attacks were multiplying against Protestant communities, it was a key role as it involved mobilizing all resources from the consistory's archives to respond to the judicial authorities. Alongside the vulnerability that came with this mission, he was also personally confronted with anti-Protestant measures, notably those that targeted specific professions. In 1678, the 1669 ruling was applied, which stated that only Catholics could practise as apothecaries. In 1680, Protestants were banned from working as midwives. In 1681, the seven Catholic doctors in La Rochelle decided to form a college from which their three Protestant colleagues (Jean Seignette, Élie Richard and Élie Bouhéreau) were excluded. The latter failed in their efforts to counter this. It was not a favourable context. It was the year of the *dragonnades* in Poitou. Abraham Tessereau, the 'legal advisor'[37] of the church of La Rochelle, responded to the three doctors: 'The petitions are pointless'.[38] According to the Protestant legal expert, judges did not want to get involved in 'issues intertwined with religion'.[39]

Élie Bouhéreau's correspondence provides information on the advice that was given to him to secure his future: to devote himself to business in his father-in-law's company, to accept the position as philosophy professor that was offered to him by the *académie* of Saumur or to join the academy in Geneva. A *lettre de cachet* (a royal missive usually used to issue punitive orders) banished him to

du sixième et dernier livre des délibérations de celui de Saintes; dédié à Noseigneurs du Parlement de Guyenne in Élie Benoist, *Histoire de l'édit de Nantes* (Delft, 1695), III, third part, pp 687–8. **36** Benoist, *Histoire de l'édit de Nantes*, pp 751–3. **37** Jean-Paul Pittion, 'Un médecin protestant du XVII^{e}siècle et ses livres. Anatomie de la collection d'Élie Bouhéreau à la Bibliothèque Marsh de Dublin', *Irish Journal of French Studies*, 16:1 (2016), 35–58. Thomas Philip Le Fanu, 'Mémoires inédits d'Abraham Tessereau', *Proceedings of the Huguenot Society of London*, 15:4 (1937), 1–16. Abraham Tessereau was officially appointed by the colloquy of Aunis as its officer in Paris in 1675 and not in 1673 as indicated by Le Fanu, Departmental Archives of Charente-Maritime (ADCM), MS 300 j 258. **38** Ibid., p. 673. **39** Ibid.

Poitiers then to Paris. But the content of a letter from his friend Turon de Beyrie dated March 1685 clarifies things: 'You have then resolved to leave your belongings and your country [...].'[40]

Élie Bouhéreau did not bring all of the archives of his church into exile. The records of baptisms, marriages and funerals remained and were preserved by the church. Then, just like in Montauban, they were kept by the royal officers because they were 'of public use'.[41] What about the records of consistorial deliberations with appended files, such as the accounting documents related to pastors' wages and the management of the consistory's assets, were they seized by the judicial authorities before Élie Bouhéreau's departure? But other documents remained in La Rochelle since they were not mentioned in the catalogue compiled by Robert Travers that was handed over to Henry Sandis. Notably, this was the case for the sixteenth-century acts from the national synod which was held in La Rochelle in 1581 with an exceptional handwritten copy of the *Discipline des Eglises réformées du royaume de France*.[42] Were Protestants concerned about keeping one of the two founding texts of the Calvinist Reformation hidden in France?

In relation to the seventeenth century, close to eighty per cent of the resources available at the departmental archives of Charente-Maritime were documents sent to La Rochelle from Dublin in 1862! This shows the significance of these resources for writing the history of the Reformed Church of La Rochelle – but not its entire history. These sources reconstruct the history of the church's legal defence of its ownership of a plot of land in the district of La Villeneuve that permitted the construction of a temple and the opening of a cemetery, as well as the history of the church's response to the anti-Protestant policies of Louis XIV from 1663 onwards. After 1674, Élie Bouhéreau, as secretary of the consistory, was able to draft memoranda to support petitions to the council of the king via Henri de Massue de Ruvigny, the Deputy General of the Reformed Churches. He was even able to engage legal proceedings with the well-informed and well-considered advice of Abraham Tessereau, with files containing, for example, significant facts about the anti-Protestant policy of the officers of the monarchy, an exceptional collection on the *dragonnades* of 1681.[42a]

It was not only men, women and children that had to leave France under the reign of Louis XIV. Books, printed pages, and manuscripts, and family documentation were carried with them in packs, luggage, pockets and in the lining of clothing. Certificates of baptisms and marriage blessings provided proof in the Refuge countries of their Protestant faith. These precious documents were often folded into a Book of Psalms, a prayer book, or a small devotional book to

---

40 Ibid., pp 673–4.   41 ADCM, *Registres pastoraux de La Rochelle*, I. 1–65, 1561–1684.
42 Didier Poton, 'La Rochelle.1571–1581. D'un synode national à l'autre: Confession de foi et Discipline ecclésiastique des Eglises réformées du royaume de France', forthcoming.
42a See David van der Linden's chapter.

hide any sign of belonging to the Reformed Church, which could enable military and judicial authorities to qualify these men and women as 'fugitives'. They could therefore accuse them of fleeing, which was a crime under the royal legislation that banned subjects from secretly leaving the kingdom without a passport. To these must be added the dossiers that would enable Abraham Tessereau and Élie Benoist to publish well-documented works on the history of the Reformed Churches under the regime of the Edict of Nantes.[43]

The archives deposited by Élie Bouhéreau at Marsh's Library are a corpus with a common theme: the relationship between the Reformed Church of La Rochelle and the kings of France between 1563 and 1681. These documents weave a continuous thread: forcing Henry of Navarre, who would become Henry IV, to uphold the commitment that he made as protector of the Reformed Church of France then as king of France, to grant Protestants a status of religious and civil tolerance. One could also include the series of documents that cover 1598 to 1628, a period marked by defending the implementation of the Edict of Nantes, and enduring Louis XIII's policy aiming to revoke its political and military clauses following rebellion in several towns including La Rochelle. After 1628, the documents had only one purpose: defending the legitimacy of Protestant worship in La Rochelle. These documents were preserved and protected abroad in the Refuge in the hope that they would be useful if Louis XIV abandoned his anti-Protestant policy and it became necessary to once again justify the right of Rochelais Protestants to form a church, to publicly practise their faith and to live without political and social discrimination. Many refugees left, convinced that their exile was only temporary and that the Edict of Nantes would be reinstated. Negotiations with the French monarchy would recommence once more, and thus the cycle would continue. Was Élie Bouhéreau one of those anticipating this outcome in 1683? Was he still expecting this in 1685 when the Revocation of the Edict of Nantes was announced, followed by the exodus of tens of thousands of French Protestants to the countries of the Huguenot Refuge?

[43] Abraham Tessereau, *Histoire des réformés de La Rochelle depuis l'année 1660 jusqu'à l'année 1685 en laquelle l'édit de Nantes a été révoqué* (Leiden, 1688); Élie Benoist, *Histoire de l'édit de Nantes* (Delft, 1693), 5 vols; trans. in English, London, 1693, in 4°, and in Flemish, Amsterdam, 1696, 2 vol. in-fol.

Stealing and selling Dr Bouhéreau's books in the long eighteenth century

JASON McELLIGOTT

I

Tourist visitors to Marsh's Library are often told that the personal library of Dr Élie Bouhéreau survives intact where it was originally placed on shelves in what is now called the 'Old Reading Room'. This is not entirely accurate. Certainly, there are almost 2,000 volumes in the space that were owned by, and placed there by Bouhéreau in his role as the first 'keeper', the title by which the librarian of Marsh's was originally known. Yet, perhaps as much as ten per cent of the original collection has gone missing over the centuries through a mixture of theft, a sale of 'duplicates' in 1833, and the destruction of books that had been sent out to be rebound in the premises of Messrs. Thom in Middle Abbey Street, in Dublin's city centre, just days before the Easter Rebellion of 1916. The proximity of the bookbinder's premises to the insurgents' headquarters in the General Post Office meant that it was wholly consumed by fire during the fierce fighting for that area between the rebels and British forces.

This article cannot examine all of the losses from Dr Bouhéreau's collection. Instead, it will use surviving audits of the contents of Marsh's Library to focus on items stolen from Bouhéreau's personal collection between 1707 and 1828. Due to limitations of space, a consideration of the losses from Bouhéreau's collection due to the 1833 sale and the 1916 Rising will appear in a future publication. In terms of theft, the end-date of 1828 marks the point when the library finally began to take the problem seriously and brought in procedures that staunched the unauthorized flow of books out of the building.[1] In what follows, the items stolen from Bouhéreau's collection will be used to consider the scope of his personal library as originally donated. The article will also use these thefts to discuss the striking failures of the library management and trustees over a lengthy period. It will further demonstrate that this important subset of thefts from Marsh's Library can be used to track the growth of a new concept around the turn of the nineteenth century, that of the antiquarian 'rare book', as well as the development of a second-hand market in Dublin to feed this trade.

---

1 Marsh's Library, Dublin, MS ML 31. Visitation book of the governors and guardians, 1708–1924, 117th visitation, 11 October 1827; 118th visitation, 9 October 1828. This volume is unfoliated, so references to the MS give the date of the relevant annual visitation.

The existing scholarship around the theft of books during the early modern period is very thin. In the mid-twentieth century there were two articles in the *Transactions of the Cambridge Bibliographical Society* about the illicit removal of books from libraries in that small town on the edge of the Fens.[2] James Raven's important edited collection *Lost libraries: the destruction of great book collections since antiquity* contains several passing mentions of theft across two millennia, but the fifteen contributors focus on the deliberate or accidental destruction of significant collections arising from military activity or political, social, and cultural tensions.[3] A small number of instances of theft are mentioned in the relevant volume of the *Cambridge history of libraries in Britain and Ireland*,[4] and Peter Fox has described several thefts that took place during the seventeenth and eighteenth centuries from the library of Trinity College Dublin.[5] Yet, the only monograph that explores the subject of book theft during this period is *Stealing books in eighteenth-century London*, which uses the digitised proceedings of the Old Bailey to examine more than 700 instances of men and women who faced trial for pilfering a book or books from commercial bookshops and private homes. The book provides fascinating details about the motives and methods for theft, as well as shedding light on the ownership of books across different social groups, but by its very nature it can only focus on those individuals who were unlucky enough to get caught *and* brought to trial.[6] This article on Dr Bouhéreau's books is, to the best of the author's knowledge, the first attempt to track thefts from a collection in an early modern library in order to deduce patterns and meaning from an accumulation of individual expropriations.

II

Before examining what went missing from Bouhéreau's collection, it will be useful to say a little about how these books ended up in a small library in central Dublin. It remains unclear how and when Bouhéreau managed to transport his cumbersome personal library of more than 2,000 volumes out of France. There is a charming tale, apparently derived from one of Élie's granddaughters, that the volumes were saved by means of a fictitious sale to the English ambassador to France, who then forwarded them to safety in London under diplomatic protection, but there is no historical evidence for such an unlikely series of

---

2 Paul S. Walker and J.C.T. Oates, 'Charles Burney's theft of books at Cambridge', *TCBS*, 3:4 (1962), 313–26; Philip Askell, 'Henry Justice, a Cambridge book thief', *TCBS*, 1:4 (1952), 348–57. 3 James Raven (ed.), *Lost libraries: the destruction of great book collections since antiquity* (Basingstoke, 2004). 4 Giles Mandelbrote and K.A. Manley (eds), *The Cambridge history of libraries in Britain and Ireland*, 3 vols (Cambridge, 2006), ii *(1640–1850)*, pp 230–2, 481. 5 Peter Fox, *Trinity College library Dublin: a history* (Cambridge, 2014), pp 21, 44, 59, 88. 6 Richard Coulton, Matthew Mauger and Christopher Reid, *Stealing books in eighteenth-century London* (Basingstoke, 2016).

events.[7] It is not known whether the books left France in the years before 1685 because of fears for the future, or if they were dispatched in a hurry at the time of the Revocation. They may even have been forwarded to Élie months or years after his flight, as there is some evidence that he was in contact with friends or family in France long after he arrived in England and later came to Ireland.[8] The first historical evidence for their location appears in August 1705 when Bouhéreau recorded spending eight shillings to have them 'carried to the Library' in St Patrick's Close, where he and his family had already been living for almost two years in the keeper's apartment on the ground floor of Marsh's Library.[9] The Act to Settle and Preserve 'a Publick Library For Ever' was finally passed in October 1707 and Bouhéreau's books became the property of the new institution at this point in time. The books were probably only moved out of the keeper's apartment and into the public galleries on the first floor of the building after the passage of the act. In January 1708, Bouhéreau recorded in his diary that a friend named Mr D'Agniel had come 'to help me put the books of the library in order, and shall continue to do so.'[10]

The act of 1707 specifies a figure of 2,057 volumes donated by Élie Bouhéreau, but, as some were sammelbands containing two or more separate titles bound together, there may have been as many as 2,300 individual titles in the collection. The general contours of the collection that have survived into the twenty-first century have been sketched by Philip Benedict and Pierre-Olivier Léchot. They describe the library of a seventeenth-century medical doctor that contains many books accumulated by his father and earlier generations of the family. The medical books tend to be the most up-to-date titles in terms of contemporary knowledge. There is little evidence of any interest in contemporary literature, but there was an impressive range of classical literature and history in Greek and Latin. There was also much religious material and theological disputation, as one might expect, but in an intriguing turn of phrase Benedict and Léchot characterize the intellectual world of the collection as a mixture of Aristotelianism and the worldview of the French natural philosophers René Descartes (d.1650) and Pierre Gassendi (d.1655).[11]

---

[7] Newport J.D. White, *Four good men: Luke Challoner, Jeremy Taylor, Narcissus Marsh, Elias Bouhéreau* (Dublin, 1927), pp 79–80.   [8] Marie Léoutre, Jane McKee, Jean-Paul Pittion and Amy Prendergast (eds), *The diary (1689–1719) and accounts (1704–1717) of Élie Bouhéreau: Marsh's Library Z2.2.2* (Dublin, 2019), p. 501.   [9] Ibid., p. 409; Raymond Gillespie (ed.), *Scholar bishop: the recollections and diary of Narcissus Marsh, 1638–96* (Cork, 2003), pp 58–9.   [10] Léoutre et al., 'Diary and accounts', p. 353.   [11] Philip Benedict and Pierre-Olivier Léchot, 'The library of Élie Bouhéreau: the intellectual universe of a Huguenot refugee and his family' in Muriel McCarthy and Ann Simmons (eds), *Marsh's library – a mirror on the world: law, learning and libraries, 1650–1750* (Dublin, 2009), pp 165–84.

III

The act of parliament that established Marsh's Library contained detailed precautions against loss and theft: the books and manuscripts were never to leave the library premises, and nothing was to be sold, given away or otherwise alienated, save for a provision that duplicate copies of books could be sold to raise funds to purchase texts that were not already present in the library. The building and its contents were vested in the care of nine *ex officio* trustees drawn from the highest echelons of the legal profession, Dublin University, and the Church of Ireland 'as by law established'. The board was to be known as the 'Governors & Guardians' and their meetings would be quorate if the archbishop of Dublin, who was the chairman, and any two other trustees were present. In the absence of the archbishop, five trustees would have to be present for a meeting to be able to take binding decisions. The governors and guardians were free 'to make such Reasonable Rules and Orders for the better Government of the Library, as they shall think necessary and convenient.' The librarian, who was usually referred as either the 'Library keeper' or simply the 'Keeper', was subordinate to the governors and guardians and his primary task was to ensure that all those who came to the library 'conform themselves to the Rules, Orders and Directions of the Governors'.[12]

There is no indication of anything at all amiss in the library until 1738 when the then keeper, Dr John Wynne, who had been appointed to the post eight years earlier, informed the governors that 'a great number of books' had been 'very lately stolen out of the Library' and that many other books' had been damaged by having maps, pictures or text torn out of them. The keeper produced a list of these stolen and damaged books, but this document does not survive. In response to Wynne's troubling information, the governors ordered that 'if any Person shall be detected to have stolen defaced interlined or tore any book belonging to the said Library he shall be prosecuted with the utmost rigor of Law without any Expectation of pardon or composition'. A stipulation that every person found in possession of 'any book stolen out of the Library' would be prosecuted 'with the same severity' was clearly aimed at booksellers who might purchase the books, or pawnbrokers willing to provide small loans based on their value.[13] As to who was stealing the books, the insistence that only 'Graduates and Gentlemen' should be admitted says much about the Trinity undergraduates and readers below the rank of gentleman who had never attended university who were suspected to be causing problems. The Governors asked the keeper to transcribe these 1738 orders and have them posted on the front door of the library to inform readers and deter potential thieves. At each of the next three

---

12 Marsh's Library Act 1707, *Irish statute book*, https://www.irishstatutebook.ie/eli/1707/act/19/enacted/en/print, accessed 2 April 2024.   13 Marsh's Library, MS ML 31, 29th visitation, 12 October 1738.

annual meetings of the board, Dr Wynne was ordered to ensure that these regulations were 'still continued and daily executed', but they may have fallen into disuse during the following years.[14]

In October 1747, however, for the second time in less than a decade Dr Wynne provided the trustees with a list of 'a great Number of Books' that had been 'Stolen out of the Library probably by persons who Resort there to Read ... under the Denomination of being Gentlemen.'[15] To 'guard against the Thefts of such Detestable Villains for the future', the board recommended that Dr Wynne 'employ an honest Porter who may Constantly attend at the Door during the Library Hours & Watch & Search every suspected Person that may happen to be admitted'. It was also ordered that the librarian 'endeavour to Collect as soon as possible Books of the same Edition' to replace all 'those that are stolen'. This would involve purchases on the second-hand market with some of the £10 per annum that was available for this purpose.

The security of the collections did not improve, and in October 1750 Dr Wynne informed the board that 'a great Number of Books' had been stolen in the twelve months since the previous visitation. This list of missing books does not survive, but a sense of the scale of the problem is provided by an order that the assistant librarian be reimbursed for the considerable sum of £7 6s. spent in 'Buying several Books since the last Visitation' to replace those 'Stolen out of this Library.' It was claimed that the culprits were 'most probably ... persons who Resort thither to Read under the Denomination of Gentlemen', and once again it was recommended to the librarian that he 'employ some proper person ... at the Door during the Library Hours who may Watch & Search every person' admitted to the building.[16]

The librarian's failure to employ a porter as per the trustees' original recommendation of 1747 was probably due to the fact that no extra money was made available to pay for this new employee. Yet, the omission may also have arisen from the very real problems that might arise for any porter who dared to stop and interrogate a gentleman or an undergraduate student. It would have been unthinkable for a porter to try to search a gentleman's possessions or even his physical person for hidden books or manuscripts. Unless a porter found himself dealing with an obviously disruptive reader from a relatively humble background whom he was sure did not enjoy the patronage of a significant individual in the social and cultural life of Dublin, the best he could do was bring his suspicions to the attention of the librarian or the assistant librarian. These men may also have been wary about trying to exert some form of discipline over

---

14 Ibid., 30th visitation, 11 October 1739; 31st visitation, 9 October 1740; 32nd visitation, and 8 October 1741.   15 Ibid., 37th visitation, 8 October 1747. Neither the 1747 list of stolen books nor the details of the books bought to replace these items survive in the library's archives.   16 Marsh's Library, MS ML 31, 40th visitation, 11 October 1750.

young men of social standing who might complain to the board or go to law to protect their good name and reputation.

The librarian was ordered to search among the booksellers of Dublin and to 'use his Endeavours to trace & find out the persons' from whom any bookseller in possession of items stolen from the library had bought 'the said Books.' The library obviously believed that the missing books were being sold or pawned by the thieves soon after being removed from the premises. There was also a suspicion that the guilty party or parties were likely to be known to the booksellers about town, probably because they were in the habit of selling individual books or small numbers of volumes on a regular basis.

It is not known whether the librarian finally employed a porter and searched the book stalls and bookshops of Dublin, but the thefts continued to be of concern to the board. In 1752, the trustees ordered the librarian to have readers sign a declaration that they would do no harm to the books. In future, nobody was to be admitted unless he had subscribed his name to this declaration.[17] A sense that the keeper was not as active in tackling problems in the library as he should have been is confirmed by the order three years later, in 1755, from the governors that 'every person who comes to Read in the Library & who is not known to the Librarian' should sign his 'Name & Place of his Abode' on the parchment scroll which contained this readers' declaration.[18]

There was no visitation in 1756, but in the following year the board 'having found that several Books' had been stolen since last visitation resolved that 'no Person whatever not known to the Librarian or his Assistant be permitted to read in this Library except in the presence of the Librarian or his Assistant.'[19] Dr Wynne was clearly still allowing some people who were not known to him or his assistant to use the collections. In addition, there were at least some readers who were permitted to use the books without adequate oversight, whether because they were allowed to access the shelves unattended or remained in the library when neither man was present in the building. The phrase in the 1757 records about the trustees 'having found that several Books' had been stolen suggests they made this discovery during their annual inspection of the site and had not been informed in advance by the keeper.[20]

The surviving archives of the library paint Dr Wynne as a man who was either cavalier about the security of the library or, perhaps more likely, simply ineffectual in carrying out his duty of care. Yet, there is an illuminating example that shows he could be very diligent, one might almost say zealous, in his protection of certain types of records that he valued. At some point before 1760 Wynne became concerned that Roman Catholic readers might abuse their access

---

[17] Marsh's Library, MS ML 31, 41st visitation, 10 October 1751; 42nd visitation, 12 October 1752.   [18] Ibid., 45th visitation, 9 October 1755.   [19] Ibid., 47th visitation, 13 October 1757.   [20] Ibid., 13 October 1757.

to the building by tampering with or destroying the papers relating to the privileges enjoyed by the French Huguenots under the Edict of Nantes (1598).[21] These documents, which might conceivably be important legal documents if the Huguenots ever returned to France, had been deposited by the first keeper, Dr Élie Bouhéreau. Wynne had on his own initiative moved them 'for greater Security' from their place in Bay A4 of the second gallery to 'a Closet which is kept constantly locked'. To thwart the machinations of the 'papists' and to protect the history of the Protestants of France and their possible future legal status, the key to this closet was always in the custody of either Wynne or his assistant. This would not be the last time that sectarian animosity would interact with the story of theft in Marsh's Library.

Soon after Wynne's death at the age of eighty-two in January 1762, the Governors elected Thomas Cobbe as keeper and he duly took the oath prescribed by the act of 1707 to protect the library collections and entered the recognisance of £500 to replace any items which went missing.[22] The appointment of the 29-year-old graduate of Trinity College Dublin as keeper might have been expected to bring some dynamism to the running of the library but he does not seem to have been very active, or perhaps it would be more accurate to say that his energies may have gone into his many other duties, which included being a colonel in the militia and a governor of the Dublin Workhouse, St Patrick's Hospital, Dr Steevens' Hospital, and Swift's Hospital for Lunatics. During his tenure as the keeper of Marsh's Library he was also an MP for Swords, which has been described as 'the most notoriously corrupt borough in the Irish parliament.'[23] On the death of his father, he inherited Newbridge House, a splendid Georgian mansion in Donabate in north Co. Dublin designed by the leading architect James Gibbs.[24]

Thomas owed his position as keeper not to any demonstrable interest in libraries but to the fact that his father, Charles Cobbe, was the archbishop of Dublin and therefore chairman of the governors and guardians which made the appointment. The publication by the *Freeman's Journal* of a barely anonymized attack on a certain prelate's son who had secured a 'nominal superintendency' of a famous library, suggests that Thomas was interested in the post because he could do little or no work and still draw an annual salary.[25] Whatever his actual level of personal activity or interest, Thomas Cobbe must have had the assistant librarian spend a considerable amount of time in carrying out a stock check of

---

21 These papers were the archive of the consistory of the Reformed Church of La Rochelle. See Didier Poton's chapter in this volume regarding their contents and 'peregrinations'. 22 Marsh's Library, ML 31, Meeting of the governors and guardians, 2 February 1762. 23 Edith Mary Johnston-Liik, *History of the Irish parliament 1692–1800*, 6 vols (Belfast, 2002), iii, p. 438. 24 Alec Cobbe and Terry Friedman, *James Gibbs in Ireland: Newbridge, his villa for Charles Cobbe, archbishop of Dublin* (Dublin, 2005). 25 *Freeman's Journal*, 8 Sept. 1764.

the library because in October 1766 the keeper was ready to present to the governors a 'Statistical Catalogue' of all the books stolen from the library since its foundation.[26]

This twenty-one-page list is written in a very neat hand in a plain paper notebook. It was the result of a huge amount of work in checking thousands of books on the shelves against the official catalogues of what had originally been in the collections. Unfortunately, only one governor was present for the 1766 annual visitation so it was not quorate, and no business could be done.[27] Thomas Cobbe and the assistant librarian had sat for two hours with the sole attending governor as they waited for the other trustees to arrive, and during this time the three men must have discussed the very sobering document that made clear the scale of the problem. This audit survives among the archives of the library and lists more than 380 volumes of 320 separate titles which had been removed from the galleries. Of these 320 titles, 97 were missing from the Stillingfleet collection, 140 from the Marsh collection, and 83 from the Stearne bequest. There was no attempt to quantify any losses from Bouhéreau's collection in the reading room. It is hard to imagine that this was a simple oversight. Instead, it suggests that the assistant librarian and whoever else might have helped him to carry out the work did not think any books would be missing from this central location where readers and library staff tended to congregate at the table near the fire, particularly during inclement weather when the unheated galleries were very cold and uncomfortable.

Thomas Cobbe was a very wealthy, well-connected, and ambitious man but he faced serious problems as keeper. The death of his father in April 1765 meant that he was no longer the son of the chairman of the board. The keeper was expected to provide the funds to carry out repairs to the deteriorating fabric of the building, including its increasingly fragile roof, and there was only a tiny fund of £10 per annum to buy new books for the collection. Cobbe was now faced with having to replace several hundred books that had vanished from the library, as well as preventing more thefts in the future. The governance structure of the library was also very cumbersome, and it was becoming increasingly difficult to convene quorate meetings of the board. In these circumstances, and with other business to attend to that was more profitable and less troublesome, Thomas Cobbe resigned his post on 12 November at a special meeting of the governors held in the deanery of St Patrick's Cathedral. Three days later, the Revd William Blachford (1730–73), an Anglican clergyman and wealthy landowner, was elected keeper and swore the oath to protect the collections from being lost or 'Imbezzeled' and entered the necessary recognisance for £500.[28]

---

26 Marsh's Library, Dublin, MS ML 33. A statistical catalogue of all the books stolen out of St Sepulcher's Library from the time of the foundation to the 9th day of October 1766.
27 Marsh's Library, MS ML 31, 56th visitation, 9 October 1766.   28 Marsh's Library, MS ML 31, Meeting of the governors and guardians, 15 November 1766; *Freeman's Journal*,

The first visitation under the new keeper was held in October 1767 and the board recorded that they had 'inspected the state and condition of the Library' and 'found it in compleat and Elegant Order'.[29] These words should be read as a fine example of the tendency for official records in all places and all eras to remain mute about discussions that might provide evidence about incompetence, failure, or criminality on the part of the institution or its officers. In fact, the situation, far from being one of complete and elegant order, was even worse than that described by Thomas Cobbe. By March 1767, Blachford had overseen the production of his own audit of library thefts which listed not 380 volumes of 320 separate titles, but a shocking 608 volumes of 505 missing titles.[30] Blachford had, in other words, identified a further 228 volumes of 185 stolen titles. A good indication of the state of disorder and chaos in the library is that subsequent enquiries by Blachford and his assistant located 70 books that they had initially believed to have been stolen. Some of these revenants had probably been misshelved by staff and readers in the public galleries of the library, but others may have been stored in other rooms in the building, or even loaned to readers who took them off the premises and were then pressed to return them by the new librarian. It is even possible that some of the 'found' books had been stolen and subsequently located when offered for sale in bookshops or pawn shops across the city.

IV

436. That was Blachford's final tally of the books stolen from Marsh's Library. Of these, 138 were missing from the Stillingfleet collection, 165 from the Marsh collection, and 118 from the Stearne bequest. The 1767 audit is significant because it provides the first evidence for thefts from Élie Bouhéreau's collection. It lists only fifteen missing items, a tiny 0.73% of the 2,057 volumes given to the library by the first keeper.

Table 1: Titles stolen from Marsh's Library, 1707–67[31]

Collection	Period: 1707–67
Stillingfleet	138
Bouhéreau	15
Marsh	165
Stearne	118
Total	**436**

9 Dec. 1766. 29 Marsh's Library, MS ML 31, 57th visitation, 8 October 1767. 30 Marsh's Library, Dublin, MS ML 34. A catalogue of the books stolen out of Marsh's Library to March 1767. 31 This table lists books by number of titles rather than the number of volumes in an

Two of Bouhéreau's books were removed from the first shelf at ground level, but all of the others were taken from the fifth to ninth shelves which house smaller formats and are not easily reached by most readers without the use of a ladder or stool. Two of the fifteen were published in English, two in French, one in Italian, nine in Latin, and one contained Greek and Latin. The earliest of the titles had been published in 1551 and there was one from 1636, but all the others were printed after 1660. The stolen books were, in other words, among the newest of the books in Bouhéreau's personal library, insofar as the word 'new' can be applied to volumes which had been sitting on the shelves for over half a century by the mid-eighteenth century.

The missing items had been printed in a sprinkling of cities across western Europe. There were two each from Paris, Leiden, and Amsterdam, and one each from Cologne, Leipzig, Venice, Lyon, Geneva, London, and Dublin. The place of publication of one book is unknown. The strongest correlation among the books was their small size; all but two of them were in octavo, duodecimo or smaller formats. As for the subjects that were stolen, there were only three items missing from the many hundreds of volumes in Bouhéreau's personal library that dealt with theology, theological disputes, or religious controversy. His significant collection of classical texts was also untouched, apart from one Latin edition each of Aristotle and Virgil. The thief or thieves had made off with some eclectic titles that might be classified under the anachronistic rubric of magical sciences. *Magia naturalis* (Amsterdam, 1664) was an immensely popular text first published by Giambattista della Porta in Naples in 1588. It brought together a range of medical facts, popular superstition, and sheer, unadulterated nonsense to inform the reader about a range of seemingly unrelated activities and phenomena. Among other things, it claimed to teach how to clean brass, grow sweet almonds, administer aphrodisiacs, manufacture magical rings that made the wearer invisible, produce silver from lead, preserve fish, prevent reeds from growing on one's land, use a piece of the hoof of a mule to render a woman sterile, kill scorpions with human saliva, and cure drunks of their love of wine. Also missing was an edition of Claude Gadroys' *Discours sur les influences des astres*, which tried to marry traditional astrology with the work of the French mathematician René Descartes on the mechanical motions of the heavens.[32]

If the missing books were mostly an eclectic mix of titles and genres, there was a noteworthy group of four titles from the world of medicine and anatomy. A copy of the famous aphorisms of the ancient physician Hippocrates edited by the Dutch physician and botanist Adolphus Vorstius (1597–1663) was taken.[33] One would need a rather specialized interest in anatomy to make off with Gerardus Blancken's list of the medical instruments and human and medical specimens on

---

edition. So, a three-volume set of a book is counted as one title rather than three volumes.
32 Aaron Spink, 'Claude Gadroys and a Cartesian astrology', *Journal of Early Modern Studies*, 7:1 (2018), 151–71.   33 A. Vorstius (ed.), *Aphorismi* (Lyon, 1661).

display in the anatomy hall of the University of Leiden. The 1704 Latin edition of letters written by the French physician Raymond Vieussens (d.1715) who was famous for his dissections of the heart, brain and spinal cord was also a rather erudite choice for a thief. Of more general interest was Richard Lower's *Tractatus de corde* (Amsterdam, 1671), which described his clinical observations and experiments concerning the heart, spinal cord, lungs, blood vessels and blood. The book's plates showing sections through these tissues and organs were of a very high quality.[34] The fact that the volumes by Blancken and Vieussens had sat side-by-side on the fifth shelf of bookcase R1 suggests they were probably stolen by the same person. This person might also have taken the other medical and anatomy books, but it is likely that the broader set of books described in this section were stolen by several people over a longer period.

V

The audits of the 1760s provide a vivid sense of the disorganization and neglect that reigned in the library, but by laying bare the scale of the problem they provided an opportunity for a new start. It should have been possible for the trustees and successive keepers to improve security and perhaps even to replace some of the stolen books, but the situation continued to deteriorate over the following decades. An audit of 1828 shows that a remarkable 539 titles were stolen in the sixty-one years after 1767. This was an increase of almost 25 per cent on the 436 titles that had gone missing in the sixty years between the opening of the library and the 1767 audit (see plate 15).

There are several probable reasons for the increase in theft between 1767 and 1828, and these factors may have interacted with each other to make the situation worse than it might otherwise have been. The first point to note is the sharp decline in oversight of the library by the governors and guardians during the second half of the eighteenth century. It was almost entirely unknown before 1757 for the trustees not to hold a quorate visitation of the library in October, as required by the founding act of parliament. It had happened on only four occasions during the first fifty years of the library, but something then changed dramatically because it proved impossible to hold a meeting in thirteen of the twenty-three years between 1758 and 1780. Matters then got much worse because the trustees only managed to hold three quorate meetings in the fifty years between 1781 and 1831. For most of this half century, one or two trustees arrived for the scheduled annual meeting, but they were too few to make any legally binding decisions on behalf of the board. The seriousness of the problem

34 G. Blancken, *Catalogus antiquarum et novarum rerum quarum visendarum copia Lugduni in Batavis in anatomia publica* (Leiden, 1690); R. Vieussens, *Epistola nova quaedam in corpore humano* (Leipzig, 1704).

is clear from the fact that there was a solid block of ten years from 1780 to 1789 and of eleven years from 1791 to 1801 when the librarian and assistant librarian waited in the library on the appointed second Thursday in October but not a single trustee came for the meeting. The high offices of the trustees and their busy schedules as well as the unwieldy nature of the board, when combined with possible changes in the personalities and priorities of individual trustees, might explain an occasional year without a meeting, but the trend is so striking from the mid-1750s that it must have been due to some broader changes in the perceived function and significance of the library among the trustees, and perhaps among the wider public.

The library was open from 10.00 a.m. to 3.00 p.m. every day throughout the year, apart from Sundays and holy days.[35] Yet, it was closed annually for two weeks at Easter and again at Whitsuntide, as well as for the six weeks between 1 September and mid-October. These scheduled closures and 'frequent' unannounced closures meant that by 1767 the *Freeman's Journal* was able to complain that Marsh's was 'useless' as a public library.[36] It soon became a truth universally acknowledged that the collections were of little interest to anyone uninterested in theology in general, and seventeenth-century Protestant theology in particular.[37]

Marsh's Library could not compete with the circulating libraries and the more upmarket subscription libraries that emerged during the mid-eighteenth century across the city. In 1763, the bookseller Mr Hoey was charging a relatively small fee to access a circulating library at his shop in Skinner's Row where the latest novels published in London and Dublin were regularly added to his stock and could be taken home to be read. Over eighty years later, Mr Morrow's circulating library at 18 Nassau Street was boasting that it added large quantities of 'every new and popular work' to its stock as soon as they were published.[38] Subscription libraries were a cut-above circulating libraries in terms of status, sociability, and comfort. In 1830, for example, the Dublin Library in D'Olier Street was open for ten hours every day. It took twenty-five daily newspapers and fourteen reviews and magazines, as well as the transactions of many learned societies, and could boast of 12,000 'useful works'. For an annual subscription that worked out as 'not quite a penny a day', members could enjoy the 'commodiously' decorated reading room which was graced by two 'large fires' for eight months of the year. The old books and cold spaces of Marsh's Library simply could not compete with the modern holdings of these circulating and subscription libraries.[39]

---

35 These hours were stipulated at the 37th visitation, 8 October 1747, Marsh's Library, MS ML 31.   36 *Freeman's Journal*, 24 Oct. 1767.   37 *Dublin Evening Packet & Correspondence*, 29 Oct. 1829; *The Nation*, 25 Jan. 1841 and 20 June 1846.   38 *Freeman's Journal*, 24 Dec. 1763; *The Nation*, 13 Oct. 1849.   39 'Great advantages of the Dublin library', *Dublin Morning Register*, 29 Jan. 1830.

The area in which the library is situated became increasingly unfashionable during the eighteenth century as the centre of social status and prosperity shifted eastwards towards St Stephen's Green and northwards towards Henrietta Street and Mountjoy Square. By the 1760s the immediate vicinity of Marsh's Library seems to have been dangerous. The *Freeman's Journal* reported in April 1764 that a young woman passing along Bride Street at the back of the library was attacked by 'a party of Ruffians' who forced her into the lane that led to the back entrance of the building. Here she was 'ravished' by the gang and although 'her cries were truly lamentable' nobody came to her aid. The time of day or night at which this gang rape took place is unclear, but a decade later it was reported that 'about' midnight a gentleman returning to his lodgings along Bride Street saw a man 'armed with a long knife' standing at the entrance to the back lane into Marsh's Library. The gentleman had the presence of mind to knock at the door of a house for assistance and the 'villain' ran off in the direction of Kevin Street.[40]

If a multitude of external factors had caused a decrease in the number of readers, yet the incidence of theft increased between 1767 and 1828, then the explanation should be sought in the management of the library. It is possible that someone working in the library stole books, and in normal circumstances it would always be easier for staff than for readers to remove books from the premises. There is no evidence for any such activity. There is, though, evidence for lax practices on the part of the men who served as keepers during these decades. The Dublin poet and lyricist Thomas Moore was, for example, given a key to Marsh's Library during the 1790s and over a period of several years he could come and go as he pleased after normal opening hours and during the annual holidays when the library was closed to all other readers.[41] There is obviously no suggestion here that Thomas Moore was a thief, but at least one reader did abuse his unsupervised access to the collections to smuggle a very large number of books out of the library.

On Friday 4 April 1828 a young man named William Richard Underwood was summoned for the following day before the magistrates at the Head Police Office on College Green to answer a charge of 'stealing some valuable books from Marsh's Library.' The suspect did not appear on Saturday 5 April to answer the charges and was subsequently found to have absconded from his lodgings. He seems to disappear from the historical record at this point and may well have gone abroad to escape the law. A well-known Dublin bookseller, Mr Hynes of Anglesea Street in Temple Bar, had also been summoned to appear and he testified to having purchased many books from Underwood. These included twenty-six volumes for which he paid a total of £2 and a manuscript copy of a Latin Bible on vellum, which was probably medieval in origin, for which he gave

---

40 *Freeman's Journal*, 24 Apr. 1764; *Finns Leinster Journal*, 12 Mar. 1774.   41 Thomas Moore (ed.), *Odes of Anacreon* (London, 1842), pp xii–xiv; Jane Moore, 'Thomas Moore, *Anacreon* and the romantic tradition', *Romantic Textualities: Literature and Print Culture, 1780–1840*, 21

£4. The librarian of Marsh's gave evidence that this manuscript copy of the Vulgate Bible was worth £1,000. Mr Hynes claimed not to have suspected that the items had been stolen and seems to have agreed in advance of this appearance at the Head Police Office to return the items still in his possession, a courtesy for which the library had agreed to reimburse him for the money he had paid to Underwood. The young thief had probably offered volumes to at least one other bookseller, who was referred to but not named in the newspapers. This bookseller may also have returned books that were in his possession. It was widely reported in the press that of 'nearly a hundred' books stolen by Underwood, 'not more than thirty' were recovered by the library.[42] This would indicate that the stolen volumes sold quickly when they appeared on the second-hand market in Dublin.

This sordid tale of theft soon became entwined with the heightened tensions associated with the attempts of some to resist, and others to achieve, Catholic emancipation. It was reported in newspapers aimed at a Catholic audience that Underwood was a candidate for holy orders at Trinity College Dublin and a zealous supporter of the evangelical New Reformation 'who happened to stand high in the estimation of his Grace the Protestant Archbishop of Dublin', Dr William Magee. There was much glee in the Catholic press in drawing attention to a trainee Anglican clergyman on the run from the law who had enjoyed the patronage of one of the most redoubtable opponents of Catholic emancipation. Those newspapers which sought to defend Dr Magee from this acutely embarrassing incident claimed that Underwood was not a candidate for holy orders at Trinity, with some going so far as to claim that he was a Roman Catholic who had pretended to be a Protestant to gain the archbishop's assistance in reading at Marsh's Library. It was of considerable significance to contemporaries as to whether Underwood was a Catholic thief or a Protestant thief, but for the purposes of this essay the most salient fact is that the archbishop's introduction saw Underwood afforded privileges not granted to readers who did not enjoy such distinguished patronage. He first entered the library at some point in 1827 and was soon allowed to frequent the building 'during the hours when less favoured Students were excluded'. He used the fact that the librarian left him 'uneyed, unguarded, and alone' to help himself to dozens of rare books and at least one manuscript which he hid under the 'large travelling cloak' which he invariably wore when visiting the building.[43]

(2013), 30–52, at 34.   42 *Waterford Mail*, 12 Apr. 1828; *The Globe*, 11 Apr. 1828.   43 This episode was widely reported in the Irish and British press. The above paragraphs are based on reports in *Dublin Evening Mail*, 7 Apr. 1828; *Saunders's News-Letter*, 7 Apr. 1828; *Dublin Morning Register*, 8 Apr. 1828; *The Globe*, 9 and 11 Apr. 1828; *Belfast Newsletter*, 11 Apr. 1828; *Waterford Mail*, 12 Apr. 1828; *Tipperary Free Press*, 12 Apr. 1828; *Connaught Journal*, 10 Apr. 1828.

VI

The debacle surrounding Underwood's thefts inevitably led to an audit of the library collections, which showed that 539 titles had been stolen during the sixty-one years between 1767 and 1828.[44] In other words, not only did the thefts not stop after 1767, but the rate of loss increased by almost a quarter. The collections of Archbishop Marsh and John Stearne in the second gallery suffered fewer thefts in the later period. By way of contrast, a greater number of books were stolen from the collections of Edward Stillingfleet and Élie Bouhéreau during this second period than had previously gone missing. We have seen above that only fifteen items went missing from Bouhéreau's personal library before 1767, but thereafter a remarkable total of eighty-three walked off the shelves and out of the library.

Table 2: Titles stolen from Marsh's Library, 1707–1828[45]

Collection	Period 1: 1707–67	Period 2: 1767–1828	Total: 1707–1828
Stillingfleet	138	248	386
Bouhéreau	15	83	98
Marsh	165	95	260
Stearne	118	113	231
Total	436	539	975

In what follows, it will be suggested that the striking increase in thefts from Bouhéreau's collection after 1767 was linked to its strengths in learned Renaissance texts, and that the interest of thieves in these books coincided with the emergence of a bibliographical sensibility among scholars and the development of a second-hand market for rare books that fetishized the works of a small number of learned printing houses. By extension, it is likely that the increase or decrease in the rate of theft from the three other collections in the library is explained by the presence or absence of such rare titles.

It would have been extremely hard for thieves to make off with books from the reading room if the library staff had been performing their functions with a modicum of attention. This space was the heart of the building where the librarian had his office and where readers tended to congregate as it was the only place heated by a fire during the eight or nine long months of the year when the thick walls and large draughty windows meant that the first and second galleries were always colder than the outside ambient temperature. The fact that there was

---

44 Marsh's Library, Dublin, MS ML 36, List of missing books 1828–1916, at list for 1828.
45 This table lists books by number of titles rather than the number of volumes in an edition. So, a three-volume set of a book is counted as one title rather than three volumes.

a large increase in the number of books taken from this central room is clear evidence that the library staff were often absent from the room when readers were in the building, and that some readers were present in the library without any supervision at all. The writer Thomas Moore and the thief William Richard Underwood were clearly not the only readers who were left 'uneyed, unguarded, and alone' in the building for periods of time.

Twenty of the eighty-three titles stolen from Bouhéreau's collection were taken from the lower shelves, which were both easier to access and housed the taller books in folio format. The remainder were removed from the fifth and higher shelves, which house smaller formats and are not easily reached by most readers without the use of a ladder or stool. The place of publication of the books stolen before 1767 had been spread evenly across continental Europe, but those that went missing after 1767 show a strong concentration in Paris (twenty-two) and two cities of the United Provinces: eleven were printed in Leiden and the same number in Amsterdam. There was only one book on the list from The Hague and there was not a single incidence of a book printed in Utrecht being stolen, even though both cities were significant centres in the international book trade.[46] There were six books from Geneva and three from Lyon, cities which despite being separated by an international frontier were in such close proximity to each other that their book-trades sometimes acted as offshoots or subsidiaries of each other. There were only five books printed in each of the great printing cities of Antwerp and Venice, three from Basel, and two each from Rome and Mainz. There was one book from each of these small provincial centres of the book trade in France, Italy, Spain, and the German lands: Bourg en Bresse, Ferrara, Florence, Genoa, Heidelberg, Pamplona, Saumur, Sedan, and Vicenza.

In terms of the languages in which the books were written, thirty-eight were in Latin solely, and a further twenty-five were either solely in Greek or had both Greek and Latin text. Twelve were in French, seven were in Italian, and one book had text in Hebrew, Latin and Greek. The preponderance of Latin and Greek (sixty-three titles) suggests the strongly learned focus of the stolen books, which, as we shall see, were often prestigious and significant texts of the Renaissance. The books stolen from Bouhéreau's collection before 1767 had been strongly weighted towards the newest texts in his library; all but two of the fifteen had been printed after 1660. By contrast, the books stolen after 1767 were much older. Three were incunables published before 1500, thirty-seven were published between 1501 and 1599, and a further thirty-five appeared between 1600 and 1659. A paltry total of five were printed after 1660.

As had been the case before 1767, this second period saw relatively few liturgical, or theological books stolen, which seems strange if, as was often said at the time, the library was only frequented by theology students. This small

---

[46] Andrew Pettegree and Arthur Der Weduwen, *The bookshop of the world: making and trading books in the Dutch Golden Age* (New Haven, CT, 2019).

group of eight items included a *Breviarium Dominicanorum* published in Rome in 1603 for use in the rites of the Dominican order, as well as a Roman breviary containing the standard liturgy of the post-Tridentine church published in Rouen in 1642. A copy of a New Testament published in Paris in 1522 was removed, as was another edition published almost fifty years later by Robert Estienne in the same city.[47] The 1658 Amsterdam edition of the New Testament edited by the Genevan minister Stephanus Curcellaeus (1586–1659) was another casualty of theft. Bouhéreau had many copies of the psalms in different editions, but only two copies went missing from the shelves. One had been published in 1567 in Antwerp and the other was a 1687 Amsterdam edition of the influential poetic paraphrases of the psalms by the sixteenth-century Scottish humanist scholar George Buchanan.

Bouhéreau had operated a medical practice in La Rochelle and had a significant number of medical books in his personal library. The subject had formed a small, but important, core of his books stolen before 1767, but there were only two such books on the later list. A 1643 edition of the works of the ancient physician Hippocrates may have had some contemporary practical use for a medical student or qualified practitioner, but it is hard to see anything other than a specialized academic interest in ancient languages behind the theft of the first ever printed edition of 1557 of two poems about medical matters written by the Greek poet Nicander during the second century BC.

There was a subset of around eighteen books that might be classified under a rubric of hunting, fishing, war and history. These tended to be Renaissance editions of earlier Roman and Greek texts or learned commentaries upon the culture and practices of the ancient world, rather than practical guides to pastimes in vernacular languages for the amusement of contemporary gentlemen. So, a 1597 edition with a Latin commentary was stolen of the epic poems on fishing and hunting produced in Greek by the second century AD poet Oppian. The German scholar Luca Holstein's missing 1644 Paris edition of Flavius Arrianus' treatise on hunting was the first time that this ancient text had appeared in print in Greek with a Latin commentary. Some of the military books removed were relatively modern in focus. There was, for example, an account of the life of the Swedish general Gustavus Adolphus entitled *Le soldat suedois, ou l'Histoire de la guerre d'Allemagne* (Geneva, 1633), and a Parisian book that continued the story of the Thirty Years' War for a decade after the Nordic warrior's death, *Suite du soldat suedois, contenant les guerres d'Allemagne depuis la morte de Gustave Adolphe* (Paris, 1642). There was a short work of 1647 by the French military engineer Charles Common which dealt with the art of fortifications, and the military uses of mathematics and 'horologes solaires' (sundials). Yet, Lazarius Baysius's famous work on ancient Roman seafaring *De*

---

[47] Malcolm Walmsby, *Booksellers and printers in provincial France, 1470–1600* (Leiden, 2020), p. 761.

re navali was much older, having been published in Paris in 1549. The library's 1599 copy of the first century AD treatise *Strategikos* by Onasander was also missing. This was an important ancient work on Roman military tactics and the nature of a just war and was highly popular and frequently reprinted during the Renaissance.[48]

Bouhéreau's significant collection of ancient history and literature was untouched before 1767, apart from one Latin edition each of Aristotle and Virgil. After that date, by contrast, his store of Greek and Roman literature and history was heavily depleted. Several texts commonly used in schools and universities were taken, such as two copies of Euclid's geometry and three separate texts by Cicero who was esteemed as the epitome of elegance in the Latin language. There was, however, a clear preference for the oldest possible editions of ancient texts with learned commentaries by leading Renaissance scholars. Among these forty or so stolen books were: a sumptuous 1513 edition of the works of Isocrates published by Aldus Manutius; the 1515 edition of Pindar by Zacharias Kallierges, the first book published in the Greek language in the city of Rome;[49] the 1534 edition of the newly rediscovered *Aethiopica* written over a thousand years earlier by Heliodorus of Emesa; the beautifully illustrated 1552 edition of the ancient Roman engineer Vitruvius's treatise *De architectura*; the 1577 edition of the works of Catullus published by Robert Estienne; the 1595 edition of the Epicurean philosopher Lucretius's poem *De rerum natura* published in Christopher Plantin's workshop; a 1637 edition of the apocryphal letters of Socrates published in Paris; and, two volumes of the works of Ovid published by Elzevier in Amsterdam in the late 1650s.

Many of the missing texts were printed by a small number of scholarly publishers who had played a key role in the diffusion of Renaissance discoveries about the ancient world. In fact, the preponderance of titles in the 1828 audit that were printed by these erudite publishers is very striking. So, there were two books published by the Blaeu family of Amsterdam, three by the renowned Aldo Manutius of Venice, six by Christopher Plantin in Antwerp and Leiden, nine by the Elzevier family, and ten by the leading French dynasty of the mid-sixteenth century, the Estiennes. Each of these names was synonymous with the very highest technical ability in the art of printing, as well as a desire to produce the best possible editions of classical works for an audience of students and scholars across Europe. This very striking difference in the books stolen from Bouhéreau's collection before and after 1767 cannot be fully explained in terms of the personal desires or scholarly preferences of the unknown number of thieves who removed these items from the premises. It is much more likely that the marked trend after 1767 for the removal of sixteenth and early seventeenth-

---

48 James T. Chlup, 'Just war in Onasander's ΣΤΡΑΤΗΓΙΚΟΣ', *Journal of Ancient History*, 2:1 (2014), 37–63. 49 Staffan Fogelmark, *The Kallierges Pindar: a study in Renaissance Greek scholarship and printing*, 2 vols (Cologne, 2015).

century editions of scholarly Renaissance texts was linked to the development of a second-hand market for rare books, which was stimulated and encouraged by an emerging bibliographical sensibility among scholars in Dublin.[50] Across Europe, the editions produced by these publishing houses quickly came to be viewed by scholars as the most accurate, the most prestigious, and the most desirable of all those available on the market. This inevitably meant that the editions published by these men became the most valuable editions of the works of any classical or Renaissance author on the second-hand market, which surely explains the rationale for their theft in such numbers from Bouhéreau's collection in the reading room.

VII

In the wake of Underwood's thefts, the governors and guardians met and formally admonished the librarian and assistant librarian 'Hence forward to give more exact attention' to the orders 'already in force relative to the Preservation of the Books'. They reiterated their predecessors' stipulation in 1779 that 'no person for the Future, take down or read any Books but in the presence of the Librarian or the Librarian Assistants'. They also added their own proviso that 'no Person admitted to the Library be suffered to read any of the Books but at the Publick Table in the Librarians Roome' in which the Bouhéreau collection was (and is) housed.[51] The library was confident that these 'excellent' new regulations precluded the possibility of future thefts, but there were almost thirty thefts from the library between the audit of 1828 and the end of 1840.[52] However, the rate of attrition had slowed considerably and it is noticeable that only one book was stolen from Bouhéreau's collection during these twelve years. This was a very rare incunable from 1475 of Orosius' fifth-century treatise *Historiae adversus paganos*.[53]

The ninety-eight titles stolen from Bouhéreau's library between 1707 and 1840 do not change our understanding of the general contours of the first keeper's collection sketched by Philip Benedict and Pierre-Olivier Léchot.[54] An

---

50 This is considerably later than the seventeenth-century 'revolution' in attitudes towards old books in Britain identified by David McKitterick in *The invention of rare books: private interest and public memory, 1600–1840* (Cambridge, 2018), pp 109–22. More generally, see Charles Benson, *The Dublin book trade, 1801–1850: a thesis submitted to Trinity College, University of Dublin. With an editorial preface by David Dickson and an updated bibliography* (Dublin, 2021).   51 Marsh's Library, MS ML 31, 117th visitation, 15 April 1828.   52 *Bibliotheca Marsiana. Catalogue of books. The duplicate copies of the public library, Dublin ... to be sold by Auction* (Dublin, 1833), p. vi; Marsh's Library, MS ML 36, List of missing books 1828–1916, books missing between the years 1828 and 1840.   53 The 1475 edition is catalogued on the Incunable Short-Title Catalogue as ISTC i00097000 and this missing copy is logged on the Material Evidence in Incunables database as MEI 02146509.   54 Benedict

examination of the thefts over these decades does, however, shed light on the level of disorganization of the institution before 1767 as well as the collapse of good governance in the institution during the final decades of the eighteenth century. A spike in the theft of certain subjects in the decades after 1767 can be used to track the growth of a new concept, that of the antiquarian 'rare book', as well as the development of a second-hand market in Dublin to feed the fetishization of the work of a small number of highly esteemed Renaissance printers, publishers, and scholarly commentators. Underwood sold around one hundred books to at least two booksellers during the period of about a year between his first entry into Marsh's Library and his unmasking as a thief. The fact that fewer than thirty of these titles were recovered after such a short period on the market is testimony to the feeding frenzy of the bibliophiles who haunted the bookshops of early nineteenth-century Dublin.[55]

and Léchot, 'The library of Élie Bouhéreau', pp 165–84. **55** *Waterford Mail*, 12 Apr. 1828; *The Globe*, 11 Apr. 1828.

Contributors

JANÉE ALLSMAN has recently completed an Irish Research Council EPS Postdoctoral fellowship at Marsh's Library and University College Dublin. She is currently preparing a critical edition of the Bouhéreau correspondence held at Marsh's Library. She completed her PhD in French at the University of Colorado Boulder in 2021 and was a Mellon Summer Institute in French Paleography Fellow at the Newberry Library in Chicago in 2018. Her research interests focus on how differing religious conceptions of time, history, and eternity shaped competing notions of political, intellectual, and religious authority in early modern France.

AMY BOYLAN is librarian at Marsh's Library. She is a graduate of Trinity College Dublin and holds a Masters in Information and Library Studies from Aberystwyth University. She was Early Career Librarian in Balliol College, Oxford from 2017–20, and completed a library studentship at the National Library of Ireland from 2016–17.

MURIEL HOAREAU is the deputy director of the University Library at the University of La Rochelle. She is currently completing a PhD on the history of the book in the École des chartes, Paris related to the Protestant printers of La Rochelle. She co-edited *Libraires et imprimeurs protestants de la France Atlantique, XVIe-XVIIe siècle* (2021) and contributed the chapter 'De l'art de cultiver et de fabriquer des produits coloniaux : livres techniques francophones et anglophones aux XVIIIe et XIXe siècles', to *Le livre technique avant le XXe siècle à l'échelle du monde* (2017).

NOREEN HUMBLE is professor of Classics and associate director of the Calgary Institute for the Humanities at the University of Calgary in Canada. She is a Hellenist who works primarily on Xenophon and Plutarch, but also on the reception and reading history of classical texts in the early modern period. Among her extensive publications are the award-winning monograph *Xenophon of Athens: a Socratic on Sparta* (2021) and the co-authored (with J. De Keyser and K. Sidwell) *Henri Estienne: on books* (2022).

GEOFF KEMP is senior lecturer in politics at the University of Auckland, teaching and researching in the areas of intellectual history, book and press history, and politics and the media. He gained his PhD at King's College

Cambridge. He has held visiting fellowships at Churchill College, Cambridge, Yale University, Nottingham University, and Marsh's Library, Dublin. His publications include an introduction to John Locke's writings on liberty of the press in *Literary and historical writings* (2019), a volume in the Clarendon Edition of the Works of John Locke; 'Thomas Basset, publisher of Hobbes and Locke' in *Early modern publishers* (2025); and 'Locke and the language of sovereignty' in *Reading texts on sovereignty: textual moments in the history of political thought* (2021). He is general editor, with Jason McElligott, of the four-volume *Censorship and the press, 1580–1720* (2009).

ELEANOR JONES-MCAULEY is a musicologist and organist who holds a PhD from Trinity College Dublin on the subject of the church music of eighteenth-century Dublin. She also holds an MPhil in early modern history from Trinity College, for which she submitted a thesis on the topic of music and the French Revolution. Her research focuses on the relationship between music and cultural identity, and she has presented papers in Ireland and the UK on parish church music, Huguenot music books, charity school choirs, and attitudes towards Italian music in the Established Church in eighteenth-century Dublin.

MARIE LÉOUTRE holds a PhD in early modern history from University College Dublin (2012). She is author of *Serving France, Ireland and England: Ruvigny, earl of Galway, 1648–1720* (London, 2018), and one of the editors of *The diary and accounts of Élie Bouhéreau* (2019). She has also authored several articles on the Huguenot experience and eighteenth-century Irish political history. Marie works in the National Archives of Ireland.

DAVID VAN DER LINDEN is assistant professor in early modern history at the University of Groningen. His research focuses on religious conflict and co-existence in early modern France. He is the author of *Experiencing exile: Huguenot refugees in the Dutch Republic, 1680–1700* (2015). His current book project, *Divided by memory: the legacy of the Wars of Religion in early modern France*, explores how Catholics and Protestants in seventeenth-century France remembered the religious wars, and how such memories could undermine religious co-existence in local communities. In 2019 he was a Maddock research fellow at Marsh's Library, exploring the local memory culture of La Rochelle's Protestants.

JASON MCELLIGOTT is the director of Marsh's Library in Dublin. He is a graduate of University College Dublin and read for his PhD in early modern history at St John's College, Cambridge. He was a fellow of Merton College, Oxford, and worked at the Trinity Long Room Hub in Trinity College Dublin before moving to Marsh's. He has wide research interests in the field of early modern print culture and is currently writing a book on white-collar crime in eighteenth-century Dublin.

CHARLES IVAR McGRATH is professor in the School of History, University College Dublin. His many publications on eighteenth-century Ireland include *The making of the eighteenth-century Irish constitution: government, parliament and the revenue, 1692–1714* (2000) and *Ireland and empire, 1692–1770* (2012). He has published articles in *Irish Historical Studies*, *Parliamentary History*, *Eighteenth-Century Ireland*, *The History of European Ideas*, *The Historical Journal* and *The English Historical Review*, and chapters and entries in a range of edited collections and biographical dictionaries.

JANE McKEE is a retired lecturer in Ulster University and former president of the Irish section of the Huguenot Society of Great Britain and Ireland. Author of numerous publications on Huguenots in France and Ireland, she published *The Huguenots: France, exile and diaspora* in 2013 with Randolphe Vigne. Most recently she co-edited *The diary and accounts of Élie Bouhéreau* (2019) and published a scholarly edition of the *Correspondence of Charles Drelincourt and his children, 1620–1730* (2021).

JEAN-PAUL PITTION is fellow emeritus of Trinity College Dublin and a former professor of the Centre d'Études Supérieurs de la Renaissance in Tours. His pioneering research on Reformation and Huguenot history has transformed the study of Renaissance intellectual and book history. He is the foremost scholar of the print history of the *académie* of Saumur. His most recent books are *Le livre à la Renaissance. Introduction à la bibliographie matérielle et historique* (2014) and is co-editor of *The diary and accounts of Élie Bouhéreau* (2019).

DIDIER POTON is professor emeritus of the Centre de Recherches en Histoire Internationale et Atlantique at the University of La Rochelle. He has published extensively on French Protestantism, as well as early modern printing and commerce. Some of his many publications include: *Libraires et imprimeurs Protestants de la France Atlantique – XVIe-XVIIe siècle* (2020), *Les Protestants de La Rochelle* (2018), and *Vers un nouveau monde Atlantique: les traités de Paris, 1763–1783* (2016). He is currently president of the Musée Rochelais d'Histoire Protestante.

AMY PRENDERGAST is assistant professor in eighteenth-century studies in the School of English at Trinity College Dublin. She is the author of *Literary salons across Britain and Ireland in the long eighteenth century* (2015), and of *Mere bagatelles: women's diaries from Ireland, 1760–1810* (2024). She co-edited *The diary and accounts of Élie Bouhéreau* in 2019 and has published multiple articles on women's writing, life writing, and eighteenth-century Ireland.

Index

Aarau (Switzerland), 124, 130
d'Ablancourt, Nicolas Perrot (classicist), 54–6, 59
Académie française, 55, 57, 81–3, 86, 93; *see also* Conrart, Valentin
académie of Saumur, *see* Saumur, *académie* of
Académie Royale, 44, 47
Acher, Abraham (bookseller), 70
Adlercron, Meliora Bermingham (Huguenot diarist), 126
Admyrauld, Pierre-Gabriel (Rochelais merchant), 29
Aelian, 171
d'Agniel, Mr, 21, 192
d'Albret, Jeanne, queen of Navarre, 24, 28, 179–80
ambassadors and envoys, *see* diplomats
Amsterdam (Netherlands), 12, 22, 31, 34, 46, 55, 61–2, 68, 71, 86, 105, 166, 199–200, 205–7
Amyraut, Moïse (Huguenot theologian), 49, 165
Ancien Régime, 12, 28–9, 66, 186–7
d'Angennes, Julie (French courtier), fn 93
Angers (France), 49–50
Anglican Church, 11, 35–6, 38, 72, 98, 107–9, 145
   in Ireland
       relationship to Huguenot churches, 99, 102–4
       see also Dublin, Anglican churches
       liturgy, 99–100
       psalms and psalm-singing *see* Book of Psalms; psalms and psalm-singing; psalters
Anglican clergy, 193, 197, 293
   benefices and obligations, 144–6
Angoulême (France), 182
Angoumois (France), 24, 178–80, 182–3
Anne, queen of England, Ireland and Scotland, 145, 155–6, 159
Antwerp (Belgium), 205–7
Ardree (Ireland), 146
d'Argenson, Mr, 181
Aristippe, 174
Aristotle, 192, 199, 207
Arnauld, Antoine (theologian), 57–9
d'Arsellières, marquis, *see* Perrinet, Gaspar
d'Aubigné, Agrippa, 28, 93–4, 104
Augier, Paul (Dublin-based Huguenot merchant), 142
Augsburg, League of, 20, 31
Aunis (France), 22–4,
   churches of, 27–8, 67–70, 187
       documents related to, 178–83; colloquy of, 180, 183, 187;
       patois, 30–1, 78,
   see also Reformed churches, synods

Austria, 21
Aytré (France), 22, 26

Baden (Germany), 120
Baden-Durlach, princess of, 121
Balzac, Jean Louis Guez de (French writer), 37, 54–5, 171–3
Bank of England, 158
Banks, Caleb (English politician), 33, 41–2, 48–54, 59
   parents of, 49, 52, 59; *see also* Banks, Sir John
Banks, Sir John (father of Caleb Banks), 41, 54, 59
Baptists, 95
Barbaud, Jacques (Rochelais merchant), 71
Barbeyrac, Charles (physician), 38
Barbeyrac, Jean (Lockean writer), 38–9
Bartholin, Thomas (Danish physician), 46
Basel (Switzerland), 205
Basnage de Beauval, Henri (Huguenot lawyer), 79
Baudouin, Solon (correspondent of EB), fn 150
Bauldry, Paul (scholar), fn 12, 174
Baulot, Isaac (apothecary) 7, 29, 50–2
Baulot, Isaac (son), 52
Baxter, Richard (Presbyterian pastor), 39–40
Bayle, Pierre (French philosopher), fn 56, 173
Baysius, Lazarius (historian), 206
Béarn (France), 65, 69
Beaulot, *see* Baulot, Isaac
Beauval, Jacques Boucher (apothecary), 50
Bégon (intendant), 26
Belcastel, Pierre (Huguenot officer), 153, 160
Belfast Newsletter, 203
Bellona, 95
Belrieu, Jacques de, *see* Virasel, Jacques de Belrieu, baron of
Benedict, Philip, 11–12, 22, 24–5, 27, 55, 62–4, fn 70, 164–5, 172, 192, 208
Benion, Louis, fn 150
Bennis, Elizabeth, fn 127
Benoist, Élie (pastor and historian), 64–5, 71, 79–80, 187, 189
Berchaud, 178
Bern, 119–21, 125, 129, 137, *see also* Switzerland
Berton, Guillaume (Rochelais printer), 180
Bèze, Théodore de, 7, fn 76, 81–5, fn 92, 97, 102, 107, 179–80
Bible, 28, 95, 113;
   Geneva, 81–7, 97
   in English, 113
   King James, 82
   stolen, 202–3

213

bills of exchange, 137, 141, 143–4, 155
Blachford, Revd William (keeper of Marsh's Library), 197–8
Blaeu family (printers), 207
Blain (France), 70
Blancken, Gerard (anatomist), 199–200
de Blégny, Nicolas (essayist), 45–6, 175
Blomer, Margaret (Lady Northumberland's entourage), 37
Blosset, Jane (Dublin Huguenot), 105
Bodleian Library, Oxford, 33
Bolton, duke of (Charles Paulet, lord justice), 152
book theft, see Bouhéreau, Élie, books, stolen
Book of Psalms, 28, 102, 113, 188; see also psalms and psalm-singing; psalters
booksellers, 18, 49, 162, 193, 206
  Huguenot, 28, 49, 70–1
  in La Rochelle, 28–9, 96; see also Savouret, Pierre
  Dublin, 105, 195, 201–3, 209
Bordeaux (France), 41, 52, 186
Bossuet, Jacques-Bénigne (bishop), 49
Boston, 7, 23
Boucher, Jeremy (organist), 109, 111
Boucher Beauval, Jacques (apothecary), 50
Bouhéreau, Amateur (EB's son)
Bouhéreau, Blandine (EB's daughter), see Jourdan, Blandine
Bouhéreau, Blandine (née Richard, EB's mother), 12–13, fn 26, fn 28, fn 30, 135
Bouhéreau, Élie senior (EB's father), 12, 17, 81, 87
Bouhéreau, Élie (EB's son)
Bouhéreau, Élie 7–23, 26–38, 41–63, 70–1, 80–1, 85–99, 113, 116, 119–77, 182–3, 187–92, 197–9, 204–8
  collections
    books 12–13, 28, 36, 42, 44, 50–2, 55–8, 71, 154, 165–6, 171, 190–210
      list of, recommended to John Locke, 33–4, 37, 52–9
      presentation copies, 44, 71, 165–6
      purchases, 12, 156, 169
      stolen, 190–210
  correspondence, 11–13, 18–19, 23, 28–9, 31, 42–9, 51, 61, 81–98, 163, 166, fn 167, 174, fn 175, 183, 187–8
    with pastors in Aunis and Poitou, 183
  manuscripts
    records of the consistory of the Reformed Church of La Rochelle, 11, 15, 22, 177–90
    diary and accounts 13, 15, 19–21, 31, 34, 40, 59–61, 73, 116, 119–73, passim, 192
    personal finances, 12, 29, 157, 134–9, 144–7, 154, 157–8,
    proto-banker for Huguenot exile community, 132, 137–40, 142–4, 151, 158–9

miscellany of Abraham Tessereau, 14, 63–81, 187–9; see also Tessereau, Abraham
conjecture on Justin's *Epitome* (2.10), 170
death, 21, 98, 156
editor, 29
  of Valentin Conrart's 1679 Genevan psalter, 81, 85–8, 104 fn 32
  of Laurent Drelincourt's *Cantiques sacrez*, 91–7
elder of the Reformed Church of La Rochelle, 18–19, 90, 178, 182, 187–8, 196
family, 11–14, 18–21, 26, 28, 30, 32, 98, 125, 132, 144, 147, 150, 191; see also individual members
  births, baptisms, and deaths, 126–7, 135
  escape from La Rochelle, 11, 19
keeper of Marsh's Library, 21, 80, 98, 116, 132, 134, 137, 149, 154
naturalization in England, 150
notes and note-taking, 159, 161–76
  missing notebooks, 6, 161–76
ordination and precentorship in St Patrick's Cathedral, 98, 145–7, 157
physician, 13, 18–19, 26, 50, 149
secretary
  to Thomas Coxe, English envoy to the Swiss cantons (1689–92), 20, 38, 61, 116–131, 137, 150,
  and financial agent to Henri de Massue de Ruvigny, earl of Galway (1693–1701), 61, 137–41, 149–160
    disbursements to Huguenot refugees, 20, 116, 151–2
student at the *académie* of Saumur, 12, 44, 49, 150, 165, 173,
translation of Origen's *Against Celsus*, 7, 12, 62, 86, 176
tutor to the children of the duchess of Monmouth, 13, 19–20, 150
Bouhéreau, Jean (EB's son), 13
Bouhéreau, Jeanne (EB's daughter-in-law), wife of Richard Des Herbiers, 126
Bouhéreau, Jeanne (EB's grand-daughter), 126
Bouhéreau, Madelon (EB's daughter), 13, 19, 26
Bouhéreau, Marguérite (EB's daughter), see Quartier, Marguérite
Bouhéreau, Marguérite (née Massiot) (EB's wife), 11, 13, 18, fn 28, 135, 158, 182
Bouhéreau, Pierre (EB's ancestor), fn 25
Bouhéreau, Richard Des Herbiers (EB's son), 113, 116, 144
Bourbon, Armand de, marquis de Miremont, 153
Bourg en Bresse (France), 205
Bourgeois, Louis (composer), 82, 103
Boyer, Paul de la Roque (pastor), 137, 143
Boyle, Robert (chemist), 39, 40–5,
Bradley, Abraham (Dublin bookseller), 105
Bradshaw, Mr (Dublin clothier), 135

Index

Brand, Mr (payment to EB), 145–6
Brandenburg, elector of, 41
Breviarium Dominicanorum, 206
Bride Street (Dublin), 202
　church, *see* Dublin, Huguenot churches
British Library, 105
Brittany (France), 70
Brodbelt (née Lortie), Marieanne (Élie's goddaughter), 52; her husband, Lawrence, 52
Brownower, Sylvester (Locke's aide), 52
Brunel, Pierre (succentor and organist), 110, 114
Buchanan, George (Scottish humanist scholar), 206
Buckingham, 1st duke of (George Villiers), 25
Burton, Benjamin (Dublin banker), 141, 158

Cabrit, Mr (French pastor), 121
Caen (France), 72, 182
Calais (France), 40, 42
Calvin, John, 82, 183, views on church music, 82, 102, 104, 108
Calvinism, 24, 27, 70
　foundational texts of, 188; *see also* Bible, Geneva; psalter, Genevan
Calvinists, *see* Reformed churches
Cambridge (England), 47
Camisard War, 104
Canterbury (England), 22
Carolina colonial project, 47
Carter, Alice, 158
Casaubon, Isaac (classicist), 171–3
Castres (France), 182
Catholic, 21–2, 49, 50, 64, 65, 71, 98, 104, 177–8, 181–2, 186, 203, 206
　cathedral, 25, 50
　Church, 18, 70, 78, 86, 102, 178, 180
　clergy, 27, 64, 66, 77–8
　and Huguenot co-existence, 24–9, 35, 63–80, 177, 182
　League, 76, 179
　music, 102
　readers at Marsh's Library, 195
Catholicism, 11, 13, 19, 27, 42, 47, 72, 101
　converts to, 18, 186 *see also* Charas, Moyse
Catinat, Nicolas (marshal), 20
Catullus, 207
Caufredon (pastor), 101
de Champlaurier, Anne, 159
de Champlaurier, Ester, Mary and Susanne, 159–60
de Champlaurier, Marc Thibaut (Huguenot pensioner), 159–60
de Champlaurier, Pierre Thibaut, sieur (Huguenot pensioner), 159
Charas, Moyse (apothecary to Charles II), 7, 14, 34, 41–52, 174–5; Madeleine (née Hadancourt), his wife, 42
Charente-Maritime (France), 17, 31, 67, 188
Charenton, Reformed church of, 42, 52, 68, 81, 83–5; consistory of, 68, 83–4, 90–1

charity schools,
　Anglican, 111–12
　Huguenot, *see* Huguenot Charity School (Dublin)
Charles I, king of England, 39
Charles II, king of England, 40, 43–7, 120
Charleton, Walter, 46
Charpentier, François (scholar), 55, 57–8
Châtellerault (France), 179
China-China, *see* quinine
Chinon (France), 49
Church of Ireland, *see* Anglican Church
Cicero, 207
Clarke, Edward and Mary, 35
Claude, Jean (theologian), 43, 52, 65, 72, 77–8
Cleves (Germany), 37
clothing, 125, 130, 135, 188
Cobbe, Alec, 196; Charles (archbishop of Dublin), 196; Thomas (keeper of Marsh's Library), 196–8
Coghill, Marmaduke (chancellor of the exchequer), 146
cognac, 31
Colbert, Jean-Baptiste (prime minister of France), fn 58, 67
Colbert de Terron, Charles-Jean (Catholic intendant of the Aunis province), 67–8
Cole, William (physician), 46
coinage, *see* currency, Irish currency, English currency
Colladon, Ésaïs (magistrate), 85–6
Collins, Arthur (antiquarian), 127
College Green (Dublin), 202
Cologne (Germany), place of publication, 199
Colomiès family, 25
　Paul (scholar and librarian), 22–3, 29, 94
　Jean (physician) 22
　Jérôme (pastor), fn 22
Condé, Louis de Bourbon, 73, fn 76, 179
Confession of Faith (*Confession de La Rochelle*), 27, 178–80
Connacht (Ireland), 152
Conrart, Valentin, 12, 14, 18, 81–92, 104–7, 172
Constantinople (Istanbul), 120, 127
Cortex Peru/Peruvianus, *see* quinine
Costar, Pierre (scholar), 54, 56
Coste, Pierre (Locke's aide), 34–5
de Coulombiére, Captain, 142
de Courcelles, Étienne (pastor), 206
Coutras, battle of, 104
Coxe family, 41, 60, 116, 125, 127, 129–31, *see also* individual members
Coxe, Mary (née Peachell), 15, 39
　diplomatic role, 120–4,
　births and deaths of children (Marie Jeanne Violante and Philibert), 129–31
Coxe, Thomas, Senior, 38–40, 43, 49

Coxe, Thomas, English envoy to Swiss cantons, 13, 15, 20, 34, 37–41, 43, 59–61, 116, 112–27, 130–1, 137–8, 150, 165
  medical career and experiments with the Royal Society, 38–9, 49
Crespin, Jean, 63
de Crosat, Mr, 158
currency, 135, 144, *see also* Irish currency, English currency

Daillé, Jean (pastor), 83–84, 90, 165
Daillé, Jean Adrien (son of Jean), 84
Daillon, Benjamin de (pastor), 159
Dalton, Mr (inn proprietor, La Rochelle), 50
Dame Street (Dublin), 105
Dauphiné (France), 69
Davantès, Pierre (composer), 82, 103
Dawson Street (Dublin), 126
Daxelhoffer, Mr, 122
de la Bouchetiére, Mr , 137
de la Forest, Louis (pastor), fn 150
Delaizement, Daniel Henri (pastor and historian), 17, 68, 70–3, 80, 165–6, 183
Delft (Netherlands), 79, 182, 187, 189
Delmas, Louis, 22, 25, 94, 177
Delpy, Mr (payment from EB), 138
Des Maizeaux, Pierre (Huguenot author), 35
Désaguliers, Jean (pastor), 22, 26
Désaguliers, Théophile (Fellow of the Royal Society, son of Jean), 22–3, 139
Desbrisay family, 139
  Theophilus (Huguenot pensioner), 139, 158
Descartes, René, 51, 192, 199
Des Herbiers, Louis Richard (grandson of Élie Richard), 29
Desmarches, marchioness, 123
Desnain, Véronique, 18, 26, 37, 172
Deux-Sèvres, 81
Digges La Touche, J.J., 98, 105–6
Diogenes Laertius, 174
diplomacy, 15, 16, 116–31, 151
  public celebrations 122–4
  public mourning 129–30
  women's role in, *see* diplomats' wives
diplomats, 41, 47, 80, fn 90 , 116, 150, 191
diplomats' wives, 116–31
  ceremonial duties of 119–24
  conducting business in husband's absence, 123–4
  family life of, 119, 125–31
Dobrzensky, Madame de, wife of the envoy of Brandenburg, 142
Dominicans, 206
Donabate (Dublin), 196
Douen, Orentin (historian), 83–4, fn 104
Dover (England), 42
dragonnades, 11, 13, 26, 69–70, 76–9, 181, 187–8
Drake, Sir William, fn 162
Drelincourt, Charles (pastor), 81, 165

Drelincourt, Laurent (theologian and scholar), 81, 83, 85–97
Du Bartas, Guillaume, 93
Du Beignon, Madame (EB's relation), 31
Du Bosc, Pierre (pastor), 72–3
Du Moulin (physician), Louis, 40
Du Moulin, Pierre (pastor and theologian), 165, 173
Dublin, 7–9, 11–12, 14–15, 17, 31–2, fn 36, 61, 98–116, 126, 134, 139–42, 145–6, 149, 152–8, 162–3, 177–8, 187–8, 190–9, 201, 203–4, 208–9
  archbishop of, 21, 99, 154, 177, 193, 196; *see also* Cobbe, Charles; King, William; Marsh, Narcissus and Whateley, Richard
  Anglican churches
    St Andrew's, 109, 146
    St Michan's, 108, fn 111, fn 113
    St Nicholas of Myra (St Nicholas 'Without'), 110, 114, 145
    see also St Patrick's Cathedral (Dublin)
  charity school, *see* Huguenot Charity School (Dublin)
  Huguenot churches, 14, 36, 98–115
    Bride Street (non-conforming), 100, 109
    Lucy Lane (non-conforming), fn 36, 100–1, 108, 110, 159
    Peter Street (non-conforming), 101, 106–7, 109, 111–14
    Lady Chapel, St Patrick's Cathedral (conforming), 7, 9, 21, 98–101, 105–12, 114, 126, 135, 137
    St Mary's Church (conforming), 100–1, 109
  newspapers, 201, 203,
  psalter, *see*, psalters, Dublin
  university, *see* Trinity College Dublin
  workhouse, 196
Dublin Castle, 153, 156
Dubois (tutor), 35
Duelly (D'uelly) (tutor), 35
Dufour, Alain, 76
Dufour, Isaac (schoolmaster), 113
Dumont de Bostaquet, Isaac (elder of the Lady Chapel), 101
Dunshauglin (Ireland), 135
Duplessis-Mornay, Philippe, 30
Durel, Jean (pastor and translator), 100, 107
Durga (cantor in St Patrick's Cathedral), 107
Duroure, Francois (Huguenot officer), 157
Dutch Republic, 65, 70–2, 80, 212

East, Thomas (composer and printer), 103
écoles, petites, 28
edicts, royal, 14, 66, 69–70, 76, 182
Edict of Alès, 186
Edict of Fontainebleau, 19, 26, fn 63
Edict of Nantes, 13–14, 19, 24, 26, 35, 64, 66–8, 77–8, 100, 150, 180–1, 186, 189, 196

Index

commissioners of the, 66–8, 78
Revocation of, 14, 17, 19, 22–3, 26, 77, 96, 100, 104, 149, 177, 181, 185–6, 189
Edict of Nimes, 26
Edict of Revocation, *see* Edict of Fontainebleau,
Ellis, John (English undersecretary of state), 153
Elzevier family (printers), 207
England, 11, 13, 19–20, 22, 24, 26–7, 32, 35, 38, 40–7, 52, 59–61, 72, 82, 128, 132, 137–8, 140–1, 150–6, 158–60, 178, 19
English currency, 140–2
English navy, 25
Erlangen church (Netherlands), organ, 108
Established Church, *see* Anglican Church
Estienne, Robert, 206–7
Euclid, 207
Euripides, 169
Ewing, George (Dublin bookseller), 105

Falcon (inn in Bern, Switzerland), 121
Faneuil family, 23; Peter, 23
Fanshawe, Lord Richard, English ambassador to Spain, 123
Lady Anne, his wife, 123
Farnham, 65, 102
Fatio de Duillier, Nicolas (mathematician), 41
Faubourg St Germain (Paris), 42
Favre, Claude, 56
Fens (England), 191
Ferrara (Italy), 205
Finns Leinster Journal, 202
Flanc (Huguenot pastor), 17
Flanders, 21, 60, 151
Flavius Arrianus, 206
Flax, 153
Flemish, 30
Florence, 205
Floris, Josias (Huguenot physician), fn 172
Fontenay-le-Comte, 67, 182
Forcade, Mr (Dublin merchant), 135
Foullon, Madame (widow of a Huguenot pensioner), 160
Fox, Peter, 191
Fraizer, Sir Alexander (court physician), 43, 46
Charles (court physician, son of Sir Alexander), 43
Franc, Guillaume (composer), 82, 103
Francis Street (Dublin), 145
Franchard, Françoise (mother of Abraham Tessereau), 65
Freboul, Jane (EB's grand-daughter), 11
Freeman's Journal, 196–7, 201–2
French pensioners, *see* Huguenot pensioners
French Reformed Churches, *see* Reformed churches, in France
French Wars of Religion, 24, 150, 178
Huguenot psalm-singing in the, 103–6
Frisching, Madame, 121
Fronde, the, 77

Gadroys, Claude, 199
Galilei, Galileo, 172
Gallet, Mr (payment to EB), 139
Galway, Lord (Henri Massue de Ruvigny), 13, 15, 47, 61, 135–46, 149–60, 165, 188, 212
commander of William III's army in Piedmont and Ireland, 20–1, 137, 151
Huguenot Deputy General, 76, 149–150, 188
investments, 158
lord justice in Ireland, 15, 21, 141, 149, 151–3, 156
Huguenot settlement in Portarlington, 152; proposed settlement in Connaught, 153
patronage of Bouhéreau, 151–6
support for Huguenot pensioners in Ireland, 137–46, 157
philanthropy, 149, 151, 155–60
Gassendi, Pierre, 192
Gaultier de Saint-Blancard, François (pastor-historian), 65
General Post Office (Dublin), 190
Geneva, 71, 96, 173, 179–80, 96, 199, 205–6
Bible, *see* Bible, Geneva
council of, 82–6
Genoa, 205
George I, king of England, 156–7, 159
Germany, 13, 40, 108, 205
Gibbs, James (architect), 196
Gibier, Éloi (printer), 73
Gilbert, Abraham (pastor), 87, 90
Girac, Paul Thomas, sieur de, 54, 56
Glorious Revolution, 141
Godeffroys family, 23
Goldie, Mark, 37
Gombaud, Antoine, chevalier de Méré, 93
Goodall, Charles (physician), 48, 61
Goudimel, Claude (composer), 103
Goulart, Simon (pastor and historian), 63, 76
Govon, Count, envoy extraordinary of the duke of Savoy, 120, 124
Govon, Countess, 120, 124
Graevius, Johann (classicist), 171
Graffenried, Madame, 122
Grand Alliance, war of the, 138, 149–52
Grand Tour, 30, 32, 39
Grant, André (Peter St. cantor), 107, 109, 113
Grant, Charles, fn 113
Grassemare, Mr de (tutor), 35
Graunt, John (demographer), 128
Great Britain, 20, 30, 103, 108, 118, 191, 208
Greek, books in, 62, 86, 162, 171–3, 192, 199, 205–6
Greenwich, 150
Gregorian chant, 103
Greiter, Matthias (composer), 103
Grigg, Anna (John Locke's cousin), 49
Guenellon, Pieter (physician), 61
Guernsey, 26
Guillaudeau, Joseph (EB's grand-uncle), 27–8, 165–6
Guillaudeau, Pierre (EB's grand-uncle), 27

Gustavus Adolphus, 206
Guybert (EB's cousin), 150
Guyenne (France), 186

Haag, Émile and Haag, Eugene, 19, 42, 51–2, 67, 180
The Hague (Netherlands), 60–1, 72, 79, 205
Hamburg (Germany), 23, 27, 60
Hampden, John (English politician), 39, 41, 49
Hampshire (England), 156
Handel, George Frideric (composer), 60
Hanover, House of, 145
Harel, Christian (professor of chemistry), 43
Harrison, Francis (Dublin banker), 141, 158
Harvey, Matthew (brother of William), fn 39
Harvey, William (physician), 39
Hatley, Griffith, fn 39
Haÿs, Jean (Dublin-based Huguenot merchant), 142
Head Police Office, Dublin, 202–3
Heidegger, Johann-Heinrich (theology professor, father of Johann Jakob), fn 60
Heidegger, Johann Jakob (aide to Thomas Coxe, opera impresario), 60–1
Heidelberg (Germany), 205
Heliodorus of Emesa, 207
Henrietta Street (Dublin), 202
Henry II of France, 24
Henry IV of France, 19, 24, 67, 104, 179, 189
d'Hervart, Philibert (friend of Lord Galway), 153
Hespérien, Pierre (pastor), 51
Higgins, Mr (payment to EB), 146
Hippocrates, 199, 206
HMC (Historical Manuscripts Commission), 40, 45, 47, 60, 155
Hoareau, Muriel, 5, 13, 178, 211
Hoey, Mr (Dublin bookseller), 201
Holland (Netherlands), 30, 40, 47, 60, 96, 123, 132, 137, 142, 153, 155, 160
Holstein, Luca (scholar), 206
Hooke, Robert (Fellow of the Royal Society), 40
Hospital for poor French Protestants in London, 157
Huguenots, 11, 13–14, 17, 21–3, 27, 30–1, 34–6, 38, 41–2, 47, 55, 57, 63–6, 68–73, 75–6, 79–82, 98–112, 134, 139, 142–3, 149, 151–7, 159–60, 165–7, 183, 189
 and Catholic co-existence, 24–9, 35, 63–80, 177, 182
 persecutions of, 13–14, 19, 26, 35–6, 63–80, 177–89, 182
Huguenot Charity School (Dublin), 99, 101, 112–116
Huguenot churches, *see* Reformed churches
Huguenot merchants, 29–30, 71, 140, 142, 144, 157, 185
Huguenot nonconformity, 36
Huguenot pastors, 12, 64, 70, 85, 104, 183, *see also* individual parties
Huguenot pensioners, 21, 100, 137–44, 146–7, 149, 152, 154–7, 159–60

d'Huisseau, Isaac (pastor), 184
Humble, Noreen, 15, 37, fn 47, fn 55, 211
Hungary, 40
Huygens, Christiaan (Dutch polymath), 44
Hylton, Raymond Pierre, 98–100, 110, 152
Hynes, Mr (Dublin bookseller), 202–3

Iberian Peninsula, 155
Île de Ré (France), 12, 24, fn 30
Île-de-France (France), 68, 83–4
Ireland, 11, 13, 17–18, 32, 35–7, 61–2, 99–101, 108–9, 118, 123, 125–7, 132, 134–5, 138–43, 145–7, 149–60, 177–8,
 Easter Rebellion (1916 rising), 190
 and England, 20, 138, 150–3, 155–6, 159, 212
Irish Civil List, 138–9, 144, 146, 152
Irish civil war, 99
Irish currency, 140–2
Irish Military Establishment, 138–9, 141, 143, 152
Irish parliament, 145, 196
Irish treasury, 138–9, 144
Isle, Isaac, marquis of Loire (Protestant intendant of the Aunis province), 67–8, 94
Italy, 13, 18, 31, 38, 47, 52, 86, 205
 northern, 151
Ithaca, 117–18

Jacobites, 153, 156
James II, king of England, Ireland and Scotland, 123
Jansenists, 84
Jargeau (France), 180
Jarnac (France), 180, fn 183
Jesuits, 55, 57–8, 100
Jesuit's Powder, see quinine
de Jocour, Jean, marquis of Villarnou (Huguenot officer), 153
Jones-McAuley, Eleanor, 14, 212
Jonzac (France), fn 183
Jourdan, Blandine (EB's daughter), 126, 135, 153
Jourdan, Henri (EB's grandson), 156
Jourdan, Jean (pastor, EB's son-in-law), 135, 153, 155, 158
Jurieu, Pierre (Huguenot pastor and theologian), 64–5, 77–9
Justel, Henri (Huguenot *secrétaire du Roi*, royal librarian in England), 49, 54, 58–9
Justin, *Epitome of Pompeius Trogus*, 170–1, 174

Kallierges, Zachiaras, *see also*, Pindar, 207
Kampen (Netherlands), fn 71
Kemp, Geoff, 14, fn 120, fn 161, 174–5, 211–12
Kensington (England), 154
Kent (England), 47
Kevin Street (Dublin), 202
Kew (England), 39
Kildare (Ireland), 144
King, Edmund (physician, Fellow of the Royal Society), 40

Index

King James Bible, *see* Bible, King James
Kin Kina, *see* quinine

L'Estrange, Roger (English political author), 35
La Basoge, Phillipe de (Huguenot officer), pension payments to, 142–3, 159
La Bastide, Marc Antoine Crozat, sieur de (Huguenot lay theologian), 90–2
La Chambre, Marin Cureau de, 54–5, 57
La Chapelle (widow of a Huguenot pensioner), 160
La Melonière, Isaac Monceau de, 152–3
Le Clerc, Jean (theologian), 34, 41, 56
Le Fèvre, Tanneguy (classicist), 7, 12, 44, 169–74
Le Maçon, Jacques (Reformed Church representative), fn 68
Le Noir, Philippe, sieur de Crevain (pastor), 70
Le Valois, Philippe, marquis of Villette-Mursay (naval officer, descendant of Agrippa d'Aubigné), 94
Labrousse, Élisabeth, 66, 69, 77
Lambeth Palace (England), 22
Lancelot, Claude, 58
Landolt, Mr (bursar) 129
Languedoc, France, 69, 77–8
  Reformed churches of, 184
Larminie, Vivienne, 14, 18, 30, 43, 70, 134, 151, 174
Laroque, *see also* de la Roque (Huguenot tutor), 35
Lautal (schoolmaster of the Huguenot charity school, Dublin), 113
Le Clerc, Jean (Genevan refugee in Amsterdam), 34
Le Fanu, T.P. (Thomas Philip), 64, 72, 79
  notes on the Huguenot churches in Dublin, 100–2, 106–7, 110,
  notes on the Huguenot charity school, 112–14, 159–60, 187
Léchot, Pierre-Olivier, 11–12, 55, 62, 64, 164–5, 192, 208–9
Leipzig (Germany), 199–200
Lemaistre de Sacy, Louis-Isaac (theologian, biblical translator), 84
Lenzburg (Switzerland), 120
Léoutre, Marie, 13, 15, 212
Levesque, Françoise (Huguenot mother), wife of Jean Ribaut, fn 26
Liffey, river (Dublin), 30, 100
Limerick (Ireland), 122, 160
Lincolnshire (England), 40, 120
Lisbon (Portugal), 123, 155
De Lisle, Rouget (French army officer), 104
Liverpool (England), fn 25
Locke, John (philosopher), 14, 33–62, 162–4, 167, 172, 174, 176, 212
Loire, river (France), 49, 67, 94
Loire Valley (France), 33
Loiseau, Mr (musician), 108, 113
London (England), 20–2, 33–6, 38–42, 44–7, 55–6, 58–61, 65, 70–2, 80, 100, 105–8, 117–18, 127, 137–8, 141–4, 157–8, 175, 201–2

Longinus, *On the sublime*, 169–71; *see also* Le Fèvre, Tanneguy
lords justices of Ireland, 13, 15, 141, 149, 151, 154
lord lieutenant of Ireland, 36, 154, 155; *see also* Rochester, Lawrence Hyde
Lortie, André (pastor and theologian), 17, 26, 51–2, 61, 72, 94
  Marieanne (André's daughter), *see* Brodbelt, Marieanne
Loss, Friedrich (German physician), 46
Loudun (France), *see* Reformed Church, synods
Lough, John, 33, 36–8, 42, 44, 49–52, 59
Louis XIII, king of France and Navarre, 65
Louis XIV, king of France and Navarre, 11, 13–14, 19–20, 26, 42, 45, 63–79, 150, 167, 178, 181, 186, 188–9
Lower, Richard (physician and member of the Royal Society), 39, 46, *Tractatus de corde*, 200
Lucan (Dublin), 153
Lucerne (Switzerland), 124
Lucien, 56
Lucretius, 207
Lucy Lane (Dublin), *see* Dublin, Huguenot Churches
Lusk (Dublin), 146
Luther, 102
Lutheran church music, 102–3, 108
Lutherans, 98, 125
Lutrellstown (Dublin), 153
Lyon (France), 52, place of printing, 58, 170, 199, 205

Madrid (Spain), 123
Magee, William, archbishop of Dublin (Church of Ireland), 203
Magnan (widow of a Huguenot pensioner), 160
Mainz (Germany), 205
Mancel, Jacob (Rochelais printer and bookseller), 93, 96
Manutius, Aldus (Italian printer), 207
Mapletoft, John (English physician), 37–9, 44, 52
Marans (France), 68, fn 183
Maréchal de Turenne (inn in The Hague, Netherlands), 72
Marennes (France), 182–3
del Marmol Carvajal, Luis (Spanish historian), 56, 59
Marot, Clément (French poet), 7, 81–2, 84–5, 92, 97, 102, 107
Marsh, Narcissus, archbishop of Dublin, 11, 21, 44–5, 50, 58, correspondence, 154, 190, 192, 198, 201, 203–4, 212
Marshall, John, fn 34, 36, 38
Marsh's Library, 7–9, 11–13, 20, 42–4, 46, 55–6, 58, 62–3, 71–3, 76–8, 80–1, 100–1, 107–14, 132–3, 144–6, 148–50, 165–6, 177–9, 190–210, 211–12
  governors and guardians, 89, 136, 193–209; *see also* book theft
Masonic Grand Lodge of London, 22
de Massanes, Antoine (secretary in the the *parlement* of Paris), 68

Massiot family, 18
    Massiot, Louïs (EB's brother-in-law), 31
    Massiot, Marguerite, *see* Bouhéreau, Marguérite
Mathew, Mr (organist), 109–10
Merian, Matthaüs (engraver), 7
Maubec gate (La Rochelle), fn 26
Mauzé (France), fn 183
Mazel, David (pastor), 34
de la Maziere, André, 106
de la Maziere, Mr, 106
McCarthy, Muriel, 11, 13, 36, 55, 126, 145–6, 148, 157, 165, 177, 192
McElligott, Jason, fn 11, 13, 212–13
McGrath, Charles Ivar, 15, 213
McKee, Jane, 13–14, fn 104, 213
Meath, bishop of, 154
de Médicis, Marie, queen of France and Navarre, 24
Melle (France), 87
Ménage, Gilles (French scholar), 163–4, 168–9, 172
Menjot, Antoine (court physician), fn 175
Mentzer, Raymond, fn 30, 185–6
Méré, Chevalier de (French writer), 93–4
Meres, Sir Thomas (MP) 35
Merlat, Élie (pastor), 183
Merlin, Jacques (pastor), 27, 30
Mervault, Pierre (Rochelais merchant), 50, fn 66
Methodists, 98
Micheldever churchyard (England), 157
Middle Abbey Street (Dublin), 190
Millar, Henry (organ-builder), 109
Milton, John R., fn 34, 37–8, fn 41
Minerva, fn 70
de Mirmand, Henri (friend of Lord Galway), 153
Molyneux, William (natural philosopher), 62
de Monginot, François, fn 175
Monmouth and Peterborough, countess of (Carey Mordaunt *née* Fraizer), 43
Monmouth, duchess of (Anne Scott), 13, 19–20, 43, 150
    children of, 13
Monmouth Rebellion, 41
Montauban (France), 65, 179, 186, 188
de Montigny, Mr (Huguenot army captain), 152; Madame de Montigny, his wife, 152
Montpellier (France), 33, 37–9, 41, 52, 65, 67, 77, 182
Moore, Thomas (lyricist), 202, 205
Moravians, 98
Mordaunt, Carey, countess of Peterborough and Monmouth, 43
Morrow, Mr (librarian), 201
Morton, William, 9
Moulin, 40, 165, 173
Mountjoy Square (Dublin), 202
de Muralt, Béat-Louis (Swiss writer), 60–1
Murphy, Samuel (organist), 109, 111
music, *see* Protestant, worship, music
Mutus liber, 7, 29, 51
Myler's Alley (Dublin), 112

Marsh, Narcissus, archbishop of Dublin, 21, 44–5, 50, 58, 154, 164, 190, 198, 201, 203–4, 212

Nantes (France), 13–14, 17, 19, 22–7, 63–4, 66–8, 77–80, 82–3, 149–50, 180–1, 185–7, 189
Naples (Italy), 199
Napoleon, 117
Napoleon III, 177
Nassau Street (Dublin), 201
Nau (widow of a Huguenot pensioner), 160
Netherlands, 13, 23, 27, 30–1, 40, 46, 108
Nevis (Saint Kitts and Nevis), fn 52
Newbridge House, Donabate (County Dublin), 196
Newdigate newsletters, fn 40
New Rochelle (United States of America), 23
Newton, Isaac (English polymath), 22
Nicander (poet), 206
Nicole, Pierre (French theologian), 57–9
Nijmegen (Netherlands), 212
Nîmes (France), 26
Niort (France), 49, 81, 90–1, 94, 96
Noailly, Jean-Michel, fn 82, 84
Nobileau, Mr (Dublin-based Huguenot hat maker), 157
Northumberland, Lady, 37
Nottingham, Lord (Daniel Finch), 60

Oath of Abjuration of the Stuart Pretender, 145
Oath of Allegiance, 145
Oath of Supremacy, 145
Old Bailey, 191
Oldenburg, Henry (Royal Society's secretary), 40
Oléron (France), 24
d'Olier Street (Dublin), 201
Onasander's ΣΤΡΑΤΗΓΙΚΟΣ, 207
Oppian, 206
organ music, 107–11, 113–15
    Dutch, 108
Organic Articles of 1802, 177
Origen, 7, 12, 62, 86, 172, 174, 176
d'Orléans, Marie-Louise, queen of Spain, 45
Orléans (France), fn 23, 40, 42, 45, 49
Ormonde, 1st duke of (James Butler), 99–100
Ormonde, 2nd duke of (James Butler), 155
Orosius (historian and theologian), 208
Osborough, Nial, fn 36, 146
O'Brien, Barnaby, 6th earl of Thomond, fn 133
O'Shea, Maria, 161
Ostervald, Louis (pastor), 113
Ottoman Empire, 120, 127
Ovid, 207
Oxford, University of, 37

Pacteau, Pierre (Rochelais baker), 70
Pajot, Jehanne (EB's godmother), wife of Jehan Richard, fn 17
Pamplona (Spain), 205

Index

Paris (France), 12–13, 17–19, 22–5, 30–1, 41–2, 44–7, 49–50, 56–8, 66–9, 71–2, 80–6, 90–2, 96, 117, 150–1, 174–5, 177–81, 183–4, 186–8, 205–7
Parry, Mr (payment to EB), 146
Pascal, Blaise (French polymath), 93; books on EB's list, 57–9
Pascal, Henry (cantor of the Lady Chapel), 107, 109
Passebon (Huguenot tutor), fn 35
Pau (France), fn 186
Payne, Benjamin (parish clerk), fn 107
Peachell/Pechill/Péchel, Marie, *see* Coxe, Mary
Pellisson, Paul (French writer), 55, 57
Pembroke, Thomas Herbert, 8th earl of, 36
Pepys, Samuel (English writer), 41
Perrinet, Gaspar, marquis of Arsellières, 121, 138–40, 143, 153
Perroniana et Thuana, 170
Peruviani corticis, *see* quinine
Peter Street Church (Dublin), *see* Dublin, Huguenot Churches
Petty, Sir William (English economist), fn 141
Peureux, Guillaume, 86
Phaedrus, 170–1
Philip II, king of Spain, 179
Philippe I, duke of Orléans, 42
Phoenix Park (Dublin), 153
Picardie (France), 150
Pickard, Madame, 152
Piedmont (Savoy), 20, 61, 116, 137, 151, 155
Pieters, Toine, 175
Pindar, 207
Pineaux, Jacques, 82
Pipiat, Mr (Huguenot stationer) 157
Pittion, Jean-Paul, 13, 37, 51, 151–2, fn 161, 213
Plantin, Christopher (printer), 207
Plato, 175
Plutarch, 211
Poitiers (France), 11, 188
Poitou (France), 19, 50, 69–70, 76, 78, 90, 97, 181, 183, 187
  Poitou dragonnade, 78–9
Pons (France), fn 183
Pontadius, James, 93
Poey, Pierre (Huguenot merchant), 15
Pooley, Thomas (payment to EB), 145–6, 157
Popple, William (translator), 61
Porta, Giambattista della (printer), 199
Portarlington (Ireland), 101, 152, 159–60
Port-Royal authors, 55–8
Portugal, 45, 123, 155
Portuguese, 30
Poton de Xaintrailles, Didier, 6, 15, fn 196, 213
Powell, Samuel (Dublin music printer), 105–6
Prendergast, Amy, 13, 15, 213–4
Presbyterians, 40, 98, 108, 110, 177
Preston, Lord (Richard Graham), English envoy to France, 120
Preston, Lady (Ann Graham, née Howard), wife of Richard Graham, 120

Prior, Matthew (first secretary to the lords justices), 151
Privy Council, 47
Protestant, 18–19, 22, 24–30, 42–3, 49–50, 64–70, 73, 76–80, 82, 98, 134, 147, 149, 151, 174, 177, 179–84, 187–8, 212–13, *see also* Huguenot; Reformed churches
  denominations, *see* Anglican Church, Baptists, Calvinists, French Reformed Church, Lutherans, Methodists, Moravians, Presbyterians, Puritanism, Quakers
  worship, 63–98, 81–2, 184–5, *see also* psalms and psalm-singing
  music, 5, 98–115
  sermons, 27–8, 77, 101, 104, 106–7, 111
Protestant History Museum (La Rochelle, France), 180
Protestant Reformation, *see* Reformation
Protestantism, 12, 17, 23–4, 34, 49, 67, 78, 91, 96, 102–3, 166, 184–6; *see also* Protestant; Reformation; Reformed churches
La Providence (London hospital), 157
psalms and psalm-singing, 14–15, 28, 102–3, 81–115, 188; *see also* Book of Psalms; psalters; French Wars of Religion, Huguenot psalm-singing in the psalters,
  Dublin, 105–6
  English language, 103
  Genevan, 81–97, 104 fn 32
Puritanism, 112
Putland, Thomas (Dublin merchant), 143
Pyrenees, Peace of the, 77

Quakers, 98
Quartier, Louis (EB's son-in-law), 135, 137
Quartier, Marguerite (EB's daughter), 126
  daughters Marguerite-Marie and Jeanne, births and deaths of, 126
  payments from EB, 134–7
quinine, 41, 44–8, 61, 174–5

Raboteau, Jean (cousin of Théodore Raboteau), 144
Raboteau, Théodore (Dublin-based Huguenot merchant), 144
Radcliffe, Sir George (English politician), fn 133
Rasteau, Jacques (Huguenot trader), 29
Raullé, Jean (Huguenot Rochelais banker), 50
Raven, James, 191
Recherches sur les commencemens et les premier progrès de la Réformation en la ville de La Rochelle, 166
Reflexions Physique sur la Transsubstantiation, & sur ce que Mr Rohault en a écrit dans ses Entretiens, 51
Reformation, 24–5, 27, 63, 70, 72, 93, fn 108, 166
Reformation, evangelical New, 203
Reformed churches, 6–7, 11, 15, 17–18, 20, 21, 23–5, 35–6, 38, 63, 76, 78–9, 83–4, 94, 177–89, 196
  in France, 17, 21, 27, 63–80, 149–50, 160, 179–80, 184, 189, *see also* Aunis; Aytré; Béarn;

Reformed churches (*continued*)
    Blain; Brittany; Caen; Castres; Dauphiné; Languedoc; Montpellier; Poitou; La Rochelle; Saint-Yon; Saintes; Quevilly;
  deputies of, 69, 79
  in Britain and Ireland, 100, 108, *see also* Dublin, Huguenot churches
  in Germany, 108
  in the Netherlands, 108
  in Switzerland, 108
  clergy, 12, 81–3, 92, *see also* Huguenot pastors
  consistories, 27, 67, 69–70, 99, 104, 174, 185–6, *see also* Charenton, Dublin, La Rochelle
    Dublin, *see* Dublin, Huguenot churches
  liturgy, 72
  synods
    of Aunis, 68
    of Brittany, 70
    of Dordrecht, 180
    of La Rochelle, 179–80
    of Loudun, 84, 183–4
    of Poitou, 90
    of Saintonge, 90
    of Sainte-Foy 179–80
    of Verteuil, fn 183
  worship, *see* Protestant worship
Réformés, see Huguenots; Reformed churches, in France
Religion Prétendue Réformée, see Reformed churches, in France
Renaissance, 24, 205, 206, 207, 208 213
Rennes (France), 27
Representative Church Body Library, fn 107
Restoration period, 141
Ribaut, Anne (Huguenot), 26
Ribaut, Jean (Huguenot), 26
Richard, Élie (cousin of EB), 12, 18, 26, 29–31, 33, 50–4, 135, 144, 183, 187
  Eloge, 27
Richard, Jehan (maternal relative of EB), 17
Richelieu (France), 49
Richelieu, Armand Jean du Plessis, Cardinal, 24–5, 28–9, 50, 83
de Richemond, Louis Marie Meschinet, 27
Richier de Cerisy, Jacques, 12, 142–3; Madame Richier de Cerisy, his wife, 143
Risk, George (Dublin bookseller), 105
Ritter, Johann Nikolaus (organ builder), 108
Rochefort (France), 52
La Rochelle (France), 5–7, 11, 13–15, 17–19, 22–33, 35–7, 43–6, 49–52, 61, 65–72, 80–1, 93–4, 96, 149–50, 165–6, 172, 176–85, 187–9, 211, 213
  consistory of, 11, 15, 18–19, 70, 80, 174, 177–89
  Reformed Church of, 7, 11, 15, 18, 177–89
  siege of, 12, 22, 24, 150, 180
  temples, fn 17, 25, fn 26, 50, 67–8, 178, 180–1, 187–8

Rochester, Laurence Hyde, 1st earl of (Lord Lieutenant of Ireland), 154
Rocque, John (surveyor), fn 112
Rogerson, Sir John I (Dublin mayor, Irish MP), 142, fn 143
Rohan, duke of, 65
Rohault, Jacques (French philosopher), 51
Rome (Italy), 40, 77, 205–7
Rookley House (Hampshire, England), 156
de la Roque/de Laroque (Huguenot tutor), fn 35
de la Roque Boyer, Paul (pastor), 137
de Rosemont, Jean-Baptiste (pastor and translator), 42
Rotterdam (Netherlands), 70, 72–3, 158, 166
Rou, Jean (Huguenot scholar), 71, 167
Rouen (France), 50, 55, 58, 66, 171, 173, 206
Rouget de Lisle, Claude Joseph (French army officer), fn 104
Royal College of Physicians, 40
Royal Irish Academy, 13, 23, 35, 150–1, 172, 177
Royal Society, 22, 39–40, 43–4, fn 47
Royal Society of Physicians, 43
rue des Augustins (La Rochelle, EB's family home), 7, 18, 28, 33, 55
rue de Boucherie (Paris), 42
Ruvigny family,
  Muysson, Jacques, 153
  Ruvigny, Henri Massue de, marquis of Ruvigny and earl of Galway, *see* Galway, Lord
  Russell, Rachel, 156
  Ruvigny, Rachel de, 150
Rycaut, Sir Paul (English diplomat), 127
Rye House Plot, 41

Saint Bartholomew's Day, 24, 63, 76
de Saint-Blancard, François Gaultier (pastor and historian), 65
Saintes (France), 26, 183–4, 186–7
Saint-Germain, treaty of, 24
Saint-Jean-d'Angély (France), 96, 179
Saint-Just (France), fn 183
Saint Laurent, Count, 123
Saintonge (France), 22, 24, 27–8, 30, 90, 97, 178–84, 186
Saintonge-Aunis Angoumois (France), 87, 183, EB synodal representative at, 97
Saint Yon temple (France), 28, 65
Salomon (widow of a Huguenot pensioner), 160
Sal prunella, 51
Sandis, Henry, 177, 188
Sandys, Edwyn (English politician), fn 39
Sarasin (Sarrazin), Jean-François (writer), 54–5
Sarrau, Isaac (pastor), 166–7
Saumur (France), 7, 12–13, 17, 28–9, 31, 49, 51, 96, 165, 173–4, 184, 205
  académie of, 12–13, 17–18, 28–9, 31, 44, 150, 165, 173, fn 184, 187, 213
  booksellers of, 18
Saunders's News-Letter, 110, 203
Savouret, Pierre (printer and bookseller), 29, 71

Index

Savoy, 20–1, 72, 120, 124, 137, 151
   Conformist church of, 35
   Savoy-Piedmont, 151
Schadlerus, Mr (member of the Zurich clergy), 130
Schapira, Nicolas, 83–4, 86
Scotland, 177
Sedan (France), 205
Séguier, Pierre (French royal secretary), 83
Seignette, Élie (Rochelais apothecary), 29, fn 91
Seignette, Jean (Rochelais apothecary), 26, 29, 50, fn 91, 187
Seignette, Jehan (Rochelais merchant), 29
Seignette salt (*sel de Seignette*), 29
Senegal, 30
Sepmaine, 93
Shaftesbury, Lord (Anthony Ashley Cooper), 33, 37–8, 41, 43, 47, 59, Lady Margaret Shaftesbury (née Spencer), his wife, 59
Shrewsbury, Lord (Charles Talbot), 21
Sigart, Isaac (Rotterdam merchant), 142
Silent book, 7, 29, 51, see also, *Mutus Liber*
Simmons, Ann, fn 11, fn 36, fn 55, fn 126, fn 145–6, fn 148, fn 165, fn 192
Simms, Philip (Dublin engraver), 105
Simon, Richard (French Catholic theologian) 41, 49
Skinner's Row (Dublin), 201
Smith, Guillaume (Dublin bookseller), 105
Snetzler (organ builder), 110
Société Charitable des Français Refugiés (SCFR), fn 107, fn 110–11
Socinianism, 61
Socrates, 55, 57–8, 207, 211
Somerset (England), 39
Song of Simeon, 102
Soret, Adam (Dublin-based French clock maker), 158
Soret, Joseph (French-born Dubliner), 158
Soubise (France), 183
Southampton, Lord (Thomas Wriothesley), 150, 155
South Carolina, *see* Carolina colonial project
South Sea Company, 141, 158
Spain, 21, 45–7, 77–8, 123, 179, 205
Sparta (Greece), 211
Stael, Madame de, 118
St Andrew's church (Dublin), *see* Dublin, Anglican churches
Stacey, Sarah Alyn, fn 18, fn 26, fn 37, fn 172
Stearne, John (Irish physician), 197–8, 204
Steevens' Hospital (Dublin), 196
Steiguer, Mr (bailiff of Lenzburg), 120
Stillingfleet, Edward (bishop of Worcester), 36, 58
   book collection 22, 56, 197–8, 204
St Malo (France), 45
St Mary's church, *see* Dublin, Huguenot churches
St Michan's church, *see* Dublin, Anglican churches
St Nicholas of Myra church (St Nicholas 'Without' church) *see* Dublin, Anglican churches
St Patrick's Cathedral (Dublin), 7, 9, 21, 98–9, 101, 107, 109–10, 112, 114, 126, 135, 137, 144–7, 154–6, 197

   dean of, 9, 157
   French church of *see* Dublin, Huguenot churches
   Lady Chapel of, *see* Dublin, Huguenot churches
   precentor of, 144, 155
   St Patrick's Close, 137, 192
St Patrick's Hospital (Dublin), 196
St Paul's church (Covent Garden, England), 40
Stafford, Lord (Thomas Wentworth), 133
Strasbourg (France), 82, 104
Stratton Park (England), 156–7
St Sepulchre's Library, *see* Marsh's Library (Dublin)
St Stephen's Green (Dublin), 202
St Werburgh's church (Dublin), fn 109
Sunderland, Lady (Anne Spencer), 46
Swift's Hospital (Dublin), 196
Switzerland, 11, 13, 20, 27, 38, 41, 108, 116–31, 137, 150, 153, 155
Swords (Ireland), 196
Sydenham, Thomas (English physician), 39, 42, 44, 46–8, 59, 174–5
Synge, Edward (archbishop of Tuam), 156
Synge, Samuel (dean of Kildare), 144, 146, 155–6

Tacitus, 56
Talbor, Sir Robert (English physician), 44–9
Tasburgh family, fn 133
Tasso, Torquato (Italian poet), 172
Temple Bar (Dublin), 202
Tertullian, 173
Tessereau, Abraham (French royal secretary), 5, 8, 22, 43, 57, 63–80, 150, 187–9; Louise Venaud, his wife, 67
   bequest of miscellany to EB, 80
   Tessereau's father, 65
Tessereau, Mathieu (brother of Abraham), 67
Themis, 95
Thévenot, Jean (French travel writer), 55, 58–9
Thévenot, Melchisédech (French travel writer), 55
Thom, Messrs. (Dublin bookbinders), 190
Thomond, *see* O'Brien, Barnaby
Thornton, Mr (payment to EB), 145–6
Threadneedle Street (Dublin), 72
Thucydides, 56, 59
Toinard, Nicolas, 40, 49, 52, 59
Toulouse (France), 22, 25, 52, 94, 177
Tourmie (cantor of the Lady Chapel of St Patrick's Cathedral, Dublin), 107
Travers, Robert (assistant librarian of Marsh's Library), 58, fn 131, 146, 177–8, 188
Trench, Melesina Chenevix St George (Huguenot poet and diarist), 127–8
Trent (Italy), fn 173
Trinity College Dublin, 12, 21, 38, 69, 105–6, 191, 193, 196, 203, 208, 211–13
Trinity Hospital, 108
Trocmé, Etienne, 185

Trumble, Sir William (English ambassador to France), 80
Tuam, archbishop of, 156
Tunbridge Wells (England), 162
Turrettini, François (theologian), 85
Turin (Italy) 117, 150–1
Turkey, 127
Turon de Beyrie, Guillaume, marquis (friend of EB), 86, 188
Tyrrell, James (English political philosopher), fn 36

Ulm (Germany), 125
Underwood, William Richard (thief), 202–5, 208–9
United Kingdom, 23, 27
United Provinces of the Netherlands, *see* Dutch Republic
Utrecht (Netherlands), 205
Uzès (France), 42

Valkenier, Pieter (Dutch envoy to the Swiss cantons), 120, 152; Madame Valkenier, his wife, 120, 123–4
van der Linden, David, 5, 14, 212
Vatable, Pierre (Dublin-based Huguenot merchant), 140
de Vaugelas, Claude Favre (Savoyard grammarian), 54–6
Vauteau, Mr (payment from EB), 147
Venette, Nicolas (Rochelais physician), 26
Venice (Italy), 123, 199, 205, 207
Vicenza (Italy), 205
Victor Amadeus II, duke of Savoy, 151
Vienna (Austria), 118
Vieussens, Raymond (physician), 200
Vieux-Fourneau, Mr, 18
Vigevano (treatise of), 21
Vigne, Randolph, 35, 157–8, 213
Villeneuve (La Rochelle, France), 7, 17, 26, 180–1, 188
 Reformed temple of, 7
Villeneuve-d'Ascq (France), 68, 150
Villette-Mursay, Philippe Le Valois, marquis, 94
Vincent, Philippe (Rochelais pastor, EB's godfather), 17, 28, 70, 166, 178, 181
Virasel, Jacques de Belrieu, baron of (Lord Galway's agent), 152–3

Virgil, 199, 207
Vitruvius, 207
Vitry (France), 84
Voiture, Vincent (French poet), 54–6, 59
Vorstius, Adolphus (Dutch physician and botanist), 199

Walloon church, 71–2
 synod meeting of, 79
Walls, George (college friend of John Locke), 38
Ward, John (London merchant), 142
Wars of Religion, France, 178, 212
Warwick, Warwick, Lord (Charles); Lady (Mary Rich née Boyle); children, Charles and Elizabeth, 128
Weldon, Anne (née Cooke, diarist), 128
West Indies, 30
Westminster (England), 35, 40, 108, 138
Westminster parliament, 138
Whately, Richard (archbishop of Dublin), 177
Whelan, Ruth, 12, 14, 17–18, 30, 43, 69, 86, 100–1, 107, 126, 147–8, 174, 182
Wheler, Sir Francis (English naval commander), 60
White, Newport John Davis, 11, 13, 23, 32, 35, 150, 172, 177, 192
Whitehall (England), 48
William III of England, 20–1, 39, 41, 60, 72, 105, 116, 122–3, 129, 137–8, 149, 151, 154, 160
 and Mary, 36
 Williamite settlement, 160
 Williamite victories, 123, 153
 William's army, 100, 138
Wilson, Mr (payment from EB), 147
Winchilsea, Countess (Mary Finch, née Seymour), wife of Heneage Finch, 120, 127
Winchilsea, Lord (Heneage Finch), 120, 127
Wood Street (Dublin), 101
Worrall, Mr (payment from EB), 147
Wynne, John (keeper of Marsh's Library), 43, 193–6

Xenophon, 55–7, 211

Yeo, Richard, 41, 161–3, 167, 172

Zurich (Switzerland) 20, 60, 124, 129–30, 152